Disparate Diasporas:
Identity and Politics in an
African Nicaraguan Community

ILAS New Interpretations of Latin America Series

Disparate Diasporas: Identity and Politics in an African Nicaraguan Community

by
Edmund T. Gordon

University of Texas Press, Austin
Institute of Latin American Studies

Photos courtesy of CIDCA-Bluefields, CIDCA-Managua Library, and Moravian Archives, Bethlehem, Pa.

"Well" from HORSES MAKE A LANDSCAPE LOOK MORE BEAUTIFUL, copyright © 1984 by Alice Walker, reprinted with permission of Harcourt Brace & Company.

"I'm Black History" reprinted courtesy of Pachanga Records.

First Edition, 1998

Requests for permission to reproduce material from this work should be sent to Permissions, University of Texas Press, P.O. Box 7819, Austin, Texas 78713-7819

♾ The paper used in this publication meets the minimum requirements of American National Standard for Information Sciences—Permanence of Paper for Printed Library Materials, ANSI Z39.48–1984.

Library of Congress Cataloging-in-Publication Data

Gordon, Edmund Tayloe.
   Disparate diasporas : identity and politics in an African Nicaraguan community / by Edmund T. Gordon. — 1st ed.
      p.   cm. — (New Interpretations of Latin America series)
   Includes bibliographical references and index.
   ISBN 0-292-72818-2 (hardcover : alk. paper). — ISBN 0-292-72819-0 (pbk. : alk. paper)
   1. Creoles—Nicaragua—Bluefields—Government relations. 2. Nicaragua—Politics and government—1979–1990. 3. Creoles—Nicaragua—Bluefields—Ethnic identity. 4. Mosquitia (Nicaragua and Honduras)—History. 5. Nicaragua—Race relations—Political aspects. I. Title. II. Series.
F1536.B58G67 1998
972.85'32—dc21
                                        98-6180
                                         CIP

Contents

Preface   vii

1. Introduction: Race, Identity, and Revolution   1

2. Anglo Colonialism and the Emergence of Creole Society   30

3. Negotiating Modernity: Disparate Racial Politics in the Twentieth Century   51

4. Creole History and Social Memory   91

5. The Discursive Struggle over Race and Nation   119

6. Ambiguous Militancy on the Threshold of Revolution   150

7. Creole Politics and the Sandinista Revolution: Contradictions   203

8. Conclusion   253

Notes   265

Acronyms   285

References   287

Index   305

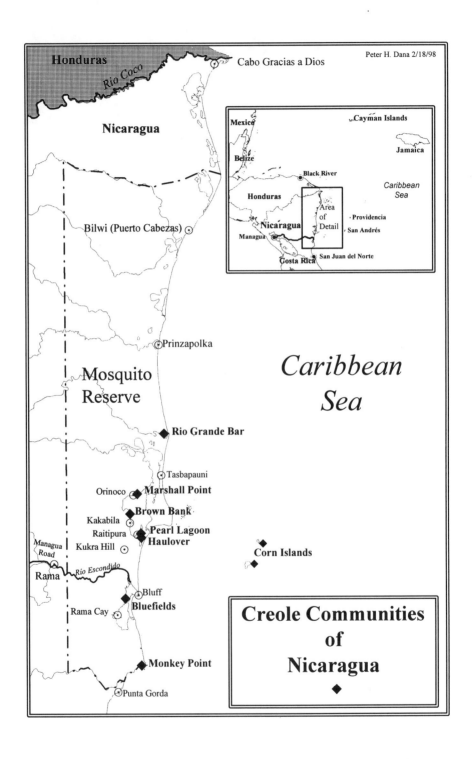

Peter H. Dana 2/18/98

Honduras
Rio Coco
Cabo Gracias a Dios

Nicaragua

Mexico
Belize
Honduras
Nicaragua
Managua
Costa Rica

Cayman Islands
Jamaica
Black River
Caribbean
Sea
Area
of
Detail
Providencia
San Andrés
San Juan del Norte

Bilwi (Puerto Cabezas)

Prinzapolka

Mosquito
Reserve

Caribbean
Sea

Rio Grande Bar

Tasbapauni
Orinoco Marshall Point
Brown Bank
Kakabila
Raitipura
Managua Kukra Hill Pearl Lagoon
Road Haulover
Rama Rio Escondido

Corn Islands

Bluff
Rama Cay Bluefields

Monkey Point

Punta Gorda

Creole Communities
of
Nicaragua
◆

Preface

I'm Black History. I'm Black Culture
I'm Black History. I'm Black Culture

We put the labor. The Indian put all the land.
They slave every effort out of us for boost their production.
Hey, could we have a little share, a people contribution,
for four hundred years of building up your nation?

I'm Black History. I'm Black Culture.
I'm Black History. I'm Black Culture.

They kidnap you long ago and disabuse your mind,
that you don't even know your name, even your language.
You were living in a blind state where you couldn't communicate.

I said they're robbing, they're robbing my culture.
I said they're robbing, they're robbing my culture.

Now is the time to reeducate yourself.
Cause we're living in a time that is reorganizing itself.
So get right up, it's time to get your supper.

I'm Black History. I'm Black Culture.
I'm Black History. I'm Black Culture.
—"I'm Black History"
Soul Vibes, Pachanga Records, 1989

This book is a study of identity formation and politics among the African
Caribbean "Creole" people who live on Nicaragua's southern Caribbean
Coast. It springs from my experiences, particularly the struggles I
participated in while living and working in Bluefields, Nicaragua, for

almost a decade in the turbulent 1980's. During those years in Bluefields I devoted much of my energy to a collective search for solutions to problems facing the Creole population, problems ranging from the community's crumbling economic base to the mutual mistrust and animosity between most Creole people and the Sandinista revolutionary government. Many of the concerns the book treats originally arose as practical problems associated with the troubled Creole/Sandinista relationship.

This book, then, was born in the context of my active participation in Nicaragua's revolutionary politics and is an expression of my continuing efforts to engage in an anthropology of liberation. It is not a conventional ethnography, and I do not consider myself a conventional ethnographer. My goals in Bluefields were to live as part of the community and to contribute to a political process—not to produce a commodified ethnographic account of the "Other." Therefore, my work was not "fieldwork" but "homework"—the work of a committed fellow resident, not a visiting observer (Visweswaran 1994; Williams 1995).

One of the book's guiding assertions is that explicitly political engagement and activity can enhance ethnographic insights, sharpen theoretical understandings, and legitimize ethnographic authority. Accordingly, I begin with a reflexive portrayal of my political convictions and involvements, how they guided my life and work in Nicaragua and gave shape to this ethnography. Here I also establish my positioning as the author(ity) of this text. I argue, however, that it is the politically engaged character of my work that most directly addresses the much-lamented crisis of ethnographic authority.[1]

As I became more deeply involved in the Creole community during the early 1980's, I found that its history offered answers to many of the questions that arose as we sought solutions to the community's problems. For example, one difficulty in the early years of the Revolution was the seeming inability of many Creoles to adjust to the state-controlled system for the distribution of basic consumer items. My and my colleagues' historical research around these issues found that, in general, Creoles had occupied an intermediary position in the labor hierarchy during the heyday of the U.S.-dominated economic enclave on the Atlantic Coast. During this period Creoles became accustomed to the ready availability and consumption of imported consumer items. After the Triumph of the Sandinista Revolution, the relative scarcity of such items and the state's regulation of access to them made Creoles feel "poor" and threatened a key symbol of their "middle-class" position in the coast's social hierarchy. This, then, was a source of their discontent and reluctance to fully embrace the new distribution arrangements.

Further research established other ways Creole politics and identity were deeply influenced by Creoles' experiences within the U.S. enclave. It confirmed my impression that the empirical details and analytical generalizations that emerged from careful reconstruction of Creole history provided an indispensable starting point for understanding what went wrong, and why, after the Sandinista Revolution reached the Atlantic Coast in 1979, hence my decision to emphasize ethnohistory in this book. This emphasis was further supported by initial historical research that revealed not only that the Creoles' story was rich and compelling but also that the distinctiveness of Creole history offered a unique perspective on many of the central theoretical and political predicaments of the African Diaspora in general.

About twenty thousand Creoles live in communities scattered along Nicaragua's Caribbean Coast (historically known as the Mosquitia). Creole culture formed within the tiny British-dominated slave society of the Mosquito Coast in the eighteenth century, nearly 150 years before the emergence of the now-dominant Nicaraguan national culture. Although they currently compose only a small minority of the area's racially and culturally diverse population, Creoles have historically played a leading role in its cultural, social, economic, and political life. Despite their longevity and centrality, however, they are missing from Nicaraguan accounts of history, culture, and politics. Surprisingly, they are equally absent from the historiography and ethnography of the African Diaspora in the Americas, even though theirs is among the oldest and most influential of Afro-Caribbean "Creole" cultures.[2] Accordingly, a principal objective of this book is to rectify this neglect by making a place in the written record for the Creole people and their unique experience.

As I recount this Creole ethnohistory and ethnography, I explore a series of interconnected conceptual themes that run through the text. These themes are at the center of current debates concerning the cultures, identities, and politics of the African Diaspora.

The first of these themes revolves around the fascinating—and often puzzling—record of intertwined processes of accommodation and resistance in Creole Nicaraguans' history. A solid and relatively conventional representation of Creole history such as Holm's (1978), which on many levels I greatly admire, goes like this. A central feature of Creole ethnogenesis was the process of accommodation by African and Amerindian peoples to their violent enslavement by the British in eighteenth-century Mosquitia. Then, through most of the nineteenth century Creole resistance resulted in one of the hemisphere's few societies where black people achieved a quasi-independent status. From the late nineteenth through the early twentieth centuries, Creoles steadfastly resisted Nicaragua's exercise of national control over the eastern half of the country. Subsequently, from the 1940's through the 1970's, Creoles accommodated Nicaraguan nationalism and state power and played a role in the consolidation of the notorious Somoza regime.

Similar readings of more recent Creole history, which emphasize such accommodationist tactics, earned Creoles a reputation among Nicaraguan Mestizos for passivity and "reactionary" politics. These denigrating generalizations persisted well into the Sandinista era, when Creole support for the United States and the Creoles' "counterrevolutionary" stance toward the Sandinistas' efforts to "liberate" them, reinforced their reputation for capitulation to dominance (see, e.g., Adams 1981a, 1981b; Bourgois 1981, 1985; Gordon 1985).

In some respects, the account that follows affirms this seesawing periodization of Creole history, from accommodation to resistance and back again. I question, however, the validity of such dichotomous representations and demonstrate, instead, how Creole politics has simultaneously embodied both accommodation and resistance. This position, in turn, is a particular manifestation of the book's central argument: Creole politics is not monolithic, internally consistent, or stable. From the moment of ethnogenesis onward, Creoles have encompassed multiple, contradictory—in a word, disparate—patterns of thought and action. These internal complexities should be viewed neither as anomalies nor as evidence of social disarray. They are historical products. More specifically, they emerge from what I call—drawing inspiration from Antonio Gramsci—Creole political common sense. My intention is to delve beneath outward expressions of Creole political thought and action to probe and analyze the historically produced quasi-explicit reservoir of shared practices and ideas that Creoles use to interpret the world around them. Rather than a history of political events, structures, or actors, this study is first and foremost a history of Creole political common sense and of the generative relationship between common sense and what we have come to understand as Creole politics.

The culminating moment in this history is the remarkably rapid shifts in Creole politics during the early 1980's, which resulted in serious and outright conflict between most Creole people and the Sandinista Revolution. In 1979 Creoles accepted the Mestizo-led Sandinista Revolution while simultaneously asserting Creole racial and ethnic rights. By 1985 most rejected the Revolution while endorsing Mestizo and Anglo power. The book explicates these transformations and seeming contradictions in Creole identity formation and politics through a critical ethnohistory and ethnography of Creole political common sense.

The logic of my focus on Creole common sense as a means of understanding Creole politics also applies to my analysis of identity formation. Too often, analysts of Creole politics, and of racial politics more broadly, have derived conclusions about a people's identity directly from observations of their political actions in one particular moment. My argument, in contrast, is that identity and politics are not necessarily coterminous and that we can learn much more about Creole identity formation by tracing its relationship not to specific political actions, but, fundamentally, to its generation from past configurations of Creole political common sense. Just as Creole common sense is multiple and contradictory, so, too, are the formations of identity that it generates and sustains. I demonstrate in these pages not only that the content of Creole identity changes over time but also that, at any one moment, it is claimed by people of great cultural, class, and "racial" diversity. This suggests that essentialist understandings of Creole, or any other racial/cultural identity, must be reconsidered.[3]

This approach also provides a useful basis for understanding the impact of dominant racialized discourse on the identity formation of subordinated people such as the Creoles. For example, I analyze at length how Mestizo elites in western Nicaragua talk and write about Creoles in the public arena. Although such discourse surely did shape how Creoles thought about themselves (i.e., how they "identified"), the pervasive effects, I argue, occurred as it shaped the content of Creole common sense, the symbolic reservoir on which processes of identity formation draw.

The contemporary racialized discourse of Mestizo elites is but one example of the inequitable conditions under which Creole common sense has been formed since the seventeenth century. These conditions, in turn, are the point of departure for understanding the evolving content of Creole identity. I am especially interested in two disparate strands of Creole identification—one "black" and the other "Anglo"—because of the implications of this coexistence for Creole politics and, more broadly, for theories of the African Diaspora. Both roots (the social memory of slavery and the idea of Jamaica, other Caribbean islands, and, more distantly, Africa as homelands) and routes (an identification with black Caribbean and North American popular culture) are the basis of the Creoles' black diasporic identity (Gilroy 1993). Paradoxically, many Creoles simultaneously identify with peoples of the transnational Anglo community. Again, both roots—the social memory of Creole participation in first British and then U.S. white dominance in the Mosquitia, and Britain as an ancestral homeland—and routes—the central commonality of English as mother tongue and shared Protestant religion—are the foundations of this identity. Hence I argue that Creole transnational-diasporic identity is not unified or essential but comprises at least two highly disparate elements.

This suggests that scholarly notions of diasporic identity as based on externally imposed or self-ascribed racial categories or even as unified and necessary products of racially specific shared memories and experiences should be reconsidered. In the Creole case, the formation of disparate diasporic identities must be understood, at least in part, as a tactical positioning implemented by the community within the context of diverse transnational racial ideologies and in confrontation with particular national racial hegemonies.

Though preeminently a constructed cultural politics, the Creoles' disparate diasporic identities are not endlessly contingent or hybrid. The generative relationship between Creole political common sense and both Creole politics and identity provides the grounds to argue for their specificity and particularity. Creole political common sense has been dynamically constructed over the course of Creole history, and its content is unique to Creoles' historical experience. Therefore, Creole identity and politics are circumscribed by and exhibit a particularity based in the unique specifics of Creole history embedded in their political common sense.

The book's organization is roughly chronological, with major thematic objectives stretching across its chapters. Chapter 1 contains a narrative of the initial years of my life and politics in Nicaragua. Simultaneously, this narrative provides a contextualizing description of the political, social, and spatial setting of my work there and indicates how the principal themes of the book emerged from my involvement in Creole struggles.

Chapters 2 and 3 provide a historical account of the Creole community from the arrival of Africans through the 1960's. These chapters also explore the relationship between the evolution of the Creoles' identities and the community's political processes. In Chapter 2 I place particular emphasis on the group's ethnogenesis as a unique form of Maroon society. Here the simultaneity of resistance and accommodation to dominance that characterized this process is first introduced as a theme that will infuse the remainder of the book. Chapter 3 presents a narrative of Creole reincorporation into Western modernity. Here I describe how Creole politics is played out within the negotiated space of a series of hegemonic projects. Both chapters are preeminently accounts of the historical formation of Creole political common sense. Thus they introduce the theme of its historically constructed and multiple character.

In Chapter 4 I present Creole accounts of their history that emphasize their multiple interpretations of key historical moments. The chapter provides a partial palliative to my authoritative account of Creole history by broadening that history's depiction and demonstrating the great variety of historical interpretations contained in "everyday" accounts of collective memory. The chapter also performs two other types of work. First, inasmuch as social memory is central to the constitution of contemporary political common sense, chapter 4 contributes to the later discussion of the diversity of contemporary Creole politics and identities. Second, it introduces the theme of Creoles' diasporic identities by presenting the selective social memories of Creole origins that are the "roots" of these disparate transnational identities.

Chapter 5 examines dominant Mestizo representations of the Creoles, of other Costeños (Atlantic Coast people), and of the coast as a region, and the ways they are situated in relation to the imagined Nicaraguan nation. The chapter describes the national and racial hegemonies and transnational ideologies that, through their effect on Creole common sense, have mediated the construction of Creole identities and politics. It completes the historical and contextualizing groundwork undertaken in the previous chapters to develop the book's culminating theme: the generative relationship between Creole political common sense and contemporary Creole politics.

Chapter 6 describes Creole political common sense during the 1970's and the early 1980's by analyzing a series of Creole social movements. Drawing on this analysis and that of previous chapters, I illustrate the manner in which contemporary Creole political common sense was historically constructed and mediated by diverse social processes. I place special emphasis on its ambiguous, multiple, and contradictory character as one effect of that diversity. This chapter also contains my argument regarding the disparate character of Creole transnational identities as part of the more general discussion of political common sense.

The ethnography of Creole political common sense and identity in the 1970's and the 1980's sets the stage for discussion of the manner in which Creole politics was generated from political common sense. Chapter 7 presents an ethnographic treatment of the transformations in Creole political expression in Bluefields during the early to mid-1980's. In this chapter I illustrate, in narrative form, how changes associated with the revolutionary process influenced the emergence of a series of sets of ideas from Creole political common sense. These in turn served as organizing principles around which explicit Creole political practices were formed and produced the series of seemingly contradictory shifts in Creole politics during the period in question.

Finally, I conclude by stepping back to reassess the book's politics and potential contributions to the Creole community, given the enormous changes that have taken place in Nicaragua since I began work there and the changes in my insertion in the community. I also briefly summarize the study's contributions to a number of theoretical debates in the literature on the African Diaspora and race in Latin America.

A final detail before I begin. While I am the author(ity) of this book, many have contributed to it and to the work from which it emerges. Years of interaction with Daisy and Charles as well as Mike Gray and Greg Jackson have deeply influenced the book's intellectual and political ideas and stances. I hope the book reflects the concerns for social justice and humanistic principles my parents, Drs. Susan G. and Edmund W. Gordon, instilled in me. Others contributed in many different ways: Prof. Hugo Sujo, Mr. Alan Stephenson, Miss Azalee Hodgson, Miss Maude Berger, Mr. George Berger, Miss Alma Archibald, Mark Anderson, Galio Gurdian, Justin Wolfe, James Brow, Kamala Visweswaran, Richard Stephenson, Noreen White, Katherine Yih, Jeffrey Gould, Philip Dennis, Rev. Vernon Nelson of the Moravian Archives, the Inter-Library Loan staff of UT-Austin, Virginia Hagerty, Kathy Bork, Carolyn Palaima, CIDCA, Ronald Hodgson, and St. Clair Drake. Over the course of the nearly twenty years that have elapsed since I first went to Nicaragua and the experience that became this book began, many others have also contributed both positively and negatively to this project; many thanks to all.

1.

Introduction: Race, Identity, and Revolution

Well.

He was a poet
a priest
a revolutionary
compañero
and we were right
to be seduced.

He brought us greetings
from his countrypeople
and informed us
with lifted
fist
that they would not
be moved.

All his poems
were eloquent.

I liked
especially
the one
that said
the revolution
must
liberate
the cougars, the trees,
and the lakes;
when he read it
everyone

breathed
relief;
ecology
lives
of all places
in Central
America!
we thought.

And then he read
a poem
about Grenada
and we
smiled
until he began
to describe
the women:

Well. One Woman
when she smiled
had shiny black
lips
which reminded him
of black legs
(vaselined, no doubt),
her whole mouth
to the poet
revolutionary
suddenly
a leg
(and one said
What?)

Another one,   the poet
duly noted by   the priest
the priest,   and the revolution
apparently   never seem
barely attentive   to arrive
at a political   for the black woman,
rally   herself.
eating
a mango   Only for her black lips
                                          or her black leg
Another wears   does one or the other
a red dress,   arrive;
her breasts   only for her
(no kidding!)   devouring mouth
like coconuts. . . .   always depicted
                                          in the act
Well. Nobody ever said   of eating
supporting other people's revolutions   something colorful
wouldn't make us
ill: only for her breasts
                                          like coconuts
But what a pity   and her red dress.
that

—Alice Walker, "Well"
(posted on my office wall, CIDCA-Bluefields, 1980's)

I would have liked to be reflexive without nostalgia. But how does one write about the defining period in one's adult life without nostalgia?

On July 17, 1981, I arrived in Managua on a plane from Miami filled with political tourists. Somehow I fell in with a group of Canadian solidarity types. Douglas, a Nicaraguan who was moving back to "Nicaragua libre" (free Nicaragua) after many years of exile in Canada, was guiding the group. He invited some of us to stay with his extended family in their Mon. Lezcano compound right next door to Alexis Argüello's father's place. The Amador family, distantly related to Carlos Fonseca, were fine people to whom I will always be indebted. I was to impose on their hospitality for four months.

Two days later we were awakened before dawn by the sound of fireworks, can drumming, pot banging, car horns, and *consignas* (political slogans). We all turned out for the long march to the Plaza de la Revolución, along with hundreds of thousands of others, to celebrate the second anniversary of the Triumph of the Sandinista Revolution.

My Spanish at the time was almost nonexistent, so I did not get much of the literal meaning of the speeches, but I thought they spoke to the world *for* me, as I believed that they precisely mirrored my politics, my dreams for humanity. Despite my bad Spanish, my memory of this and many other such occasions in those first years in revolutionary Nicaragua are not of miscommunication or lack of understanding but of being totally caught up in the flow of events, in the excitement of participating in something of transcendent value.

These were heady times, and I had a head full of agendas. I had long since decided that my goal to change the world would be best pursued from outside the United States. As anyone could see from the reactionary depths (or so they seemed then) of the Carter administration, the turn the country had taken over the succeeding decade dramatically reduced the prospects for radical social change from the inside; however, elsewhere all seemed possible. In the late 1970's I had followed from a distance and rooted for the revolutions in Grenada and Nicaragua. I attended a few solidarity events in San Francisco but did nothing more active on their behalf. Then, casting myself as a politicized expert in small-scale fisheries, I traveled to both countries in 1979–1980, looking for a place in these newly liberated societies.

I had prepared myself and been prepared by others. I felt I had much to offer. I was a young (multiracial) black man who had been brought up in a home created by intellectual and professional parents where Marxist analysis and leftist politics were de rigueur. My youth was spent in one of the oldest cooperative communities in the United States in the company of the children of WWII war resisters, pacifist Quakers, progressive Jews, civil rights activists, and biracial couples. My parents and I picketed Woolworth's, integrated swim clubs, demonstrated against the bomb, marched on Washington . . . some of my oldest memories are of one political action or another. As a young adult I had been deeply and passionately involved in the campus politics of the early 1970's, mostly through black student organizations. In graduate school I was trained by St. Clair Drake, one of the U.S. black community's great public intellectuals, and by Bridget O'Laughlin, a Marxist anthropologist and activist who abandoned a promising academic career to participate in the revolutionary process in Mozambique. By the time I arrived in Managua, I had spent a couple of years in Belize teaching elementary school, tending bar, and doing fieldwork for a dissertation in social anthropology on fishing cooperatives. I had just simultaneously completed that degree and a master's in marine sciences (fisheries). I was willing to devote my life (or at least the foreseeable future) to revolutionary change.

Grenada's Fisheries Department said it could use me but had no resources to support me. Maybe, they said, they could come up with some funds through the United Nations. I never heard from them again. The Nicaraguans also said that they could use someone with my expertise.

I was marketing myself as a fisheries expert who knew a great deal about small-scale fisheries in the Caribbean. Nicaragua has a long Caribbean coastline and an important industrial fishing industry. The Sandinistas also had the idea that rationalizing the fishing activities of small, largely subsistence-level fishermen would be an important step toward developing the region already considered a dicey area for the Revolution. I was hired by INPESCA (Instituto Nicaragüense de la Pesca—Nicaraguan Fishing Institute). Receiving the job offer from Nicaragua while living in married-student housing at Berkeley (although I was unmarried and attending Stanford) and obsessing simultaneously over an M.A. thesis and a Ph.D. dissertation was one of the most exciting moments of my life.

I began taking Spanish lessons—the kind where, instead of studying grammar, you sing songs ("De colores") and role-play—to no avail. I joined the African Peoples Socialist Party (APSP). I don't really remember whether this was before or after I got the job. Probably before. The party's attraction was multiple: I was a political animal without an organizational connection (there is no one more disconnected from everything than a graduate student writing a dissertation). I decided I needed a political organization to belong to and these folks were *organized.* They were also relatively sophisticated theoretically. I needed a black group with a class analysis. They had one. They thought that socialism was the answer to the capitalism-induced "troubles of the world." They also thought racism was important and not completely an artifact of class oppression. So did I. They believed that poor black people (this was before "African" Americans) in the United States, by virtue of their multiple oppressions, would lead the rest of the oppressed in waging antiracist and socialist revolution. Sounded good to me.

The African Peoples Socialist Party also had what they represented as a long-running association with the FSLN (Frente Sandinista de Liberación Nacional—Sandinista National Liberation Front). They supported the revolutionary effort in Nicaragua and defended the newly formed Government of National Reconciliation. They also believed that the FSLN was indebted to them. (I never figured out what this debt consisted of. I guessed that it had something to do with arms, but no one ever told me specifically.) What a great combination—good revolutionary politics and a secret, ultraradical in with the Sandinistas as well.

When it became clear that I really was going to live in Nicaragua, I began talking to the "chairman" of the APSP about the kind of relationship the party could have with the FSLN. We knew there were black people living in Nicaragua and that they resided mostly on the Atlantic Coast. We had also begun to hear stories about the problems the Revolution was having with blacks and other people of color in that area. Being black and therefore "experts" on blackness and also fancying ourselves as a vanguard party of black and other oppressed peoples, we figured we were in a good position to give the FSLN advice on its problem. We thought that we could also learn something of value for the black liberation movement in the United States. Military training was an aspect of this, but also of interest to us was how the particular race-based demands of blacks could be harmonized with the other aspects of organizing and executing a socialist society.

In early 1981 I received word that there had been a serious confrontation between the Afro-Amerindian Miskitu people on Nicaragua's Atlantic Coast and the FSLN. The APSP had an auxiliary group composed mostly of white lesbian feminists who were extremely political, organized, and hard working. (Actually, as far as I could tell, they were the core of the organization in the Bay Area.) Some of these folks had been monitoring the Nicaraguan newspapers and provided me with a translation of the reports of this incident. The disaster took place in the Moravian church at Prinzapolka in February 1981. Four Sandinista military and four Miskitu were killed in a confrontation in which the former were attempting to arrest some Miskitu on charges of separatist activity. It looked as if, contrary to our best theorizations, what we took to be Nicaragua's socialist revolution was beginning to founder on the rock of racial contradictions rather than being led by them. I was charged by the APSP to go to Nicaragua to initiate party-to-party talks and to offer the services of the APSP in helping resolve these problems. Once in the country and once I became more familiar with the exact nature of the problem, I was to devise a plan to achieve this end.

So I put my personal relationships on hold. (Actually, as with most graduate students, the most significant had ended.) I finished my degrees in June. In July, after visiting my parents, I left for Nicaragua. I thought I was going for at least five years. I was gone for almost ten.

After all the July 19 celebrations were completed and the country got back to work, I started in earnest on my various agendas. I went to INPESCA looking for Sergio Martínez, the head of Ecosistemas Acuáticos (Aquatic Ecosystems), who had offered me employment. He was nowhere to be found and no one else knew anything about my situation. All I could do was wait until he got back. Opinion was divided about when that might be. After a number of weeks, I finally got the word from someone in INPESCA that Sergio Martínez was back in the country and had actually been there for some time but was avoiding me. Evidently, he was reluctant to break the news to me that INPESCA no longer was responsible for *pesca artesanal* (artisanal fishing) on the Atlantic Coast and that he was not in a position to hire me for the job he had offered. I was referred to a number of other governmental ministries that might be interested in employing me.

Simultaneously, I went in search of the APSP's political connections so that I could get started on our project to "save" the Atlantic Coast. I met a number of times with a Peruvian who had been one of the party's principal contacts in the Bay Area before the Triumph. He got me in touch with the FSLN's DRI (Dirección de Relaciones Internacionales— International Relations Directorate) and I think he even went to one of my original meetings with them. I had letters of introduction and had begun working on a proposal for the project. My plan was to have an APSP cadre come down and live in Bluefields, the town on the Atlantic Coast with the largest concentration of blacks in the country. I felt that black APSP members and I would have a natural, self-evident affinity with Nicaraguan blacks to which the latter were sure to respond. We would work to politicize black people in Bluefields by "opening their eyes" to the racism inherent in U.S. imperialism. We planned to point out U.S. whites' history of neocolonial exploitation of people of color overseas. We especially wanted to clarify for them the racism against blacks inherent in U.S. society and free them of what was turning out to be a distressing tendency to view the U.S. government and white people as models and allies rather than as enemies. I was seeking a formal party-to-party relationship with the FSLN under which we could carry out this and other initiatives that could contribute to the success of the Sandinista Revolution and black liberation worldwide.

Unfortunately, I was not getting anywhere with either of my agendas. Managua was very hot, very dusty, and extremely decentralized. The city had no center; it was like a doughnut. The old downtown had been destroyed by the 1972 earthquake and, because of the Somoza regime's corruption, it was never rebuilt. There were government offices in all parts of the city, and it was difficult to get around. I hadn't mastered the bus system and was afraid taxi drivers would take advantage of me. I did a lot of walking—from office to home to office and home again. I did a lot of waiting: *fulano de tal* (so and so) was not in but would soon be back; *fulana de tal* was out of town; *fulano de tal* had unfortunately forgotten our appointment; *fulana de tal* no longer works in this ministry; this ministry no longer handles this set of issues; come back this afternoon, tomorrow, next week, next month; there is nothing we can do for you, don't come back here; go to this ministry; go to that office; go see *fulano de tal*; I don't know whom you should see.

I managed to borrow a typewriter and spent my free time typing up my vita, working on the APSP project (it was looking really good), and reading the newspaper in the shady tiled courtyard of the Amador family compound. I didn't get to visit cooperatives, talk to revolutionaries about their work, or tour the countryside, as other political tourists were doing. I was too afraid that if I didn't spend every day visiting offices in this dispersed and disorganized bureaucracy, I might miss an opportunity to advance my position. I did not want to go home. What was I going back to? Given my lofty goals, an academic job, even if I could get one, seemed revolting and almost treasonable.

The most promising of the ministries to which I had been directed was the Instituto Nicaragüense de la Costa Atlántica (Nicaraguan Atlantic Coast Institute—INNICA). INNICA was created in late 1980 to govern the Coast. It had taken over responsibility for small-scale (artisanal) fishing in the area. I figured they would also be interested in the APSP project. I started making regular pilgrimages to its offices in the distant and posh Las Colinas area.

INNICA had its Managua headquarters in a house presumably confiscated from a former member of the Somocista *alta burguesía* (elite). I got nowhere fast there either. The young woman who was assigned to listen to my problem seemed barely able to understand me, never mind the complexity of my "progressive" agenda. A number of times I traveled the long distance in the hot sun and dust with no concrete results.

I had been at this game for more than a month. I was running out of money and hope and I was confused. The situation seemed contradictory to me. Here was a national revolution that I understood to be the embodiment of my politics. I supposed that the Sandinistas were universally on the side of the oppressed, that we shared a common conception of what constituted oppression, and that they were in the vanguard of the opposition to such oppression worldwide. I understood that they were fundamentally opposed to American imperialism. This meant to me that they rejected not only the class aspects of this form of oppression but also its cultural and racial features as well. Here I was— a skilled black man, steeped in the racial politics of the capitalist, racist beast itself—offering my political and technical expertise for a minimal charge to a revolution I thought should value it and so obviously needed it; and yet clearly I was not being embraced by these revolutionaries with whom I believed I shared so much.

I have since come to understand some of the things that were so perplexing to me in 1981. Among the reasons I was having so much trouble were a number that have little to do with the major themes of this book. For example, I have come to understand that my APSP connection was a liability. Almost immediately after the Triumph, the FSLN attempted to portray itself as the leadership of a nation in the international community of nations. This meant that it was cutting its ties with small, radical fringe *grupúsculos* (tiny groups) like APSP. These groups were seen as potentially embarrassing hindrances rather than as allies. This was one reason my attempts at consolidating party-to-party relationships through the project I had proposed were never seriously entertained. (I was not told this at the time.)

Another of the problems I had in selling myself as a fisheries expert had to do with changes in the state's lines of authority regarding the Coast. INNICA was in the process of consolidating its power over government activity on the Coast and was engaged in a sometimes fractious effort to wrest control of these activities from those ministries that had previously been in charge of them. Therefore, INPESCA did not have the authority to hire me to work in artisanal fishing on the Coast. INNICA could have, but its efforts to develop small-scale fishing were being handled by economists and not by fisheries experts. They saw no pressing need to hire someone with my skills and my dubious "imperialist" connections.

On top of all this, I was presenting myself as a highly qualified fisheries expert. Such *técnicos* (technicians) generally were arrogant, well dressed (in expensive *guayaberas*), sweet smelling, well spoken, wore Ray-Bans, carried *mariconeras* (men's wallets), and rode in cars. I, on the other hand, was humbly intimidated, relatively unassuming, dressed in button-down short sleeves and painter's pants, a light-skinned black with a mid-sized Afro, always a little sweaty and a little ripe ("stink of sun," as Creoles would say) from walking across town, wore no sunglasses, carried a floppy old leather bag, and was inarticulate. To top it off, I was a gringo without clear institutional ties. Who is this black hippie? Does he really have these degrees? He sure doesn't look like it. What is he doing here? Whom is he really working for? The *African Peoples Socialist Party* from the United States? He wants to go to the *Atlantic Coast*? Nobody in their right mind wants to live there.

The basic reasons why the Sandinista reaction to me seemed so contradictory do speak directly to major themes of this book. These reasons slowly became apparent to me and are being fully articulated for the first time here. For the Sandinistas who were considering my case, I not only was strange (in multiple senses of the word), I was also potentially dangerous. The issues of race and culture that the APSP and I assured the Sandinistas we would raise for them on the Atlantic Coast were viewed quite negatively. The Sandinistas had not considered the possibility that they themselves or their policies could be interpreted as racist. They thought of racism as a secondary mode of oppression characteristic of the United States and South Africa—not of Nicaragua. For them racism was an epiphenomenon of class exploitation. Now that the American imperialists had been routed from the Coast and the country was on the road to socialism, racism was no longer a relevant issue for that region. They reasoned that questions of racial and cultural identity undercut the class and national basis for unity under the auspices of the Revolution and raised the specter of separatism for the strategically critical Atlantic Coast. What I was proposing to them smacked of *divisionismo* (divisionism) and was to be avoided at all costs.

Moreover, since Mestizos had a racialized notion of Creoles, they were in constant fear of the potential for race-based politics on the part of blacks. The Sandinistas had just recently had a problem with a black Costa Rican, Kalalú, who had stirred up feelings of racial solidarity among blacks in Bluefields, and they did not want a repeat performance. Furthermore, I was insisting on my blackness, the APSP was a bunch of blacks, and we wanted to work with blacks. Nicaragua's racial ideologies were such that it was difficult for Mestizo Sandinistas to identify with us or the problems we were enunciating. It was even harder for them to believe that these *black* North Americans had something of value to offer the Mestizo vanguard of the politically exemplary Sandinista Revolution. In their revolutionary righteousness, most Sandinistas felt that, by definition, the Revolution could not be racist. They considered expression of doubts in this regard to be tantamount to treason. My racial politics and agenda and that of the APSP were so totally out of sync with the Sandinistas' that we were viewed as dangerous agitators, potential threats to the Revolution. Hilda Bolt, the person from the DRI who was responsible for me, was trying to contain me, to get from me as much information as possible without giving me formal recognition and then get rid of me. To the rest, the APSP and I were pariahs.

Fortunately, the people at INNICA asked Galio Gurdian, a University of Chicago–trained anthropologist who spoke fluent English, to meet with me to see if he could decipher what I was really after. Galio was in the process of creating INNICA's research organ, the Centro de Investigación y Documentación de la Costa Atlántica (Center for Atlantic Coast Research and Documentation—CIDCA).

Though wary of me at first, Galio gave me a job. I thought that I had been hired for my fisheries expertise. Years later I found out that this was not the case; my black activism and my association with the APSP played no positive role either. (After a while Galio gently intimated that there was no chance my project would fly.) I was hired because I had conventional academic credentials as an anthropologist and because I was one of the few qualified social scientists in the country not already indispensably employed by the state or associated with a competing tendency in the FSLN. In fact, CIDCA's initial staff of social investigators was composed of myself and two other internationalists, an Uruguayan and another gringo. The rest of INNICA conceived of us as a group as eccentric, slightly dirty (I swear I took a shower twice a day every day), and disheveled hippies, with liberal rather than radical political tendencies.

There were some initial contradictions within the CIDCA group. Guillermo, the Uruguayan, was big on class analysis. We spent many weeks sitting around the CIDCA office reading and arguing about whether or not the FSLN's growing problems with the Miskitu were based in ethnic differences or the counterrevolutionary attitudes of an emerging Miskitu bourgeoisie. Initially, Guillermo didn't have much time for secondary phenomena like race and culture. In the first month or so, all this discussion was pretty academic. I can't remember if he had ever visited the Atlantic Coast; if he had, it was only a short trip. I certainly had not. My only contact with Costeños took the form of casual greetings exchanged at the office with a few who were employed by INNICA. I was so raw that my initial written offering, a piece on the overexploitation of coastal resources by foreign capital (ultimately published in *Barricada*), mistakenly located the main colonial Pacific port on the Caribbean Coast.

Nevertheless, in a relatively short time, we at CIDCA were able to hammer out a position of critical support for the FSLN's attitudes and policies toward the Coast. We argued that racially and ethnically based differences and demands of Costeños had to be taken into account in any analysis of the problems the Revolution faced in that region. We also felt that, rather than being divisive, the struggle against racism and ethnocentrism under the revolutionary umbrella could serve as a unifying factor between Mestizos and the Amerindian and African-descended groups of the Coast in the face of the white supremacy of U.S. imperialism.

Well. It should have been obvious to us, but I recall being surprised when the positions of INNICA's leaders continually demonstrated that they neither fully understood nor completely shared our views—even though the FSLN's political discourse was extremely eloquent in its denunciation of exploitation and oppression and in its solidarity with the struggles of subaltern peoples everywhere. One indicative incident centered around a photo of children of a number of the different coastal ethnic groups on the front page of INNICA's new publication. The photo was obviously intended to preach ethnic harmony within the Nicaraguan nation and the Revolution. The caption named each of the ethnic groups represented in the photo: Miskitu, Sumu, Creole, and so on. The Mestizo child was identified as *blanco* (white)! INNICA's brown-skinned Mestizos identified racially more closely with the white imperialists they were battling than with brown and black Costeños.

In those days we at CIDCA were responsible for producing drafts of position papers and speeches to be presented by INNICA's *comandantes* (commanders) to explain the situation on the Coast and the FSLN's position on it to the outside world. We worked particularly hard preparing such items for the United Nations Conference on Human Rights held in Managua in December 1981. We were fashioning a position paper positing the multiethnic character of Nicaraguan national identity and championing the fight against the vestiges of racism inherited from the Somoza regime. I was pleased and not a little surprised when, after reading one rendition of this argument, Comandante Ramírez stated that he entirely agreed with our stance denouncing the racism that continued to exist in Nicaragua. My surprise turned to chagrin when he neatly and unknowingly turned our argument on its head.

Well. He noted that he was pleased to find that we agreed with an impression that he had lately formulated himself. He was now convinced that the problems the Frente was encountering on the Coast were in large part the result of Costeño racism against Spanish speakers from the Pacific! Claims of reverse racism coming from the mouth of a *comandante de la revolución.*

In perhaps our small CIDCA team's most prescient act, some time in mid to late 1981, we proposed what we thought was a revolutionary solution to the problems the FSLN was having on the Coast. We wrote a heretical position paper calling for the establishment of an autonomous government on the Atlantic Coast that also implicitly critiqued INNICA's policies toward the region. We handed it along the chain of command to the powers that be. We received no response whatever to our proposal. Unfortunately, the revolutionary merit of ideas and practices lay in the eye of the beholder. This type of "liberal" proposal was considered counterrevolutionary and we became even more marginalized within INNICA.

The most serious and contradictory problem I faced in that first year working out of CIDCA's Managua offices had to do with the *traslado,* the relocation in early 1982 of the Miskitu communities situated along the Río Coco on the Nicaraguan border with Honduras. A military decision had been made to remove these people; INNICA was to plan and implement the move.

We foreigners on the CIDCA team were involved in some of the early low-level discussions of the *traslado*'s implementation. Afterwards we were almost totally excluded from discussions on security grounds or because we were opposed to the move or perhaps for both reasons. One plan was to resettle these thousands of Miskitu families throughout areas of the Atlantic Coast that were predominantly Mestizo. The idea was not only that the social base of the counterrevolution would be removed from the border area but also that the problematic Miskitu would acculturate, become Hispanicized campesinos, and eventually be integrated into the nation/Revolution.

I was shocked by the *traslado* decision; however, it was only the most extreme manifestation of a pattern of ideas and practices regarding Costeños that seemed totally inconsistent with my understanding of the Sandinista Revolution's most basic principles. The resort to short-term military solutions rather than longer-term political ones in dealing with ostensibly counterrevolutionary Coast people, while extremely unfortunate, was at least defensible, given the escalating military response of American imperialism.

The strict equation of Mestizo racial/cultural identity with Nicaraguan and revolutionary identities, however, was puzzling; so was the Mestizo Sandinistas' inability to recognize racism and ethnocentrism in the vexed relationship between Mestizos of the Pacific and the racial/cultural groups of the Atlantic Coast. The attempt to make "sense" of these perspectives and practices on the part of Mestizos and to understand their impact on the politics and common sense of Creoles is an important objective of this book.

During my entire stay in revolutionary Nicaragua, the *traslado* was the most serious test of my and my CIDCA colleagues' strategy of critical support of the Revolution. It was a defining moment. Many Miskitu fled across the border to Honduras as their opposition to the Sandinistas solidified. Most of the French internationalists went home, at least partially in protest over this issue. In general, this was a period of mounting contradictions, as the Sandinista-led process of social and political change intensified and opposition sectors consolidated. I briefly wondered whether this might be a good time for me to head back as well; however, I was committed to the struggle for revolutionary change, and my experience with radical politics in the United States had taught me that contradictions were to be expected—though not condoned. Also by this time, I was spending more and more time on the Atlantic Coast. Drawn to it, I stayed.

The CIDCA collective's position of critical support placed me in a very contradictory position. I supported the Revolution's basic principles, publicly advocated and worked hard to further them. Simultaneously, I struggled to produce intellectual work with practical implications that challenged many of the attitudes and policies of the state, the FSLN, and its Mestizo *cuadros* (cadres) toward the Atlantic Coast. Maintaining the political space for this high-wire act in a country being attacked by the United States and in a state of civil war was very difficult. That we were able to persevere in these circumstances for almost a decade is a tribute to the integrity and commitment of our working collective and the astute guidance of CIDCA's director. It is mostly attributable, however, to the Sandinistas' willingness to tolerate loyal but opposing opinion, even when the temptation to stamp it out, given the Revolution's struggle for survival, was the strongest.

During my time in Nicaragua, I also attempted to work with the people of the Atlantic Coast, especially Creoles, to help them clarify and fulfill their collective political, economic, and social aspirations. The Creole project was not straightforward; in many ways it was as contradictory as the FSLN's vis-à-vis the Coast. In part this was an artifact of the paradoxical character of Creole politics and identity.

> No, I'm not a gringo. I'm black!
> —Edmund Gordon

> No, I'm not an American. I'm one of the 22 million black people who are the victims of Americanism. One of the 22 million black people who are the victims of democracy, nothing but disguised hypocrisy. So, I'm not standing here speaking to you as an American . . . no, I'm not. I'm speaking as a victim of this American system. And I see America through eyes of the victim. I don't see any American dream; I see an American Nightmare.
> —Malcolm X
> (sign on my office door, Regional Government Building, Bluefields, 1980's)

I had already written and theorized extensively about the Atlantic Coast before my first visit there in fall 1981. Most of the details of that trip are now mixed up in my memory with those from innumerable other trips made from Managua to Bluefields, across the breadth of the country. That first journey was made in relative comfort, riding shotgun in an INNICA Land Cruiser. Leaving Managua at dawn, we drove five hours across the country. I had been looking forward to this trip. All I knew of Nicaragua after several months of residence was Managua, which, despite its charms, has to be one of the least-attractive cities in the Americas. The changes in terrain, climate, and ecosystem as one proceeds from west to east are dramatic, and the drive, made at top speed over the narrow but paved highway, was exhilarating.

We arrived around midday at Rama, the raw river port gateway to the Atlantic Coast. Bendaña, a Mestizo *técnico* who would later become head of the Southern Regional Government, climbed out of the driver's seat to go see about tickets for the "Express," the wooden riverboat that would take us six hours down the brownish green Río Escondido to Bluefields on the Caribbean. I sat in the car with the door open in front of the restaurant of the famous Hotel Amy—a large, ramshackle, unpainted, Chinese-owned wooden structure that sat terraced over the brink of the steep riverbank. I surveyed the ebb and flow of travelers bustling through the mud, trash, and vendors on the unpaved Rama streets. I alternately gazed at those sitting at small tables in the cavernous interior of the Amy restaurant—talking, joking, sipping cold Victorias, slowly adding to the rows of empty beer bottles on the tables in front of them while they waited for the Express to arrive.

Welcome to the Coast.

A dark and slender young woman stepped up and asked me if the car was returning to Managua that day. I am not sure how I responded. I had met my first "genuine" Costeña on the Coast. I was favorably impressed. This was Daisy. Two years later, among other positive results, our marriage significantly altered my place in Coast society.

Bluefields has changed so much since the day in 1981 when I first arrived that it is difficult for me to remember what it was like during the early 1980's. The Contra war that raged in the area during the mid-1980's triggered a massive emigration of Mestizo campesinos from the hinterland, doubling the town's population from around sixteen thousand when I first arrived to over thirty thousand by the time I left. This demographic revolution transformed the town from a compact, genteel Creole port and administrative center to a sprawling provincial Mestizo market town in a decade. The free fall of the town's economy during this period was topped off by the disastrous Hurricane Joan in 1988, which destroyed more than 80 percent of the town's buildings. Both left a Bluefields that retains important aspects of its historic character, but that also has been rapidly and significantly transformed.

Architecturally, Bluefields was very different from the cities of the Pacific. It reminded me of Belize City, though not so flat, or dirty, or smelly, or crowded, or commercial, and with little vehicular traffic. It is built on a series of low hills on the western bank of the enormous shallow expanse of Bluefields Lagoon, which is its major means of communication with the rest of the world. The center of town in 1981 was composed of small shops, restaurants and *comedores* (restaurants), two movie theaters, some small hotels, banks, and government offices occupying confiscated shops. None of these buildings were more than two stories and most were constructed of cement. The major streets were paved with hexagon-shaped cement paving stones.

Aberdeen Street, the thoroughfare running east and west on the south side of downtown, ran down to the public market. The final block before the lagoon was a chaotic welter of outdoor vendors hawking their wares from enormous bamboo baskets under small, wooden, zinc-roofed stands set up on the curb. They overflowed onto both the sidewalk and the street, partially blocking the doors of the more solid commercial establishments behind them. At the bottom of the street was the government-built enclosed market, where there were more booths brimming with products and which led out to a small wharf on the lagoon. Here the goods for sale arrived in everything from dugout canoes (dories) to fifty-foot wooden boats. A block and a half south of the market, just down from the corner where Duarte meets Commerce Street (the major north-south thoroughfare through downtown), the squat cement *cuartel* (police station and jail) sat on a rise overlooking the lagoon.

To the north of downtown, another thoroughfare led to the municipal wharf. It always swarmed with boats and people and was the place where larger craft from the communities up the Coast and down from Rama delivered passengers and goods. Smaller, dilapidated wharves jutted out into the shallow, muddy harbor at the end of streets as they reached the water side and from the back of commercial establishments. The shoreline was littered with garbage and the detritus of sunken, rotting, and rusting boat hulls.

Dominating the center of Bluefields physically, socially, and spiritually was and is the Moravian church complex. The tall, graceful, red-roofed steeple of the church was the preeminent symbol of the town and was pictured in innumerable publications. The massive concrete structure of the Moravian High School anchored the center of the complex and seemed to symbolize the stolid, conservative, and pervasive influence of the church and its ethic on the town.

The principal Creole barrios, the oldest portions of the town, radiated south (Cotton Tree) and north (Pointeen, Beholden, Old Bank) along the lagoon from the downtown area. These barrios were almost entirely black. Mestizos, Creoles, and Miskitu resided inland in the newer, more ethnically integrated, barrios to the west of downtown. Most Creole residential structures were small "West Indian cottages": wooden-framed clapboard structures with wooden floors raised on posts off the ground, steeply pitched corrugated "zinc" roofs, porches off the front and painted, if at all, white or pastel colors. There were some larger wooden houses of the same basic design. In my day, most of these were in advanced states of disrepair.

Most Creole residences had swept yards with flowers and perhaps a few food plants cultivated in them or in containers on the verandah. If there was enough space in the yard, usually there would be some fruit trees as well—mostly coconuts and limes or perhaps breadfruit. Houses were generally placed close together, though none shared common walls. It was not unusual for several houses belonging to adult family members to be clustered on a single lot that had been inherited jointly.

Only a very few buildings located in the town's center were hooked into the puny municipal water system. There was no sewage system at all in Bluefields. Most people had outhouses and obtained their water from their own open wells. As a result, in a massive testing of well water during the mid-1980's, every well tested except for one (and including mine) turned out to be contaminated with fecal matter.

My impressions of Bluefields were and still are dominated by its wet lushness (it seemingly rains all the time); the pungent, muddy squalor of its streets and pathways (the omnipresent litter was mostly mango and other fruit seeds and skins, plastic *gaseosa* [soda] bags, and, outside of downtown, pig shit); and its intimate socialness. The last came from its small size, the crowded closeness of its housing, the "yard" orientation of its inhabitants, and the absence of vehicles. If you wanted to go somewhere, and there was always somewhere to go, you walked. If you walked, you always saw someone you knew and needed to talk to. In Bluefields in the 1980's it took two to three times longer to get some-where than it should have because travel was such an intensely social affair.

That first trip, I stayed in the Hotel Bluefields. It was being converted from a nunnery to a government-run guest house. There was no running water at all. The rooms were stuffy and hot, and at night there were a lot of mosquitoes. But after the alienation of Managua—the language, the intense demand for political orthodoxy, and Mestizo culture—I knew Bluefields and the Coast was the place for me.

Though I now understand that I was initially hired by CIDCA as an anthropologist, the principal focus of my work during the first five years of my stay in Nicaragua was artisanal fishing. I thought of myself as a fisheries expert, not an anthropologist. My specialty was "development" through small-scale fishing. In 1981 INNICA was working on the implementation of an artisanal fisheries project in the communities of the vast Pearl Lagoon, whose southern tip is about twenty-two miles north of Bluefields. I made several trips to these communities during the latter part of that year and in early 1982 and spent a total of a couple of months headquartered in the Creole village of Pearl Lagoon. It was beautiful—set on the banks of the enormous lagoon and with tidy wooden houses surrounded by gardens; flowers, coconut, breadfruit, and mango trees; laid out along broad, verdant streets mowed by grazing horses and cattle. I made my first Costeño friends in this village of about two thousand. I also got my first lessons in the disjuncture between how I identified myself in relation to what I perceived to be the African peoples of Pearl Lagoon and their perceptions of me.

I arrived on the Coast wearing my Pan-African identity on my sleeve and expecting to be immediately identified as an insider, a distant but clearly related member of the large African racial and cultural extended family. In general, people were friendly and outgoing with me; however, the nickname I was almost immediately given and which stuck with me was "Gringo." For years, I would cringe when the greeting "Hey, Gringo!" was shouted on the streets of Bluefields by one of my acquaintances visiting the town from Pearl Lagoon. After I moved permanently to Bluefields in early 1982, a few people there used that name for me as well. In those early days there were also some who referred to me as "White Man." I protested both. Imagine my mortification! No, I was not a white man. I was black, like them! One of the millions of black people throughout the African Diaspora victimized by racist American imperialism.

I managed to keep the "White Man" to a minimum, though I was never able to get a young Creole/Miskitu who ended up working with me (and who, it turns out, was my future wife's cousin) to totally desist. He refused to admit what was to me my obvious blackness. In fact, he thought it ridiculous that I could be black, but bowing to my energetic protests, he began calling me "Green Man," and still does.

This problem of identity was especially painful and embarrassing because I rapidly came to consider myself the "ultimate" insider and developed quite a stake in that positioning. To this day, I have a problem taking seriously the purported expertise of any non-Creoles on Creole matters. At the time, it was difficult for me to get my mind around this problem of identity—the seemingly paradoxical Creole inability to recognize early on who I *really* was and to be in solidarity with me because of our commonalities in blackness and African heritage. In fact, thinking through this personal conundrum of how I was perceived by Creoles quickly led to the related question of how it was that Creoles conceived of themselves and perceived themselves in relation to other groups. This set of questions became a central aspect of my intellectual work in Bluefields. It is a central feature of this book.

It took me a while to realize that the name "Gringo," while not a nickname of respect, was not necessarily being used derisively. For Creoles, being white and "American" (i.e., North American) was not necessarily bad. Contrary to my expectations, given their decades of exploitation of the area and its people, U.S. whites were generally respected and honored by the residents of Bluefields. So while I was not being accepted into the community as a fellow black person, I was amicably accepted as an "American." This was a relatively unexpected and very contradictory state of affairs for me.

It also had implications for another related set of expectations I had of Creoles—that a strong part of their identity would be tied up in their obvious Africanness and diasporic identification. After all, this was the age of reggae. Hadn't they been listening to Tosh and Marley—"No matter where you come from . . .", "Africa Unite . . ."—as I and everyone else in the Diaspora had. In fact, many had, very closely; however, they were also listening to Jim Reeves, Merle Haggard, and other country and western artists. Strolling through Old Bank and Beholden on balmy Saturday evenings, you had to nimbly shift cadence as you passed in front of houses from which these two musics alternately wafted through open windows and doors into the street. As time went on, I learned that among many Creoles, African origins were downplayed or even denied, and transnational identities and solidarities were just as likely to be shared with those of the Anglo Diaspora as with those of the black Diaspora.

Categorizing me as a gringo or white man also was indicative of what was for me the very surprising indeterminacy of phenotype or "race" in identity formation for many Creoles. I am not very dark or "Negroid" in my looks; however, I am never mistaken for a white person here in the United States. In fact, many Costeños have told me I look like a lot of Creoles, especially those from Corn Island—at least before I open my mouth.

One of my Creole friends told me in the early eighties that a group of political tourists from the United States had recently come through Bluefields. Among them was an African American woman. A little Creole girl saw them passing by and asked her mother, "Mommy, why is that white woman so black?" As we shall see, for many Creoles, the most salient index of social identities is not necessarily phenotypical. In this case, a particular mix of nationality, culture, class, and geographic space rather than "phenotype" or "color" can (but does not always) make whiteness.[1]

> It is wrong to say that the Sandinista revolution today is a revolution made only to benefit the Spanish speaking peoples of the country. To be successful it must be a revolution of all the people of Nicaragua. This is something that the people of both the Atlantic and Pacific portions of the country must recognize if the opportunity for a better future for everyone is not to be lost. The ability of persons of disparate racial and cultural groups, each with its own identity and pride in its identity, to come together to undertake mutually beneficial revolutionary activities is a question of utmost importance to those of us who believe that world revolution is the only answer to imperialism and the world wide human suffering associated with it. I ask our brothers in Nicaragua to take a step forward toward an affirmative answer to this question. It is further of the utmost importance that the Creole and Indigenous populations of Nicaragua take the initiative, as we the Black, Brown, and

Red in the U.S. are now beginning to do, to understand their history and its relationship to North American Imperialism (or Colonialism as we in the U.S. experience it) and how we all have been and are being exploited and manipulated by it.

—Edmund Gordon
(unpublished 1982 paper on General Sandino's operations on the Coast)

I was asked by CIDCA to create and head its regional office in Bluefields. I moved permanently to the town around April 1982. By this time I was partnered with Sasha. Her mother had dropped Sasha off with me in Managua for a yearlong stay. The mother was unable to take care of the four-year-old in Havana, where she had gone to study. Sasha was not biologically mine, and I was no longer with her mother, but she was my daughter. She and I moved to Bluefields and found lodging with an older Creole couple whose son had befriended me in Pearl Lagoon. Kevin and Mabel Whitiker were fine people and lived in one of the cleanest and best-organized houses I have ever had the pleasure of living in—anywhere. (Miss Mabel would wake Mr. Kevin at four o'clock every morning to begin the day's chores, which generally included scrubbing the porch and the outhouse as well as a concentrated cleaning of a particular area of the house selected for that day.)

Much of what I know about "traditional" Creole culture I learned from the Whitikers. They were Creoles of the old school: genteel, pious, hard working, clean, neat, strict, judgmental—Victorian? Thirty-one, with a child but unmarried, I was still a young man in Miss Mabel's eyes and I lived by her rules: lunch at twelve, dinner at six, front door locked by nine. When I got married, I had to move out, even though, since Daisy was attending school and living in Managua, I would have preferred to stay with them. Miss Mabel said it would not look "right." I think the Whitikers were rather proud of their "American" lodger, although I don't think they ever understood my politics or why I had this little girl along with me.

The Whitikers' house stood on an unpaved street/swamp on which horses sometimes grazed in barrio Tres Cruces, just north and west of downtown, close to the park, a block north of the Palacio (municipal building). In my day you did not get muddy approaching the house because the fine high sidewalk that the barrio had recently built passed directly in front. The house was built in typical West Indian style with a front gate in a fence made of beaten half sheets of roofing zinc and a short concrete walk that led up steps and onto the creaky and weathered wooden front verandah. Much to Miss Mabel's chagrin, her Obeahman brother, Solomon, held court there daily for a while sitting and watching the world pass by and selling "somethings" (small yellow plastic tape-covered packets of folded notebook paper with a scripture verse written on it—I looked) to those who knew enough to seek him out.[2]

Inside, the living room ran the length of the original house. Miss Mabel had carefully furnished it with four low rocking chairs, a coffee table with a large plaster German shepherd on it, a black and white television set, some other pieces of miscellaneous furniture, and a curved glass–fronted cupboard. A bare light bulb hung from the ceiling. The cupboard showcased some of her most prized possessions—miscellaneous china, glasses, a few glass or porcelain figurines. The central piece was a china plate with a picture of the Moravian church painted on or glazed into it commemorating the 125th anniversary of the launching of the Moravians' missionary work on the Coast.

The television set was another prized possession. We watched Costa Rican channels every night through a piece of rose-colored glass clipped to the front of the set to simulate color reception (or relieve eye strain—I can't quite remember the explanation). There we sat rocking into the night—Mr. Kevin dozing and Miss Mabel chatting and flicking mosquitoes (which were thick in Bluefields) off of herself, Mr. Kevin, and me with a dish towel in a regular rhythm. Around nine o'clock Miss Mabel would pack the two of them off to bed in their room—in which Sasha also had a small bed—on the other side of the wall that divided the original house in two. I would then retire to my small room, created when an addition had been thrown up on the back of the house to make a small dining room and kitchen area and my bedroom.

A bathhouse was connected to the back of the house and the ample outhouse was about ten feet from this door. This outhouse was *clean*—scrubbed every morning, ashes and lime dumped in it to keep it smelling fine. In the small yard beside the outhouse was a small coconut tree, some flowers, and various food plants. As in most of Bluefields, there was no running water. After a while I took on the morning chore of filling the large plastic tubs—one in the kitchen, the other in the bathhouse.

What a pleasure to live with the Whitikers. Miss Mabel was a fine Creole cook. We ate the Creole everyday standards—rundun and coconut rice and beans regularly. But Miss Mabel also reveled in serving a wide variety of Creole food and she baked. She insisted on cooking with the traditional coconut oil, even though many of the town's less-discriminating chefs were using vegetable oil or lard by this time.

The Whitikers were devout Moravians, as were many Creoles. Every Sunday one or the other would go to church. (One of them stayed behind to guard the house from intruders.) Once a week, when it was her turn, Miss Mabel and other female members would clean the church. Mr. Kevin, dressed in a suit and tie, often served as an usher. They were very serious about their religious commitment, very proud to be Moravians, and strict supporters and adherents of the tough moral code that all Moravians were expected to live by.

Yet for all the propriety, regularity, and Victorian domesticity of the Whitiker household, other equally characteristic aspects of Creole lifestyle intruded into my everyday life with them. Mr. Solomon with his Obeah on the front verandah—a constant source of irritation to Miss Mabel but tolerated. Miss Mabel religiously buying "dooky" (numbers) tickets at the back door. Mr. Kevin selling lottery tickets in the street for a living. Scandalous neighbors whose uncontrolled sexuality was a constant target of Miss Mabel's ire. The young daughters of a neighbor who one by one got pregnant out of wedlock. The unattached older neighbor who shacked up with a taxi driver for a few months. Tension and disputes with a *"vaga"* (disreputable) daughter-in-law. Recriminations against a son who had left for the United States never to return, abandoning his wife—a "decent girl." Breaking a broomstick on the head and back of another son for drinking or smoking ganja or for disrespect or laziness or other offenses. Trips to the herb doctor midwife Mommy Jones to seek gynecological assistance. Repeated admonitions to me never to eat or drink in anyone else's house because someone was sure to slip "something" in my food or drink. Fear of duppys (ghosts) and spirits at night and accounts of encounters with them. Surreptitiously smoked cigarettes.

Thursday through Sunday nights from 7:00 PM to 1:00 or 2:00 AM, the house reverberated with the sounds of Dimensión Costeño, soon to become the most popular band in all Nicaragua. They played in the Blue Soul, the nationally famous nightspot just up the street in the park. *Rancheros,* Spanish ballads, reggae, and *soca.* The songs I remember the best, unfortunately, are the misogynistic ones, the Bluefields calypsos. Falling to sleep to "Come down, Brother Will, come down / Come see what the man have done / Grab up the knife / Stab up he wife / See how the blood de run / Ah, Ah. Ah, Ah," or "Brown skin girl stay home and mind baby," and the voices of revelers in the street.

After having lived with Mr. Kevin and Miss Mabel for some time, it surprised me to discover that, despite all the investment in time and resources they had lavished on their home, they did not own it. The house and land, like many others in Bluefields, were owned by the famous Crowdell family. As far as anyone could tell, there was only one member of that family still living. He had not visited Bluefields for over twenty years and was rumored to be permanently residing in a government mental institution in the United States. A friend of the Crowdell family was charged with collecting rents for him. Nobody seemed to know what she did with the money. Nevertheless, month after month for decades the Whitikers had paid the rent on their domicile. It struck me that this was precisely the kind of situation that the Revolution was waged to address. I said so to the Whitikers, who responded ambivalently. They condemned the Sandinistas' confiscations in general terms and continued for a number of years to pay rent, though many others had long since ceased to do so.

Miss Mabel had also spent many years of her youth working for "white" foreigners at the Bluff (the port facility at the entrance to Bluefields Lagoon) and in Bluefields. She cared for their children and worked in their kitchens. She described a relationship of servile subordination reminiscent of that of generations of black domestic workers in the United States. She was laid off from work after seven years with one family because she had injured a finger at work and could not do all that was expected of her for a time. It appeared paradoxical to me that she remembered these times fondly, and when I asked her, she explained that she got along well with her employers.

Both the Whitikers had only good things to say about white "Americans." They could not understand why the Sandinistas were "picking a fight" with them. They also were very skeptical about Mestizos in general, especially those from the "interior." They bemoaned the ways in which the "Spaniards" kept the Coast from advancing. At the same time, I remember being shocked the first time I heard Miss Mabel, who to my eye was very dark (she claimed to be a Creole/Sumu mix), talk in disparaging racialized terms about "those blacks in Beholden and Old Bank."

In 1982 the Whitikers, like many other Creoles, were bitterly opposed to the Sandinistas and their Revolution. I found this hard to fathom. They seemed to me to have everything to gain from it and little to lose. Most Creoles like the Whitikers were poor by First World standards or even those of Pacific Nicaragua's urban areas. Many like the Whitikers had experienced firsthand exploitation and subjugation by light-skinned local elites and foreign whites. These seemed to me to be precisely the kinds of people who had the most to gain from the Revolution.

I also kept hearing about a time not so long before my arrival when large sectors of the Creole community had supported the Revolution. I heard tales from some young men about their taking over a U.S.-owned fishing enterprise before the Triumph. Others spoke about a group of Creole men who had taken control of Bluefields in the name of the Sandinistas after the Triumph. This group supposedly had a strong black nationalist orientation and had closed down the major industries of the area, including the sugar mill and fishing plants, intending to place them in the hands of the black workers. I heard that Creoles organized by the FSLN in Comités de Defensa Sandinista (Sandinista Defense Committees—CDS) worked together in their barrios to build sidewalks, footbridges, and drainage ditches, clean their neighborhoods, and vaccinate the children.

I immediately thought the more recent problems must have had something to do with race. After all, I understood the problems that we as blacks experienced in the United States almost exclusively in racial terms. Though there were some Creoles I spoke to who mentioned Mestizo domination and arrogance, this did not seem to be the major problem for most. In fact, what I kept getting from the Whitikers was depressingly similar to what I was hearing on The Voice of America and reading in the newspaper clippings my sister was sending me from the United States. The Sandinistas were a bunch of atheistic, war-mongering, anti-American communists who were running the country into the ground with their antidemocratic and unjust policies.

This was all very confusing to me. It seemed so contradictory. If Sandinista racism was not the problem, what could have happened to so rapidly sour Creoles on the Revolution after their initial enthusiasm? Why would poor black people reject a revolution waged against all forms of oppression and back the United States, the center of imperialist racism and class oppression? The search for answers to these paradoxical questions led to my practical and scholarly interest in the processes of Creole identity and politics. This became the major focus of my intellectual work during my years in Bluefields and is the principal theme of this book.

The discordance that existed between the Sandinistas and the Creole community in the mid-1980's created a duality in my personal and intellectual life. At times this duality was more wrenching than that which DuBois so eloquently describes in "The Souls of Black Folks" and which I had experienced as a black American. Working for the revolutionary government and living in the Creole community, I was caught between two forces, neither of which I completely agreed with nor whose logic I totally understood. During this period of war and political turmoil in Nicaragua, one's social and political allegiances were a very serious matter—life and death for some. My radical politics and job with the Sandinistas made me suspect in important sectors of the Creole community while my social and political identification with Creoles made me suspect for many Sandinistas. Both sides found it very hard to place me in this crucial respect.

CIDCA-Bluefields was initially housed in the Casa de Gobierno (Government House) in Bluefields. This was an enormous house on the park that had been confiscated by the Sandinistas after the Triumph. During this period INNICA was dissolved and control of the Coast was "regionalized," giving the regional government in Bluefields, headed by a Creole *comandante,* Lumberto Campbell, a certain amount of autonomy. With the demise of INNICA, CIDCA became a semi-independent organization dedicated to social research. It was funded by the revolutionary government and associated with the regional governments of the North and South. Through my work in fisheries development in the Pearl Lagoon area, I had become experienced in working with the NGOs (nongovernmental organizations) that funded our projects. Consequently, I was made fisheries adviser and director of special projects for the regional government.

In this capacity I spent a lot of time in the communities of the southern Atlantic Coast as a representative of the revolutionary government. It was difficult, if not impossible, for me not to be closely associated in the people's minds with the government. This was somewhat problematic for my relationship with Creoles, but not too bad, because many Creoles worked for the revolutionary government as civil servants while maintaining an uneasy political distance from the FSLN. There were also, however, revolutionary Creoles who were actively political—holding FSLN party positions and loudly espousing their political views. These persons were viewed by many Creoles as traitors. I felt strongly that I did not want to be lumped in with this sector of the community. It would have impeded my efforts to influence politically important sectors of the Creole community and also would have cut me off socially from them. Unfortunately, this placed me in the exceedingly uncomfortable position of only partially revealing my politics. At its most benign, this meant that I often avoided clearly stating my position when it could have been construed by Creole or Miskitu listeners as problematic. Occasionally, it required my seeming to support statements and positions that were contrary to those I actually held.

This was very awkward. It was made worse by some of the activities in which I felt compelled to engage. For example, during this period, government workers were strongly encouraged to demonstrate their identification with the Revolution by marching through the streets of Bluefields shouting political slogans in the frequent demonstrations protesting U.S. imperialism, the Contras, and so on. This kind of political exuberance was not really my style. Moreover, one of the objectives of these marches was to demonstrate to the Creole population, considered by the local FSLN cadres to be politically underdeveloped, the strength of revolutionary support in the community. In other words, the FSLN was attempting to rub Creole noses in the strength of the former's politics and simultaneously solidify the identification of the marchers with their position.

I was very self-conscious about this and tried to avoid these demonstrations. This was difficult because I also had to maintain my viability with the Sandinistas. So, maneuvering in a way that seems ludicrous now, I marched toward the middle of the crowd so no one could see me or straggled at the end, trying to blend in with onlookers. In general, I tried not to be too blatantly identified with the party or state bureaucracy. For example, I traveled to the outlying communities in public transportation rather than with government delegations or on government boats (though this was also in part an effort to lessen the chances of getting gunned down in a Contra ambush). It was, however, impossible totally to avoid public demonstrations of support for the Revolution. I was "mobilized" in the militia and trained publicly with them. I cut sugarcane with "mobilized" workers in Cukra Hill, and the like.

There were many reasons, despite my discomfort, why I ultimately could not allow myself to be identified with the FSLN's opponents, regardless of my criticism of the former's policies. I believed wholeheartedly in the basic objectives of the revolutionary process. Moreover, this was not the time or place for criticism of the loose-cannon variety. The Revolution was struggling for its existence against tremendous odds. The Atlantic Coast during much of the 1980's was a war zone. "Low-intensity" warfare raged between the Sandinistas and the U.S.-supported Contras. The day-to-day realities of life in a war zone can only be appreciated by those who have experienced it. I had never before been in a situation where the stakes were so high. People paid a very dear price for their principles. They struggled for what they believed in. People with whom I worked fought, and some died. Friends of mine fought, and some died. Members of my immediate family fought, one died. You cannot be neutral under such circumstances, and ultimately I was not. I supported the FSLN and the Revolution of the Nicaraguan people and worked to the best of my ability for its success. Even after all the changes, the failures, and the disappointments in Nicaragua, I still support revolutionary social change there and elsewhere. This book cannot but reflect this positioning.

I could not, given my job and my politics, operate in the southern Coast and not be *pintado* (painted) in many Creoles' eyes by the brush of revolutionary politics. Despite my fears of being marginalized from the Creole community for this reason, however, over the years I became more and more integrated into and identified with it. During most of the 1980's, a good number of Creoles supported the Sandinistas. So my work with the government did not count too heavily against me. Ultimately, I had Creole friends and acquaintances of all political persuasions with whom I worked and interacted socially. My Creole language skills gradually got better. Daisy Garth and I were married. This gave me family connections that were very important in creating an organic connection and opening up a meaningful identity for me within the

community. We set up an independent household and we had two
children. I felt that I had almost become a "real" Creole. To my great
pleasure, these pretensions were substantiated by a foreign social scientist who refers to me in her work as "a Creole working with CIDCA"
(Freeland 1988:45). (There are no greater authorities on cultural and
ethnic authenticity than those of us in the Western social sciences. Who
am I to dispute this categorization?) I lived with Creoles, I socialized
with them, the work environment I created was peopled by them. I
identified with Creoles almost viscerally, in part because of what I
perceived to be language, racial, and cultural affinities between myself
and the Creole community and because of my racial politics. For a host
of reasons, however, I was always an outside insider in Bluefields, and my
interactions with Creoles were always colored by each of the various
ways they perceived me to be different from themselves.

My close identification with the Creole community caused severe
strains with Bluefields' Sandinistas. First, despite the fact that I struggled
to differentiate myself, I was a gringo to them, too. For all Sandinistas
this was a negative. As a politically sensitive war zone, the Atlantic
Coast was off limits to most foreigners. A special permit (which was
difficult to obtain) was needed by foreigners to visit the area. Even those
who were able to visit were closely watched. Most were unable to visit
anywhere but Bluefields in the South. Often, no foreigners at all were
allowed in during periods of arms movements or troop maneuvers.
During the nine years I lived in the area, I don't think there were ever
more than five Americans living there. Most of the time there were only
three or four.

My biggest problem, however, was not being a gringo; it had to do with
my identification with the Creole community and the critical nature of
my support for the Revolution. An indication of this was the difference
between the deferential treatment allotted two American women who
lived there and that accorded me. They socialized, married, and identified with the Mestizo Sandinistas. They also identified completely and
seemingly unquestioningly with the entirety of the Sandinista project
and quietly and competently carried out their roles within the party
structure. As far as I could tell, they were completely trusted and fully
incorporated into Sandinista inner social and political circles.

On the other hand, my black/Creole identification, lack of sufficient
deference to orthodoxy and party hierarchy, my critical perspective, and
being a male got me into trouble. I was seen by many Sandinistas as
uppity, divisive, racist, liberal, antirevolutionary. Though not directly
confrontational, I was disparaging of the party structure on the Coast. I
was at war with INPESCA, which wanted to proletarianize the small-

scale independent fishermen. I was attempting to give the government an understanding of the basis for the discomfiture of the Creole population with many of the policies and personalities of the Sandinistas.

Paradoxically, my relations with many Creole Sandinistas were perhaps even more problematic than those with Mestizo Sandinistas. The former had their own problems in the struggles for power within the party and deeply resented a gringo outsider holding the positions of regional director of CIDCA and director of special projects within the Regional Government that they coveted for themselves.

My standing in the regional government deteriorated significantly after CIDCA-Bluefields, while I was director, published a report detailing human rights violations that ended up being a significant factor in the dismissal of the head of state security in the region. The war was worsening, security tightening, and we became a target of that agency. Ultimately, pressure from a number of constituencies in local party and government structures forced my removal from my position as director of special projects. Feeling pressured and that it was better for capable locals to hold such positions, I also resigned as head of CIDCA-Bluefields. As time went on, the military threat grew more and more serious and, correspondingly, state security and the army grew more powerful. My mobility in the region and my access to power became more and more circumscribed. Toward the end, in the late 1980's, I was confined to Bluefields by the Ministry of Interior. In the early years I had commanded the resources and the authority to travel almost anywhere in the southern Atlantic Coast. Now I was no longer able to travel even across the lagoon to the Bluff.

This series of events began in 1985. It was at this point that I began thinking of myself as an anthropologist again, though, looking back, I had continued to do critical social analysis during my marine biologist period. I dedicated much more of my time to Coast history and socioeconomic research. This is also when I began to contemplate the possibility of this book.

This book, then, is not a neutral offering. For one thing, it is a product of a politicized activist scholarship of which I am quite proud. The action aspect of our research at CIDCA, rather than hindering our intellectual production, enhanced it. It made us responsible for our ideas. They had consequences. They had enormous potential to concretely affect peoples' lives. This kind of scholarship forces one to be much more careful with ideas than in other kinds of intellectual production, where the only consequence of mistakes or bad analysis is mild reproofs from colleagues. The viability of ideas was also put to the test in ways not possible for work directed only at academic audiences. We watched, often with a great deal of discomfort, the results of our thinking unfold before our eyes.

For another, this book is thoroughly saturated by all the various things that I am and was perceived by others to be. The perspectives, political and otherwise, that I brought to Nicaragua and have adopted since that time thoroughly mediate my depictions of Nicaragua in this book. How Creoles, Sandinistas, and others in Nicaragua perceived and interacted with me had important consequences for how I perceived and portray them as well. This "cross-fertilization" was compounded by the length of time I spent in the country and by the kind of activist scholarship in which I was involved through CIDCA.

Our scholarship was undertaken in constant interaction with its objects. For example, I circulated versions of the Creole history I worked on for many years to my friends and acquaintances and engaged in countless discussions with all kinds of people about Creole history. I never hesitated to argue for my perspective. My studies of small-scale fisheries were based on work and conversations with fishermen. The studies were turned into projects, which were then implemented in interaction with these same fishermen. My ideas, many of which had come from the fishermen themselves, became the subject of discussion with them as we attempted to implement these programs. Much of the work I did for CIDCA was also circulated in the form of projects, reports, and monographs to the local government and FSLN organ. There they were studied and debated. Some were accepted; many were rejected.

Because we purposefully intervened in the everyday lives of Coast people, we influenced the ways in which they thought about their world, and we also observed and wrote about those perceptions. The ideas that I had helped develop became part of the reservoir of ideas and practices available to the Bluefields community in our effort to make sense of our world. Simultaneously, the ideas and practices of all those in Bluefields had an impact on how I understood the world.

This "reverberation" factor was clearly brought home to me as I read through a book by another Western social scientist reporting the situation in Bluefields in the mid-1980's. There was a section quoting from a top Creole Sandinista official making an astute analysis of the situation and using the precise words I had written in a report he had reviewed some time before. We had talked at length a number of times on the subject about which he was being interviewed. It was not that his answer to the researcher's questions did not represent what he thought—it did; however, the ideas we generated at CIDCA from our interactions with the people of Bluefields, of which he was one, had a definite influence on how they, including this official, thought about themselves and their world. These practices of identity and politics are what I, in turn, have recorded in this book. My muddy footprints are all over the supposedly pristine perspectives of my friends-neighbors-acquaintances-informants.

This book was partially written before I sat down to conceptualize it. It is a product of the multiple activities in which I engaged during my decade's residence in Nicaragua. Its central questions are refinements of ones I formulated while trying to situate myself and my ideas during the tumultuous 1980's among Nicaraguans.

I know that my identity and politics seemed contradictory, ambiguous, multifaceted, and confusing to many of the Creoles and Sandinistas with whom I lived and worked. It was the realization of how I was perceived by these others, as black and American, single male and father, educated elite and poor, Sandinista and black, racial-cultural rights and socialist politics, that helped me understand that subject positions, political ideas, and social roles have no necessary logical and linear relation. I now know that they can be arranged in innumerable ways and negotiated such that coherence can be claimed for almost any combination, and that the combinations that emerge have everything to do with the historical meaning they have acquired in specific conjunctures and power relations.

I would like to make a claim for collective rather than individual authority for the perspectives that this book takes. While I lived in Nicaragua I participated in a loosely defined and organized but nevertheless tangible political project with a number of others. In this book I strive to speak from a position staked out by these Creoles who were co-workers, friends, and family. We struggled to uphold the liberational objectives of the Sandinista Revolution while taking a critical stance toward it, simultaneously proud of their/our Creoleness/blackness and willing to struggle for their/our rights as a people and a region. The book is written from what I understand that committed positioning to be and is meant to be a part of the struggle of this group of people with whom I lived and worked for the better part of a decade. As such, it owes much to the key members of this group: Mike Sloan, Gregory Jackson, Daisy Garth, and also Noreen White and Miss Azalee Hodgson, Miss Mary Ugarte, Will and Brunilda Cassanova, Hennigston Hodgson, Dicky Stephenson, Algren Morgan, Alicia Slate, Hugo Sujo, Hennigston Omier, Percy González, Angélica Brown, Alan Stephenson, and others.

2.

Anglo Colonialism and the Emergence of Creole Society

Slavery, the key generative historical experience in most constructions of African or black diasporic identities and the central metaphor for black politics of resistance, has had a profoundly equivocal place in the formation of Creole identity and politics. Two popular representations of slavery performed by Creoles in the 1980's as part of the annual parade to celebrate Bluefields' designation as a city clearly illustrate this ambiguity.

In the first, young Creole men, many of whom were members of Bluefields' loosely organized rastas, marched chained together along the city's main streets. They were barefooted and dressed only in loincloths and their chains. A young man, also Creole, in dress shoes, a suit, tie, and hat herded them along, rifle in hand.

In the second, a young Creole played a slave coachman driving an elegant horse and buggy. Seated inside the buggy were a well-dressed light-skinned Creole couple. The coachman was shirtless, dressed only in tattered pants. He was in blackface—his upper torso and face smeared with oily soot or charcoal.

From the mode of presentation, it was clear that the Creoles who planned and performed the first tableau identified with the slaves, whereas those performing the second identified with the light-skinned masters inside the buggy. Though perplexing and seemingly contradictory, this juxtaposition of images is not exceptional, or even anomalous, in contemporary Creole consciousness and identity. Nor is it merely a contemporary phenomenon. To the contrary, I contend that disparate identities and politics have been a persistent theme in Creole history since ethnogenesis. This pattern complicates the placement of Nicaraguan Creoles in standard historical narratives of the African Diaspora and disrupts facile assumptions about black resistance to racial terror and ideologies.[1]

The first objective of this chapter, then, is to document and analyze the genesis of multiple Creole identity and the community's early political processes and to trace the emergence of these contradictory patterns within Creole "common sense." Here I particularly want to suggest that, rather than being typified by either resistance or accommodation, this common sense and the politics generated from it were characterized by a complex amalgam of resistance and accommodation to and collusion with dominant colonial power.

My second objective in chapter 2 holds also for chapter 3 and stands in partial tension with the first objective. Not only am I fully aware of this tension, but I want to direct the reader's attention to it, to highlight a central concern that guides my approach to scholarship on the African Diaspora. Despite the disparate character of Creole identity and politics, Creoles have historically experienced and represented themselves as a (single) people. My objective, then, is to provide a historical account of Creoles as centered political actors in this respect. The importance of this aspect of my argument goes beyond its role in my analytical reading of Creole history. It also speaks to my political concerns and those of a particular constituency within Nicaragua's Creole community as outlined in the introduction.

Pursuing this objective, I raise a strategically authoritative narrative of Creole history in which I unabashedly construct an "authentic" past for the Creole community.[2] The narrative aims to (a) open a space for Creole participation on the international and national stages of competing national identities (i.e., races, ethnicities, and nationalisms), and (b) connect Creole peoples' origins, experiences, and struggles to those of others in the African Diaspora, thereby lending more weight to their identity claims and fortifying their position in Nicaraguan identity politics.

Though my objectives in these chapters are somewhat in tension, my attempt to realize them simultaneously represents an effort to allay the endless debates around the fragmented and contingent character of African Diaspora history and identity (e.g., Mercer 1994), on the one hand, and totalizing Afro-centric accounts (e.g., Holloway 1990), on the other. My narrative of Creole history seeks to open up Diaspora history, challenging monolithic essentializing notions of black identity and politics but nevertheless demonstrating that identities are generally lived as fixed and periodically provide a standpoint for the deployment of temporally centered identity politics.

In general terms, the critical Creole history begun in this chapter and completed in chapter 3 is a key element of my ethnographic analysis of contemporary Creole political common sense. Elements of the Creole past—events, experiences, ideas, practices, and institutions—contribute, frequently in residual forms, to the conscious and unconscious repertoire/reservoir of Creole common sense. These elements are often difficult to locate or verify in contemporary Creole culture and society and therefore are best described and analyzed in a recounting of the community's past.[3]

Attempts to document and analyze the origins and early history of Nicaraguan Creoles are few and far between. John Holm's (1978) well-written and highly informative dissertation on Mosquito Coast Creole language is largely descriptive and focuses on sociolinguistic issues. Michael Olien's journal article (1988) is necessarily short on detail and seems to argue that a homogeneous Creole group emerged from a biological process of racial admixture and passive cultural assimilation. Characteristic of such reasoning, Olien (1988:9) writes, "Miscegenation continued between the Whites and Blacks, and to a lesser extent the Indians, producing the English-speaking coastal population that later became known as Creoles. The primary characteristics that set this population apart from other coastal populations were the Black-White admixture and the ability to speak English. Culturally, the Creoles emulated the British, not the Indians." Olien's position is similar to that of other ethnographers of the Mosquitia (e.g., Helms 1971; Nietschmann 1973), for whom the only authentic cultures are indigenous or European. It shares with other accounts of Diasporic history (e.g., Elkins 1959; Stampp 1956) a fixation on biological notions of racial identity and a neglect of the enslaved's agency in the creation of Diaspora cultures.

This chapter presents a different perspective on Creole ethnogenesis. In it I portray Creole identity as emerging from the collision of cultures within the context of racial slavery and colonial power in the Mosquitia of the eighteenth to early twentieth centuries. I particularly want to show how this identity emerged, not from a specific biological admixture but as a consequence of people's often contradictory tactical maneuverings within and against specific relations of power. The chapter also emphasizes the manner in which the content of Creole identity, that is, the salient "racial" and cultural features of its members, rather than remaining a static entity after its emergence, changed over time as sociopolitical conditions changed and as racially and culturally different peoples interacted with or were incorporated into the group.

Finally, this chapter, and this book, take the history of Creole identity and politics seriously. They were not just the epiphenomena of the social and biological relations between other more basic groups (indigenous or Anglo), but processes specific to a group of people who dynamically created their own culture and complex common sense and who, so centered, have played a role in the unfolding of Nicaraguan and Caribbean history.

African Arrivals and the Mix

Though Africans visited the mainland and offshore islands of the Honduran and Nicaraguan Caribbean Coast (the Mosquitia) with European pirates during the sixteenth century, it was not until the mid–seventeenth century that they began to inhabit the area. Some of the first of these settlers were associated with the 1629 English Puritan occupation of Providencia, an island 110 miles east of the Central American Coast.

In 1641 the Spanish attacked and destroyed the Providencia settlement. Though they captured many of the English and African settlers, some of the latter fled to the mainland, where they took up residence (Newton 1966:302), joining the indigenous peoples there and becoming part of the Miskitu Indians' African ancestral group.[4] Other Africans, arriving in groups from shipwrecked slavers or as individuals fleeing slavery in other areas of the Caribbean and Central America, probably settled with the Miskitu during this period as well (Hodgson 1766:30; Holm 1978:181).

During the late seventeenth and eighteenth centuries, British colonists expanded their political control and economic activities in the area. In 1747 the British government appointed a superintendent for the Mosquitia, under the auspices of the governor of Jamaica, to oversee its interests and those of its settlers. Trade with the Spanish colonies in the interior of Central America became the colonists' most important economic activity. They also fished sea turtles and set up lumber works (cedar and mahogany) and small plantations (sugar, cotton, and indigo) (Romero Vargas 1994:411). The British imported Africans through Jamaica and utilized them alongside Amerindians as slave labor employed in these activities (Bell 1899).

By the mid-eighteenth century there were Anglo-dominated British/African/Amerindian communities dotting the Caribbean coasts of present-day Honduras and Nicaragua. Major settlements included Black River, Cabo Gracias a Dios, Bluefields, Corn Island, Bragmans Bluff, Punta Gorda, and Pearl Key Lagoon, among others (Hodgson 1766:8). The Mosquitian social formation consisted of two separate but interrelated race/culture- and class-segmented societies—the first composed of indigenous communities, the second of multiracial/multicultural immigrant communities.

The Miskitu Indians dominated the first. In the 1750's approximately seven thousand Miskitu lived in small hamlets along the Caribbean Coast and up the major rivers of the area (Hodgson 1766:34). They had subjugated neighboring culturally distinct indigenous groups such as the Rama, Kukra, and Ulwa, who lived on the southern and western outskirts of their territory. The Miskitu also exacted tribute from indigenous groups living along the Caribbean Coast from present-day Panama to Belize (Sorsby 1969).

Throughout the eighteenth century the Mosquito Kingdom was organized around leaders who controlled different sections of their territory. These leaders, though independently powerful, considered themselves subjects of the British monarchy. The legitimacy of their ranks (e.g., king, governor, general) was gained in part through commissions granted by the governor of Jamaica, the superintendent of the Mosquitia, or, at times, by visiting British military authorities. The British differentiated between those Miskitu who were supposedly "pure Indians" (Tawira, or straight hairs) and those who were African Amerindian (Zambo). While there is little concrete evidence that the Miskitu differentiated among themselves on racial grounds, it does seem that the terms the British used named political divisions the Miskitu recognized (Hodgson 1766:8).

The immigrant settlements were more racially differentiated and stratified than those of the Miskitu. In 1757 Hodgson recorded 154 white persons, 190 free "mulattoes" and "mustees,"[5] 20 freed slaves, and 780 African and Amerindian slaves as "inhabitants of the Mosquito Shore (exclusive of the Natives)" (Hodgson 1766:8). A small elite composed of British white male entrepreneurs dominated these settlements. Members of this elite were the owners of means of production in land, ships, and, most important, slaves (White 1789:64). They also employed other whites as ship captains, sailors, traders, carpenters, fishermen, slave drivers, and so on. The most important of these entrepreneurs also held the leading political and military positions in the colony. They were the patriarchal heads of the leading families with dominating access to the labor and sexuality of women regardless of racial or cultural identity.

Slaves, who in 1757 outnumbered "free" inhabitants by more than two to one, were at the very bottom of the race and class hierarchy. Amerindian and African slaves evidently lived together in close proximity and worked together on the same tasks (Hodgson 1766:9). By the 1780's the numbers of slaves held by the British in the Mosquitia had more than doubled, to 1,808. Slaveholders now uniformly referred to slaves as "Negroes," though many undoubtedly were of mixed African, Amerindian, and European ancestry. In the 1780's, even without including those members of the free colored population who were of African ancestry, of those persons living outside of indigenous communities in the Mosquitia, persons of African descent outnumbered whites by more than four to one.[6]

Miscegenation between African, Amerindian, and British peoples was common in eighteenth-century Mosquitia. Though the offspring of female Amerindian and African slaves ordinarily remained slaves, European masters/parents freed some of the offspring of such unions. These people, along with the children of Europeans and free people of African and Amerindian descent, formed the third category of "inhabitants" in Hodgson's 1757 report—free "mulattoes" and "mustees." This group was continually augmented by the trickle of "colored" merchant mariners, soldiers, itinerant traders, craftsmen, and so on, who migrated to the Coast from Jamaica and other areas of the Caribbean (Long 1970:549). These free people of color constituted a slightly larger portion of the population of the British establishments on the Coast than did whites throughout the eighteenth century, though they were vastly outnumbered by the slaves (Hodgson 1766:8; Romero Vargas 1994:478).

This free colored population occupied a middle position in the Mosquitia's racial hierarchy, though it was itself stratified internally by class and color. At the bottom were manumitted or Maroon "unmixed" Mosquitian former slaves of African descent. Their status was so low that Hodgson lists them in his census of the Mosquitia as a special category under "slaves" rather than as free persons. The bulk were racially "mixed" "freemen" who lived as traders, wood cutters, turtle fishermen, mariners, and peasant farmers. A few owned slaves themselves (Romero Vargas 1994:419–420).

The Golden Age: The Emergence of Creole Identity and Politics

By the terms of the Treaty of Versailles and the Convention of London signed between Britain and Spain in 1783 and 1786, respectively, the British government agreed to abolish the superintendency and evacuate their Mosquito Coast settlers. Disgruntled and bitter, the settlers left in 1787, taking with them as many of their slaves as possible.[7] There were, however, many, especially those of color, who did not leave, or, if they left, soon returned. While reconnoitering the Coast of the Nicaraguan Mosquitia for the Spanish in 1790, engineer Porta Costas found "English" families of color living at Bragmans Bluff, Walpasixa, and Pearl Lagoon as well as white Englishmen living with the Miskitu king at Sandy Bay and with the Miskitu admiral up the Río Grande.[8] The largest nonindigenous settlement, however, was led by Col. Robert Hodgson, Jr.

Sometime before the evacuation of the Mosquitia, Hodgson transferred his center of commercial operations to Bluefields Lagoon from Black River. In 1785 he engaged in conversations with the Spanish viceroy of Santa Fe (in Bogotá, Colombia) in which he offered to represent Spanish interests on the Coast and which eventually led to his appointment as governor of the area. As governor he implemented a plan to win over to the Spanish side the Tawira, a subgroup of the Miskitu, as well as other Indian groups (such as the Rama and Ulwa) who had been subjugated by the Miskitu (Porta Costas 1990:58).

Porta Costas visited Hodgson at Bluefields in 1790. He found a settlement that, though grander, was in many ways similar to British establishments on the Coast before the evacuation. At its head was Col. Robert Hodgson, the patriarchal head of a "family that composed the entire population." This included his two sons, his wife, thirty individuals of different nationalities—English, Americans, French, and so on—and two hundred slaves.[9]

Over the years Hodgson and his father (the first British superintendent of the Mosquitia) had acquired grants of land from the Miskitu kings that included Bluefields and most of the Río Escondido valley, and the two Corn Islands (Romero Vargas 1994:489, 501). He headed up a commercial enterprise that included the cutting of mahogany and digging of sarsaparilla for export, trade with the Indians up and down the length of Caribbean Central America for tortoiseshell and other products, and trade with the Spanish throughout colonial Central America. The products he gathered were traded to Cartagena, Jamaica, North America, and England. Bluefields was now an important commercial port (Porta Costas 1990:59).

Hodgson's political machinations and attempts to divide the Miskitu eventually backfired. On September 6, 1790, six hundred Miskitu under Adm. Alparis Dilson and his brother Sulera (both Tawira), who were allied with King George II (a Zambo), surrounded Hodgson's establishment in Bluefields. That afternoon Hodgson's house in Bluefields was attacked by "Zambo-mosquitos." The residents were spared only because they respected Mrs. Hodgson, who was former leading colonist William Pitt's daughter. Hodgson's slaves and the Miskitu sacked the establishment's storehouses. On September 10 Hodgson and his family abandoned Bluefields. The Hodgsons' former slaves, who had played an active role in the fall of their masters' establishment, stayed on (Ayón 1956:I:254–256; Romero Vargas 1994:499).

The alliance between the Tawira admiral and the Zambo king soon disintegrated and war broke out between the two groups. Zambo Colonel Caesar, an ally of King George II, ruled five Zambo Miskitu villages in southern Pearl Lagoon. He took Hodgson's former slaves from Bluefields to Pearl Lagoon so that Alparis Dilson could not take control of them (Porta Costas 1990:57; Romero Vargas 1994:250).

After the death of both Alparis and Sulera and the defeat of the Tawira Miskitu, King George II turned his attention to the elimination of the remaining vestiges of Spanish presence on the Coast. In 1800 his forces attacked and routed the Spanish settlements founded after the British evacuation (O'Neille 1802 in Costa Rica 1913:584–585). All slaves were freed by the victors (Sorsby 1972:152). The mainland Mosquitia under the domination of the Zambo Miskitu was free of direct European colonial presence and would remain so for forty years.

Meanwhile, Robert Hodgson, Jr., had died in Guatemala without ever returning to the Coast (Romero Vargas 1994:488); however, his wife and two sons, William and Robert III, returned to Corn Island. There, in 1793, they raised cotton by utilizing the labor of 145 slaves and 30 transient Indians (José del Río 1793 in Costa Rica 1913:532–533). By 1808 the last of the "white" Hodgsons living on the Coast were dead. Those of their Corn Island slaves who did not escape and remained on the island moved to San Andrés (Parsons 1956:19). The communities formed by the Maroons (Hodgson's former slaves) at Bluefields and Pearl Lagoon, augmented by those at Corn Island and San Andrés, became the foci of Creole ethnogenesis.

The first decades for the free blacks and coloreds at Bluefields and Pearl Lagoon village were perilous. The British evacuation of the Coast did not mean that slavery as an institution had ceased to exist. The African-descended residents of these villages had not been officially manumitted and lived in a time and place in which blackness was the universal sign of servitude and in which slavery persisted in the Caribbean among English, free coloreds, and Spaniards (Dunham 1851; Roberts 1965:117–118, 166). The relative isolation of Bluefields and Pearl Lagoon contributed to the continued freedom of these Maroon communities; however, these former slaves' efforts to maintain their liberty and the protection of the Zambo-Miskitu also played an important role in their development as free communities.[10]

For example, in 1804 persons arrived from England at San Andrés seeking to recover from Bluefields "the Negroes who were slaves of Hodgson." With the help of Tomás O'Neille, the island's Spanish governor, they "arranged for sending an armed schooner to seize and carry off the Negroes; *but these latter undertook to defend themselves*" (Roque Abarca 1804 in Costa Rica 1913:651; emphasis added). The schooner evidently returned again to take the Maroons. This time Zambo Miskitu leaders, armed with weapons and a letter from the subinspector of Guatemala, Roque Abarca, prohibiting Spanish ships from carrying off the blacks, warded them off: "they gave to the captain my [Roque Abarca's] letter upon the point of a lance. They returned to land and waited armed." O'Neille later asserted that Hodgson's former slaves had been sold to the residents of San Andrés and tried again to claim them, to no avail (Roque Abarca 1804 in Costa Rica 1913:651).

The Maroons at Bluefields also utilized guile to remain free. In 1816 they told Cap. Jacob Dunham, a U.S. trader, that Col. Robert Hodgson had sold them their freedom, for which he was to be paid in yearly installments (Dunham 1851:92). This would have made them legally free and exempt from any attempt to re-enslave them. They also claimed to be the direct descendants of Robert Hodgson, thus asserting both their freedom and a high-status association of blood and color.[11]

A contributing factor to the Maroons' successful defense of their freedom at Bluefields and Pearl Lagoon may have been their prosperous trading activities. While some traders from Jamaica did contract to pursue runaway slaves from the sea island cotton farms on San Andrés and Corn Island, many were loath to jeopardize their positions in the valuable commerce that these Maroon communities at Bluefields and Pearl Lagoon enjoyed with merchants from Jamaica, Curaçao, and the United States (Dunham 1851:78–79). By the early 1800's the islands of San Andrés, Providencia, and Corn Island served as important trade intermediaries with Jamaica, Curaçao, the United States, the mainland Coast, and even the Spanish colonies inland (Roberts 1965:103; FO 53/15, fol. 76 in Olien 1988:11; José del Río in Costa Rica 1913:535). Bluefields was a significant entrepôt in this trade. The village was described as the "meeting place of the Indian Nations." Trading up the Río Escondido was undertaken by residents, Indian groups, and colonial Nicaraguans (Roque Abarca 1804 in Costa Rica 1913:651; José del Río in Costa Rica 1913:536, 537).

Orlando Roberts, who was a trader on the Caribbean Coast of Central America for many years, provides a description of commerce at Pearl Lagoon in the 1820's. Jamaican and U.S. traders had established stores there (Roberts 1965:109):

> The agents in charge of these stores constantly reside at English Bank and are visited by different tribes of Indians and by the Mosquito-men, from all parts of the Coast; bringing tortoise shell, gum copal, caoutchouc [rubber], etc; skins, paddles, canoes, and various articles to barter for duck, check [cloth], cutlass blades and other goods adapted for the Indian trade. The inhabitants employ themselves in turtling during the season, and in raising provisions, hunting, and fishing during the remainder of the year. They maintain a friendly correspondence with the regular Indians; are in general fair and honorable in their dealings with them and with each other and are truly hospitable to those Europeans or other strangers who happen to come amongst them.

The freedom (from slavery, from colonial law, and of trade) and the relative prosperity of the Coast attracted a constant trickle of immigrants. Free black and colored traders, adventurers and turtle fishermen arriving from Jamaica, Cayman, and San Andrés slowly augmented the black and colored population on the Coast. After 1834 and emancipation in the British Caribbean, there was an influx of freed slaves, particularly from Jamaica (Parsons 1956:16; Wullschlagel 1990:130). As before, the population of African descent was further increased through constant intermarriage with and acculturation of the local Miskitu and Rama Indians (Roberts 1965:108). The colored population was also augmented through intermarriage with white sea captains and traders who visited the area.[12]

With the isolation from direct colonial oppression in the first half of the nineteenth century, the communities at Bluefields and Pearl Lagoon flourished and what is now known as Miskitu Coast Creole culture solidified. During this period a slowly expanding segment of peoples of African and mixed descent on the Mosquito Coast began to refer to themselves as "Creoles." The first reference we have of people described as "Creoles" in the Mosquitia is found in British trader Orlando Roberts's descriptions of Pearl Lagoon [English Bank] and Bluefields circa the 1820's. Speaking of the village of Pearl Lagoon, he says (1965:108, emphasis added): "the principal settlement is . . . composed of people similar to those at Bluefields, it may also be considered an English settlement. The people are principally *Creoles*, Mulattoes, and Samboes[13] from Jamaica, San Andrés, and the Corn Islands; many of them have married Indian women, and everything considered they live in a very comfortable manner" (Roberts 1965:108, emphasis added).

Extrapolating from Roberts's usage, it seems probable that only the lighter-skinned mixed elite were considered Creoles initially; however, by mid-century the term had been extended to encompass the entire free English Creole-speaking nonwhite population born in the Americas and living in the Mosquitia. Bell (1899:17), commenting on Bluefields in the 1840's, stated that "the colored people call themselves Creoles as 'nigger' is a term of opprobrium and 'mulatto' is of doubtful significance."

The group identity included people of African and mixed descent. The latter category consisted of both European African and European Amerindian people, in other words, those persons who had previously been labeled "mulattoes and mustees" and some African Amerindian people (acculturated "Zambo Miskitu"). Most observers, however, continued to differentiate between "colored" and "Negro" Creoles.[14]

Brother Amadeus Reinke, a Moravian missionary sent on an exploratory voyage to the Coast in 1847, provides us with the clearest statement from this period of the racial and color categories composing Creole identity. Discussing the Coast population, he gives the following description: "add to these [Indians], English settlers, German Immigrants [*sic*], and Creoles, (brown people and Negroes, the descendants of

former slaves,) the number of inhabitants may probably be 12,000"
(Reinke 1848a:410). The tendency for the term "Creole" to signify only
the lighter-skinned English speakers of mixed descent, however, continued through the nineteenth century. An example is the following
statement by a missionary in the 1870's: "Indian, Negroes, *and* Creoles
assembled at the appointed place" (Lundberg 1875:308).

The term "Creole" was used primarily to designate English Creole
speakers of African descent; however, it also named persons of European
Amerindian descent who spoke English Creole and were born on the
Coast (Feurig 1862:349).[15] In the 1860's many of the most important
members of the Creole elite in Pearl Lagoon (e.g., Henry Patterson, John
and Thomas Fox, and Michael Allum) and Corn Island (e.g., Newton and
Benjamin Downs and Michael Quinn) were half "Indian" (Lundberg
1875:336). We know that Henry Patterson was half Amerindian, half
European, and presume that the other "half Indians" were a similar mix.
Since the Miskitu of the Lower Pearl Lagoon basin, the Amerindian
source of this mixture, were largely Zambo, however, these Creoles were
likely also of partial African descent.

The name "Creole" sprang from its earlier usage to describe slaves and
whites born in the Americas.[16] Creoles were native-born possessors of
the new language and culture created by Creole slaves and freedmen.
The significance of the assumption of "Creole" as a racial/cultural
identity in large part lay in its evocation of similarities between Creole
culture and the culture of the group's former British masters.[17] This
close identification of Creole with English was signified by the name of
the principal Creole village at Pearl Lagoon, English Bank, and by the fact
that even white observers like Roberts (1965) considered these settlements to be British.

In the first half of the nineteenth century, the emerging Creole
population began to exercise considerable economic, political, and
social power in the Mosquitia. An elite group of Creoles, composed
predominantly of lighter-skinned "colored" recent immigrants and the
mixed descendants of former white masters like Hodgson, filled the
vacated positions of the British settlers. These persons were the local
authorities in their own communities and the surrounding areas and
functioned under the suzerainty of the Miskitu king. From at least the
1820's, the king appointed magistrates with executive and judicial
authority from among the Creole population.[18]

In the 1840's, two interrelated series of events culminated in Bluefields'
becoming the capital of the Mosquitia and triggered a dramatic increase
in Creole political power in the area. The first was the reinitiation of the
British presence on the Coast. In 1844 the British appointed Patrick
Walker consul-general and British resident to the Mosquito Coast and

designated the Mosquitia as a British protectorate. The consul-general was posted at predominantly Creole Bluefields, the closest major Mosquitian settlement to the strategically important mouth of the Río San Juan.

The second was the transfer of the principal residence of the Miskitu king from Waslala on the Río Coco to Bluefields in 1845. King Robert Charles Frederick, who was under the influence of the British superintendent and others at Belize, British Honduras, sent his daughter Agnes and eldest son George to live in Bluefields, presumably to get an English education.[19] When George was crowned by the British colonial authorities at Belize in 1845 at the age of fourteen, Bluefields became the king's domicile. The king's residence was to remain in the Creole-dominated southern Mosquitia, either in Bluefields or Pearl Lagoon, for the remainder of the monarchy's existence. The combination of the kings' and the British consuls' residence in Bluefields made that town the capital of the Mosquitia.

Under Walker's influence, the young king moved to "modernize" his government, creating a number of new institutions in which the local Creole elite played leading roles. Chief among these was a Council of State, which proposed laws that were then enacted by the king. The members of the council included two white men, five Creoles from Bluefields, and no Miskitu.[20] This Council of State established English law and promulgated a bill creating a militia in the Mosquitia.[21] Members of the Creole elite were appointed to key posts in the military and placed in a number of other positions of importance in the incipient civil service.[22] No Miskitu held any of these positions. With the transfer of the king's residence to the southern Mosquitia, the kings (and later chiefs) became increasingly isolated from the rest of the Miskitu population and were culturally Creolized.[23]

In 1860, by the terms of the Treaty of Managua, Great Britain renounced its protectorate and recognized Nicaraguan sovereignty over the southern portion of the Mosquitia. The treaty specified that an area extending from Río Punta Gorda in the South to the Río Hueso (north of contemporary Puerto Cabezas) in the North be designated as a reservation for the Miskitu Indians: the Mosquito Reserve. The Miskitu, however, had the right to incorporate their reservation into the rest of Nicaragua whenever they desired to do so and were to receive from the Nicaraguan government an annuity of five thousand dollars for ten years. The treaty also stipulated that the Miskitu Indians could exercise self-government within the reserve, though the head of this government was now to be designated "hereditary chief," not king. It made no mention of rights within the reserve for any other group.

Creoles, however, held political power in the reserve. Of the forty-three members of the General Council of the Reserve created in 1861, thirty-two were Creole, four were Rama Indians, four were white Moravian missionaries, and only three were Miskitu. These same three were the only Miskitu members of the eighteen-member Executive Council, of which twelve Creoles were members (Municipal Authority of the Mosquito Reserve 1884:7–8, 18–19). Creoles occupied the bulk of civil service posts in the Mosquito Reserve from its formation to its termination in 1894 and, aside from the British consuls and the Moravian missionaries, were the king's closest advisers and companions. Creoles actually ruled the reserve in the chief's minority or absence.[24]

During the first half of the nineteenth century, the Creole elite became economically powerful and some were even slave owners. Slavery on the Miskitu Coast was officially abolished by King Robert Charles Frederick in 1839, effective January 1, 1841; however, manumission was not actually accomplished until August 1841, during a visit to the Mosquitia by Superintendent McDonald of Belize, seven years after the abolition of slavery in the British West Indies. In a joint act presided over by the Miskitu king and the British superintendent on August 10, they liberated forty-four slaves at Bluefields and twenty-eight at Pearl Lagoon. These slaves were probably employed as domestic labor and in the thriving turtle fishing industry of that time. Subsequently, at Corn Island on August 27, during a public gathering called by the superintendent, they liberated ninety-eight slaves who had worked on the island's cotton farms.[25]

In both Pearl Lagoon and Bluefields, the liberated slaves represented about 10 percent to 15 percent of the total population of the villages in 1841.[26] All of the slave owners were Creoles and hence people of color with at least some African heritage. In Bluefields seven of the ten (and all but one of the largest slaveholders) were surnamed Hodgson. These slaveholders, then, were descendants of the Mosquitian Maroon slaves who had actively defended their own freedom and who, earlier in 1841, had accepted into the village as free persons Maroon slaves from San Andrés.[27]

The Creole economy was based on subsistence fishing and agriculture on "plantations" scattered around the lagoons and up nearby rivers. Creoles' cash needs were met by intermittent labor as sailors or stevedores or preeminently by fishing for tortoiseshell. Wealthier Creoles who were the owners of means of production in turtle fishing (large seagoing dugout canoes, harpoons, ropes, and provisions) hired Indian and poor black labor for their fishing excursions, often developing relations of debt peonage. Some Creoles were also able to operate as traders, or agents for foreign traders exchanging imported goods with the local population for local products like tortoiseshell, sarsaparilla, rough dugout canoes, and skins.[28] By the mid-nineteenth century, Creoles, especially those on the offshore islands but also those living at Bluefields and Pearl Lagoon, had developed a thriving coconut industry exporting to the United States (Parsons 1956; Wullschlagel in Oertzen, Rossbach, and Wunderich 1990:130).[29]

Creoles also played an important role in the india rubber boom, which took off in the Mosquitia during the 1860's. Many poorer, darker, and younger Creoles roamed the forests bleeding rubber from trees to sell to local and foreign traders. Others served as middlemen between Amerindian rubber gatherers and these foreign traders. A few of the Creole elite were able to amass substantial fortunes as entrepreneurs in this industry.[30]

As with the British settlers before them, Creoles utilized their position of relative political and economic power to exploit poorer and blacker persons of African descent as well as indigenous people, whom they considered their inferiors.[31] For example, Creole accumulation of wealth in the rubber trade was facilitated by an intensification of the system of debt peonage. The Creole elite played a key role in the promulgation of the Mosquito Reserve's vagrancy laws, which made it a crime for any one to "idle about the public highways and other places, and refuse to labour when requested to do so." They also helped enact Reserve legislation that stated that "all persons owing debts to merchants shall be compelled to work if they cannot otherwise satisfy the demand against them" (Municipal Authority of the Mosquito Reserve 1884:23–26, 58–61).

Numbering around one thousand persons at mid-century, the Creoles were only a small portion of the Coast's population.[32] By the 1860's, however, they had consolidated their exercise of dominant social, political, and economic power over other nonwhite ethnic groups in the southern Mosquitia (the Pearl Lagoon basin south to San Juan and including the offshore islands). They were able to maintain this structure of power relations until the 1890's. Throughout the nineteenth century, however, Creole political and economic power was increasingly exercised under and in collaboration with, first, British colonial and then U.S. imperialist power.

As early as the 1820's, British settlers, woodcutters, and traders intruded into Mosquitian affairs using their economic power to encumber or forge alliances with influential local individuals and families and to manipulate the Miskitu king. The British in Belize, attracted by the area's rich mahogany reserves, were particularly influential in what is now the Honduran Mosquitia (Naylor 1967:61–62). British traders from

Jamaica, dealing mostly in tortoiseshell, played a similar role in what is now the Nicaraguan Mosquitia.[33] Under the British government's protectorate, which lasted from 1844 to 1860, a succession of British consuls essentially governed the Mosquitia through the Miskitu king and the Creole-controlled executive council. Despite the recognition of Nicaraguan sovereignty over the Mosquito Reserve, the British consul remained extremely powerful in the regulation of its affairs until the mid-1870's.[34]

The U.S. government was also interested in establishing control of the possible interoceanic canal through the Río San Juan. The California gold rush in 1849 made a fast and economical route from the East Coast to the goldfields a priority for the United States. Britain resolved U.S./British conflict over the area in 1860, when it ceded control of the Mosquitia to U.S. clients Nicaragua and Honduras.

North American traders and entrepreneurs also played an important role in the Mosquito Reserve, especially during and after the india rubber boom beginning in the 1860's. In increasing numbers over the decades, U.S. citizens settled in Bluefields, Pearl Lagoon, and other villages along the Coast, where they set up trading establishments. By the late 1870's, North Americans had fully displaced the British in terms of economic and social influence on the Coast.[35]

Another power in the Mosquitia—the Moravian Church—also emerged during this period and greatly influenced the Creole community. Established on the Coast in 1849, during its first thirty years the Nicaraguan Moravian mission concentrated its activities in the predominantly Creole communities around Bluefields and Pearl Lagoon.[36] Moravian missionaries exercised a great deal of political power. At various times they housed and educated the Miskitu kings and chiefs and members of their families.[37] The missionaries also held a variety of positions in the Mosquitian government.[38] The wardens of the Moravian mission to the Mosquitia served in the offices of treasurer and receiver general for the Moskito Reserve. The king and all of the state functionaries received their salaries directly from them.

The Miskitu chiefs' principal adviser and the leading political figure in the reserve from 1875 through the "Reincorporation" in 1894 was a Creole, James W. Cuthbert, Sr., who immigrated to the Coast from Jamaica at the instigation of the missionaries. A carpenter, he built many of the mission buildings and was a "native assistant missionary."[39] Moravian missionaries also provided religious services, interpreted at official state functions, and hosted many of these functions in their buildings.[40] For all intents and purposes, the Moravian Church functioned as the national church of the Mosquitia (De Kalb 1893:268).

Race, Class, and Culture in the Creole Reserve

Mosquitian society during the nineteenth century was stratified according to socially defined differences of race, color, culture, nationality, and class (not to mention gender). Indigenous peoples formerly subjugated to the Miskitu, such as the Ulwa, Kukra, and Twaka, were considered by the Creoles to be "wild," premodern, and outside the influence of civilization. The Rama people, who were in closer contact with the dominant populations of the Coast, had slightly higher status. The formerly dominant Miskitu were next in the Mosquitian social hierarchy; however, because of their inability to speak English, dispersed settlement patterns, marginal integration into the European proto–world economy, and non-European cultural patterns, the Miskitu fell below the Creoles. These latter were more urbanized, English speaking, nominally Christian, and, in general, practiced a more Europeanized culture.

At the pinnacle of the Mosquitian social formation were Anglo males. At the beginning of the era these were the few British civil servants, land- and slave owners, woodcutters, and traders who remained on the Coast or trickled back in after the British evacuation in 1787. By the 1880's there was a growing community of U.S. traders, merchants, and entrepreneurs who had recently arrived to get rich quick in the rubber boom. By dint of their economic and political power and the status afforded by their white skins and "civilized" culture, the Anglos who composed this tiny sector of the Mosquitian population were the objects of desire of and emulated by its black, red, and brown residents. The British consul, with an arrogance that only the conceit of inherent superiority can produce, claimed that even the king, the most powerful personage in the Mosquitia, yearned for what he could not embody—whiteness: "The king *of course* desires to have a white woman for his wife" (Christie in Sorsby 1989:41, emphasis added). The Moravians found that "the English language causes much trouble both to teacher and scholar as it is an unknown tongue to them [the Miskitu]; but still none want to learn the art of reading Mosquito."[41]

Economic, political, and social power in Mosquitian society was closely correlated with cultural/racial identity. Therefore, for Creoles identification with and emulation of British colonialists and American imperialists became essential factors in the exercise of power and in the formation of their political common sense. A major portion of the Creole community, especially the elite, saw themselves as the torchbearers of Anglo civilization on the Coast. They spoke English when the vast majority of nonwhite inhabitants of the Coast did not. They were

Christians, at least nominally, whereas, well after the arrival of the Moravian missionaries, most other residents of the Mosquitia were not. They thought of themselves and other Coast peoples saw them as British subjects, members of the New World branch of the British Empire and the nearest thing to the English "master race."[42] They believed themselves to be the rightful leaders of the Mosquitia as a consequence of being more "civilized" than the rest of the largely indigenous peoples of the Miskitu Coast.[43] Claims to Creole identity were a form of upward mobility in the Mosquitia: "There are also some half-Indians [living at Bluefields] but they wish to be considered Creoles, and not Indians."[44]

Even whites viewed the Creoles as more "civilized" than the rest of the Mosquitian inhabitants. Some allied themselves with leading Creole families in order to jointly and more effectively exploit the indigenous population.[45] James Stanislaus Bell, a longtime British resident of the Mosquitia, describes this relationship between such cultural emulation and political accommodation with surprising perceptiveness: "I have no fear at present of this southern portion being visited by similar evils [Miskitu unrest]; for the majority of its population [Creoles] affect civilization and have become used to something like subordination."[46]

A reciprocal element of this increasingly hegemonic conception of Creole identity was the Creoles' pejorative perceptions of other groups considered less Anglo and hence inferior to themselves. The Moravian accounts of the period are filled with examples of such Creole attitudes: "several Indian boys and girls attended the day-school . . . The feeling of dislike between the two races, however, soon manifested itself, there being constant strife between the Negroes and the Indians. The cause of this is the contempt entertained by the Negroes for the Indians, arising from the pride of the former."[47]

Such Creole "pride" in Anglo superiority was, however, partially subverted by a glaring contradiction. The Anglo supremacist ideology on which their superiority over other Mosquitian people was based could be deployed against them. Most Creoles were not white. Some were nearly white, a few perhaps "European" phenotypically, but most were brown and black (Bell 1899:20). All, in the eyes of the members of other groups, no matter how lofty their station, were stained by their Africanness.

This placed the Creoles at a disadvantage relative to the indigenous people of the Coast. These latter may have been "uncivilized," but they were not perceived to be of African descent. The contradictions between the Creoles' relatively high cultural and economic status and their low racial status is neatly exemplified in the following description of the relation between a Creole man and his Miskitu wife: "Cupid's wife has some difficulty in reconciling herself to her position, and the [Miskitu] girls used to jeer at her on account of her jet-black husband, but her answer was always quite satisfactory, namely, that he gave her plenty of meat to eat and lots of cloth and beads" (Bell 1899:181).

White assessment of Creoles was not as ambivalent. While they recognized the redeeming features of the Creoles' cultural similarity to European practice, their perceptions of Creoles were saturated by the dominant idea of white supremacy. In contrast to the Creole elite's lofty opinions of themselves, racist British whites considered them, as blacks, to be inferior—ignorant, tending to the savage, and incapable of regulating their own affairs.[48] Consider, for example, British Consul Christie's much-quoted assessment of the Council of State in 1848. Christie refers to its members, who were among the most powerful and highest-status citizens of the Mosquitia (at least two of the four were former slaveholders) as "these ignorant and needy African and Creole Councilors" and goes on to say that, as "ignorant as these members of Council are, they are probably about the best of the black and brown inhabitants of Blewfields, and their office gives them position among their ignorant fellows."[49]

The Moravian missionaries also held racially stereotypical views of the Creoles. They complained repeatedly that, apart from their moral depravity (Creoles were supposedly ravaged by their polygyny and drunkenness), "the greatest difficulty lies in the supineness of the Creoles, who manifest a want of energy" (Reinke 1848a:413) and "their natural indolence." They further stated that "our Brn. and Srs. are particularly anxious to accustom the people at Bluefields, chiefly consisting of Negroes, to habits of industry."[50] For whites in the Mosquitia, Creoles, no matter how Anglo-cultured, were inferior because they were, at least partially, racially identified as African.

The Nicaraguans also took advantage of the Creoles' racial Achilles' heel by never failing to protest Creole power in the Mosquitia and decrying their foreignness and racial inferiority. Rallying resistance to the threat of British incursion into Lake Nicaragua in the 1840's, a Nicaraguan official exclaimed: "Nicaraguans! Some English pirates, at the head of a handful of African slaves, have dared to attack the rights of our dear country. Country men, run all of you to sustain it, and drive back from it the chains with which these African slaves, who wear them, wish to bind our country" (Trinidad Munos in Jenkins n.d.:23)

Creole appropriation of the dominant ideology of Anglo racial and cultural superiority had another dissonant feature. Skin color and level of "Africanity" were important bases of social hierarchy within Creole society itself. This is dramatized by the continued discursive differentiation between "colored and Negro" Creoles. Color and culture were closely articulated with class and the basis of considerable divisiveness within the group. A Moravian missionary visiting Bluefields in 1847 attests Pfeiffer and Reinke (1849:166):

During the week the catechist is engaged in instructing the young
king and in keeping a small school, which, however, is only fre-
quented by colored children. The sum required for each pupil being
a shilling a week, the consequence is, that the numerous Negro
children, whose parents are for the most part poor, are entirely
excluded from the benefits of Christian instruction. There is also a
strong party [divisive]-spirit prevailing between the colored and the
Negro population, which can only be overcome by the reconciling
influences of the Gospel.

A strongly marked color line and animosity across it clearly existed
within the Creole communities of the mid-nineteenth century. This
was due in part to the fact that recently liberated black slaves, many of
whom were African born, lived side by side with their upwardly mobile
former colored and Creolized masters (Bell 1899:25).

Paradoxically, people who saw themselves as so different came to
share a common identity. The descendants of the black former slave
populations of Bluefields, Pearl Lagoon, and Corn Island assumed Creole
identity evidently within a generation after emancipation. This may in
part be explained by the powerful role played by the Moravian missionaries and other whites in the external construction of this identity and
the tendency of white foreigners to lump all persons of African descent
together into a single racial/cultural category. Color distinctions and
differentiations based on family lineages, however, continued to be
made within the group.

Despite Creole complicity with Anglos and the appropriation of
Anglo status and culture, the contradictory, multiple character of Creole
cultural practice, politics, identity, and common sense was already
manifest in the nineteenth century. Although Creoles identified with
and emulated Anglos, they also developed an identity and culture that
was different and oppositional. The collective memory of their African
past exerted a strong influence on them, as evidenced by the fact that
African-derived practices and sensibilities were central to the constitution of Creole culture and identity (see, e.g., Pfeiffer and Reinke 1849:166).
While Creoles, especially the elites, were emulating Anglo culture, large
sectors of the community simultaneously (re)created African and African-influenced cultural traditions. Though Creoles called the language
they spoke English, it was Miskitu Coast English Creole, whose syntax,
phonology, and morphology exhibited strong African influence (Holm
1978). They were Christians but, much to the chagrin of the Moravian
missionaries, they continued to practice their own African-derived
religion (Lundberg 1854:158; Wullschlagel 1856:34–35): "Last night, a
dance was held in a neighboring house, with tremendous noise and

uproar, in honor of the dead. And these are people to whom the Gospel has now been preached for eight years!" (Feurig 1857a:299). Bell (1899:19), in reference to Bluefields circa the 1840's, states that the inhabitants "though somewhat kept up to the mark by Europeans trading and living among them, yet were slowly relapsing into the superstitious gloomy half savage state into which blacks, left to themselves, always sink back. They . . . practiced obeah and wakes in the regular African fashion." He goes on to describe a number of Creole cultural practices such as foods, culinary arts, music, dances, and keeping of oral history, which he considers to be of African origin. Bell further states that white attendance during some of these practices was prohibited. Bell as a child asked "an old African Obeah man . . . to tell me one of his wake stories, but he turned a horrid eye on me, and said, 'go way, Buckra bway, you too popisho [foolish; derived from "puppet show"]'" (1899:30–31). Taken together, these African-based practices were crucial mechanisms for the maintenance of an identity separate from the Anglo.

There was no doubt in the minds of the Moravian missionaries that they were up against determined Creole resistance to their brand of cultural colonialism:

We have also many mockers and scoffers at religion. (Pfeiffer 1850b:406)

The heathenish dances and other riotous amusements began already a week before Christmas; and on Christmas-Eve, while we were holding a preparatory service, the disturbers of our peace commenced drumming and dancing with great spirit, and continued their noisy mirth for three days and nights. On the morning of Christmas-day, I held an early service, which was numerously attended. . . . While thus engaged, the drumming and shouting was renewed *for the evident purpose of interrupting us.* Two of our magistrates went out to endeavor to induce them to be quiet; but only partially succeeded. What grieved us most of all was the discovery which we afterwards made—that only 14 of our 100 Sunday scholars had kept away from these heathenish performances. (Pfeiffer 1850a:361, emphasis added)

The simultaneity of cultural resistance and accommodation, often by the very same people, is quite clear; however, Bell, in reporting the rituals surrounding Christmas Eve in mid-nineteenth-century Bluefields noted (1899:39): "the horse's jaw-bone, the teeth rattled with a stick, and two other sticks beating on a bench, with the drum and the wild snatches of song by the women, provide the stimulus for the weird and mystic

African dances, at which the younger men and the young women of the period look askance, as savoring too much of African slavery." This passage alerts us to the possibility that admiration for European culture was not the only motivation for acculturation. Former slaves were eager to abandon the symbols of their servitude whatever they might be.

In addition to accounts of decades of Creole resistance to their attempts at cultural conversion, the Moravians provide documentation of other forms of Creole "everyday" resistance. The Moravians constantly bemoaned the fact that even though the Creoles seemed to be idle much of the time they were nevertheless unwilling to labor as servants and wage workers for them. When they could be induced to do so, Creoles were often more than the Moravians could handle. In a detailed account of their exploratory trip to the Mosquitia in 1847, two Moravian missionaries found themselves at the mercy of four Creole sailors. The missionaries clearly thought themselves to be superior to these black sailors and felt that they should be able to control and command them. These seemingly subservient (but resourceful and independent) men, however, through a series of ploys, including deception, obstinacy, malingering, prevarication, and alternative logic, were able to maintain command of the situation. The following passage describes just one episode of this kind among many during the trip:

> When the necessary preparations appeared to have been made we gave them orders to get "under weigh," but now they discovered that they had forgotten to cook their rice and plantains. We had no other resource but to wait, for we were dependent on them in a greater measure, as they well knew, and their only reply to our impatience and remonstrances was "Massa, you tink we can do mitout provishan; you tink we goin to eat it raw." It would have lost labour to have proved to them that there had been time enough before hand for all this.

Flowing from the disparate contents of their political common sense, which provided the logic for both, however, their posture of resistance was followed in suitably contradictory fashion by an act of extreme accommodation. The sailors, now exploring on shore along the Río Punta Gorda with their employers, in the missionaries' words, "come to our assistance, and convey us on their backs over the shallow water near the bank, until we reach the settlement" (Reinke 1848b:444–461, 521–527; idem 1848c:549–557).

3.

Negotiating Modernity: Disparate Racial Politics in the Twentieth Century

> The collective will is a result of the politico-ideological articulation
> of dispersed and fragmented historical forces.
> —Laclau and Mouffe (1985:67)

This chapter offers a narrative of Creole cultural politics from the halcyon days of Creole society in the mid- to late nineteenth century to the doldrums of the Somoza dictatorship in the 1960's. Over the course of the century, external "modernizing" forces of economic, political, and cultural dominance penetrated and transformed Creole society. These forces initiated power relations on the Atlantic Coast, which were configured and articulated in multiple ways and which varied through time. In general terms, they can be thought of as constituting dual but entwined processes of rule and hegemony.[1] The first involved the transformation from indirect British colonial rule through the generation of an incipient "Anglo" hegemony mediated by the Moravian Church and dominated by U.S. whites. The second consisted of the coercive institution of Nicaraguan national rule and the gradual formation of an incipient national hegemony arbitrated by the Moravian Church and the Nationalist Liberal Party (Partido Liberal Nacionalista, PLN). Because Creoles were actors in the construction of these dual hegemonic processes, in each of which both negotiation and consent (resistance and accommodation) became the basis for domination, Creole politics during the period was even more disparate than during that covered in chapter 2.

At first glance, Creole politics during this period seems to be divided into three distinct epochs: a phase of collusion in the encroachment of U.S. Anglo economic and cultural power from the 1860's through 1894, followed by one of overt resistance to Nicaraguan national rule from 1894 through the 1930's, and ending with a phase of apparent acquiescence to that rule from the 1930's onward. One objective of this chapter is to document, critically examine, and explain these shifts in the character of Creole responses to change, adversity, and subordination.

Documentation of the first two phases is important to my effort to provide a strategically authoritative narrative of Creole history. Creole exercise of power and resistance has largely been erased, both in the few historical accounts and, equally important, in popular memories of Creole history. Going against the grain, I document a rich history of multifaceted Creole actions in terms of both regional leadership and contestation of subordination, actions often intended to achieve a radically alternative sociopolitical order. As the reader learns of the Cuthberts and the Pattersons, of Francis Mena and J. O. Thomas, Sr. and Jr., of the Twenty-five Brave and General George, it is my hope that the pervasive images of Creole political marginality and passivity will be definitively shattered.

Yet to the extent that this chapter highlights the largely untold story of Creole leadership and resistance, the contrast with the Creoles' willing subjugation to Anglo power in the late nineteenth and early twentieth centuries and their acquiescence to Nicaraguan rule after 1930 appears baffling. Here, as in chapter 2, I challenge the zero-sum assumptions about resistance and accommodation that make this situation seem paradoxical—assumptions that equate resistance with readily observable actions of contestation and acquiescence with the absence of such actions, assumptions that take for granted the contrast or mutual exclusivity of the two.

I contend that such assumptions obscure more than they reveal. The initial period of accommodation to Anglo power was also a period of ascendant Creole activism and even nationalism. Among some sectors of the Creole community, these contained postures of resistance to the incursions of white U.S. entrepreneurs. Elements of these resistant politics were antecedents of what I call Creole ethnic populism—an important component of contemporary Creole common sense. The epoch of ostensible Creole resistance after 1894 also involved the profound incorporation and reinforcement of subordinating premises. Aspects of these were precursors of what I refer to as Anglo ideology, another key facet of contemporary Creole common sense. Similarly, apparent acquiescence in the post-1930 period obscured much subtle political maneuvering, cultural initiative, and civic organization—what Scott (1985) calls "everyday resistance"—which helped Creoles recapture something of their previous status as regional elites.

Attention to the multivalent and contradictory character of Creole politics during this epoch makes the seeming incongruities of Creole history more comprehensible. It also advances my theoretical argument about politics by directing attention to Creole common sense as an unexamined key to understanding the complexities of Creole politics.

For example, during the period of "resistance" to Nicaraguan rule, values of the Moravian Church and U.S. entrepreneurs that rationalized Creole subordination to them became deeply ingrained in part because they complemented anti-Nicaraguan feelings. These values formed part of the reservoir of common sense alongside notions of autonomy, cultural pride, and ethnic militancy that upheld General George as a hero. As we will see in later chapters, these disparities at the level of Creole common sense persisted and reemerged to guide Creole politics. As I argue later, they are one key to understanding the Creoles' troubled relations with the Sandinista state after 1979.

The historical production of diversity in the reservoir of Creole common sense is also the point of departure for the second major analytical theme in this chapter—Creole identity formation and its relationship to Creole politics. The closer one gets to the fine-grained details of Creole history during this period, the more bewildering the question of Creole identity formation becomes. Here I show that Creoles displayed, over a period of roughly forty years, at least eight strands of identification, all of which at one time or another formed the basis of an identity politics. At various points in time, Creoles as a group represented themselves as British colonials, small producers, members of the Liberal Party, Mosquitian nationals, Nicaraguan nationals, Afro-Caribbean blacks, Miskitu Indians, and Costeños.

These modes of identification were not simply political positions. None of them were invariably central to the Creole community's politics. Nevertheless, they existed within the reservoir of Creole common sense as possibilities for tactical deployment in the generation of Creole politics at specific social conjunctures. Here again, many of these historical and disparate forms of identification were forerunners of those I will discuss as part of the ethnography of contemporary Creole common sense I present in later chapters.

Modern Penetrations and Creole Collusion
The Moravians: Capitalist Culture and Anglo Hegemony

During the last half of the nineteenth century, the penetration of Central America's Caribbean Coast by Euro-American culture and capital accelerated. In the southern Mosquitia the arrival of the Moravian missionaries in the 1850's as well as coconut exports and the rubber boom of the 1860's and the 1870's were important elements of this process. The modest penetration of U.S. capital transformed Bluefields into a bustling rubber trade market town, the seat of the Mosquito Reserve's incipient state institutions, and the center of Anglo-European and African culture on the Coast.[2] The population of the village grew steadily, and by 1873 there were about one thousand inhabitants (Levy in Pérez Valle 1978:130).

The rubber trade was the leading edge of capitalist penetration. Prompted and financed by a few foreign buyers, Mestizo and Creole middlemen entered even the most isolated communities of the Coast and joined these previously isolated social groups to a monetarized economy and international capitalist economic practice. Symptomatic of the transformation in the political economy of the area were changes in Creole commercialization and consumption patterns: "Thirty years ago perhaps a hundred half-barrels of flour were sold on the Coast, now at least two thousand barrels are imported annually. This shows how people have become accustomed to the use of flour and bread, instead of coarse plantain, yams and cassava, which used to be their main articles of food" (Lundberg 1880:318).

These experiences set the stage for a subsequent period of rapid and unprecedented change on the Coast over the last two decades of the century. During this interval, dominating North American culture and capitalist economic relations entered the Miskitu Coast in full force. While there were coercive aspects to this penetration, the way was smoothed by the collusion of the Creoles, who sought advantages for themselves in the new circumstances, and by the cultural leadership of the Moravian missionaries.

The opening salvo in this process of rapid social change—modernization—was the "Great Awakening." Over a decade, large numbers of Costeños of all cultural groups were spectacularly converted to Christianity. The Awakening began in 1881 among the Creoles, Indians, and "Spaniards" living in Pearl Lagoon Town and spread through the whole Coast (Martin 1881:74).

In the fifteen years between 1879 and 1894, membership in the Moravian Church increased over fivefold in the Mosquito Reserve. In the Creole communities of Bluefields and Pearl Lagoon, the number of Moravian Church members more than doubled, from 654 to 1,528. In 1879, before the Awakening, about two-fifths of the Creole population of Bluefields were church members and two-thirds regularly attended services. By 1894 approximately two-thirds were members and an even higher proportion regularly attended services (Anonymous 1880:338; P. A. 1894:408).

Church membership was not a matter of simply attending worship services regularly but required a great deal of personal initiative, commitment, and change. Members were held to the strictest norms of piety. Not only did one have to be well versed in the Bible and the general teachings of the church, but one had to attend regularly and punctually all the various church rituals and functions. Moreover, there was a very strict code of personal conduct that included prohibitions against smoking tobacco, drinking alcohol, dancing, and swearing as well as graver sins such as "fornication" out of wedlock and adultery. The missionaries attempted to transform not only Creole religious practice but the very lifestyle of the community by dictating proper clothing styles, the arrangement of living spaces in houses, forms of interaction between family members, recreational activities, and, perhaps most important, the types of economic activities and forms of labor appropriate for the Creole community.

In Bluefields and Pearl Lagoon, the Moravian mission became the principal institution of civil society. It was the only organized European religious institution in the Mosquito Reserve. The Moravians instituted a strong Sunday school program, held regular prayer meetings during the week, organized choirs, and started Bible study groups for young people. They also operated the only schools in the reserve, conducting well-attended elementary schools in Bluefields and Pearl Lagoon and in 1892 opening a high school in Bluefields (Anonymous 1892:638). As a result of these educational efforts, a large portion of the Creole population was literate.

The power of the Moravian Church in the acculturation of Creoles into what Jean Comaroff calls "British Protestant culture and intellectual traditions" (1985:131) can scarcely be exaggerated.[3] The missionaries were clear about their intentions and the transformations they had wrought (P. A. 1900:353, original emphasis):

> How agreeably surprised have not many young missionaries been when, on coming here with preconceived notions of a somewhat primitive Negro congregation, brightly attired in dresses of many colours, they found themselves face to face with our civilized, tastefully dressed Bluefields people, versed in many of the arts and sciences. But above all, by means of the schooling imparted to them and the good English literature thereby made accessible to them, the formation of *character* in the people of this town has made almost phenomenal progress. Nothing but a healthy evangelical spirit could have brought this to pass.

Even though many missionaries were German, aided by their colleagues of color from Jamaica, they went out of their way to reinforce British patriotism and colonial subordination in their Creole congregations. For example, they celebrated Queen Victoria's Jubilee in 1887. The missionary Sieborger at Pearl Lagoon described his effort that day as follows (Sieborger 1887:182, original emphasis):

I endeavored to bring before the congregation what the English
Government has done for our Moravian missions, and what a
special thanks this country [Moskito[4]] owes Her Majesty for past
and present protection. I told them that even the present treaty,
ensuring them their own territory, would be simply waste paper if
England did not endorse it. I related to a most interested audience
what I knew of the personal life of Her Majesty, after which we
rose and sang with might and main, "God save *our* gracious
Queen."

Pictures of the queen were then distributed to the congregation.

As the Creoles became more Anglicized, there was a corresponding
decrease in cultural resistance, as represented by the strength of
"Africanized" cultural practice among them. The gradual disappearance
of marathon drumming, dancing, and ritual alcohol consumption from
traditional Creole Christmas celebrations, which the Moravians had
fought against for decades, epitomized this process.[5]

The Moravians' cultural hegemony had a profound effect on Creole
identity. Riding a wave of structural economic change brought on by the
rubber and, later, banana booms, the missionaries provided the cultural
basis for Creole claims to civilization and modernity. This became an
extremely important aspect of Creole identity. Even though in their
blackness Creoles bore the mark of the primitive, under the influence of
the Moravians, culturally they became the local epitome of the modern.
For the Creole community the claim to modernity was a corollary to the
claim to Anglo cultural and national identity. This, then, legitimized the
group's assertions of its superiority over the remainder of the nonwhite
inhabitants of the Mosquitia and its affinity with high-status Anglo
outsiders.

U.S. White Entrepreneurs, Creole Nationalism, and Anglo Hegemony

During the 1880's the process of transformation of the economies of
Pearl Lagoon and Bluefields accelerated. Members of the Creole elite, in
collusion with U.S. entrepreneurs, began cultivating banana plantations
up the Río Escondido from Bluefields and exporting the fruit to the
United States (Martin 1882:309; Pérez Valle 1978:138).

The advent of commercial banana production in the Escondido Valley
created an economic boom that further transformed Creole productive
activity.[6] Many Creoles grew bananas for the U.S. market on their own
small plantations or on lands rented from others (Romig 1892:446). A
number of Creoles with familiar names such as McCoy, Tayler, Taylor,
Hodgson, Waters, Forbes, and Hooker established businesses in retail

dry goods and groceries, saloons and billiard parlors, print shops, and the like (*Bluefields Messenger* 1890). Some few, such as Henry Clay Ingram, J. O. Thomas, Sr., and John Taylor, were also able to take advantage of the rapid increase in commercial activity and establish major mercantile businesses (Taylor 1889; Pérez-Valle 1978:242). Some members of the Creole elite became wealthy and cosmopolitan enough to send their children overseas to Jamaica, the United States, or England for schooling (*Bluefields Messenger* 1890; Keely 1893:166). Creole economic efforts were soon overtaken in importance, however, by those of North American adventurers and entrepreneurs and immigrant Chinese retailers.

By the 1890's, U.S. whites had transformed the reserve into an enclave of the U.S. economy. By 1894, U.S. capital investments in bananas, lumbering, natural rubber extraction, gold mining, coconuts, transportation, and commercial enterprise totaled at least $2 million and perhaps as much as $10 million. The reserve's annual trade with the United States was worth an estimated $4 million a year. U.S. whites controlled between 90 percent and 95 percent of the area's production and commerce (Morrow 1930:4; Baker in Laird 1971:26).

Accommodation to the enclave economy severely undermined the relative economic independence of the Creole community. Many remained petty commodity–producing peasants but were far more dependent on imported consumer goods than previously. Their cash demands were also satisfied through wage labor for the white entrepreneurs. Though many found jobs as lower-level managers with some authority over Mestizo and indigenous people, Creoles were compelled to accept a subordinate role in new, radically different and exploitative relations of production.

Nevertheless, collusion with powerful Anglo outsiders paid initial political dividends for Creole elites. Through the early banana boom years of the 1880's, the Creoles remained in control of the Mosquito Reserve's government: "Br. Cuthbert, [is] the Attorney-General of the Reserve, and the leading man among the government officials. . . . the Vice Governor [Charles Patterson] . . . is an intelligent man, and a support to Br. Cuthbert in efforts to promote the moral and social elevation of the people. . . . the Chief Jonathan Charles Frederick . . . is only the nominal head of the government, and knows but little of its affairs" (Romig 1892:441–442).

Encouraged by the rapid economic growth, the Creole-dominated Mosquito state expanded its size, complexity, and role in an increasingly complex and multifaceted social formation. Simultaneously, an incipient Mosquitian nationalism began to emerge among the Creoles of the reserve. In the 1870's, the Creoles had already begun to insist on the reserve's autonomy from Nicaragua. By the 1880's, the Moravian missionaries reported the emergence of Mosquitian national sentiments among the Creoles. The *Bluefields Messenger,* launched by Jamaica-born Creole Markland Taylor in 1890, was infused with nationalist discourse. In the inaugural issue Taylor urged fellow Creoles to "subscribe to a journal of native growth, a medium by which the material interests of our town and *country* will be promoted, and which will bring us into closer contact with the civilized world. We have already subscribed to foreign industry [bananas]. Now let us prove ourselves as ready and willing supporters of a cause that is emphatically our own. *Native enterprise! Home industry!*" (emphasis added). Articles in the *Messenger* commonly referred to the reserve as a "country," and J. W. Cuthbert, Jr.'s, Pearl Lagoon–based musical group was advertised as the "Mosquito National Band."

In 1894 leading Mosquitian nationalist Creole J. O. Thomas wrote of the Mosquito Reserve as "a state of free men who are to govern themselves—not as an unsettled horde of wandering savages not yet formed into a civil society; not as a voluntary association of robbers or pirates; but as members of this country or state . . . the Mosquito Indians, and all persons residing among them before the treaty of Managua, enjoyed, occupied and governed a definite state belonging to them and exercising an internal as well as external sovereignty" (in Oertzen, Rossbach, and Wunderich 1990:376). A Moravian missionary noted that "a remarkable unanimity of patriotic nationalism prevailed amongst the mixed population of his kingdom" (Moravian Church and Mission Agency 1894:320).

Creoles constructed this emergent national identity in relation to other nationalisms. Courtney De Kalb (1893:281, 285), a contemporary white U.S. observer, pointed out that the common loathing of "those of Spanish blood" (Nicaraguans) was a central feature of the "distinctly national" bond among residents of the reserve. Central American independence from Spain and the advent of Central American and Nicaraguan nationalism and states during this period must certainly have had a stimulating effect on the florescence of Mosquitian nationalism among the Creoles.

The full flowering of Creole-led Mosquitian nationalism was impeded by the legal limitations inherent in the reserve's status as a reservation within Nicaragua's sovereign territory. Legally, there could be no citizens of the Mosquito Reserve, because the reservation did not have the sovereign powers to grant citizenship. Thus, Creole Mosquitian nationalism had no juridical basis. Moreover, reserve residents were "subjects" of Nicaragua but not citizens. Those Creoles who had been born under the British Protectorate or in other areas of the British West Indies claimed to be British colonial subjects and retained "uncompromising

British prejudices" (De Kalb 1893:281; see also Harrison in Oertzen, Rossbach, and Wunderich 1990:404).

The uncertainty surrounding the Creoles' national identity posed serious problems for the legitimacy of their rule within the reserve. Since the initial days of the Treaty of Managua in 1860, the Nicaraguans had loudly claimed that foreigners, preeminently *"negros de Jamaica"* (blacks from Jamaica), rather than the indigenous Miskitu, controlled the reserve. The Nicaraguans considered Creoles, regardless of whether they had been born in the reserve, to be foreigners and, perhaps more important, to be racialized interlopers (*"los negros"*) in the Mosquitia.[7] The Nicaraguan government used the claim that Jamaicans controlled the reserve government as the basis for violating the treaty, delegitimating the reserve's government, and asserting Nicaraguan territorial claims over the region, this despite the fact that all but a few government officials had been born in the Mosquitia (Thomas in Oertzen, Rossbach, and Wunderich 1990:377–378).

As Creole political power reached its zenith during the 1880's, competition between the Creole elites of Bluefields and Pearl Lagoon emerged (Wunderich 1990). By the 1860's, the center of political power had shifted from Bluefields to Pearl Lagoon. The chief now resided there and most of the top positions on the executive council of the Mosquito Reserve were held by Creoles from the latter town, which caused resentment in the former (Erskine in Oertzen, Rossbach, and Wunderich 1990:340; Gollan in Oertzen, Rossbach, and Wunderich 1990:343); however, the tensions extended beyond the political to include economic differences.

Pearl Lagoon's economy was based on trade with the surrounding indigenous population. Creoles from the town interacted extensively with the predominantly indigenous population of the reserve. They also maintained very close ties to the Moravian missionaries. The elites who ran the government were conservative defenders of the reserve's socioeconomic status quo and its British colonial status. In contrast, by the mid-1880's Bluefields had become the center of an international trade in bananas and the residence of a number of foreign whites with whom the Creole elite of the town had developed business relationships. The more "progressive" Bluefields Creoles defended big foreign business and the region's emerging position as an enclave of U.S. capital (Wunderich 1990:75). The split weakened Creoles' ability to maintain their position of power in the Mosquitia. Some of the Bluefields elite even supported incorporation of the region into Nicaragua when white U.S. entrepreneurs became dissatisfied with the Mosquitian state. This division among the Creole elite reflected the rapid changes in the basis of the incipient Anglo hegemony from British colonialism to U.S. imperialism.

Ultimately, the reserve government came under direct attack from the resident white entrepreneurs. In part, this was an artifact of racist attitudes the latter brought with them from the United States. They bristled under the jurisdiction of the reserve's "nigger government" and in general held attitudes of disrespect and disregard for the Creole and Amerindian inhabitants of the region (Morrow 1930:7; Curzon-Howe to Hopkins in Oertzen, Rossbach, and Wunderich 1990:372; Harrison in Oertzen, Rossbach, and Wunderich 1990:409).

Dissatisfaction on the part of U.S. whites also had to do with the reserve government's "attitudes toward the economy," which protected the interests of small independent Creole and indigenous producers and partially inhibited unbridled capitalist expansion (Wunderich 1990:75). This was exacerbated by the difficulty the reserve government experienced, given the restriction of its reservation status, in creating legislation, state structures, and physical infrastructure that could keep up with the demands of the rapidly expanding economy (Curzon-Howe in Oertzen, Rossbach, and Wunderich 1990:372).

In a protest to the U.S. government, the white entrepreneurs accused the reserve government of abuses and irregularities (Seat in Oertzen, Rossbach, and Wunderich 1990:365; Madriz in Pérez Valle 1978:178), and there was talk of making the Mosquitia into a U.S. colony (Cabezas in Pérez Valle 1978:160). Within little more than a decade from the onset of the banana boom, this contradiction was resolved by the U.S.-supported military incorporation of the Coast into the Nicaraguan nation, with negative consequences for the Creole population.

By 1894, on the eve of this incorporation, the Creoles had formed a strong sense of Mosquitian nationality and simultaneously acquiesced to Anglo hegemony forged by the Moravian missionaries and white U.S. entrepreneurs. Creole acquiescence was the basis for their ascendancy to a position as the leading Coast group in economic, political, and social terms. Simultaneously, it was the basis of their subordination to powerful white outsiders and, ultimately, of their fall from power.

Incorporation into the Nicaraguan Nation

The "Overthrow"

The final blow to the position of the Coast's Creole community came in 1894 with the "Reincorporation" of the Mosquitia by the Nicaraguan government. By the 1890's, Bluefields had become an irresistible plum for the Nicaraguans. The town and its hinterland constituted the most economically dynamic area in the entire country. It was booming demographically as well. A census taken by the reserve government in 1889 found 2,083 persons living in Bluefields, 90 percent of whom were black and 506 foreign born. In twenty years, Bluefields had grown from a village of thatched huts to a town of "325 substantially built houses, two hotels and several public and private boarding and lodging houses, 25 shops and stores" with streets lined by street lamps.[8] By 1894 Bluefields's population was reported variously at between 3,500 and 4,000 "negros, americanos y zambos" (De Kalb 1893:255; Moravian Church and Mission Agency 1895a:467; Vitta in Pérez-Valle 1978:237). Finding the government bankrupt on being elected to the Nicaraguan presidency, in 1893 José Santos Zelaya initiated a concerted effort to bring the Coast and the area's robust international trade under national control (Morrow 1930:5).

Nicaraguan troops occupied Bluefields in February 1894, initiating what the national government called the Reincorporation. The "Overthrow," as the Creoles termed it, threatened the political and economic interests of the Creole community, which, despite its divisions, immediately assumed a posture of active resistance. Within a month of Nicaragua's military occupation of the reserve, approximately 1,750 Creoles (close to the entire adult population) signed a petition directed to the queen of England asking for the resumption of the English Protectorate over the Mosquitia. They complained (Great Britain, Foreign Office 1894:89–104): "We will be in the hands of a Government and people who have not the slightest interest, sympathy, or good feeling for the inhabitants of the Mosquito Reservation; and as our manners, customs, religion, laws and language are not in accord, there can never be a unity."

Besides petitioning the British and U.S. governments, Creoles resorted to armed violence in an attempt to thwart the Reincorporation.[9] In the weeks following the Nicaraguan occupation, rioting erupted in Bluefields (Moravian Church and Mission Agency 1894a:321). Calm was restored when British troops occupied the town, ostensibly to protect foreign lives and property. In the following month, the Nicaraguans established nominal control of the town amid plotting, turmoil, and bitterness on the part of Creoles and the North American merchant community (Madriz in Pérez-Valle 1978:183–209).

In July an armed, predominantly black, group seized control of Bluefields and the Bluff. They forced Nicaraguan officials to relinquish the government, and Chief Robert Henry Clarence and his council reassumed their authority over the government (Moravian Church and Mission Agency 1894b: 373; Castrillo Gámez in Pérez-Valle 1978:209–211). Simultaneously, armed Creoles moved to retake Corn Island, Pearl Lagoon, and Prinzapolka. The Nicaraguans were convinced that the Creoles wanted to proclaim an independent republic (Báez in Pérez-Valle 1978:218).

During the events, however, North American troops landed in Bluefields. They quickly assumed military control and reestablished "order." The United States did not support the reconstituted government and took steps to discourage the uprising by, for example, preventing U.S. citizens from aiding the Mosquitian cause (Reyes in Pérez-Valle 1978:219). In general, the U.S. government supported the Reincorporation as a means of ending all British claim to the area and securing undisputed access to the possible Río San Juan canal route (Moravian Church and Mission Agency 1895b:465). Equally important, as a consequence of their ideas of white supremacy, both the U.S. and British officials on the scene dismissed the predominantly Creole reserve government's right and ability to rule (Curzon-Howe in Oertzen, Rossbach, and Wunderich 1990:372–375).

In late July and early August, Nicaraguan forces retook Bluff and Bluefields without a fight. Chief Robert and his people, unable to obtain support from the British or the U.S. whites, put up no resistance to the reoccupation (Cabezas in Pérez-Valle 1978:220). Many Creoles, including the principal figures in the reserve government, either fled the country or were arrested by Nicaraguan officials and sent to Greytown, where they were given the choice of exile or standing trial in Managua (Moravian Church and Mission Agency 1894b:373). All were ultimately pardoned, though some, including J. O. Thomas, Sr., and J. W. Cuthbert, Sr., never returned. Chief Robert Henry Clarence fled the reserve as well, ending up in Jamaica, where he died a number of years later.

Legally, the Mosquito Convention, in which the headmen of Atlantic Coast Miskitu communities assembled by the Nicaraguans denounced the government of the reserve and agreed to subject themselves to direct Nicaraguan authority, consummated the Reincorporation (Harrison in Oertzen, Rossbach, and Wunderich 1990:416–424). The convention granted a number of "special privileges in accordance with our [the Miskitus'] customs and the nature of our race" (Decreto de Reincorporación in Pérez-Valle 1978:227). By the terms of the convention, all revenues produced by the Coast were to be reinvested for the benefit of the Coast, thereby maintaining its economic autonomy; all "indigenous persons" were to be exempted from military service; no tax was to be levied on the Miskitu; And the Miskitu could elect their own local mayors and police and remove them from service when they saw fit.

After the Overthrow

During the first half of the twentieth century, the dual penetrations of Anglo capital and culture and the Nicaraguan Mestizo state and national culture consolidated. Both sets of forces were attracted to and guided by ideas of the region as an unpopulated reserve of boundless material resources and a source of potential wealth for themselves. The Nicaraguan state and U.S. capital operated in a relatively coordinated fashion, due in large part to Nicaragua's position as a client state of U.S. imperialism; however, there were always simultaneous discord and contradictions between them that provided spaces within which opposition could be articulated and mobilized by Creoles.

U.S. capital, varying from large international corporations to small-scale speculators, developed an "imperialist" relationship with the region. Foreign (U.S.) capital, armed by the coercive arm of the imperial nation (the U.S. Navy and Marines),[10] was the mechanism for control of the region's ample natural resources and markets. At the turn of the century, the enclave economy of the southern Atlantic Coast boomed. In 1905 the U.S. consular agent at Bluefields remarked that "Bluefields is the most important town in Central America as far as American interests are concerned."[11] At the turn of the century, U.S. firms and individuals dominated commercial trade in Bluefields as well as the majority of the services and industries, such as bottlers, shipyards, tanneries, ice plants, hotels, and transport companies.[12] U.S. companies owned the most important lumbering enterprises and mines. In the banana industry, land exhaustion, disease, fluctuations in banana prices, the international consolidation of the tropical fruit industry, and policies of the Nicaraguan state resulted in the vertical integration of the fruit companies and a concentration of capital. The major player in this process was the Bluefields Steamship Co., operated by the Weinberger brothers with the United Fruit Company as a major shareholder.[13]

The Nicaraguan state developed an "internal colonial" relationship with the Atlantic Coast. After the military conquest, it ruled the area and its noncitizen (non-national) population from its Pacific national "center" and utilized the coercive mechanisms of the state as the engine for the extraction of surplus for the benefit of that center. The weakness of the state, however, and the inability of Mestizos for many years to form civil institutions that could incorporate the Costeño population prevented the Nicaraguan nation from moving beyond a situation of coercive rule to one of national hegemony in the area.

The Reincorporation also transformed the political configuration of the Atlantic Coast in a number of important ways. After 1894 the Zelaya government rapidly moved to bring the Mosquitia under its control. Over the ensuing decade and a half, the Zelaya regime replaced the laissez-faire economic policies of the reserve government with a series of taxes, tariffs, and concessions aimed at generating income for the Nicaraguan state (Moravian Church and Mission Agency 1895b:466). The Creoles and foreign residents felt that these measures were unjust and strangled the economic vitality of the Coast.[14] As an added affront to Creole sensibilities, the income generated by these measures was rarely reinvested in the Coast, violating one of the basic and most positive tenets of the hated Mosquito Convention.

The system of monopolistic concessions instituted by the Zelaya regime in which companies and individuals paid the state for the exclusive right to undertake economic activities on the Coast was particularly problematic for Creoles. These concessions extended to almost every aspect of economic activity and product from rubber and coconuts to liquors to dynamite to sugar and meat. They squeezed many Creoles out of business and in general had a negative impact on the community's standard of living. Adding insult to injury, Zelaya used these concessions to enrich himself, his extended family, and his associates.[15]

The most controversial concession granted the steamship company exclusive navigation rights for banana purchases on the Río Escondido and its tributaries.[16] The company took advantage of the lack of competition by paying independent banana growers the lowest price permitted by the concession; simultaneously, it offered higher prices to larger U.S.-owned companies, particularly those operating in the Cukra area and those few in the Escondido Valley that had negotiated contracts with the Bluefields Steamship Co. This was intensely resented by Creole growers caught in the double bind of imperialist and internal colonial rapine. The viability of their small plantations was threatened in the squeeze by low prices for their bananas and high tariffs on imported necessities.[17]

The national government was also reluctant to recognize land rights established under the Mosquito Reserve. While many of the Creole elite were able to obtain legal recognition of their pre-Reincorporation landholdings through the Nicaraguan courts, the bulk of the Creole community experienced difficulties in this regard.[18] The Zelaya government in particular was exceedingly liberal in the sale and granting of lands on the Atlantic Coast to foreign fruit companies and Pacific Mestizo military and government officials.[19] The seizing of lands that had been worked by Costeño families and communities for many years was commonplace.[20]

The Harrison-Altamirano Treaty signed between Great Britain and Nicaragua in 1905 provided Creoles an opportunity to voice their displeasure and the possibility of partial redress. The British formally recognized Nicaraguan sovereignty over the former Mosquito Reserve. The Nicaraguans exempted Creoles and Miskitu born in the reserve before 1894 from military service and direct taxation. They also granted Costeños two more years to legalize their pre-1894 land claims and guaranteed communal lands and a minimum eight-manzana (about fourteen-acre) agricultural parcel per family (Pérez-Valle 1978:268–269).[21]

The letter excerpted below, sent by the former vice-president of the Mosquito Reserve and others to Vice-Consul Chalkley, British representative to one of several land commissions established by the Nicaraguan government, is an example of the many letters sent to these commissions that document the seizure of Creole and Indian lands:

> We the people of Bluefields and the Rama Indians beg to lay before you, our grievances . . . All our land possessions are grappled up by the Spaniards and turned into pastures leaving us void of forest land to even yield us fire wood. . . . farms, belonging to several of the native inhabitants of Bluefields are also devastated and laid waste . . . in the District of Pearl Lagoon, the cultivated farms of the natives are wrested from them and devastated, without compensation. Along the sea-beach, all the coconut farms made by the natives are cut down and laid waste by the Spaniards. In the City of Pearl Lagoon, the Governor enters upon the bone fide lands and cut down all the fruit trees despite the protestations of the owners. We cannot exist any longer. We are without support for our families.[22]

Despite the treaty and the land commissions, many Costeño individuals and communities were able to recover only a small portion of their lands.

Following Reincorporation, the national government, which viewed the Coast as conquered territory, moved immediately to establish and control the state apparatus. Much to the chagrin of the Creoles, the state renamed the area the Department of Zelaya, after the hated dictator, and installed civil servants from the Pacific side of the country in a range of political positions (Ruiz y Ruiz 1927:73). A few members of the Creole elite participated in the local municipal governments at Bluefields, Pearl Lagoon, and Corn Island;[23] however, by law the police had to be Spanish-speaking Nicaraguan citizens, and the top regional positions were filled exclusively by Mestizos from the Pacific. In 1911 U.S. Vice-Consul Lee observed in this regard that "every office is filled by the so-called 'Spaniards' from the interior, who treat the 'Creoles' as inferiors and exploit every avenue of 'graft.'"[24]

The departmental government chronically operated without funds, and clientelism, nepotism, bribery, extortion, and general corruption were rampant.[25] Government officials and their associates abused the Costeños, particularly those from the indigenous communities, by levying all sorts of extralegal taxes and often engaging in outright thievery (Grossman 1988:14; Harrison in Oertzen, Rossbach, and Wunderich 1990:409).[26]

The Nicaraguan state was very uneasy about the "foreign" character of the Coast's population. In an attempt to hasten the cultural national-ization of the region in 1900, the Zelaya government began enforcing national laws stipulating that all schools, state supported and private, teach exclusively in Spanish. Unable to comply with the law and a specific target of government enforcement of it, the Moravian Church was forced to close its schools.[27] The closing of the schools undermined aspects of Creole culture that distinguished the group as more "civi-lized" than others on the Coast; Creoles saw the closings as direct attacks on the foundations of their distinctive way of life.

Incorporation into the expanding enclave economy and the Nicara-guan nation wrought long-term transformations of Creole society. Creole culinary, material, and economic desires and practices changed in ways that reflected their intensive interaction with missionaries and entrepreneurs who were the bearers of Anglo culture. By the early 1900's Creole production of subsistence crops had declined to the point that U.S. Consular Agent Clancy could claim that "no beans, rice or corn is cultivated in this section [Bluefields], and all that is consumed must be imported." Five years later, a U.S. consular official stated that "people . . . rely upon the United States solely for all they consume and wear."[28]

The enclave economy also affected Creole demographics. The accel-erated pace of incorporation of indigenous peoples into the enclave economy had a major impact on acculturative processes that had been proceeding over the past half century. This was particularly the case in the Pearl Lagoon area, where Miskitu and other indigenous peoples closely interacted with Creoles. The Creolization through acculturation of Miskitu people in Pearl Lagoon town during this period and in neighboring communities, particularly Haulover and Tasbapaunie, sig-nificantly increased the Creole population.[29]

The population of African descent was also augmented by blacks and coloreds[30] who migrated from the Caribbean, mostly from Jamaica, the Cayman Islands, and the Bahamas as well as the southern United States to work as miners, stevedores, sailors, small banana producers, and so on (Araya Pochet and Peña 1979:35).[31] These immigrant blacks, many of whom were phenotypically more "African" than the Creoles, were called "Negroes." They were usually unskilled or semiskilled workers, or peasant agriculturalists and members of the Anglican and Baptist denominations and speakers of various Caribbean Creole languages (Harrison to Kimberley in Oertzen, Rossbach, and Wunderich 1990:404; Ruiz y Ruiz 1927:73).

Most Creoles were small landowners, skilled workers, small boat captains, pilots, and, especially in Pearl Lagoon and Corn Island, peasant agriculturalists and fishermen (Ruiz y Ruiz 1927:73). They served also as functionaries, secretaries, clerks, foremen, and lower-level managers in the North American enterprises.[32] In general, Creoles were better off materially than the "Negroes" and held a higher position than the latter in the Coast's social hierarchy. They were also lighter skinned, better educated, members of the Moravian Church, and speakers of Miskitu Coast Creole.

On the basis of these and other differences, the two groups of African descent considered themselves distinct; however, there was considerable overlap between them, especially since most light-skinned, higher-class West Indian immigrants socialized and identified with the Creole elite. The social-cultural-racial distinction between Creoles and Negroes survived on the Coast for decades in part because significant numbers of black immigrants from the Caribbean and the southern United States continued to arrive through the 1930's.[33]

These "Negroes" contributed substantially to the growth of Bluefields's population of African descent and ultimately to that of the Creole population. From a population of about two thousand in 1889 (*Bluefields Messenger* 1890), the black population grew to approximately four thousand by 1925 (Ruiz y Ruiz 1927:72); however, Creoles composed only about 60 percent of the Bluefields population,[34] a substantial decrease from the approximately 90 percent of the population in the 1880's.

The influx of West Indian blacks also had a cultural impact on the Creoles. The Moravian missionaries began reporting that their "spiritual work" in the community was being hampered by "Obeahism" and other cultural practices associated with Africa and reintroduced by the black immigrants.[35] Over time the "Negroes" and their offspring, through intermarriage and mutual cultural interchange, became Creoles and adopted the less-pejorative ethnic designation in place of the racialized "Negro" identity. As we shall see, however, distinctions based on color, religion, and class and based in part on this original division continue to stratify the Creole community.

The imperial and colonial domination of the Creole population by U.S. capital and the Nicaraguan state had an extremely deleterious impact on the Creoles' social position. From a point at or very near the top of the social hierarchy of the Miskitu Reserve, Creoles fell to a middling one, superior in their own eyes to the "semisavage" indigenous and Negro population but subordinate and perhaps inferior to Hispano-Nicaraguans and U.S. whites. Creoles and Negroes were generally lumped together by members of these latter groups on the basis of their presumptive "African" racial characteristics. As a group they were seen by both U.S. whites and Pacific Mestizos as uncivilized and in other ways inferior and were treated accordingly.

For U.S. whites, many of whom came from the South,[36] where apartheid had been codified in Jim Crow laws and racial violence was the order of the day, the second-class status of Creoles was self-evident. Residential areas in company towns were segregated, as were social clubs and even church services (Karnes 1978:111). A Moravian missionary observed in 1926 that whites "still look upon our church as a 'colored church,' and will not, therefore, attend" (Society for Propagating the Gospel 1927:65). The U.S. businesses paid their Creole employees less than their "Caucasian" ones as a matter of course and reserved the prestigious positions such as bookkeepers and managers for the latter.[37]

Nor were blacks and whites judged equally before the law. In one notorious case, the Creole editor of the local newspaper was shot by a U.S. white who was subsequently acquitted of the crime by an all-Mestizo jury. According to a Creole commentator:

> The moral of this case need not be deduced it is obvious; suffice it
> to say that it is now upheld as a principle that the Anglo Saxon is
> to be held as sacred by the Creole and that the former is perfectly
> justified when molested to set aside the usual forms of law
> whereby redress is usually sought, and take the law in his own
> hands. This was the main argument for the defense, and it had the
> desired effect.[38]

As elsewhere where patriarchy is articulated with racial supremacy, white males took advantage of their power and status to initiate exploitative relationships with Creole women. This situation was described by the U.S. consul to Bluefields as follows: "white men consider it 'chic' to act in the manner of the late Mr. Lahue, and after tiring of the [Creole] woman, let her and the offspring of the liaison shift for themselves, while they again go forth in search of new prey."[39]

Pacific Mestizos were racist in their own way. They believed themselves to be inheritors of "Hispanic" civilization and therefore to be members of the "Hispano-Nicaraguan race" and thus superior to the Creoles. In addition, they disparaged the latter's foreignness: "an African people who feel not even a drop of love for Nicaragua" (Ruiz y Ruiz 1927:38).

But hostility ran both ways. Creoles were extremely resentful and disparaging of Mestizos, whom they saw as culturally inferior and as usurpers of their historical rights. In 1911 a group of Bluefields residents stated, "There exists today considerable ill feeling and bitter hatred between the Nicaraguans and native (or Creole) peoples."[40] Mestizo workers, who streamed to the Coast during the banana boom, resented the competition for jobs from blacks. In 1912 serious clashes broke out on U.S.-owned banana plantations between black and Mestizo workers and several blacks were killed.[41] In the 1920's, riots broke out in the

Puerto Cabezas area in which, again, Mestizos killed a number of blacks and promised more of the same if foreign black workers did not go home.[42]

Frutos Ruiz y Ruiz, head of a presidential commission that visited the Atlantic Coast in 1925 and wrote a report that presented a hierarchized analysis of Coast peoples and cultures from the Pacific Mestizo perspective. In a section entitled "Coast People's Civilization," this report sums up the Mestizo viewpoint on these matters (1927:126–127): "In first place is the culture of the Hispano-Nicaraguans . . . In second place the foreign [white] culture . . . After comes the culture of a few Creole mulattoes . . . Last come the Miskitu, Zambo, Zumos, Rameños, in a semi-savage state." Writing specifically about Creoles (p. 132) Ruiz y Ruiz states that

> the blacks and mulattoes do not have their own religion, language, or culture: imported at one time from Africa or from Jamaica they speak English and profess the Protestant religion and morals educated by the Moravians without themselves giving signs of being able to have their own civilization. As they have some mixture with the white race, they have exercised some predominance over the aborigines, but on the whole they are dependents of the imported culture, and erudite men are rare.

Mestizos used these ideas to marginalize Creoles and other Costeños from government employment and to justify their absence from positions as professionals and businessmen. Ruiz y Ruiz (1927:112–113) claims that, rather than needing employment in government positions, Costeños "need for the civilized people of Nicaragua to come to their lands, interbreed with [them] and elevate the race, and impose the Nicaraguan civilization and language." Interestingly, Ruiz y Ruiz ranks U.S. whites second to Hispano-Nicaraguans in the social hierarchy, largely because of the low educational level of most white residents. U.S. whites, however, had no illusions about the relative status of the two peoples. Vice-Consul Samuel Lee summed up his opinion of Mestizos as follows: "a mongrel and generally degenerate race of people, who will never be able to do anything more than 'play at government.'"[43]

Creole Resistance under Nicaraguan Rule

Creole response to the network of power relations imposed by the social forces operating on the Coast during the first half of the twentieth century ranged from enthusiastic embrace through acquiescence to passive opposition and active resistance. Creoles emerged from this era as poor, marginalized, and colonized Nicaraguan nationals, an exploited labor force and market for metropolitan capital, and as devout adherents of missionizing international religious institutions. Creoles were not, however, just manipulated by these powerful social forces but also used them to forge a relatively advantageous place for themselves within Coast society. They held more positions in the state, lived better materially than other Costeños, and savored their status as the most "modern and civilized" of the Coast's "native" groups. At the same time, Creole opposition and resistance to domination took myriad forms and were waged from a variety of subject positions.

Culture and group identity were key realms of Creole resistance. One of the most fundamental concerns of the Nicaraguan state in its attempt to establish its sovereignty over the Mosquitia was to nationalize its inhabitants and their culture—to construct a national hegemony on the Coast. Especially during the Zelaya period, much emphasis was placed on forcing Costeños to learn to speak Spanish and to practice what Mestizos defined as Nicaraguan culture. Creoles fought this with every available means. The Moravian Church had decided soon after the Reincorporation that it would be best for the church's survival as an institution to encourage the Creoles to nationalize; however, missionaries found Creoles very resistant to their attempts to teach Spanish in the schools. According to the Moravian missionaries, "Considerable pressure was needed to induce the parents to pay the small price for the [Spanish] books, and the strictest discipline required in order to get the children to open their mouths to read and learn" (Mission Board 1900:354–355). Many Creoles kept their children out of school and held classes in their homes.

For many years most Creoles also refused to accept Nicaraguan citizenship. The Moravian missionaries related that, when their schools were closed by the Zelaya government, an attempt to mount a petition protesting state educational policy failed for this reason: "some political oddity or other spread the report that whoever signed this petition would be obliged to acknowledge himself a Nicaraguan—and this our Creoles do not want to do at all" (Mission Board 1900:354–355). Two decades later, many Creoles remained just as intransigent about their refusal to accept Nicaraguan Mestizo culture. A group of distinguished Creole and Miskitu stated this clearly in a letter to the U.S. secretary of state: "Having always been in constant intercourse with the nations of Anglo-Saxon civilization, training, and religion and being of a different race we cannot under existing conditions assimilate or amalgamate with the people of Latin civilization."[44] Most Creoles continued to insist on their cultural and political ties to the British and continued to believe well into the twentieth century, as leading Creole J. O. Thomas wrote in 1915, that "some day by some mysterious means they would receive their independence supported by the British government or that of the United States."[45]

Creole identity and politics were created, nurtured, and emerged in correlation with the gradual expansion of the Creole public sphere. The Moravian Church and its institutions were crucial in this regard, though the church supposedly refrained from explicit political involvement. During the period under discussion, the Young Men's Union of the Moravian Mission played an important role in convening Creole men across social lines and placed its organizational weight behind particular political positions from time to time.[46] The Young Women's Union played a similar if less public role.[47] This latter organization must have been even more important in mobilizing Creole women's political perspectives because it was one of the only public venues for the social interaction of women outside of worship services.

There were a great variety of other "social organizations" operating in Bluefields during this era: bands, literary societies, lodges, secret societies, athletic clubs, and social clubs (*Bluefields Messenger* 1899:2; Meza Briones 1991; Green in Oertzen 1993:458–459). The single most important Creole organization, however, was the Union Club. This organization, established in 1902, had most of the influential elements of the Creole community as members. Though it was the focus of the Creole elite's social life, the Union Club was also crucial to the development and implementation of Creole politics. Under cover of its social function, strikes were planned and implemented, political organizations spawned, protest letters written, and political candidates launched or endorsed.[48] The Union Club was the very hub of Creole political activity for over sixty years, until it closed its doors in 1965. For all intents and purposes, it functioned as the Creole political party.

Creoles mounted stout economic resistance to forces within the enclave economy that threatened their position as relatively prosperous independent producers. They refused to be reduced to an agricultural proletariat. This created labor problems in the early years of the banana boom, before large numbers of West Indians and Nicaraguan Mestizos arrived and filled this niche. In 1893 De Kalb noted in exasperation (1893:264): "Personal independence is insisted upon with an accompaniment of insolence, which is a great detriment to the progress of the people. . . . service of any sort is usually rendered only as a favor into which one must wheedle the people by infinite cajolery. It is not in appearance merely, but in fact, that the money consideration is the less powerful inducement."

Some Creoles and many Negroes did eventually come to work for the banana and lumber companies. They engaged in class-based labor organization across racial lines, often under the auspices of the Liberal Party, and Creoles participated in labor unrest in 1896, 1922, and 1925 (López 1982:180; Ruiz y Ruiz 1927).

A central economic issue around which Creole politics coalesced during the first half of the twentieth century arose from many Creoles' position as small producers. They fought hard and long to preserve the viability of small-scale banana production in the face of state intervention and the monopolistic tendencies of international capital. When in 1904 the Zelaya regime granted the Bluefields Steamship Co. a monopoly on navigation in the Río Escondido Valley, Creole planters, who made up the bulk of small producers, organized along class lines with Jamaicans and a smaller number of Nicaraguan planters to resist this threat to their viability. Through the Union Club the planters formed an association and bought transportation equipment from a rival fruit company. They agreed not to sell to the Bluefields Steamship Co. and attempted to break the monopoly by collectively transporting bananas to the Bluff for exportation on a boat they had chartered from a competing company. Though they were supported by Governor Estrada, the central government enforced the monopoly by seizing Planters Association shipments, destroying their bananas, and sinking their barges.[49]

Resentment over the Bluefields Steamship Co. concession simmered for a number of years. In 1905 a delegation from the Planters Association to President Zelaya undertook the long journey to Managua to protest the concession.[50] In 1909 the Planters Association organized another "strike" against the Bluefields Steamship Co. concession. The planters refused to sell their bananas to the company and began destroying fruit on plantations belonging to the company and to planters who continued to produce for it.[51] The Zelaya government declared martial law and government troops arrested five hundred planters and their family members, allowing the Bluefields Steamship Co. to recommence its operations and undercutting the momentum of the strike.[52]

In late 1909 Bluefields seethed: "The most bitter feeling exists here and along the rivers against the Bluefields s/s co." as well as against the Zelaya government.[53] In October Juan B. Estrada, Liberal governor of the Coast, defected to the Conservatives and led a revolutionary movement centered in Bluefields against the Liberal Zelaya government. U.S. Consul Moffat reported that the uprising was the result of Costeño and U.S. white anger at what they considered to be the excessive duties, tariffs, taxes, and the monopolistic concessions of the Zelaya government.[54] Creoles believed that the Atlantic Coast as a region was being looted to pay the expenses of the Pacific region, with nothing being invested for the benefit of the former.[55]

On taking power in Bluefields, Estrada abolished the government concessions (with the exception of those held by U.S. whites living in the area) and called for the establishment of an independent republic on the Atlantic Coast.[56] Creole leaders were involved in the planning of the revolution and the Creole community enthusiastically supported the separatist cause.[57] Many joined the rebellious military forces and lent it financial and other material aid.[58] The central Creole role in fomenting the revolution and its regional (Costeño) rather than racial/cultural emphasis are brought out by a speech made at the Union Club immediately after the revolt: "to show . . . that their protests were not born of personal or racial reasons, the Creoles looked cautiously about for a man native to the country to lead them to establish peace and prosperity. When Estrada's name was suggested, the idea was acclaimed vigorously."[59]

U.S. whites in the area were also enthusiastic supporters and financiers of the revolution. Some U.S. whites even volunteered for the revolutionary army.[60] The rebels quickly took Bluefields and set up a provisional government.

The rebellion rapidly developed into a struggle for domination of the whole country, however, with Estrada allied with the Conservatives against the Liberals. Conservative Mestizos led by Gen. Emiliano Chamorro squeezed black supporters and their cause out of what was now a full-scale national rather than a separatist revolution.[61] In the words of U.S. Consul Moffat: "Chamorro, allied with the Conservatives in the interior, cares nothing for the needs of the Coast. The interior and Managua are all he and they are striving for. On the other hand Estrada, with the native Creoles, Mosquito Indians, the best class of Nicaraguans and all the foreigners with their allied interests, are fighting for the separation and supremacy of the Coast."[62]

With Estrada's forces in control of Bluefields, the United States landed the Marines, ostensibly to protect North American lives and property.[63] The Managua government attempted to rally its forces in part by claiming that the "entire trouble on this Coast has been caused by the Americans and Negroes."[64] The "neutral" presence of the Marines in Bluefields, however, aided the revolutionaries, whose forces the Liberals otherwise would have routed (Langley 1983:62). In 1910 the Conservatives took over the national government from the Liberals and installed Estrada as president. Not surprisingly, no more was heard from the now-ruling Mestizo Conservatives about Atlantic Coast independence. The Conservative Party ruled Nicaragua for the next eighteen years.

In the era following the Reincorporation, a common form of Creole protest was to write group letters to the governments of the United States, Great Britain, and Nicaragua. The sense of outrage and betrayal after the Estrada revolution inspired just such a protest letter to the British government from the Creoles of Pearl Lagoon. It lists complaints against the Nicaraguans characteristic of Creole political preoccupation during this period. The Creoles' central position was "that the Mosquito Coast has never been incorporated with Nicaragua neither by law nor fact." This is followed by what was now a conventional litany of complaints and accusations against the Nicaraguan government, including the illegality of the Mosquito Convention, Nicaragua's violation of the treaties concerning the Atlantic Coast, overtaxation, involuntary military conscription, land expropriation, and lack of freedom of speech.[65] The letter concludes with a plea to the British to help the Creoles restore their former state of independence, a theme that became standard in Creole communications of this sort: "In view of the numberless grievances and the present state of unrest and dissatisfaction which reigns and a constant fear of serious occurrences we humbly pray that such measures will be taken to rid us from [our] common enemy: Nicaragua."

The years of Conservative rule were unhappy ones for the Creole community. The revolution engendered large losses in property destroyed (particularly on the Río Escondido) and debts unpaid. As a consequence, credit, essential for the banana and other industries, dried up. The banana plantations on the Río Escondido, many now in operation for several decades, suffered from soil exhaustion and disease. World War I closed the Atlantic Coast off from European lumber markets. In Bluefields during much of this period unemployment and economic depression reigned. New threats were being mounted to Costeño land tenure rights, particularly in the North Coast, where large U.S. companies were opening new banana lands. The Conservative government on the Atlantic Coast was corrupt, inefficient, and provided few or no services.[66] Lawlessness on the Coast was notorious. The Conservatives attacked the Moravian Church, which remained highly influential in the Creole community.[67] Under these conditions, Creole dissatisfaction simmered while sympathy for the Liberal Party grew.

The Creole political response was varied and conjunctural. In April 1919 fifteen members of the Creole elite signed a letter to the U.S. consul decrying the general lawlessness of the Coast. They petitioned for U.S. government intervention and, by implication, called for independence under U.S. protection.[68]

In October of the same year, however, at least a third of those Creoles who had signed the first letter petitioned the Nicaraguan government to make Bluefields the terminus of a proposed transcontinental railroad. They provided a list of grievances against past regimes, including noncompliance with treaties, unjust taxation, monopolistic concessions, and so on, to justify their request. Incongruously, they also claimed affinity with the Conservative government based on common allegiance to some very liberal-sounding principles of the "Revolution of

October 1909": "free Government, liberty, justice and equity, commerce, industries, communication and the moral and social welfare of the Country." Moreover they claimed "that this department is now enjoying peace, liberty and representation in the national Congress, that monopolies have been abolished, that education and religious liberties have been maintained, . . . under the present [Conservative] regime."[69] Creole elites were becoming willing to play party politics at the national level and clearly could play both ends when they thought it justified or convenient.

The most important political activity of black people on the Atlantic Coast during this period was their participation in the local branches of the Universal Negro Improvement Association (UNIA), the international movement of black racial redemption and African uplift led by Marcus Garvey. There were at least five branches of the movement organized on the Coast, two of which were in Bluefields.[70] In the early 1920's the movement was extremely popular in Bluefields. A Moravian missionary observed: "I do not think that anything during my stay here in Bluefields has taken the people so quickly than this new movement. The majority of our male church members and a goodly number of the female as well are active members of the 'Black Star Line.'"[71]

The same missionary professed concern that the UNIA was "threatening to become a danger to our people."[72] The movement was certainly a threat to the missionaries themselves. It competed directly with the Moravian Church for the hearts and minds of the Creole population. The missionaries commented in 1923 that "the open hostility of the UNIA . . ., and the mission of the African Orthodox Church they have started here with an ex-Anglican priest at its head, and their day school with a good enrollment . . . must be reckoned with."[73]

The Moravians were also much concerned with the "anti-white" nature of the movement,[74] though it appears that at least some Creoles were willing to engage in a variety of racial exceptionalism when it came to the white missionaries: "Some of our best people have said to me openly: 'our American missionaries, the Michels, the Cruickshanks and Br. Shimer are fine people and we love them. But we are terribly anxious lest later on missionaries with colour prejudice be sent out.'"[75] Others, however, were more critical of the Moravians. Tensions between the black community and the Moravians became particularly acute after a former superintendent of the mission, Guido Grossman, sent a circular to Bluefields condemning Garvey as "un-Christian." Grossman was himself denounced in a letter from Bluefields blacks published in *Negro World*. The letter berated him for engaging in a "wicked conspiracy" against Garvey "when he was here, sucking the last dime from the colored people of his church, he proclaimed himself a 'neutral.' Instead of being a neutral, he was more of a hypocrite—flinging stones and hiding his hand . . . the whole Nicaragua Coast is much surprised at Mr. Grossman's unchristian action . . . but know that from the beginning Mr. Grossman was only using 'diplomacy' to safeguard his interests" (Mynot 1925).

An indication of the popularity of the UNIA during this period was the celebration of the "Negro National Holiday" on August 31, 1922. One thousand members and associates of Bluefields' two UNIA branches turned out to march in the parade commemorating the day. Those participating represented a quarter of Bluefields' entire four thousand blacks. The strength of the movement is further demonstrated by the fact that all stores in Bluefields were closed in honor of the day and the organization (Bury 1922).

Africa and the return was a central theme of the celebration, with a number of songs such as "Africa, Our Home" and "Our Home in Africa" being sung at meetings along with more conventional Protestant hymns. The overall objective of the organization, in the words of a Creole member was, "a redeemed Africa and an emancipated Negro race" (Bernard 1926).

The direct political impact of the Garvey movement in Bluefields is unclear, however. Despite its principles of race unity and its seeming popularity in all sectors of Bluefields' black community, there were serious internal divisions in the local movement. The two Bluefields chapters were divided along lines of color and class. One was headquartered in the Union Club and was composed principally of the Creole elite. The other had its "Liberty Hall" in Barrio Beholden and was composed of poorer and darker Negroes and some Creoles. Though attempts were made to cooperate in the name of blackness, these differences for the most part impeded joint activity. Nonetheless, the heightened racial consciousness and organizational experience gained from participation in the Garvey movement prepared Creoles for the pivotal role they were to play in the political upheavals that wracked the Coast during the 1920's and the 1930's.

In 1925 a letter was sent to the Conservative president of Nicaragua, Carlos Solórzano, by Bluefields Creoles who, adopting a regional identity, had recently formed the Liga Nacional del Litoral Atlántico (National League of the Atlantic Coast). The letter protested "unjust treatment" by those who ran the national government. It went on to say that, whatever their differences, all these leaders "maintain the idea that the Atlantic Coast is a conquered and disaffected province that must be governed with an iron hand and obliged to pay tribute. . . . the Coast was turned into an object of merciless political and industrial exploitation by ruinous monopolies and concessions granted to the president's favorites and unscrupulous foreigners" (Creoles to President Solórzano in Ruiz y Ruiz 1927:133).

Perhaps in response to Solórzano's reputation as a moderate Conservative[76] or, more likely, because Creoles thought it the better part of valor to mask more radical tendencies, this group of Creoles listed a number of relatively new grievances and demands, which were integrationist in tone. They claimed to have accepted the changes in government effected by the Reincorporation and to be "loyal citizens of the Republic of Nicaragua." After arguing that "economic autonomy" for the Coast was guaranteed by the Mosquito Convention (Creoles to President Solórzano, in Ruiz y Ruiz 1927:134, 135), as most such documents had in the past, a relatively new complaint appeared. Creoles now were concerned about participating in the regional organs of the national government: "Another matter directly related to the subject of this petition is that of the governmental employees and officials of the Atlantic Coast, who, with very rare exceptions, are sent from other parts of the country without taking into account that these [positions] are owed to the true residents of the Coast" (Creoles to President Solórzano, in Ruiz y Ruiz 1927:137).

In an important integrationist departure from past Creole political discourse, the letter observed that, if the national government responded positively to their complaints and complied with their interpretation of the Mosquito Convention "the work of the real nationalization of this Coast would be advanced more by this one step than all that has been done up to now" (Creoles to President Solórzano, in Ruiz y Ruiz 1927:139). The letter documents at least two other innovations, both of which were associated with the growing Creole participation in national politics: the formation of an incipient Atlantic Coast political party, the League; and political horse trading on the level of national politics.

Six months later, in February 1926, prominent Creoles writing to the U.S. government as members, with prominent Miskitu, of the Miskito Indian Patriotic League adopted a more traditionally resistant position listing a series of now-standard grievances, emphasizing their independent national identity, and calling for independence.[77] The letter is innovative in one respect. Creoles identified themselves with and as Indians: "We the undersigned Miskito Indians, aborigines of this section of the American continent . . . together with natives of amalgamated Indian ancestry . . . [members of] the Miskito Indian Patriotic League." Interestingly, the attempt to identify politically as "Indian" or Miskitu took place during a period when the UNIA and the diasporic identity of blackness were still quite strong among Creoles in Bluefields.

Solórzano's coalition government was overthrown in a military coup headed by the Creole's old nemesis, Gen. Emiliano Chamorro of the

Disparate Diasporas

Conservative Party. On May 2, 1926, a small group of Creoles known as the "Twenty-five Brave" attacked and took over the *cuartel* (military barracks) in Bluefields. This military action is represented in most narratives of Nicaraguan history as the initial battle in the nationwide constitutionalist revolution in which adherents of the Liberal Party fought for deposed Liberal vice-president Juan B. Sacasa's constitutional right to the presidency. The Creole revolutionaries, however, had other objectives.

Two days after the triumph at Bluefields, a group of Bluefields' leading Creoles (writing this time as Creoles and not as Miskitu) sent a letter to the U.S. consul at Bluefields in which they pleaded for U.S. intervention in support of their military initiative and their independence through the reestablishment of the Miskito Reserve.[78] The first signature on the letter, which was signed by a number of the Twenty-five Brave and other Creoles, was that of their leader, Gen. George Montgomery Hodgson, a Creole dentist who had fought on the Conservative side in the 1909 revolution. After the initial ineffective plea to the United States, the insurgent Creoles led by "General George" cast their lot with the constitutionalist struggle of the Liberal Party.

The alliance between the Creole-led Costeños and the Mestizo Liberals was born of convenience, as illustrated by the 1927 admonishment of one Creole leader to another to "trust none of them [the Liberal Mestizo generals] but use them just as they are using us."[79] In addition to leading the original attack, General George planned and led a number of other crucial engagements.[80] He was made a general in the Liberal Army but became ill and died while in the field with his troops in 1927. With him died any real chance for Coast autonomy.

The Creoles' plea for U.S. support was wildly unrealistic, indicating a romanticized notion of that country's commitment to anticolonial and democratic principles. They were soon rudely awakened. The U.S. Marines, who had left Nicaragua just the previous year, returned to Bluefields and the rest of the country, supposedly as a neutral presence to safeguard North American lives and property. As the Moravian missionaries observed, however, the U.S. troops "from the beginning were not neutral, but assisted in every way the conservative party, so the liberals were hindered in their movement."[81]

The position maintained by the U.S. government provoked much bitterness on the part of the Creole community.[82] The Creole inhabitants of Pearl Lagoon protested the actions of the U.S. troops to the British consul at Bluefields: "these American Marines march with their arms through town evidently to intimidate us. . . . we have absolutely no faith in the good intentions of these marines . . . they seem to be allied with these other troops [Conservative] which persecuted us for no cause whatever."[83]

U.S. military support of the Conservatives became such an important factor in the conflict on the Atlantic Coast that the Creole insurgents developed a strategy of civil action to combat it: "The procession should proceed quickly going through the town stopping on its way at the American Consulate, when a petition should be presented protesting against intervention . . . This is the only way we can fight the Americans—Silence gives consent—We in the fields can only shoot and it would be just what they would want if we shot down any Americans."[84]

After the conflict had spread to the Pacific portion of the country, the United States forced a peace. In national elections in 1928 supervised by the United States, the Nicaraguan electorate returned the Liberals to power. The problems and demands of the Atlantic Coast seem to have played no role in this process. Months before the elections, members of the Creole community were already at it again. Bitter after another failure to ameliorate their situation through revolutionary struggle, they fired off yet another letter to the British consul at Bluefields. The immediate catalyst for the letter was a new export tax on bananas; however, recycling verbatim phrases from previous such letters and speaking in the name of the Indians as well, these Creoles listed a series of reformist demands and dropped the radical demand for independence:

> What do the people of the Coast want? . . . We want to see the end of a political system comprised of bribery and corruption. We want to see the end of political dominance; politicians who under the pretense of serving the country, merely line their own coffers out of the schemes and taxation imposed upon their fellowmen; politicians who have no regard whatever for the needs of the nation; . . . We want education, participation in our government; a government which spells peace, progress and decency, instead of moral degeneracy, financial ruin and devastation.
>
> Having always been in constant intercourse with the nations of Anglo-Saxon civilization and training, we cannot under existing conditions be satisfied.[85]

The U.S. military, which occupied Nicaragua until 1933, much of the time engaged in a running battle with Augusto César Sandino. It also supervised the creation and training of a national guard. This was to be a nonpolitical military force, which the United States hoped would keep the peace, end the political turbulence that had wracked Nicaragua in the preceding decades, and guarantee North American interests in the country (Society for Propagating the Gospel (1929:80). In 1937 the head of the National Guard, Anastasio Somoza, a Liberal, took control of the government. He, his sons, and their associates ruled the country for almost half a century as their personal fiefdom.

Quiescence

In the late 1930's there was a shift from the politics of discontent, public agitation, and active resistance characteristic of the Creole community during the forty years immediately following the Overthrow to a politics of clientelism, integration, and accommodation, which reigned from the late 1930's through the 1960's.

The public debate that erupted in 1930 between Alfred W. Hooker, who represented a new wave of Creole politics waged on the national level, and a group called the Creoles of Bluefields, who clung to many of the old attitudes, not only illustrates conflicts among Creoles but also reflects a move away from an independent Creole politics waged principally against the Nicaraguan state.[86]

In 1930 in a printed circular, Hooker accused leaders of the Creole community of being unpatriotic in pushing their claims against the Nicaraguan government and in trying to obtain British assistance to do so. He also claimed that the Harrison-Altamirano Treaty was no longer valid. Creoles organized in the Creole and Indian League under the auspices of the Union Club and calling themselves Creoles of Bluefields wrote a scathing open letter in response, which was published in a local newspaper. In time-honored fashion they claimed that they could not be traitors because they had never sworn allegiance to the Nicaraguan government, that Nicaragua and the Miskito had been "TWO DISTINCT NATIONS," that the latter had never been colonized by the former but instead had been "clandestinely overthrown." The bitterness about past betrayals by Mestizo allies (Conservative and Liberal) in revolutionary struggles was plainly stated: "You would that we all become true Nicaraguans. Does Nicaragua want us as such? Yes; when there is trouble in the country. When our services are urgently needed then we are 'patted on the back,' praised and handed out promises on a silver platter. When the danger is over, we are entirely ignored except when it comes down to the matter of TAXATION." Despite the militancy of the rest of the document, however, they emphasized a key component of an emerging integrationist theme in Creole political discourse: that compliance with past treaties, rather than pulling the two portions of Nicaragua farther apart, was precisely what was needed to draw them together: "You would like to nationalize the Coast, but cease your vain endeavors, friend. The Coast will be nationalized just as soon as the government righteously complies with the terms of the Mosquito Convention and the Harrison-Altamirano Treaty."[87]

The major difference between their article and pre-1920's Creole political discourse was that by this time it was clear to all except the most romantic that a return to the golden past of Miskito independence was only a dream. Paradoxically, the most that could be hoped for was compliance with the treaties that had been the basis of their demise.

In 1935 the Creole senator Horatio Hodgson presented the "Memorial of the People of the Department of Zelaya to That Just and Honorable Assembly, Our National Congress."[88] Although it includes complaints about taxation and lack of treaty compliance, it also signifies the important extent to which Creoles and other Costeños had become integrated into the Nicaraguan nation.

First, the "memorialists" referred to themselves as "the people of the Department of Zelaya," choosing a regional rather than a racial/cultural or national position. Perhaps more important, they also situated themselves as Nicaraguan citizens—"the people of this littoral . . . every one of which is a loyal and patriotic Nicaraguan"—and petitioned the government through proper channels. They even commented sympathetically on the national government's previously scorned attempt to enforce the use of Spanish as a means of nationalizing the Atlantic Coast: "Zelaya's aim was to compel the people of this Department to learn the Spanish language. We admire his intention." Their demands were for those services due any sector of the national polity, such as roads, phone system, hospitals, and education. They even called for better government regulation of the large foreign corporations that had engaged in "a most destructive exploitation of the natural resources of this department." The authors couched their discourse in terms that acknowledged their citizenship within the nation and eschewed the demands for independence that had been a consistent feature of Creole discourse since the Reincorporation.

The message delivered by Sen. Horatio Hodgson is one of the last documents of Creole political discourse that I have been able to find from this period. Though there may have been some before the 1970's, it is clear that the intensity of Creoles' public political expression was much reduced in this intervening period. As a result, it is difficult to analyze Creole politics in this era. Nevertheless, I will briefly discuss some of the factors that led to and perpetuated the decline of overt, collective resistance among Creoles for approximately forty years.

In the first place, transformations of Creole politics were likely influenced by the increased precariousness of Creoles' economic lives. The worldwide depression of the 1930's wrought many changes on the Atlantic Coast, chief of which was the withdrawal of North American capital and an end to economic expansion (Dozier 1985:216). This created a prolonged period of depression, which lasted until the early 1970's in southern Zelaya. Resident U.S. whites, who had supported the Creoles in post-Reincorporation political struggles, abandoned the area, leaving the Moravian Church and the products of U.S. media as the sole representatives of Anglo culture on the Coast.

Economic depression had a series of consequences for the Coast's black population. Many blacks abandoned the hinterland, where they had spread during the enclave economy and concentrated in Bluefields, Puerto Cabezas, Pearl Lagoon, Corn Island, San Juan del Norte, the Mines (Siuna, Rosita, Bonanza), and Waspam (Ruiz y Ruiz 1927), and migrated in large numbers to Managua and the United States. Within these urban settings, some Creoles used the educational opportunities available, particularly in the Moravian and other missionary schools, to attain prestigious positions in Coast society—as professionals, skilled workers, and office workers. The competition with educated Mestizos for these jobs was intense, however, and Creoles were at racial and cultural disadvantage in obtaining them. Simultaneously, the Negro group melted into the Creoles and withdrew from the ranks of unskilled wage labor now associated with Mestizo peasants and indigenous villagers. Most poorer Creole families, even in the urban centers, lived off a combination of migrant skilled labor in the northern mines or Managua, subsistence agricultural production, fishing, and forms of domestic petty commodity production such as baking or the making of coconut oil.

It is possible that economic hard times had a chilling effect on Creole politics, as the community was forced to focus on issues of everyday survival. Creole political quiescence, however, was principally related to increasing economic and cultural integration into the Nicaraguan nation—the creeping institutionalization of Nicaraguan national hegemony on the Atlantic Coast. In the 1940's an unpaved road was pushed through from Managua to the riverhead port of Rama to provide a more direct commercial and social link between Bluefields and the Pacific. As the enclave economy based on foreign capital languished, the economic connection to the Pacific became predominant. Moreover, the Spanish language and Nicaraguan history were taught in all the schools and Creoles born on the Coast after the Reincorporation were automatically Nicaraguan citizens. Creoles who had been born in the reserve and who had burned with Miskito nationalism in their youth were now older and dropping out of public life. Under these circumstances, many Creoles came to accept the "fact" of their Nicaraguan nationality.

The nationalization and political quiescence of Creoles were augmented by the articulation of the three major institutional forces impinging on their daily lives; the Nicaraguan state, U.S. government and commercial culture, and the Moravian Church.

Perhaps the most important factor in the diminution of Creole oppositional politics after the 1930's was the Liberal Party's consolidation of political power under the Somozas. The Somoza dictatorship produced a prolonged period of relative political stability in Nicaragua, from the 1930's through the 1960's. The domination of national political processes by the Somoza dictatorship precluded tears in the national political fabric, which had provided space and opportunity for the intensification of Creole politics in the past. Moreover, many Creoles had come to see their interests represented in the Liberal Party, which became their venue for political expression. This convergence of interests had taken place over a long period, but was consolidated in the constitutionalist struggle of the mid-1920's. Nicaraguan Liberal philosophy, which included constitutional government, government by consent of the governed, the rule of law, property rights, laissez-faire economics, modernization, and separation of church and state, coincided well with the perceived interests of those acolytes of modernity, the Creoles (Hodges 1986:8).

These principles were clearly manifest in the discourse accompanying the twentieth century's central ritual performance of Creole community solidarity and politics: General George's funeral. In his "Oration Delivered at the Grave" of General George, Leonard E. Green associates Creoles as a racial group with the ideals of liberalism and the Liberal Party (Green in Oertzen, Rossbach, and Wunderich 1991:462–463):

> [General George] *was* a Liberal in the sense of being a believer in, and lover of, liberality in the recognition of the majesty of the law, in supporting of that majesty by all legitimate means and in the equal distribution of justice among the people regardless of color, race, creed or any other qualification whatsoever. . . . he fought to destroy utter disregard for the law, utter disrespect of the rights of the people, utter disregard for public order. He fought so that all those corrupt conditions might be superseded with their antithesis.

There were other aspects of the Somoza regime that made it attractive to Creoles. The Somozas spoke English to the people on their visits to the Atlantic Coast and, for the most part, did not interfere with their cultural life. Over time they became skillful in manipulating and buying off Creole leaders when necessary to keep things under control. Many Creoles were members of the National Guard, the central Somocista institution (Society for Propagating the Gospel [1929:80].

The legitimacy of the National Guard for Creoles was based in part on the Somozas' rabid anticommunism . It characterized any threat to the regime as part of an external communist attack on the nation and hence a danger to the religious freedom and overall social and economic well-being of all Nicaraguans (Chamorro Z. 1983:11; Millet 1977:225).

Under the Somozas, Nicaragua's national hegemonic project became increasingly tied to that of Anglo hegemony. The U.S. government, fixated on the "Communist threat" to Latin America, instituted such programs as the Good Neighbor Policy and the Alliance for Progress. Through these it distributed food and clothing on the Coast, collaborated with the Moravians in the provision of medical assistance, bought surplus Coast products, and financed large-scale projects, such as the road to Rama (Society for Propagating the Gospel 1943:45–54; The Moravian 1963:1). North American newspapers, magazines, movies, radio programs, and popular music recordings remained regular features of Creole life. The growing number of Creoles with family members living in the United States also served to maintain strong ties to that country. The pro-U.S. feelings generated in the Creole community served to legitimize the Liberal Somocista government, which initially came to power in the 1930's with the support of the United States and for decades maintained Nicaragua as a highly visible client state of the United States and bulwark against communism in the area.

The Moravian Church played an important role in rehabilitating the U.S. government's reputation among Creoles and strengthening the community's relationship with the Somoza regime. During this period the missionaries were mostly U.S. whites.[89] They unabashedly championed U.S. positions and programs, at times passing out U.S. government literature from church offices and echoing its shrill anticommunism (Society for Propagating the Gospel 1944:47–48). In fact, the U.S. Good Neighbor representative used the Moravian Church offices as headquarters for operations on the Atlantic Coast (Society for Propagating the Gospel 1943:43).

The Moravian Church's accommodationist position vis-à-vis the Liberal Party was clearly manifested in its positive relationship with the Somozas (Society for Propagating the Gospel 1928:98). The Moravians were adamant about their alleged political neutrality and actively taught their adherents respect for authority, political disengagement, and subservience to established governments.[90] To this end, they taught Spanish and Nicaraguan history and civics in their schools. They consulted often with government officials in Managua concerning educational and other matters. When any of the Somozas came to Bluefields, they were honored by the Moravians at special services or receptions (Society for Propagating the Gospel 1954:17). The description of one of these receptions shows the popularity of the elder Somoza with the Moravians as well as the people of Bluefields (Society for Propagating the Gospel 1946:52–53): "a union service of all Protestant groups had been planned for our church. The President graciously accepted our invitation, with the result that great crowds filled the sidewalks and street in front of the church, as well as the church itself."

The Moravians even seem to have gotten on well with the Somozas' feared National Guard. In 1930 they reported the latter as being "friendly to us everywhere along the Coast" (Society for Propagating the Gospel 1930: 104). A Creole ordained Moravian deacon whose leadership responsibilities in the Bluefields congregation spanned more than twenty-five years was also a captain in the National Guard who "enjoyed the confidence of the President of the Republic" (Society for Propagating the Gospel 1938:44).

In general terms, the decline of overt protest among Creoles was facilitated by the mutual articulation of the three powerful social forces that impinged on their daily lives: the Somocista state, the U.S. government and commodified culture, and the Moravian Church. If in the era immediately following the Reincorporation fissures between these institutions created political space for Creoles to maneuver, their consolidation and coordination from the 1930's to the 1970's inhibited mobilization and facilitated the nationalization of the Creole population. Their hegemonic effects were evident, not only in Creole support for all three, but in aspects of their common sense. For example, the strong sentiments against communism I found among Creoles in the early 1980's had their roots in the rabid anticommunism practiced by the United States, the Somozas, and the Moravians. Simultaneous contradictions between the three influenced Creole commonsense notions of their difference and independence. Their historical and contemporary affiliation with the power, symbols, and rituals of Anglo culture embodied in commodified U.S. culture and the Moravian Church served to reaffirm and strengthen their identity and deflect Nicaraguan nationalism's enormous hegemonic pressure to assimilate to Mestizo culture.

Central Moravian Church, Bluefields, early 1900's. Then, as in the 1980's, the Moravian church stood at the geographic and social center of everyday life. (CIDCA-Managua Library)

Calle Commercial, Bluefields, early 1900's, at its southern terminus looking north toward what was then the old Miskitu Chief's Palace and in the 1980's the Cuartel at the top of the rise. This is the main thoroughfare of Barrio Cotton Tree, one of the city's four main Creole barrios. This portion of this street was dominated by houses of the Creole elite. (Moravian Archives, Bethlehem, Pa.)

Bluefields, Moravian Day School, circa 1900, a key institution in the construction of Creole common sense for more than a century. (Moravian Archives, Bethlehem, Pa.)

"In a banana plantation," Casa Alemán, Bluefields. Postcard from Bluefields demonstrating the centrality of the banana industry and racial inequality to the area during the early twentieth century. (Moravian Archives, Bethlehem, Pa.)

Gen. George M. Hodgson, the central heroic figure in contemporary Creole social memory and military leader of the 1926 movement for Atlantic Coast independence. (*La Información*, Sept. 15, 1927:1)

"The Twenty-five Brave," Creole fighting force assembled by General George, which engaged in the initial actions of the 1926 insurgency. (CIDCA-Bluefields Archive)

4.

Creole History and Social Memory

Corn Island, small, lush, and white sand–fringed, sits in the blue Caribbean about sixty miles east and north of Bluefields. Though in recent years the numbers of Miskitu have increased dramatically, the bulk of the island's inhabitants belong to a small number of Creole families whose roots reach back almost two hundred years. I have always been attracted to the island by its physical beauty and (as a seafood fanatic) its thriving lobster-fishing economy. The African Caribbean cultural influence there and the island's annual community celebration of the end of slavery have made it an extremely interesting place for me as well.[1] During the late 1980's, in conjunction with a CIDCA-Bluefields' effort to produce a series of informative monographs on the region, I spent time on Corn Island trying to learn more about the people and their history.

After a few interviews, a number of things became apparent. First of all, people were not particularly forthcoming about their history. They seemed not to want or to be able to reach back much farther, in terms of specific events, than their own experiences and perhaps those of their parents. Even the genealogies I collected usually did not go back farther than the speaker's grandparents. The only glaring exceptions were European and sometimes Amerindian ancestors; Scottish great-great-grandfathers and Rama great-great-grandmothers were remembered and highlighted. On the other hand, African and slave forebears were few and far between in these accounts.

There were, however a number of standardized events that kept popping up in most peoples' accounts of the island's history. Isleños also made continued reference to a definitive written history of the island, which many, especially the middle aged and aged, had seen and read but copies of which were lost or misplaced and whose author they did not remember. Many of the most knowledgeable Isleños insisted that if I wanted to know the real history of the place I had to consult this text. Thinking that I had stumbled on a reference to the lost diary of a Baptist

*clergyman who had recorded more than eight decades of his experiences
on the islands during two centuries of Corn Island history, a diary I had
seen referenced in an obscure monograph on San Andrés, I began to
pursue this text in earnest.*

*After much traipsing around the island I finally found a copy of this
venerable document in the possession of an aged schoolteacher. Following her into her small house and waiting with increasing anticipation
as she located it, I was handed a worn translated mimeograph of a short
work by Eduard Conzemius, well known to me and to most others with
an academic interest in Coast history. Les îles Corn du Nicaragua (1929)
was what Isleños claimed as the definitive history of the island. They
had recounted partial but relatively accurate versions of it in most of my
interviews on Island history. I was never able to elicit oral histories of
the island that went much beyond the basic details contained in this
text and ended up constructing a short history of the island based
mostly on traditional historiographic materials.*

*I later found that the pastor's diaries had been burned after his
grandson died. The Baptist grandson's Seventh-Day Adventist brother-
in-law had destroyed them, along with a quantity of other, to him,
irrelevant and perhaps irreverent old papers.*

> Well, as far as what I could understand and what I see, is not much
> information them in the school about it. If they even refer to it, it
> either be mostly on a superficial level. They say, "Well, a fleet of
> slaves drift from Cabo Gracias a Dios" and that is all. They don't
> mention nothing about the real history or organization of black
> people, nothing at all. Yeah. Briefly we get history about all the
> different man them; down to the Japanese Dynasty, the Chinese
> Dynasty. We don't get none about ourselves as yet.
>
> —Terry García interview, 1991[2]

> I wonder if I could contribute so much to *you* with that. . . . Well,
> the recent history that I would know about, that I live. I could tell
> you about when the first, um, when they first start lobstering in
> Corn Island.
>
> —James Johnson interview, 1991

> Everybody is making up their own history now.
>
> —L. Williams interview, 1991

For most Nicaraguans, the distinct colonial histories of the Caribbean
and Pacific portions of the country are the principal explanatory device

for understanding what for them are obvious contemporary cultural and economic differences between the two. History as social memory also provides a reservoir of key symbols utilized in the everyday processes of mutual construction and maintenance of identity boundaries between groups within these regions. For Atlantic Coast people in general and Creoles in particular, history is a crucial terrain for thought and political practice.

Creoles, however, have an ambiguous relationship to their history. While they are quite conscious and proud of the history of the Atlantic Coast and of themselves as a people, their historical knowledge is generally not detailed or elaborated. Both written and oral Creole historical narratives have tended to be embedded within general accounts of Atlantic Coast history rather than being accounts specifically focused on Creole histories. This is undoubtedly related to Creoles' tactical subordination to regional (Costeño), seminational (Mosquitian), or transnational (Anglo/Afro-Caribbean) identities as they have engaged in identity politics over the years. Moreover, Creole communities have no canonical versions of Coast or, especially, Creole histories, no accounts of Creole history that most Creoles are familiar with or on which they can generally agree.

Oral accounts lack historical authority for Creoles. Bluefields' Creole community is literate and well educated by Nicaraguan standards, a fact of which most Creoles are proud. For them an authoritative history of the Coast would be one that is researched, written, and published by professional (read *foreign*) historians. Though oral histories of the Coast as recounted by older Creoles have a certain level of credibility, that credibility is based on the teller's personal experience of the narrated events or close relationship to another teller who experienced them. These remembrances, because they are neither written nor "scientific," have not reached canonical status nor have Creoles standardized them, as other African American peoples are reported to have done with their memories.[3]

Over the last fifty years, no definitive printed treatment of Atlantic Coast history and the Creole place in it has been generally accessible to the community. The most important reason for this lack of accessibility is that, until recently, Atlantic Coast history was not taught in the schools, much less the history of Creoles as a group. Additionally, other than newspapers, no printed texts are produced on the Coast, and it has been difficult for Creoles to obtain reading materials, particularly materials that address their realities. Most reading matter has come from the Pacific portion of the country or from the United States; neither is a particularly fertile source of printed material concerning the history of

Coast peoples.[4] Finally, while Creoles are generally literate, they are not text oriented in practice, so that, while textual knowledge is revered, written narrative is not a central, everyday aspect of Creole culture.

The lack of a canonized version of Creole history has produced a number of important effects. On a practical level, it has made the task of eliciting Creole accounts of their history difficult indeed. Because I was a powerful outsider/insider, known to be both well educated and a possessor of authoritative knowledge of Coast history, Creoles were unable to understand why I would be coming to them for their accounts of that history. Only the old, operating from the authority of personal experience, the brash and radically irreverent, or those I could coax would provide more than an extremely abbreviated historical account.

More important, the relatively open character of Creole history makes the Creole past an especially malleable terrain for memory politics. Because it has not been authoritatively standardized, Creole history can be retold and reinterpreted in ways that reflect the narrators' perspectives without being brought up short by an authoritative version of the "facts."

There are, however, events, personages, and social relationships that recur in Creole historical accounts. These discursive fragments are important components of Creole political common sense.[5] Competing versions and interpretations of Creole history are woven within and around these relatively agreed-upon historical elements. They are variously interpreted and reinterpreted, combined and recombined, selectively employed, elaborated, simplified, omitted, and emphasized in patterns that flow from the positioning of their narrators. Creole collective histories and social memories, crucially important components of Creole common sense, are multiple and often contradictory.

The presentation of Creole collective history that follows has many agendas. First, having claimed authority for my "academic" account of Creole history, I want also to interrupt that authority by acknowledging alternative histories produced by Creoles. The Creole narratives that I have chosen were produced in two genres—the printed and the oral. I use the elements of Creole history that emerge from the oral accounts and constitute the most salient elements of Creole popular (social) memory to organize the representations made in both genres. Second, this chapter does important work in my ethnography of Creole common sense. It highlights the events, personages, and relationships that Creoles of the 1970's–1980's themselves considered central to their history and were, therefore, salient commonsense elements in the construction of Creole identity and politics during this period.

This chapter contributes in another, related, way to my discussion of the politics of Creole common sense and to the historiography of the

African Diaspora in general. Unlike in many social scientific compilations of oral history (e.g., Price 1983), I have made an effort to consult not only the individuals the Creole community named as historical authorities but also a range of individuals some of whom (young, relatively uneducated, verbally maladroit) would most certainly have been counted by the community as among the least historically knowledgeable. In this way I hoped to obtain a broader and more "everyday" notion of the collective memories that stem from such individual knowledge. This methodology helps accentuate the great variation in Creole interpretations of their history. This in turn provides insight into the multiple constitutive possibilities available in the generation of Creole politics and identity.

There are only two extensive published Creole historical texts, one by Donovan Brautigam Beer and the other by John Wilson, produced during the period in question (the 1970's and 1980's). Both touch on all the themes central to Creole oral social memory of the group's history, albeit sparsely. This meager treatment of Creole history contrasts sharply with the extensive materials they present on the international struggles between the British and the Spanish over the Atlantic Coast, the detailed discussions of the origins of the Coast's indigenous populations and of Miskitu society and politics. Creoles are present in these written narratives but in a decidedly secondary position, as interlopers rather than legitimate players. This, in part, is a function of the larger objectives of these two works. Brautigam Beer deals with the history of the Coast in general, and Wilson specifically with that of the Moravian mission to the Coast. Nevertheless, the relative absence of Creole presence in these published histories generated by Creole scholars is a perplexing problem that I will take up again in later chapters.

The oral accounts of Creole history are compiled from conversations with a large number of community members from a variety of economic, gender, age, color, educational, and social positions in Bluefields' Creole community. The accounts have important differences that are in part a product of the disparate subject positions of the narrators. To assist the reader in locating the narratives, I have included in the endnotes a brief description of each narrator, including age, political positioning, and economic status, after the first quotation from each. It should also be noted that more than a decade separates the publication of the two written narratives and my conversations with most of the oral narrators. Social, economic, and political conditions had changed dramatically on the Atlantic Coast and in Nicaragua over that space of time, and this certainly had an effect on the specifics of the historical memories presented in each form.

The published texts were also influenced in important ways by their methodology and audiences. Both were written in a scholarly genre and were therefore constrained by their construction around the historical authority of colonial and church archival texts. Brautigam Beer's text was published in installments in the daily newspaper *La Prensa*, a mouthpiece of a leading faction of the Conservative Party and the Mestizo elite. It was also published within the context of the Somocista Mestizo state, which actively practiced censorship of the press and other forms of political repression. These circumstances were not conducive to a free interchange of ideas. In some ways it is remarkable that Brautigam Beer was able to publish a history of the Coast that was at all critical of the region's relationship to the Nicaraguan nation. Published in the nation's premier newspaper in Managua, the capital, Brautigam Beer's text is exemplary of Creole social memory as expressed in a public sphere dominated by Mestizos.

Wilson's work was prepared and presented as a thesis for the completion of his *licenciatura* in theology at the Seminario Bíblico Latinamericano in Costa Rica. Because it was written with the idea of some level of public distribution in Nicaragua, Wilson must have been sensitive to some of the same pressures as Brautigam Beer; however, the authoritative audience that he was the most conscious of was the Moravian Church, particularly its U.S. missionaries and administrators.

Social Memory of Creole History

Almost all accounts of Creole history, be they oral or printed, contain a narration of a slave ship or ships wrecking off the Caribbean Coast of Central America near Cape Gracias a Dios. The shipwrecked strangers are universally reported to have joined the indigenous people already living in the area. This narrative also appears in innumerable non-Creole historical accounts of Miskitu origins from the seventeenth century on and is taken as a central narrative in the origin accounts of the contemporary Miskitu population.

Brautigam Beer and Wilson take this as the origin story for the Zambo-Miskitu and not the Creoles. For both, however, it is an important event in the generation of a black presence on the Coast. Wilson claims that the slaves (no race or other identity is reported) came from Jamaica, whereas Brautigam Beer posits a specific African (Senegambia) origin for them. The version of their origin that appears in most Creole oral histories maintains the connection between these events and the origins of the Miskitu; however, these shipwrecked persons are often also considered to be ancestors of the Creoles, as in Herman Dixon's account (interview, 1991):[6] "They did bring the Jamaican them as slavery, you see. The first people them was here was the Miskitu Indians and the Sumu. The ship get wrecked in Cape. Well, the black was on the beach and the first people they meet up was the Miskitu Indians and there is where they mix them cross, and that's why we all have in Miskitu Indian blood." In most oral versions of this event, the shipwrecked former slaves who arrive from across the sea are assumed to have originally embarked from Jamaica.

Almost all Creole historical accounts agree, despite enormous variation in the details, that as a group their principal ancestors were Jamaicans of color; however, Creole social memory varies concerning the initial origins of the group's black ancestors. For many, especially older Creoles, the connection between these ancestral Jamaicans and Africa is not self-evident and the possibility of the African origins of these black ancestors is unknown, ignored, or denied. Miss Lucy Williams, famous for her practical expertise in Creole folklore in general and dance in particular, told me (interview, 1991):[7]

> We call ourselves Creole and people say if you are black you come from Africa. But we are, Creoles, a very mixed group. Many of us that you see here, our ancestors is—we don't find them in Africa. We find them in different parts where Africans were. For instance, many of our people on the North [Puerto Cabezas] are Jamaicans or from Limón. Many of our black—we don't have any pure black people here in Bluefields.

Some younger, well-educated Creoles or those who identify as rasta are more likely to claim African origins for the ancestors. Burt Hodgson exemplifies this position; however, his version of African origins is clearly tempered by memory of West Indian and Anglo origins as well (interview, 1991):[8]

> We know that our old ancestors come from Africa. But the first encounter was with English people in the West Indies and finally they keep on the journey looking for mainland and that is how they end up here on the Central American mainland. Here we had some cultural mixture. Racial mixture, I should say, and that mixture is what comes out in the Creole man. So it's a kind of mixed culture. It was mixed between the English people that was here and also the Miskitu people.

Some, like René Hodgson, claim that, besides the shipwrecked blacks, others of the Creoles' ancestors were brought as slaves, again principally from Jamaica (interview, 1991):[9]

> It's two version that they had how we Creole people reach here. One is that we came as slaves when a ship was—you know they come when they used to sell the slaves. And they had, like, a

shipwreck or something like that and the slaves came into the north part of the Atlantic Coast and they mixed up with—amongst the Indians and that's how Creoles got here. And they have another version that is not exactly—that they had a auction, see like, then brought the black people as slaves to work here in the Atlantic Coast. And they gave the specific case of Corn Island where they had native people here working as slaves then. And that's how they come in.

For many Creoles the connection of Creole ancestors to the institution of slavery does not presuppose African origins, as it would for most blacks in the United States. Berta Blanford clearly demonstrates this in her memory of her family's history (interview, 1991):[10] "more and more I am convinced a lot of the influence of the, not Afro, but more say, Jamaican influence here. And especially in my family, I found out that my great-grandfather by mother side was a Jamaican . . . He came here, I imagine as a slave worker. Because she [her mother] mentioned an English family that he used to work with."

Other Creoles claim that their ancestors came to the Coast from Jamaica as free immigrants, though some of these accounts, like Thomas Jackson's, still include slavery as an aspect of Creole history (interview, 1991):[11] "as custom you know, our old people always tell us about their days then. They claim that our descendants is Jamaican, Caymanian, you know, black people that came out here after the emancipation of the slaves. Some of our great-grandparents they was slaves." Some, however, like Kevin Whitiker, do not (interview, 1991):[12] "The Creole people really come from Jamaica. Jamaica and Caymans . . . They came here with the banana people."

Both of the printed historical accounts agree that slavery as an institution existed on the Atlantic Coast and that the black slaves who were brought by the English to labor there were an important ancestral population for the Creoles. Wilson briefly states in his work that the Creoles "are the descendants of the negroes and mulattoes brought as slaves from Jamaica by the English colonists during the 18th century. Later there was a mixing between these Creoles and the Miskitu and Rama" (Wilson 1975:109; all translations are mine unless otherwise noted). He makes no specific mention of an African origin for these ancestors.

Though it does not occupy a prominent position in his history of the Coast, Donovan Brautigam Beer does construct a narrative of Creole origins that is similar in many ways to that presented in chapter 2. After describing the Miskitu expulsion of Colonel Hodgson and his family from Bluefields in 1790, Brautigam Beer goes on to say that "Hodgson's slaves adopted the name of their master . . . These families, with other mulattoes imported from Jamaica, etc., are, in part, the foundation of many of the present inhabitants of the Coast who are called Creoles." He also alludes to the fact that slavery continued to exist at Bluefields after 1800, an assertion I have seen nowhere else in the secondary literature:

> On the other hand, Colonel Hodgson had two natural sons with a pretty daughter of the Rama Indians, . . . in 1820 these two Mestizo youths ruled over almost all the population of Bluefields, . . . they were able to subject their deceased father's slaves, although many of them had fled. One of these youths, George, had consecutively seven women, and with them twenty-five children. These are the parents of the group of Hodgsons who are considered "the legitimate Hodgsons." This family and that of the Wilsons is the largest in the city of Bluefields, . . . Lately, many of them have mixed with those of Ethiopian [African] descent, and up to today, the legitimate Hodgsons and their mixtures and the slave Hodgsons argue among themselves over their genealogy. (Brautigam-Beer 1970a:3 [June 1])

Despite its centrality to written Creole history, slavery is not a central theme in Creole oral history. Many Creoles claim that slavery never existed as an institution on the Coast. For them what might seem to outsiders to be the contradictory relationship between the blackness of some of their ancestors and the absence of slavery is resolved by their shipwrecked and runaway status. For others the status of slavery in Creole history is more ambiguous. Lucy Williams told me (interview, 1991):

> And that's why there are so many Hodgson. . . . See, when the first Hodgsons came all the men that they brought to work with them— call them slaves—they were adopted. Had to use the Hodgson name and that's how the slaves they caught too [got their names]. . . . So some were not pure Hodgson. Some were slave Hodgsons.

So there was slavery here on the Coast?

Not to my knowledge.

For many younger adults such as Burt Hodgson, on the other hand, there was no doubt that slavery was a central experience for their ancestors (interview, 1991): "So far I believe that the black people came this side because they brought them as slaves."

It is significant that the only popular narratives of slavery times that I can remember from a decade of conversations with Creoles are accounts of their ancestors' escape from slavery through shipwreck or the famous manumission event at Corn Island. There is a celebration held by the Isleños every August 27 in which the freeing of the island's slaves is celebrated. Creoles narrate this event telling how, depending on the version, the Miskitu king or a British dignitary freed the slaves after calling them together on the beach. Other than these tales, I never heard any oral narratives of slavery times or accounts of slavery as an institution on the Coast. I was told about one specific slave ancestor by members of a Corn Island family. Otherwise, even though many Creoles were willing to admit that they must have had slave ancestors, specific ancestors were always free Creoles, Europeans, or Amerindians.

In Creole accounts of their history, great emphasis is laid on the process of racial mixing that produced the contemporary Creole population. As Lucy Williams said (interview, 1991): "We are a mixed group. We can't call ourselves pure." The European and Amerindian role in this process is particularly emphasized. Most Creoles are certain that a vital part of their history as a group is to be found in their origins in the indigenous community. This is an important part of the significance of the shipwreck/intermarriage narrative.

The written texts and the oral histories agree on this point. Herman Dixon (interview, 1991): "The real name of the Creole is Sambo because we all mixed with Indian [Miskitu] or with Rama, Sumu or with the Philistine Spanish, see . . . so we not no more black, real black that is why they call us Creole."

Many Creoles chronicle the historical coming together of Amerindian and Europeans as an important aspect of Creole history. Again this propensity increases with the age of the speaker. Lucy Williams (interview, 1991): "My great-grandmother from my mother's side was a Rama Cay Indian and she married to one of the Hodgsons, British, . . . three Rama Cay ladies populate this. One married to Jaensky. One married to Hodgson and another one married to Ingram. And there formed the Ingram, Hooker, and the Jaensky, the Germans on the hill up there."

In general, oral histories, especially those that include family genealogies, emphasize the European origins of the Creole group. Creoles stress in particular the group's ties to the "English" as an ancestral population and the central role of the English in Coast history. James Johnson made this statement during one of our many conversations (interview, 1991):[13]

The teaching on that was . . . telling us that we descend from
people from Caymans and from Providence. And you, you know,
try to follow that up and, and they would carry you right back to

Scotland, you know. They would trace you right back to Scotland and Englishman. That is what . . . we thought. At least I thought the Englishman was like me because that is what they taught me, that I was descended from Englishmen.

Many Creoles were able to name individual white ancestors separated from them by many generations. These same people did not specify their black and brown ancestors any deeper than three generations. Interestingly, there are indications in James Johnson's statement that the historical relationship between the English and whiteness was not self-evident for many Creoles. The following narration of Creole origins further highlights this, as well as Creole perceptions of the British colonial identity of the Coast and Costeños. Kevin Whitiker (interview, 1991):

You had king, you know. The king was Miskito. Miskito people. Originally, I say, from England. England had a lot to do with it.

Who was from England?

Both the Indians and the Creoles. Both of them.

Were originally from England?

That's right.

So the Miskitu and the Creoles came from England to here?

That's right.

So then they came from England to what, to Jamaica and Cayman and then from there to here?

Exactly, because all—most of those poor people that died, they still believed that here supposed to be for England. They still have that belief up until when they died. You see what really happen, they used to get aid. They used to get a lot of aid from England.

Creole social memory also includes admixture with other whites, particularly Germans and white Americans, as well as people of color principally from places such a Jamaica, Cayman, San Andrés, Providencia, Roatán, Belize, and the islands of the French Caribbean. Lucy Williams (interview, 1991):

Because there were some Caymanian women here. Like this same
Miss Ida . . . she and Miss Musso and several black women from
Cayman were here as cooks and washerwomen. The Germans
came and the white men came and picked these women and had
children with them. You understand. Because Miss Musso had the
Kandlers. The other women had the Haffa, Australian [Austrian].
And that is how those mixture begin. And those are black, black
women. . . . Those were some of the first missionaries that came to
build. And they took wives among the black women.

A central feature of Wilson's and Brautigam Beer's Coast histories is
the narratives of British influence and presence on the Coast. Brautigam
Beer in particular chronicles British policies toward the area, conflicts
with the Spanish and the exploits of British superintendents, particularly Robert Hodgson, Sr. and Jr. Creole oral history is much less specific
in this regard. There is general acknowledgment of British colonial
control of the region. The assumption is universally made that the
Mosquitia, until the Reincorporation, was a part of the British Empire.
Creoles also remember that the Miskitu king operated under the paternalistic authority of the British. Aside from the freeing of the slaves
at Corn Island and the signing of treaties regarding the Coast with the
Spanish, however, I heard no narratives of specific events naming the
British as protagonists. The following synopsis provided by Frank Parsons is typical (interview, 1991):[14]

First it was rule by the Miskitu. Then the Spain came and like they
take it away from the Miskitu. Then the English people come
afterwards. They were the one were ruling afterwards. Good. Well,
I understand that the treaty that they had with the Nicaraguan
government and the Coast then. That, well, you must always look
after the Indian people because, well, you know, they is descendant
from here, and all that. Sign then that they must all the time look
for leave them out nothing . . . The English government make a
treaty with the Nicaragua government to take care of the Indians
them . . . That's why the Spaniards get to come in here, you see.
Afterwards they sign up a treaty and then for so much years but it
look like time pass. But I don't [know] what happened. Probably
because England is so far that . . . I hear somebody said that the
English people did, well, give the United States to look over here
because, well, they are close and they are too far away to see
everything go good on the Coast.

Creole written histories of the Coast documented the succession of the Miskitu kings; however, their major focus was on British manipulation of the kings and chiefs in the international struggle over the Mosquitia. Brautigam Beer is particularly scathing in this regard (1970:2 [June 5]): "The genealogical history of the Zambo and Miskitu 'kings' was invented in the 19th century by some English subjects from Jamaica and Belize. In the years 1838 to 1841 they invested that odd dynasty with nominal sovereignty to give the appearance of legality to various acts of sale and cession of land in favor of individual Jamaican merchants." Referring to the Miskitu kings disparagingly as "Los Reyes Moscos" (The Fly Kings) he claims that (1970:2 [June 2]) "King George, as with all the 'kings' of the Mosquitia, did nothing to improve the social situation of his subjects, and from his noble lineage, there were illustrious issue who, like him, persisted in attending innumerable parties, washing the brain with 'firewater,' losing, in Christian rum, the sense of responsibility and mission that every leader needs besides other virtues that make men great."

Brautigam Beer also maintained that in the late nineteenth century the Miskitu king was a powerless figurehead (1970a:2 [June 12]): "the reserve . . . is not governed by the Indians. The territory and the government were virtually in the power of a circle of foreigners completely unfamiliar with their customs. It is true that the nominal head of government was an Indian (mixed) and that some of his race took part in the General Assemblies, but the Executive Council was formed exclusively of individuals of this aforementioned circle." According to Brautigam Beer, these foreigners were ""Creole and white Jamaicans" (1970a:2 [June 11]).

Creole oral accounts of the Miskitu kings and their relationship to the Creoles are much less detailed but in general more favorable than written accounts. Most Creoles believe the Miskitu kingdom to be indigenous and to predate English colonial control of the Coast. They also credit the kingdom with a level of status and autonomy denied by the written accounts, although many accept the idea that the king was not completely independent. One indication of this is that Creoles never spoke to me of the reserve or the Miskitu chief. Reference was always made to the historical power of the Miskitu king. James Johnson (interview, 1991): "Well, I read about the Miskitu king. Well, I know it was an imposed king. But goddamn it to hell, at least you had a king! Eh! Somoza wanted to be king once. Someone from up Matagalpa propose him was to be king or emperor or something like that" [laughs].

Creole oral historical accounts also posited a close relationship between the Miskitu kings and the Creole community. In my discussions with Creoles about these kings, reference was often made to the Creole defenders of the last kings who lived in the community. Creoles also spoke of the power of the members of the group who were the kings' close advisers, thereby establishing a close historical link between the Creole community and the Mosquitian centers of power. Lucy Williams (interview, 1991): "My ancestor was an adviser to the Miskito king. My old man Forbes. My great-grandfather who was from Cartagena. Why because being from there he could speak Spanish and English. But he was a black man. Black man."

One area where almost all Creoles agree is the central and beneficial role played by the Moravian Church and its missionaries in Creole history. While the Moravians' role in the spiritual formation of the community was considered to be important, the missionaries' educational and civilizing role was emphasized in most accounts. Donovan Brautigam Beer's narration of the historical impact of the Moravians is characteristic of the position of many, especially older and better-educated, Creoles. He characterizes the arrival of the first Moravian missionaries as the most important event in the history of the Atlantic Coast during the nineteenth century (1970a [June 6]):

> With justice we recognize the Moravians' outstanding intervention, without equal in the lives of the inhabitants of the Coast. . . . in addition to their religious teachings, where they organized a church they also founded and built a school. They organized one of the best choruses in Central America, which year after year intoned the greatest works of the immortals of music. They produced the richest compilation of useful data for the history of our Atlantic Coast for the period from 1847 to 1900, . . . They brought the first doctors to watch over the health of the people. They changed the population's natural way of life and overturned their scarred consciences, bending a great multitude to the soft and light yoke of the sainted gospel, introducing for their work teachers, philosophers, pedants, linguists, herbalists, lexicographers, composers, entomologists, authors, and, above all, missionaries.

Wilson's thesis documents in detail the history and influence of the Moravians on the Coast. He also emphasizes the educational activities of the Moravians, pointing out that much more attention was paid to the educational formation of the Creoles than to that of the indigenous peoples of the Coast.

In the oral accounts I heard, although the Moravians' historical influence on Creoles was much emphasized, there was little memory of their arrival or of specific events involving missionaries. There were two exceptions. The first was the memory, mostly among older women, of missionaries who had married local women and whose progeny were members of the community. The second was the death at the hands of Augusto César Sandino's troops of a Moravian missionary in the early 1930's. In a number of oral narratives, the Creole role in the missionaries' efforts to educate the Miskitu is remembered and emphasized as a key aspect of the historical relationship between these two groups.

The event in Atlantic Coast history that Brautigam Beer places second in importance only to the arrival of the Moravians is the Reincorporation. This is in many ways the opening event in significant history for most Creoles. In Creole social memory, events dating from this historic moment elicit much richer and more complex oral narrations. Creoles' reluctant social memory of events and relationships before the Reincorporation may be related to their greater distance from the present. The past is much more immediate if there are living members of the community who have personally experienced it and can narrate it from that perspective. I suspect, however, that close attention to pre-Reincorporation facts concerning Creole arrivals calls into question Creole standing as a pre-Nicaraguan autochthonous group and undermines the group's national claims and that these events are therefore downplayed. In other words, Creoles can claim that, at the dawning of significant history, represented by the Reincorporation, Creoles were Costeños.

Social memory of the Reincorporation varies greatly in levels of detail. Some Creoles I talked to claimed never to have heard of the Reincorporation. Kevin Whitiker (interview, 1991): "I don't know anything about that." Most, however, were aware of this series of events as a tranformative moment for Creoles as a group. It was recognized as the point at which Nicaraguan dominance was asserted over the British/Miskitu/Creole Mosquitian social formation and Creole resistance to this dominance began. Burt Hodgson (interview, 1991): "It was said also in history that the black man was the one who fought against the Spanish dominion capacity and who help the Indian people here when the Spaniard tried was to take over the Atlantic Coast." Francis Sui Williams, a noted Creole scholar, describes the Creole role in the Reincorporation and its aftermath as follows (interview, 1991):[15]

So they [the Zelaya government] maneuver and they took over the Coast by force of arms. There was a brief rebellion by the Creoles of the black people who managed to reconquer the Coast, for maybe about a period of about a month they held it. And with the intervention of an American battleship, I think it was the *Marblehead*, they came in and they took over the Bluff and Bluefields and handed it over back to the Nicaraguan army without firing a shot. The Creoles, the black people, discovered that it was useless to keep up an armed struggle because they didn't get the support or the help that they expected from England. So that put an end to that rebellion and a couple of the outstanding leaders were arrested, sent to Managua, and tried as rebels. The Nicaraguan government even accused some of them as traitors to the country. So from 1894 the Coast is a legal part of Nicaragua.

When this Coast was incorporated, the very first Nicaraguan government under which we lived started treating us as a conquered province. As a vanquished people that had to be punished and exploited. And that is exactly what the very first Nicaraguan government started doing. Started punishing the people, exploiting them, committing all sorts of cruelties. Taking away their properties and discriminating them racially and politically.

All the functionaries were sent from Managua, governors, mayors, judges. Every position worthwhile, military, civil, all those people were sent from Managua, and a lot of what we call the Mestizos, the Ladinos, started migrating towards this Coast and they started picking up the best of our lands. They came with the idea of exploiting and getting rich as quick as they could.

I personally compare it to what took place in the United States after the Civil War. I understand that some politicians used to go down to the South, the famous carpetbaggers, no, and started taking advantage of the situation of the vanquished. Something similar happened here in the Nicaraguan Coast. All the government, the different Nicaraguan government kept up that policy towards the Coast from 1894 until I would say, until the beginning of the revolutionary government.

Young Creole men, especially those most critical of the Sandinistas in the late 1980's, identified the events of the Reincorporation with Creole independence struggles during the 1920's and placed historic figures of that era as the major protagonists of the Reincorporation. In many Creole accounts of the Reincorporation, all Mestizos are not judged harshly. Rather, the agents of the end of Mosquitian independence are seen as the Nicaraguan state and its unsavory leaders. The following account by Herman Dixon features these ingredients and includes the common notion of the United States as the ultimate arbitrator of the conflict over the Coast (interview, 1991):

You see afterwards they come together, all of them. They say they are Coast people all of them together because they used to fight against the Spaniard, Philistine here. And there is where they unite together and make the Coast be for the Coast people. For the

Miskitu, Sumu, Rama, black Garifuna, and everyone that is staying here. But they didn't want the Philistine to come in, you see, so they used to fight against the Philistine.

Well, my great-grandfather was one of the forty brave [Twenty-five Brave]. Hardy Archibold. He was one of the forty brave. Well, now, the Coast started from Nuevo Mundo that is ahead of Nueva Guinea come down. So Chontales, Rama, Nueva Guinea belongs to the Coast. Well, that fight against the Spaniard. Afterward, well, they leave it like that because those people stay in that side, you see. So they can come to the Coast and work the Coast, you see.

So, first when it was independent. The Coast was independent. . . . The younger generation, afterwards, they leave the Spaniard make them come in. They used to come in one by one because they did afraid of the Coast. And after they start come and they start work and thing like that, no one trouble them, you see. Because we realize then that, well, some of them is from Chontales and so forth so they can come and work the land because we have plenty land here. And, well, just so the Creole here get in with the Spaniard, you see, and it's a lots of Spaniard get in with Miskitu and they get in with the Sumu and they get in with the Rama so everything mixing up.

They come and they start it. Because, you see, when the United States make the plan with Somoza, Old Somoza. If he kill Sandino that he can, he will rule because he was just a general, you see. Well, he did it, you see. So, well, he give him was to rule the Coast, too. So there is where we stop being independent.

So that is the Reincorporation or the Overthrow?

United States make the deal with Somoza was to throw Sandino. Because Sandino he was ruling in León and León was the capital first. So, well, after he win out and take over the Coast, people was so easy they start to send down this Philistine to be in the military and just so until they throw out all the Creole and leave just the Spaniard.

Brautigam Beer's account of the Reincorporation is much more sympathetic to Mestizo Nicaraguans than are any of the oral accounts. Paradoxically, in a tone reminiscent of the political discourse of a sector of the Creole community during the 1970's, he applauds the Reincorporation, specifically its foiling of the antipatriotic pretensions of the British and "Jamaican Negroes." He disagrees, however, with the way in which it was undertaken. He provides an account of the signing of the

Mosquito Convention clearly taken from archival descriptions decrying the way in which the Miskitu delegates were coerced into signing. On the other hand, he characterizes the event as "the most glorious" moment of the Zelaya administration (1970a [June 13]).

A central and related focus of Creole social memory is the treaties that the British and the Nicaraguans signed regarding the Coast. The Treaty of Managua, the Mosquito Convention, and the Harrison-Altamirano Treaty tend to run together in Creole memory. The Mosquito Convention is clearly the most important of the three for Creoles. As can be seen from the following and the Parsons quotation above, Creoles remember that the Nicaraguans agreed to a number of provisos favorable to the residents of the Mosquitia. They generally agree that the Nicaraguans did not comply with these treaties. This was the source of much resentment. Burt Hodgson (interview, 1991):

> If we refer back to the treaties, because there were more than one. It seems, or this is what I was told, and what I want say that I heard it but I converse with old people that, after the English people they were tired of exploiting the indigenous people that was here, they decided to leave these people, to abandon them to go back to England. Well, someone had to take care of them because they seems to be self-protected. So what they did they come to some kind of agreement with Managua being to the proximity of the Atlantic Coast to Nicaraguan territory and they signed some treaty. That's how that becomes to be part of Nicaragua. But that treaty if we make research, there are certain agreements that was stated in the treaty which have not been complied. In the law indicates.
>
> Probably that is where our feelings start growing to be some sort of self-independence or autonomous because we were not being treated the way we should be. First that the Managua government was to pay in concept of taxes something like US$40 million per year, which they did not comply with, and also look about the development. The development of the people here both intellectual, cultural, and etc. And none of those things have been accomplished.
>
> One happened sometime around 1890. I am not sure of when the other one was signed. We was also told that these was even trick in the sign of one of those treaty. You know that they took up a lot of Indians and Creole people and they drunk them and mostly was Indians, though, and they just make them sign or just put their fingerprint because they were not.

According to Herman Wilson (interview, 1991):[16]

They never lived up to the contract, or to the treaty from the start . . . That would be 18 [pause] when the Coast was turned over to . . . Reincorporation. They promised that we would have our own caciques and we would have our own tax and our own. All we would have to do is the foreign, international treaties and so on, well, would be carried out by Nicaragua. But we would handle our own system, monetary system and so on. And they never did live up to that.

In the written texts these treaties are not nearly so central and are remembered differently. For Wilson the significance of the Treaty of Managua is religious rather than political (1975:197): "Now that the Mosquitia had for all intents and purposes fallen under Nicaraguan sovereignty, the missionaries who before had had the backing of Great Britain and the Miskitu kings felt threatened by the new situation . . . the Catholic priests began a strong campaign of proselytizing." Brautigam Beer, unlike most Creoles, in general characterized the treaties favorably (1970a:2 [June 10]; 1970a:2 [June 13]).

Creole social memory of resistance to the injustices of incorporation and broken treaties is also extensive. One example is the memory of the UNIA's presence and operation on the Coast. During the mid-1980's Creole youth, influenced by the popularity of reggae and rasta theology and lifestyle, engaged in a major revival of Garvey memories. They interviewed a number of older Creoles about the movement, painted t-shirts with Garvey's likeness, and so on. Herman Wilson recounted his memories of the UNIA (interview, 1991):

When I was a boy, what I remember going to their meetings. They were a, apparently were a pretty fanatical group. I remember they used to sing certain songs that Marcus Garvey were in the confidence and UNIA, had different rhymes to make up in songs. Their idea, I imagine, was to integrate the black people. One of the idea was to send them back to Africa. I used to go with my grandfather.

Memories of the Garvey movement included differences of color and class that divided the Creole community. May East, a UNIA member, told an interviewer:[17]

[The UNIA was] a black movement of black struggle for equal rights and justice. . . . Marcus Garvey was the head of this movement. He came from way across the sea to show us that we are black descendant from Africa. It was he who taught us to be proud of our God-given color and that black existed before white. He also

said that if black people all over the world unite together we would
be more strong to fight the white world. No matter where you
come from, if you are black your origin is in Africa.

I tell you, girl, the black people of Bluefields or the so-called
Creole did despised us. They never join the movement, only we
black ones that our parents were Jamaican or small island people.
They call themselves black Indian. If the black people did support
the movement, the Spaniard wouldn't get so much show in this
place. They took it all away. I could tell you that the Creole of this
country are the ones that have this town to what it is today. They
don't belong to nobody because they are not Indians nor Spaniard.

Only the oldest Creoles who directly participated in the Union Club
remember its elitist members' embrace of the UNIA. As May East stated,
many older Creoles recalled social segregation of elite and other Creoles.
In fact, in discussing the Union Club (interview, 1991), Herman Wilson
claimed that

they didn't consider themselves black.

That's all the so-called elite of the Creole element. That was
strictly by invitation. So the little lower group they formed the La
Patria Club. That's the blue-collar workers and so on belonged. The
other club there. The Union Club strictly formal with their dressed
and everything else . . . They used to have a base there and they
used to play billiards and [unintelligible] occasionally.

They sold out [their house] to the Moravians. They started
wrangling among themselves and didn't get by too well . . . I know
I used to be outside on the street watching them dancing inside.
Well, I was small then, too, schoolboy when they was really strong.
But later on they didn't have any so-called elite society among the
Creole race.

Older Creoles like Herman Wilson also have vivid memories of other
individuals and groups organized to fight for Creole and Coast rights:
"Creole and Indian League they had. Well, they used to have meetings
at the same UNIA hall and so on but that was mostly to fight the central
government for our rights . . . Crepe Hodgson was one of the leaders in
that. Sam Howell and Tommy Howell . . . He [Crepe Hodgson] was
really dedicated. And for that reason probably he died almost a pauper.
He wouldn't accept any bribes or anything."

The central historical figure in Creole social memory is Gen. George
Hodgson. His military campaign initiated with the Twenty-five Brave is
read as the quintessential act of Creole resistance to Mestizo Nicaraguan

dominance. During my time in Bluefields, I heard many accounts of their exploits from young and old alike. A few were personal memories of the events recounted by older Creoles, most of whom were children in the mid-1920's; most were narratives garnered from older relatives who claimed to have personally experienced at least a portion of what they had recounted. As can be seen from the narratives reproduced here, many narrators of General George histories are concerned with establishing the veracity of their accounts and utilize the claim of their source's firsthand experience as an authenticating device. This concern with demonstrating the accuracy of the General George accounts is not present in the narrations of other historical moments and demonstrates their importance to Creoles. The series of historical events in which General George is the heroic figure is so central to the group's popular memory that for many of its younger members other crucial historical moments are read through them. Thomas Jackson (interview, 1991): "Spaniard didn't begin to come around here until after the death of some mens that was around here they used to call the 'Twenty-five Brave.' General George and a small troop that he had along with him." René Hodgson (interview, 1991):

> One thing I were worried about was where my surname came from, Hodgson. I used to investigate and ask people. They said Gen. George Hodgson came here first and he mixed up with—so I went back and investigating. They had a little book here that they to— just when the Revolution took over—they were selling named *Campos azules* that spoke about how General George came when he came here and more or less it said how Hodgson came in and how and now I have that surname Hodgson and things like that. I have been trying because I wanted to know my own roots and things like that. Up to now we don't have no type of documentation.

In the following narrative by Ronny Green (interview, 1991), the story of General George is the main narrative device for the telling of the entirety of Creole history and the establishment of the Creole place in the Coast's ethnic hierarchy:[18]

> Well, I study more or less, my old, how he named, people say told me about Creoles. My grandfather told me that the Creole, what I say, well, the Jamaican people them, you know, what come here on the Atlantic Coast. Them come, not like a slave, they say, they came like the Indian people them, the Rama. Them say the Rama were ruling here in Bluefields [unintelligible] were the king. The

king did name King Clarence. After, when them come here, them
say that the Spaniard the Liberation [Liberal] and the Conservative
them, them did got a little problem. I mean say fight. So the Rama
people them, them went. You understand.

The Creole people them stay. And when they came as student,
pardon, as teacher and then there is when they stay and start get in
with the Indian them and start make up the Creole, you know.
They start live up with one another and the Creole people they stay
and fight for they land, that is why we got rights on this Atlantic
Coast. Because we did got our general. You understand. General
George Hodgson. My grandfather told me everything, you know. So
I could tell you . . . That is why I say with this autonomy government if them did know what is autonomy government we would
get our old people and make them tell we the reality of our history
on this Atlantic Coast. Understand? We got rights just like the
Rama, the Sumu, the Miskitu, and the how he name?

All right . . . Him [Green's grandfather, who had been General
George's boat man] told me that when the Creole people them start
fight, a lot of them run, he say. Because the Creole people them
were farmers one time. You understand. Everybody live on the
Coast them used to plant. And when the Conservatives and the
Liberation they start fight, everybody start run.

He say the Rama them used to live up in the Rama River. Not in
Bluefields, he say. Who were most in Bluefields, he say, were the
black people them what come out from out. Okay. He say that
General George is other one what stand and fight for the right for
the Creole people them. The Miskitu them, them never got no
leader because them leader was the king what was in the park and
the king went, them say, he went to England back. That how them
say. All right.

Then when the general start fight and kill people them. Him,
including the Creole. Them fight because—not only Creole people
fight with him, you know. You got Creole, you got Miskitu, you
got the Sumu, you got everybody mix up in one group. You understand, so when fighting, they fight up in Pearl Lagoon up in Gun
Point.

So him [Green's grandfather] told me, he say at one point
Sandino leave from in the North, up in the Pacific side and he went
Pearl Lagoon killing out the black people them. You know. You see
black people them used to run, too. Them used hide. You understand. So the general facing Sandino up Pearl Lagoon and he beat
him. You understand. He beat Sandino. He kill out a lot of Sandino
man. He catch him live and when he catch him live he send the

two of his bodyguards to kill Sandino. But you know, them didn't kill him. You understand.

So when they let go Sandino. Must be about two weeks after when you hear Sandino fighting up in Puerto Sandino. That's how they call it, Puerto Sandino. Sandino fighting the whole—with the Yankee. You understand. That where them chop off white man head and all them thing.

Okay. He [Green's grandfather] say when this Coast, this Coast was for the Creole peoples, the Miskitu was one people. There was no one no Spaniard. He say it our own people was ruling on this Atlantic Coast, so I asked him, I say, "What about, what happened to our general?" He tell me say, "Well, they kill the general. And from they kill the general there is where black people just. They say how their braveness just gone, it's gone. You understand."

And the old people hiding it from we right now. Because I all the time find out from them, then. I all the time tell them, "What happening? What happen about our general?" They don't tell me nothing. So they just tell me sometime, "Take it easy and keep silent. But we got rights!" they say, "because our Creole people fight." Not because we come [from] out. We come but we never come here as no slave. You understand. We come here like, say now, like teacher. We teaching. We teaching the—the how he named—Indian them. You understand.

So when we come here. Say—well, we did going back. But what happen, them say, with this same problem with—this same fighting between—all of us just stay here. And by we children them. We got rights. Just fight for our rights. And when we get it, them say kill our general. And when they kill our general, we just take it easy, just so.

But we for more rights than the Spaniards them on the Atlantic Coast. And now we don't see nothing. We don't see no rights. You understand. Who them what got more rights is the Spaniard. We can't even talk because right now I would a want a piece of land . . .

This Atlantic Coast what them call Zelaya. It not supposed to name Zelaya because General Hodgson—them say we did got our general. Zelaya was, them say, a conquistador from the Pacific side. Came from Managua coming on the highway. That's how him run all the Rama Indians up in Rama River. Because there was only belongs to Rama. You understand. So by the Rama them was afraid for fighting. The Rama them and they running about in the bush and they stay up Pilla Pilla, Diamante all up in them riverhead. Till them reach Rama Cay. All up in Río Indio all Tourswani . . .

So he [Green's grandfather] told me, the general he leave from

there with him twenty-seven brave and went Rama and run back—
how he name?—Zelaya, you understand. So him say, when Zelaya
gone back Managua, him come back again, and when the general
dead, them say, the people say you know, Somoza, old Somoza is
what put it Zelaya, Zelaya Sur. So I tell them, "Why them call it
Zelaya Sur?" "Because," them say, "in memory of a general what
named José Santos Zelaya." "But tell me something, my General
George Hodgson fight against him. Why them put it Zelaya and
they no want to put it General Hodgson?" So then now them tell
me, "Know what keep hush up because this thing done make."
And I say, "No, man. We going to fight for that until where we
get." I'm tell you with this autonomy, I say we could clear it up.
But what happen, I know what is the meaning of autonomy.

General George's untimely death was an event of mythic proportions
for Creoles: it symbolized the death of the prominent political and
economic role of Creoles on the Coast. I was told numerous versions of
the circumstances of the general's death. Most involved a conspiracy in
which various combinations of U.S. Marines, General George's wife, and
Mestizos participated. A favorite is that his wife was romantically
involved with a marine and they poisoned the general. The following
version by Burt Hodgson is a variation of this account (interview, 1991):
"What I know is what my grandparents told me about him . . . What I
know he fought a lot here for this Atlantic Coast. And what I was told
also that he was tricked. The—he was tricked to death, also, General
George, through his wife."

The works of Brautigam Beer and Wilson paint a negative picture of
the Zelaya regime but treat the following period of Conservative rule as
one of relative prosperity and democracy. In marked contrast to popular
memory of this period, neither mentions Creole resistance to Nicaraguan rule. Although both texts treat the Revolutions of 1909 and 1926,
neither accords Creoles political agency. Both texts characterize them as
national confrontations between the Conservative and the Liberal Parties. Both also give considerable play to the role of U.S. intervention in
Nicaragua during this period. The only hint of local agency is the
following vague statement concerning Costeño liberalism from Wilson's
thesis (1975:228–229): "It was not in Granada, the cradle of conserva-
tism, nor in León, cradle of liberalism, but once again in the Atlantic
Zone, in the historic city of Bluefields, cradle of liberty and Nicaragua's
purest republicanism, that raised the cry of revolution."

Brautigam Beer's history ends with the beginning of the 1926 Revolution. Wilson, however, covers its effects and those of subsequent national events on the Moravian mission. A key element of his narration

is the rise of General Sandino and the Sandinista movement's interaction with the Moravians. Calling the Sandinistas "guerrillas," he narrates the principal event in Creole memory of the original Sandinistas (1975:234):

> The Moravian work in Nicaragua, in the midst of these bloody encounters, also suffered the attacks of the Sandinistas now that they intended to end all types of foreign domination. They considered the missionaries to be spies. The following event proved these assertions. In Musawas lived the missionary Karl Bregenzer. The Sandinistas, suspecting that he was passing along information about their movements, executed him on April 2, 1931. The fact should be noted that before his execution, Bregenzer, with his Spanish New Testament in his left hand, inasmuch as his right hand was tied to one of his executioners was able to preach to them about the road to salvation. Some refused to listen to him while others listened attentively. Once he was executed, the Sandinistas burned the parsonage and totally destroyed every trace of the property.

Creoles remember the first thirty years after Reincorporation as a time of social differentiation and demographic change as well. Herman Wilson provided this account of Creole origins, which emphasizes Jamaican laborers as an important source of Creole peoples and the origin of class differentiation within the community (interview, 1991):

> [The Creole people got started] from slavery. And after that they had a little migration from Jamaica and the West Indies after slavery was abolished and the United Fruit Company had introduced a lot of people in the banana plantations, mostly from Jamaica. Well, they were considered as the lower class; they used to work strictly on the plantation. And the higher class was the people in Bluefields, who used to work in the company offices and stores and the other town jobs. And they maybe had a little fairer skins than the Jamaicans that were brought in. So just a shade make a big difference in their way of thinking or looking at you. So the real Creole is from introduced labor and slaves. We didn't have too many slaves here but you had a lot of imported labor. . . .

> *I thought the important families you have here now—the Wilsons, Hodgsons, Bent, Dixon—were here before the 1880's.*

> Well, they came from migration, too, mostly from England when

England was in power and they either married or had illegitimate
children. And, naturally, when they went back home or when they
died they leave their children certain properties. They helped them
a little with their reading and writing. So that was the aristocrats of
the Creole race. All right, once the missionaries came, well, they
had more access to education and a different style of life. Of course,
they learned from their masters, too. More or less that where they
came from.

We had several groups like the Vogels, for instance, supposed to be
German. And they had the Jaenskys, they were Germans. And we had
the Downs and Jacksons and so on. They were all foreigners that
settled down here and had children here and many of them never did
go back.

Mr. Wilson went on to talk about the Creole elite and emphasized
their origins in alliances and mixture with powerful outsiders. He also
placed the height of their prosperity in the 1920's. This coincides with
the impressions of many other Creoles that their community was at its
most prosperous during this period, just before the international depression and the withdrawal of U.S. capitalist enterprise from the Coast:

If you go Christian Hill there that was something to see. That was
something. I believe their [the elite Creoles'] real best time was
middle 1920's to the middle 1930's. That was their best, best time I
would say. Before that some of them they were pretty all right, too,
but there were less people in that category. Mostly foreigners that
come and married the natives and they had a head start and things
and own property. Practically every Creole had their own property
anyway. Plenty of them sold out and the old people died.

The Somoza period, which followed immediately on the heels of this
era of great significance for Creoles, does not stand out in Creole social
memory. Most Creoles remember it as an uneventful time on the Coast
marked by the withdrawal of U.S. capital and business. Times were
generally hard economically but tranquil politically. The first Somoza,
Anastasio Somoza García, was remembered by many as a paternalistic
figure. Kevin Whitiker describes how Bluefields people reacted to his
assassination in 1956 (interview, 1991): "Man, I mean to tell you
everybody was really sad, all the bells they toll and everything, everybody was really, really, really upset."

In general, the forty-five-year Somoza family dictatorship is remembered by Creoles ambivalently. As Kevin Whitiker explained (interview,
1991):

you see what happened, when this "Pedrón" and them had this place, before Somoza take it over . . . you had a hard time, you had war here every minute, things breaking out this way and breaking out there and after Somoza take it over, everything was quiet, no more of that, and that is what the people they wanted. So everybody didn't care if Somoza didn't move from there. Everybody was contented then. But of course you got some people that say they did want it to change, because he was there too long. I myself, to tell you the truth, was figuring that he should give somebody else a chance, you know . . .? Because one person reigning that kind of way, somebody else wanted to take a chance, too . . . that was my thinking about it. And I was glad after he gone and everything.

The written texts have nothing to say about the Somozas. In Wilson's work the Somoza period is treated as one of relative tranquillity in which the Moravian Church was able to operate unimpeded on the Coast and its area of influence and the variety of services it offered Costeños grew.

There is no single shared chronological narrative of Creole history, though some Creoles clearly are capable of producing one;[19] however, social memory of their history does provide members of the community with a collective image of the past. This is not a history in the sense of a sequential narrative of the Creole past. Creole social memory is a swirl of significant events, persons, and relationships. From this swirl, a series of themes common to many Creole accounts of the community's significant past emerge.

White and black Creole ancestors arrived on the Coast from a rather vague elsewhere (most commonly England and sometimes Africa) via Jamaica and other islands in the western Caribbean (Cayman Islands, San Andrés, Providencia). Once on the Coast, they mixed with Europeans (English, German) and Amerindians (Rama, Miskitu). They had a historically positive relationship with the British monarchy and the Miskitu and a negative relationship with the Spanish and, subsequently, the Nicaraguan Mestizos. These Mestizo Nicaraguans, especially embodied in the figures of Zelaya and Sandino, are remembered as having taken away Creole independence. Through force and treaty, a succession of Mestizo governments have appropriated the Coast's natural resources for the benefit of the Pacific, leaving Creoles in comparative poverty and underdevelopment.

Creoles remember that they have historically fought against this and other forms of Mestizo oppression. Gen. George Hodgson is the outstanding Creole historical figure and is remembered chiefly for his resistance to Mestizo tyranny and championing of Coast independence.

He is also the founding father of the liberal revolution, which culminated in the oppressive but stable and paternalistic Somoza regimes.

Creole social memory resides in and is a key component of the community's political common sense. Residual elements of social memory in common sense are utilized by Creoles to construct common meanings and are integral to imagining the community (Alonso 1988). They provide the basis of the structure of feeling, which, more than anything else, holds the Creole community together. As we shall see, contemporary Creole politics and identity derive their legitimacy and veracity from their articulation with specific aspects of Creole social memory.

5.

The Discursive Struggle over Race and Nation

Daisy and Charlie and I were talking about racism in Nicaragua and how it is manifested. Even though most Creoles will tell you that it exists, it's hard to pin down. Most have a hard time remembering specific instances when someone was overtly racist toward them. So that day when Daisy, who is a Creole from Bluefields, recounted a story about her experience with racism in Managua, I made a mental note of it. Recently, I asked her to tell the story again.

The incident took place when Daisy, then in her mid-twenties, went to Managua to study at the National University. It was a difficult time for her. In the 1980's there was no university on the Coast. Costeño students who wanted to pursue a professional degree were forced to go to Managua or León to study. Many students did not make it. The expense, even with a government scholarship, was often more than the student's family could afford. The universities did not board and finding acceptable living circumstances was difficult. The transition to big-city living after living in a small isolated town or village was problematic.

And then there were the attitudes of the faculty and students toward Costeños. Early on in her time at the university, Daisy had a conversation with another student that, though somewhat cruder than usual, exemplified these attitudes.

When pushed to do so, many, and especially older, Creoles related such experiences to me, though they might not immediately have come to mind. These incidents call into question the assumptions of Nicaraguan Mestizos and others that racism doesn't exist in Nicaragua:

This is someone who was always in my face, she was in my classroom, she was always around. . . . we had this guy who came in to talk to us . . . he was talking about the Miskitu and how Miskitus are lazy and stuff like that. So we were kind of in the Coast atmosphere. And then I kind of talk to him about that. That that wasn't true and tried to point a few things out.

After that class then she came to me and said, well, she always wonder whether you needed a passport to go to the Coast because people told her that people live there in trees . . . So I told her, "No, you don't need a passport . . . You just get on the bus and go". . . . People told her that people live in trees there. So I said to her, "Well, no, I have a house; I don't live in a tree and everybody I know have a house nobody live in trees."

And then she said to me well, she can't believe that I am from the Coast because I was so *fina* [fine features, i.e., as in the Caucasian phenotype]. I was so *fina* compared to the Coast people what I imagine she seen on TV or the newspaper because I don't think she had seen too many [Costeños] . . . . So then I said to her I thought that was—I, you know, I tell her "that was a racist statement and I disagree with it." And then she said "Why?" she said, "because it's true, because I see unos negros negros y vos no sos—vos sos bien finita y hablas el español muy bien" [some black blacks and you are not—you are very fine featured and you speak Spanish very well]. So I kind of got so upset because I knew that talking to her wasn't going to do anything. So I just told her to move away from me. She was racist and I wasn't going to take that.

She didn't even know what I was talking about. So then she went to Marta [a Mestiza friend]. Complain to Marta, and Marta say, "What did you tell her?" And she said "Well, I was just asking her whether you needed a passport and whether people lived in trees and I also told her that she was *fina* and she speaks Spanish good—and then she got upset." So Marta said, "Well, she got upset with right. How you going to go tell the woman that. That is racist." Then she said only Marta and I saw that racist. She was just asking questions.

. . . She thought she was being very nice to me. She told Marta, "I told her she is different from them because she is intelligent and nice-looking." Marta told her "that is what is racist" and she didn't understand that.

All or nearly all initiatives and contributions, even when they take on manifestly alternative or oppositional forms, are in practice tied to the hegemonic: . . . the dominant culture . . . at once produces and limits its own forms of counter-culture.

—Raymond Williams (1977:114)

A central idea of this book is that Creole political common sense, from which Creole identities and politics are generated, is constructed through a number of articulated historical processes. Among the most important of these are Pacific Nicaraguans' discursive representations of the Atlantic Coast, its "minority" inhabitants (Costeños), and their relationship to the Nicaraguan nation. These representations support the Nicaraguan system of class, race, and ethnic stratification and Nicaraguan nationalism within which Costeños maneuver and which plays a significant role in the formation of their political common sense.

This chapter analyzes this representational process through a presentation of the Creole and Miskitu place in the political maneuverings and national imaginings of three distinct sectors of political elites over the course of two decades. This analysis indicates that, while there are often basic similarities between them, Mestizo racisms and regionalisms are multiple. On the one hand, the ways in which Nicaraguan elites represent Creoles and Miskitu as marginal and inferior are different. The racialization of Creoles as "African" and their simultaneous association with internationally prestigious "Anglo" cultures make them "non-national" and therefore more alien and threatening than the "subnational," "Indian" Miskitu. On the other hand, the distinct character of each elite's political struggles and the specific sociopolitical conjunctures within which each operates have produced a series of qualitatively different racist discourses about Creoles and about Miskitu.

This chapter follows critical analyses of nationalism in Latin America that focus on forms of racial and cultural exclusion practiced against peoples of African descent that are both promoted and denied by notions of *mestizaje,* the idea of the creation of a unique people through particular forms of racial and cultural mixture (Hanchard 1994; Stutzman 1981; Wade 1993; Wright 1993). In Latin America, elite constructions of national identity typically praise and promote processes of *mestizaje,* imagining the citizenry as a homogeneous group of mixed European and indigenous (and, occasionally, African) peoples unified by Spanish language and culture, as well as indigenous folk traditions seen as particular to each country. Within this frame, the indigenous past is often glorified as the ancestral spirit of the nation, even if contemporary indigenous peoples continue to be viewed as primitive, marginal, and—insofar as they retain distinct languages, cultures, and identities—a threat to the integrity of the nation. Constructions of *mestizaje,* however, rarely acknowledge the contribution of peoples of African descent to the racial makeup of the nation, whether in reference to its precarious present or its hallowed past (Wade 1993; Wright 1993).[1]

In important aspects, Nicaragua has followed this general pattern. During the twentieth century, and particularly during the Somoza regimes, the state and elite consolidated what Gould (1993:395) refers to as the "myth of a mestizo Nicaragua, a collective belief that Nicaragua had been an ethnically homogeneous society since the 19th century."

The Mestizo as symbol of Nicaraguan national identity simultaneously claims Spanish cultural heritage and glorifies indigenous roots in the pre-Columbian civilizations of the Chorotega and the Nicaraguas (Cuadra 1971).

Importantly, the "myth of a mestizo Nicaragua" refers to the Pacific portion of the nation rather than to the Mosquitia, with its very visible indigenous and black populations. Within the unique "moral topography" (Taussig 1987:253) or "culture of geography" (Taussig 1993:51) constitutive of Nicaraguan history and nationalism, problems of racial and cultural difference are intimately linked to problems of region and territory. My analysis thus treats the question of the position of indigenous and black peoples within the nation as tied to the question of how the Mosquitia as a region has been constructed within Mestizo discourse.

In Nicaragua, indigenous people, particularly the Miskitu, have figured much more prominently in this discourse than have Creoles, whose African heritage and Anglo-identified cultural practices have made them particularly suspect as full-fledged citizens of the nation. This contrasts with the situation in other Latin American countries with significant black populations, such as Colombia, where Indians are seen as "more foreign and distinct" than blacks (Wade 1993:20). Such differences point up the value of careful ethnographic analyses of the discourse of race and nation and the place of blacks within that discourse in Latin America.

The Somoza Regime and the Atlantic Coast

During the late 1960's and the early 1970's, after a decade of steady growth, unstable commodity prices, world inflation, international economic recession, the collapse of regional trade accords, and internal structural problems precipitated a crisis in Nicaragua's agroindustrial economic project. This crisis, which began slowly but was exacerbated by the catastrophic 1972 Managua earthquake, triggered rising rates of unemployment, inflation, indebtedness, state corruption, and a generalized decline in the standard of living. Simultaneously, the Somoza regime, now under the direction of Anastasio Somoza Debayle (Tachito), used its military and political position to enhance the economic position of its adherents at the expense of other sectors of the national bourgeoisie and to squelch any opposition (Bulmer-Thomas 1987:195–229; Chamorro Z. 1982:44–45)

Under these circumstances, the Atlantic Coast became the object of renewed economic attention. National planners saw it as a potential source of exportable industrial products, most notably lumber, wood pulp, paper, and seafood, as well as a potential site for tourism (Anonymous 1969a:6; Vilas 1990). Attempting to realize this potential, the Somoza-dominated Nicaraguan state, with the financial and technical support of foreign and nongovernmental agencies, undertook a series of grandiose development projects. Additionally, the Somoza family itself made a number of large and well-publicized investments in everything from fisheries to agriculture to transportation to tourism.

The Coast, which had moved in and out of the national spotlight over the previous three decades (see Ramírez 1942), was brought to national attention in a number of other ways in the late 1960's. A series of devastating fires and hurricanes received sensationalized coverage by the Managua-based national media. International territorial tensions and outright disputes—with Honduras over an extensive area in the Río Coco region, with Colombia over Caribbean islands and reefs, and with Costa Rica over the Río San Juan—also attracted national notice. All this combined with the launching of the Bay of Pigs invasion of Cuba from Puerto Cabezas, the need to provide agricultural lands for displaced peasants uprooted by the enclosure of Pacific lands for cotton cultivation, and the international attention focused on "minority" peoples by the U.S. civil rights movement to place the Atlantic Coast in the national eye by the late 1960's.

Novedades (the official Nationalist Liberal Party newspaper) published numerous articles and editorials about the Coast and Costeños during this period. In 1969 President Anastasio Somoza Debayle, exhibiting unprecedented interest in the area, made at least three official visits to the Atlantic Coast. The Somoza regime's project with regard to the Coast was "transformist" inasmuch as Costeños were represented as marginal "others" who must be culturally assimilated as Mestizos into the Nicaraguan nation and, in this sense, transformed.

In speeches delivered to Coast audiences, Tachito portrayed the Atlantic Coast as an unincorporated and vast resource-rich area with huge economic potential for his regime and the nation (Anonymous 1969a:6). The Somocista state's major preoccupation was "works of cultural and material progress for the Atlantic Coast" (Anonymous 1969b:1). Indigenous Costeños were represented as impediments to regional and national development and progress. They needed to be "educated" and in other ways made over so that they could effectively participate in national "progress." In this discourse the idea of Costeños as essentially uncultured and backward—suffering from "cultural underdevelopment"—comes through strongly.[2] The "modern" and "civilized" Mestizos from the Pacific were seen as the source of knowledge and culture necessary for the Costeños' development and incorporation into the modern Nicaraguan nation.

In a speech given to a largely Miskitu crowd in Waspam, a market

town on the Río Coco, Somoza proposed a total makeover of the Miskitu
population with the clear objective of "developing" them into Mestizo
campesinos:

> in this isolated region . . . the Pilot Project taught your youth how
> to read and to adopt healthy attitudes, it taught you, the elders, to
> feed your children healthfully, and to read. In sum, it did all it
> could to incorporate in this Nicaraguan tribe [the Miskitu] all those
> new technological advances that a people need so that from there
> an ordered and healthy development will take off . . . We have
> come to begin a struggle that is to settle you, who by tradition and
> custom, are nomads, . . . with technical assistance, with the incor-
> poration of new agricultural methods, the land where you will be
> settled . . . will be a productive one.[3]

Somoza described the Miskitu way of life in only two words—*tribal* and
nomadic—words laden with negative connotations of backwardness
and lack of civilization. He presented Miskitu lifeways, in the main, as
a series of absences, a featureless entity, a lump of clay that could and
would be molded into a utilitarian, valued, and modern form.

Somoza's paternalistic and disparaging prescription for overcoming
the Miskitu's "cultural underdevelopment" and resultant poverty was
based on the stereotypical perceptions of Amerindian cultures held by
many Mestizo Nicaraguans. An explicit enunciation of such representation is found in one of the few descriptions of Miskitu lifestyles among
all the developmentalist rhetoric about the Coast in *Novedades*. It
paints a highly stylized, mythical, and generic picture of a primitive
paradise with Stone Age people indolently living off the natural abun-
dance of the land (Anonymous 1969d:16):

> they [the Miskitu] indolently while away their frugal existences . . .
> a nomadic people with their own tongue, who live off of the fruit of
> a palm and use a bow and arrow to fish, inappropriate weapons for
> today's civilization. . . . a mysterious people whose origin is an
> enigma . . . the exuberance of our tropical forest and the tumultu-
> ous currents of our rivers, whose imposing landscapes give the
> impression that some primitive epoch has stayed behind in them,
> reluctant to submit to the natural process of evolution.

Despite the disparaging character of many of his remarks, Tachito
took pains to indicate that he was not prejudiced against indigenous
Costeños. In a number of speeches, he mentioned appreciatively the
backing he received from Atlantic Coast voters in his campaign. Further-

more, in various speeches to Costeños, Tachito claimed that he and his government did not discriminate along racial lines: "humanity, regardless of where it comes from, what color it has, and what race it claims, this humanity, when it is given an unselfish hand [read *Somoza*], responds with such force and virility that it gives hope that someday we will all live in peace and contentment."[4] Moreover, when speaking to Miskitu audiences during his trip to the Coast in 1969, Tachito read small portions of his presentations in Miskitu. This populist gesture in no way negated his pejorative view of Miskitu people, but, to a certain extent, it legitimized the Miskitu language and identity.

This leads us to the core of Somocista perceptions of Costeños. On the one hand, Nicaraguans are the possessors of "Hispanic civilization" (*Revista Conservadora de Pensamiento Centroamericano* 20 [1966:1]). On the other hand, Nicaraguan racial heritage is "Indo-Hispanic" (CODECA 1966:8). The nation's indigenous roots are not denied and at times are even selectively glorified by Mestizo Nicaraguans. It follows, then, that, although their Indian racial purity is a liability, Amerindian Costeños have Nicaraguan national potential. For example, during a 1969 speech inaugurating the construction of a vocational school in La Rosita, a mining town in the interior of the Atlantic Coast region, Tachito stated, "this vocational institute . . . represents the removal from cultural underdevelopment of *we the Nicaraguans*, whom God placed here before the Spanish and the English came" (quoted in Anonymous 1969c:4, emphasis added).

The Miskitu's principal national debility lay in their lack of Hispanic civilization. The manner in which such phrases as "cultural underdevelopment," "cultural progress,"[5] and "low cultural level" are used in Somocista discourse with reference to indigenous peoples of the Coast supports this assertion. "Culture" was conceptualized in this discourse in much the same manner Raymond Williams (1983:90–91) claims it is utilized in Italian and French—as a "general process of intellectual, spiritual and aesthetic development" and as the high-status "works and practices which represent and sustain" this developmental process understood as moving from the primitive to the "cultured" or "civilized." Indigenous Amerindian people were represented as not having a culture of their own in the contemporary anthropological sense of "a particular way of life" (Williams 1983:90). They, instead, were thought of as living in an almost generic primitive condition, which would drop away as they developed culturally and which they must overcome if they were to develop economically.

In this case, what it means to be "civilized" or "cultured" is to adopt the modern ways of the Nicaraguan Mestizo. This is strongly evident in Alba Rivera de Vallejos's (a Mestiza Nationalist Liberal Party deputy from Waspam) plea to Somoza (Rivera de Vallejos 1969:13): "I beg you for these new generations [of Costeños], who are trying to leave their former primitive condition. . . . to surrender to these groups marginalized in days gone by the message of civilization." For this reason, a distinctive Miskitu way of life is never referred to as "culture" in Somocista discourse and Miskitu language is referred to as a dialect rather than a language. It is also the reason why there are no substantive ethnographic descriptions of indigenous ways of life in the extensive Somocista materials I have reviewed for this book. For all intents and purposes, Miskitu culture, in the anthropological sense of a unique and valid way of life, did not exist for the Somocistas; others of the Coast's indigenous inhabitants were unmentioned and invisible.

Creoles presented a different set of problems for Somocista nationalists. African-descended blacks were racially outside the national pale, as most Mestizo Nicaraguans did not think of themselves as having any African heritage. As elsewhere in the world, African heritage was generally disparaged; however, in cultural terms, Creoles, though undoubtedly considered by the Somoza crowd to be "underdeveloped," were associated with and assumed to be headed toward Anglo "civilization." Persons of African descent as opposed to Amerindians stood as radically other, *non-nationals* to the Nicaraguan racial and cultural identity (CODECA 1966:7-8).

Accordingly, Creoles are ignored in official Somocista discourse. There is no mention whatsoever in speeches by Somoza or those of other Liberal Party officials from either Coast of Creoles, Creole culture, or even English (or English Creole) as a language spoken on the Coast. Nor are Creoles mentioned or referred to in the articles describing state visits to the area, or in any other article in *Novedades* during 1969. This is the case despite the fact that Tachito visited overwhelmingly Creole Bluefields, the largest and most important town on the Atlantic Coast, where he spoke to what must have been predominantly Creole crowds.[6] He also visited Puerto Cabezas and the communities of the mining district, all of which had substantial Creole populations during this epoch. Creoles remained essentially invisible in Somocista national discourse.

The Emergence of an Alternative Bloc

Nicaragua's continuing economic stagnation and Tachito's increasing reliance on repressive measures to concentrate political and economic power in his own hands, especially after the earthquake of 1972 (Millett 1977:229–237), stimulated the emergence of a growing opposition. The movement sprang from a sector of the elite that slowly forged alliances with the Catholic Church hierarchy, anti-Somoza elements of the urban middle and working classes, and portions of the peasantry. Central to this emerging civil struggle ("war of position") was the elaboration of an alternative set of ideas and practices (an "alternative hegemony") that could be the consensual basis for the formation of a new alliance (a "historical bloc") that would contest Somocista domination of the country. A group of progressives from the Nicaraguan economic and social elite (the bourgeoisie) and middle-class professionals played the leading role in the emergence of this reformist political project, which was based in a social Christian ideology similar to that of the Christian Democratic movements prominent elsewhere in Latin America. Pedro Joaquín Chamorro Cardenal, a member of one of Nicaragua's elite Conservative families, became the leading figure in this alternative alliance and his newspaper, *La Prensa,* its principal voice (Chamorro Z. 1982)

The key elements of this group's emerging alternative hegemony were demands for "the democratization of state structures, decentralization of economic power, and the achievement of social justice" (Chamorro Z. 1982:53). For example, in a 1973 editorial, P. J. Chamorro C. blasted the lack of "equal opportunity," "despotism," and "nepotism" in Somoza-dominated Nicaragua (Anonymous 1973:2). These central ideas were similar to the foreign policy rhetoric of the liberal wing of the U.S. Democratic Party during this era. The anti-Somoza opposition used them in their appeals to the United States to end its support of the Somoza regime.[7] Paradoxically, within the country these ideas were also combined with a strong emphasis on Nicaraguan nationalism to represent the Somozas as the local agents of imperial power. In another editorial P. J. Chamorro scolded the U.S. Republican administrations for their "economic domination of small countries" and their continual "intervention" in Nicaraguan affairs to maintain the status quo (Chamorro C. 1973a:2).

As part of the process of reinterpretation and negotiation involved in the struggle to create and forge a new national consensus around them and their ideas, intellectuals of this opposition bloc attempted to alter the hegemonic ideology of Nicaraguan nationalism. More specifically, they transformed the conflation of race, class, and ethnicity on which the ideology of Nicaraguan nationalism was based, particularly as this applied to Costeños of Amerindian and African descent.

In what follows I use materials from *La Prensa,* the national newspaper published and edited by Pedro Joaquín Chamorro, to document these emerging ideas about the Atlantic Coast and Creoles in particular. I have concentrated on the years between 1969 and 1972, the crucial formative period of this reformist political project. The Nicaraguan political scene during the remainder of the 1970's was dominated by its consolidation during a protracted struggle with the Somoza regime. By the late 1970's the alternative ideas forged by this opposition group had succeeded in becoming the hegemonic discursive cement that held together an alliance poised to challenge the rule of the Somocista state in an all-out military confrontation ("war of maneuver") led by the FSLN.

Alternative Hegemony and Representations of the Atlantic Coast

There were important basic similarities between Somocista representations of the Atlantic Coast and those of the reformist national bourgeoisie. For both, the Atlantic Coast region was only tenuously integrated territorially and culturally into the Nicaraguan nation. In fact, a number of *La Prensa* articles referred to the area as being almost another country: "In Santo Tomás I felt the uneasiness I have felt at all frontiers. At daybreak I prepared myself to continue the voyage, I would enter something like the second part, the other part, and, here I don't want to be harsh, another country" (Alemán Ocampo 1969:1b). The alternative bloc also represented the Coast as a vast area rich in natural resources and economic potential. This made the lack of territorial integration particularly painful to Mestizo Nicaraguans in general and was a matter of concern for Pedro Joaquín Chamorro C., who editorialized on this subject in *La Prensa* (Chamorro 1970a:2).

As in Somocista discourse, the Coast's vast potential was contrasted with what was considered to be its poor, backward, and economically marginal state (Balladares 1969:16). For the emerging opposition group, however, the Coast "problem" was another front in the battle with the Somocista bloc. They associated the Coast's lack of development and hence the problem of its material incorporation into the nation with government inaction and corruption (as well as capitalist rapine) rather than with the uncivilized nature of its sub- and non-national "others." Chamorro went as far as to say that Costeño resentment of the Somocista state's indifference toward them was the major cause of whatever separatist sentiments existed on the Atlantic Coast (1970:2): "Costeños are amassing a kind of resentment because of this real abandonment, . . . which has now lasted a good number of years, and from resentment some of them, without even knowing it, move on to expressing a certain estrangement from the rest of Nicaragua, feeling like an almost separate fraction of the country."

Between 1969 and 1972, *La Prensa* was full of articles and editorials hammering away at government neglect of the Atlantic Coast and the greed and corruption of government and military officials. For example, *La Prensa* on October 9, 1969 (p. 1), screamed:

THE EVENTS OF THE COAST GUSH BLOOD
High functionaries' interests; bribes of fifty thousand monthly and armed persons who buy turtles.

The personal interests of high government functionaries who take advantage of their position and the acceptance of bribes by high-level military officers are two of the influential factors in the irrational exploitation of our natural riches in the Atlantic Coast, without any benefit to the public treasury.

There were also many articles decrying the exploitation of Costeños and the overexploitation and exhaustion of the Atlantic Coast's natural resources by national and international capital (which was supposed to be regulated by the Somocista state). For example, *La Prensa*'s Bluefields correspondent denounced U.S. and Canadian mining companies operating in the northern Coast with the authorization of the state (García 1971:20): "These companies have never complied with the famous Article No. 85; as a result, many Nicaraguans of the Miskitu, white, and colored races have been treated badly in pay, food, and medical assistance . . . humble Nicaraguans who are exploited and viewed without mercy." He also took on lumber companies operating in the southern Coast in the following terms (1970:1): "The forests of this zone are exhausted because they do not comply with the Reforestation Law; this is also the case in the mines, whose product is exported without leaving behind money in the payment of taxes nor any other benefit."

Many of these articles directly tie Somoza family economic interests to those of the foreign companies plundering the Coast.[8] While Somocista discourse emphasized the British and Costeño threat to Nicaraguan political and cultural sovereignty over the Atlantic Coast, *La Prensa* emphasized the U.S. and Somocista threat to Nicaraguan economic and political sovereignty over the area (R. Sevilla in Ramírez 1942:55; S. Zúñiga in Ramírez 1942:69). This dovetailed nicely with the opposition's nationalist critique of U.S. imperial support of the Somoza regime.

La Prensa, and P. J. Chamorro in particular, also picked at a Somoza soft spot, the decade-old loss of previously held territory north of the Río Coco to Honduras. In a series of articles about the Miskitu communities of the Río Coco, published in 1970 under the title "Pobreza y esperanza en nuestra frontera recortada" (Poverty and hope on our trimmed border) Chamorro blasted the Somoza regime for the loss of this territory (Chamorro C. 1970c:16). It was for him yet another example of the damage to the territorial integrity of the nation and to the welfare of Costeños occasioned by the Somoza regime's inability to govern the Coast and the nation.

The strong relationship between the threat to the territorial nation posed by the undeveloped, unintegrated Atlantic Coast and its premodern subnational and foreign non-national occupants found in Somocista discourse was muted in the emerging alternative discourse. As part of the opposition's attack on Somocismo, the problem of the economic and territorial integration of the Atlantic Coast into the nation was blamed on the inefficiency, lack of will, and corruption of the Somocista regime in combination with wanton exploitation by allied international capital. The opposition's idea that the national state should intervene to exercise control over the territory against national and imperial capital for the benefit of Costeños was new. Shifting the blame for the Coast's under-development from the Costeños themselves to the ineptitude of the government and exploitive economic relations served as a basis on which the alternative bloc could assert its corrective potential.

Additionally, the alternative bloc clearly championed Costeños' interests as a basis for recruiting them. *La Prensa*, in fact, became a vehicle for Costeño voices criticizing government and company activities on the Coast. For example, in a 1972 article, the newly elected Creole mayor of Bluefields, Frank Hodgson, made a statement that could never have appeared in *Novedades*, even though he was a Nationalist Liberal Party member (in Barreto Pérez 1972:12): "This zone is very rich but the riches have been extracted from here and nothing was left for us. The foreign and national companies exploited the zone without leaving us, the Bluefileños, any benefits."

In 1970 *La Prensa* published a letter from a group of Miskitu *tuno* (gum) workers who complained of exploitation by a U.S. company associated with the husband of the regional Nationalist Liberal Party deputy (Anonymous 1970c:2):

In Waspam there is a *"tuno"* processing plant that is owned by a North American [U.S. citizen] named H. W. Kerr, who, despite the fact that he has become a millionaire here on the Río Coco at the expense of us Miskitu, has no compassion for us. We the Miskitu who go into the forest for months to extract the sap of these trees, who are exposed to falling from the trees, exposed to all the dangers that can exist in the mountains, nevertheless, when we take this gum to sell it to this wretched gringo, he throws up a number of obstacles, he tells us that it is badly cooked, or that it contains 75% moisture, or that it has a lot of dirt or rocks in it and in the end he pays us 1.60 or 1.65 a pound.

The creation of a place where Costeños could speak in their own defense and the emerging equation of the interests of Atlantic Coast racial/

cultural groups with the national interest were two of the most striking new aspects of alternative discourse regarding the Coast.

The opposition's modified stance on the source of the Atlantic Coast's territorial ambiguity and antiracist international influences provided discursive space for a renegotiation of Costeños' relationship to Nicaraguan cultural nationalism. This space coincided with the alternative bloc's practical political aspiration: to make of these national others credible supporters in the country's political struggles. To accomplish this, however, the idea of Nicaraguan nationalism had to be renegotiated. The Somocista discourse's ethnocentric, assimilationist, and marginalizing rhetoric, in the case of the Miskitu, and its silence, in the case of the Creoles, had to be eschewed and a more inclusive, positive discourse about Coast peoples elaborated.

La Prensa published many articles that illuminate the process by which the Costeño place in the construction of Nicaraguan cultural nationalism was reconfigured. In 1970 alone, *La Prensa* published three series totaling fifty articles about the Atlantic Coast in addition to its regular news reportage on the area. According to Pedro J. Chamorro C., these series represented "one more contribution to the real integration of the Atlantic Coast into the rest of the country . . . to make this yearning a reality, before everything else a real spiritual integration is needed, this presupposes the knowledge and teaching of its history within the homeland's history . . . [with these articles] I believe *La Prensa* has placed the first stone in this road" (1970b:2). Chamorro's "Nuestra frontera recortada" series of eight articles written after a five-day trip he made to the lower Río Coco is a compelling example of the effort by intellectuals of the alternative bloc to reposition the Miskitu within the Nicaraguan nation.

It is important to note that this undertaking was part of this group's larger project to redefine Nicaraguan nationalism. A central aspect of this process was group members' location of national identity in the personage and culture of the Mestizo campesino. To distinguish this identity from that of other nations of Hispanic heritage, these intellectuals excavated and glorified the peculiarly Nicaraguan indigenous roots of this Mestizo culture (see, e.g., Cuadra 1971). In this process, the construction of "the new Indo-Hispanic history of Nicaragua" (Cuadra 1971:20) differed from the formerly dominant conception of Nicaraguan national culture as re-created Hispanic culture to which subnational indigenous races assimilated.

In the first of his "Nuestra frontera recortada" articles, Chamorro wastes no time in declaring the Miskitus' Nicaraguan identity (1970c:1b): "The man was a Miskito, that is to say, one of the 15 or 20 thousand

Nicaraguans who belong to this mysterious race." Throughout the series and in an accompanying article by columnist Horacio Ruiz (reporting on a public presentation by Chamorro of his trip's findings), this assertion is supported by reinterpretations of Miskitu history and culture. After declaring the Miskitus' Nicaraguan identity, Chamorro reinterprets the group's own social memory of its origins in western Nicaragua and makes their history that of the nation (1970c:1b): "Where are the Miskito originally from? . . . This is a mystery . . . They seem to come from the indigenous Chontales race, displaced to the northeast of the country by other migrations." This places the Miskitu not only as Indians and thus racialized subjects of national potential, but as Indians, from the Pacific portion of Nicaragua with a historical relationship to Nicaraguan territory and a traceable blood relation to the Mestizos: "los nicaragüenses que ostentan la rectoría del país" (those Nicaraguans who proudly hold the leadership of the country).[9] Chamorro also directly confronts the Miskitus' historically problematic intermixture with Africans and others through repeated reference to the Indian phenotypical and cultural features that he claims have been preserved despite this history of miscegenation:[10]

> The Miskitu are an indigenous people who have mixed their blood with Europeans, Asians, and other indigenous groups. But they have maintained almost unaltered the firm facial lines of their tribe.[11]
>
> Now very mixed with black, other types of Indians, and whites or Anglo-Saxons, they nevertheless maintain the common trait of language; and the "tribal unity" of which we have spoken, maintained for generations, serves as a social link between all their communities.[12]

Chamorro further establishes the Miskitus' worthiness for Nicaraguan national identity by representing their culture not only as indigenous and "pure" but as a culture valid in its own right, and in some respects nearly "civilized." Gone are the references to the Miskitu language as a mere dialect composed of pirated vocabulary (in Ruiz 1970:2b): "they have such a tribal pride that they continue to consider their sonorous and complicated tongue as the principal and most adequate form of expressing their thoughts."

Horacio Ruiz, after listening to recordings of Miskitu music made by Chamorro, characterized it in terms similar to those used to describe the country's glorified Indian ancestral civilizations and the cultural greatness of the Nicaraguan people (1970:2b):

In all justice, this children's song is so beautiful that it could be an example of the purest Nicaraguan folklore. . . . This single fact places the Miskitu, at least in this aspect, at the level of the most nobly situated American tribes.

Another song that is very pure, without any influence from Saxon hymns, is the beautiful psalm that the Miskito intone "to deliver the soul" of a person who is dying. . . . how is it possible that a people who, it could be said, are still hunters, can create songs like this one in which . . . one can hear elements of the greatest spiritual heights that have been reached by men much more cultured and "civilized"? . . . It speaks to the great instinct of the Nicaraguan people for the grand and elevated in all its manifestations.

Chamorro's descriptions of the Miskitu were in implicit conversation with alternative bloc intellectuals' writings that lamented various deficiencies in the Nicaraguan national character, for example, divisiveness and lack of national unity, an "inferiority complex" in the face of other nationalisms and cultures, and a tendency to assimilate toward dominant foreign cultures.[13] Chamorro and Ruiz portrayed the Miskitu as in some ways more exemplary in their nationalism and patriotism than were Pacific Coast Mestizos. They depicted the Miskitu as having preserved their culture and identity pure and intact, despite their interaction with dominant foreigners (Ruiz 1970:2b): "Dr. Chamorro reminded us that the Miskito, whom he called 'a legendary people,' have never been conquered by anyone and their strong unity has survived all foreign penetrations of our country." They also emphasized repeatedly the Miskitus' strong "tribal unity" and "pride in being Miskitu," which they associated positively with nationalist patriotism (Chamorro C. 1970c:1b; Ruiz 1970:4b).

Chamorro and Ruiz's inclusion of this romantic (almost Rousseauean) notion of Indian unity, pride, cultural purity, and anti-imperialism not only bestowed national status on the Miskitu but was consistent with these intellectuals' larger project to critique and reformulate Nicaraguan national identity in their own interests. The emphasis on Miskitu aboriginality, purity, and patriotism was clearly an attack on Somoza, who was continually depicted by the opposition as "the last marine" and as unpatriotically subservient to foreign interests.

The nationalization of the Miskitu, however, did not mean that they were the same as, unified with, or had equal standing within the nation to those (the Mestizos)"que ostentan la rectoría del país": "This is a people different from us . . . Misquito first by race and tradition and

Nicaraguan afterwards" (Chamorro C. 1970c:1b). Not only were the Miskitu characterized as different from Pacific Mestizos, these differences had a pejorative cast to them. Despite the inclusionary rhetoric of Chamorro's articles, in many respects he, and others writing in the pages of *La Prensa*, represented the Miskitu in much the same way as they were represented in Somocista discourse, as primitive, poor, marginal, and undeveloped subnationals. For example, he depicted them as living in "communities that have lived for hundreds of years in the most complete misery and total abandonment." For him the Miskitu was only slowly emerging "from the infra-underdeveloped life that he has suffered for centuries" (Chamorro C. 1970c: [July 5]:2; [July 12]:2).

Like the Somocistas, Chamorro claimed that Miskitu development would come with the intervention of the benevolent Mestizo state and more contact and assimilation with "developed" Mestizos from the Pacific. His characterization of a Miskitu with whom he interacted as "the little brown [*moreno*, i.e., black] man [who] could not say it in [proper] Spanish" (1970c:1b) demonstrates the differentiation, paternalism, racism, and feelings of superiority with which he and other alternative bloc intellectuals continued to view the Miskitu, despite their reconceptualization of their place in the nation.

The alternative bloc's intellectuals also reconfigured the African Nicaraguan's place in the nation. While *Novedades* ignored this group, *La Prensa*, which had a correspondent reporting regularly from Bluefields, was filled with articles about Creoles and folkloric aspects of Creole culture and published a number of articles, essays, poetry, and artwork by Creoles. For a significant number of those writing about the Atlantic Coast in *La Prensa*, the area was "the black Coast" (Alemán Ocampo 1969:1b). In fact, one article claimed that on "the Atlantic Coast . . . . 70% of the population is black or of black origins" (Pérez-Estrada 1970:1b, 5b).

Repeated references to the United States' problematic race relations in articles about Nicaraguans of African descent suggest that the interest shown by *La Prensa* in Coast blacks and the blackness of the Coast was related to the influence of the surging international discourse about blacks and the problems of racism during this era.[14] To ignore Nicaraguans of African descent would have left the alternative bloc's Pacific Mestizos open to accusations of racism, which would have gone against their democratic pretensions and their perception of Nicaragua as a racial democracy.

This interest must have been compounded by the emergence during the 1960's and 1970's of an educated and "cultured" Creole sector of intellectual interest to Pacific Mestizo intellectuals. Perhaps most important, the latter saw the former as potential allies and leaders of

Costeños in the movement against the Somoza regime as well as conduits to the influential foreign-dominated missionary churches.

In a sharp break with the Somocistas, *La Prensa*'s discourse about the country's blacks explicitly considered them to be Nicaraguan: "black nicaraguans . . . the African ancients, today Nicaraguans" (Anonymous 1972:7; Pérez-Estrada 1970:5b). Creole inclusion in the nation was contingent on a re-representation of both Nicaraguan and Creole history and culture. An important aspect of this process, just as with the Miskitu, was the linking of the Creoles' historical and cultural heritage to that of true Nicaraguans (Mestizos).

In "El Negro en Nicaragua," a seminal article published in *La Prensa* in 1970, Francisco Pérez-Estrada discussed at length the historical place of blacks in the Nicaraguan nation:

> The African population came to Nicaragua indirectly and involuntarily. They were brought in small part by Spanish conquistadors, and in more appreciable quantities they arrived fleeing from the English domains. . . .
> The primitive black group was brought to work in indigo and cacao and left behind as a mixed product a mulatto population, which has now been absorbed.[15]

In other words, small numbers of Africans were present in Nicaragua from the earliest colonial times and were a component (albeit a small one) of the ancestral Nicaraguan population. Most phenotypical traces of this African component of Pacific Nicaraguan heritage disappeared through a long process of assimilation and "blanqueamiento" (whitening): "Impelled by physiological necessity, the Spaniard joining with the [black] slave gave origin to the mulatto, who in successive mixing went along losing his characteristics of color and human type until he was incorporated definitively into the new society of Nicaraguan whites and Mestizos" (Aguilar Cortés 1971:2). According to Pérez-Estrada, however, there remained areas of Nicaragua, the Atlantic Coast being the most important, where contemporary evidence of the historical territorial presence and genetic contribution of blacks existed (Pérez-Estrada 1970:1b).

Pérez-Estrada also strains to establish the lingering cultural influence on Pacific Nicaraguans of these "antiguos africanos" (ancient Africans). He points out the African origin of the Mestizo "marimba, de origen bantú probada" [marimba, of proven Bantu origin], the use of "pasto africano" [African pasturage] in the cattle industry, and the historical "contribution" of African manual labor to the Nicaraguan economy.

A number of other contributors to *La Prensa* were able to discern the

African influence on Latin and Nicaraguan music. Reporting on a concert given by a Senegalese dance group, one commented that "the drums of Senegal also awoke all who slept for centuries beneath the fandango, the rumba, the samba, the merengue, the May pole, the black salt of the Caribbean. Drums that sleep muted in the roots of our milpas [cornfields] igniting the Indian drums with their fire: . . . Africa is not far, but tangled in our history" (Anonymous 1971:2b).

Those writing about blacks in *La Prensa* were slightly more successful in identifying "authentic" African cultural features on the Atlantic Coast. Despite what he refers to as a cultural stripping process, Pérez-Estrada was able to identify a few African survivals in contemporary Coast culture. He mentions a leaf called "Zulu" used for perfume, and alligator teeth, ox eyes, and seahorses, whose use as good luck fetishes on the Atlantic Coast is supposedly of African origin (1970:5b). The nationally famous and notoriously sexual Creole May Pole dance, as well as other aspects of Creole expressive culture, were described and pronounced to be of African origin by other *La Prensa* writers (Anonymous 1972:7): "With charged African rhythms, to the song of the drum and the bongo, hundreds of dancers dance around the May pole, in the typical style of black Africans."

The "discovery" by the opposition's organic intellectuals of African historical presence within the national territory and population as well as the continued existence of African phenotypes and cultural practices among Mestizo Nicaraguans linked Creoles to the nation in important ways. It established (albeit tenuously) Nicaragua's national African racial and cultural heritage and thus provided "primordial ties" as a rationale for the inclusion of Creoles, now constructed as African, in the Nicaraguan nation.

Somocista nationalist discourse, though largely silent on these matters, identified Creoles not with Africa but as a cadet branch of the imperial British and Creole culture—as a "low" or corrupted form of "high" Anglo culture (e.g., S. Zúñiga in Ramírez 1942:69). This association with the British, who were seen as not only imperialist but also denigrating of Hispano claims to culture and civility, was extremely damaging to Creole national pretensions (e.g., Ortega 1950:3). In contrast, articles in *La Prensa* represented the connection between the British and the Creoles as superficial and an accident of history rather than as based on an innate or profound link between the two.[16]

For example, Pérez-Estrada carefully explains that though "the blacks of Nicaragua's Atlantic Coast" still remain "inclined" toward the British, they should not be blamed for historically contributing to the latter's pretensions in the region. The Creoles merely chose an affiliation that "could in some way benefit them" (1970:1b). This characterization of the Creoles' association with the high status and nationally threatening British as utilitarian rather than organic diminished this barrier to Creole inclusion in the Nicaraguan nation. Moreover, the portrayal of Creole history and culture as emerging from a nonimperial, low-status, African heritage was less of a challenge to the status of Nicaraguan nationalism and was therefore less nationally problematic. This further eased the Creoles' nationalization process.

Alternative bloc intellectuals also established Creole difference from the British and cultural connectedness to the rest of Nicaragua by publishing Creole poetry, prose, and painting as well as articles about their music.[17] This presentation of the work of Creole artists not only established the existence of an autochthonous "high" culture produced by Creoles in the Coast but also demonstrated the relatedness of Coast "culture" in language, genres, and styles to Nicaraguan "high" cultural traditions.

The revision of Nicaraguan history, however, and contemporary imagining of the nation as multiracial in ways that provided space for the inclusion of people of African descent begged the question of racism. Black/white turmoil in the United States, besides being an important impetus for the alternative bloc's repositioning discourse about blacks, alerted Nicaraguan intellectuals to the threat of this phenomenon. The existence of racism against blacks was antithetical to the newly minted African/Nicaraguan linkages and the idea of one harmonious multiracial nation. Accordingly, the discursive nationalization of blacks was accompanied by the simultaneous construction of Nicaragua as a racial democracy where the incorporation of blacks into the nation had never been and should not be a problem. In the words of one alternative bloc intellectual, Juan Munguía Novoa, "In Hispanic America . . . . where Spain brought the Christian concept of human persons as carriers of eternal values; there has never been racial discrimination" (Munguía Novoa 1970:3b). Another described "Spanish America, where the spirit of equality of all men is a reality" (Aguilar Cortés 1971:5). Despite these assertions, the fear of blacks' "ansias de poder" (yearnings for power) and "black power" (Pérez-Estrada 1970:1b) as possible destabilizing factors was the source of Pérez-Estrada's admonition that, "as we have Nicaraguan blacks, we have to take into account this phenomenon. Because, even if it is true that there is no hostility against them, a sentiment of discrimination does exist, even though it is not open or strong. Our attitude must be one of incorporation, treating them as the citizens they are and giving them the same opportunities as everyone. Otherwise this will bring about a strong political problem" (1970:1b).

The nationalization of Nicaragua's Creoles was an ambiguous and contradictory project, however. Despite the extensive coverage of

Bluefields in *La Prensa*, many of the top alternative bloc intellectuals, such as P. J. Chamorro and Pablo Antonio Cuadra, made no reference to the Coast's black population in their writings about the area. They wrote about "Costeños" (a category that included but was not exclusive to Creoles) and the "Miskito," but not about Creoles.

Those writers who focused on the southern Coast and wrote extensively about the Creole population generally referred to them in racial terms as "*negros*" or in regional terms as Costeños rather than in ethnic (cultural) terms as Creoles.[18] This suggests the construction of a racial identity for Creoles in which their place in the nation was conceptualized as that of a subaltern racial minority. From this perspective, Creoles were national only because of their historical and contemporary spatial location within the national territory. This was in marked contrast to the Miskitu, whose cultural link to the core national group was the basis of their status as part of the national cultural community.

The racialization and inferiorization of the Creoles was further manifested in the opposition's intellectual discourse about Creole "Africanness." While Creole Africanness was much ballyhooed, all these writers found it difficult to come up with cultural practices that they could identify as part of a valid and significant "African"-based way of life, as they had for the "Indian" way of life for the Miskitu population. Pérez-Estrada, for example, had great difficulty in this regard and qualified his meager offerings by stating that only very small numbers of Africans ever inhabited the Pacific and that few African cultural survivals were to be found anywhere in Nicaragua (1970:1b): "In regard to [the survival of] their original culture, it does not seem to have been too great. [They were] isolated from anything that would have brought them together [and] spread out to conceal their escape."

In those cases in which an "authentic" Creole culture (whether of African derivation or not) was located and reported, it was often merely a celebration of the folkloric in that culture, for example, the May pole and the greasy pole (Anonymous 1972:7; Velásquez 1972:6). Moreover, most of the Creole cultural practices and attributes discovered by the alternative bloc intellectuals were garnered from international racial stereotypes of people of African descent, which Mestizos considered to be innate "genetic" Creole features. For example, Creole athletic prowess is continually lauded in *La Prensa*. There are numerous articles about the exploits of black baseball and basketball players. The following description of a basketball game between a team of "Atlantic Coast *morenos*" and a team of Mestizos from the Pacific makes clear the stereotypical nature of these representations of their sporting superiority: "The Enag, with greater experience and ball handling, began by dominating the game; however, the greater speed and physical superiority of the Bluefields team gradually undermined the resistance of the agriculturalists, who by the end were defenseless in the face of the supersonic incursions made by the Costeños on their basket" (Anonymous 1969f:13).

Pérez-Estrada's racial Darwinism supports not only similar stereotypical assumptions about Creole physical attributes but also essentialist ideas about racial politics and Nicaraguan race relations (1970:1b): "The black, assigned only to physical force by his dominators, was doubly selected. On the one hand, there was the approval of the slaver, who required optimum physical conditions; on the other hand, the environment distinct from that of their origin imposed a survival [of the fittest process] whose results we now see in the distinguished performance blacks had and have in American sports in general, as well as in Nicaraguan sports."

An incipient travel literature emerged in the pages of *La Prensa* during this period as counterpart to tourism advertisements that fetishized the Atlantic Coast as a natural and sensual tropical paradise. The highlight of these travel pieces is invariably a stereotypical description of the exotic black (African) practices to be found and consumed there:

> I [went] to know Bluefields at night. It is tumultuous in the night, it is full of blacks who dance calypso . . . It is night full of rhythm, of love for music, of small, little houses replete with blacks who contort themselves to the rhythm of tropical music, eroticism in every movement, without immorality or indiscretions, sex can never be indiscreet, simply feeling the music, bodies stuck together, hands stretching above shoulders, hips revolving, who wouldn't laugh? How enthusiastic they were, and I only watched.
>
> At night we are in an improvised nightclub. . . . There is alcohol, music, and romance, but more than anything, music. It penetrates with cadenced rhythm the blood and spirit of this original people. The music absorbs your mind, feelings, and movements. A giant Creole contorts his gladiator's body like a feather.[19]

The difference between the characterizations of Miskitu culture by Chamorro and that of Creole culture in the pages of *La Prensa* is striking. On the one hand, descriptions of the Miskitu are Rousseauean in their characterizations of them as noble savages: loyal, proud, patriotic, stoic, unified, culturally pure, with some cultural features that are on the level of Western high culture. These cultural features, from the perspective of alternative bloc intellectuals, were associated with the elevated planes of the spirit and mind and were tied to the loftiest elements of Mestizo culture. The descriptions of Creoles, on the other hand, emphasized the exotic, savage body—hedonistic, sensual, libidinal, rhythmic, powerful, athletic—as well as base folkloric popular culture. These physical attributes and instinctual practices were all stereotypically inscribed in the blood and on the figure of the racialized, mindless black body and were only weakly related, if at all, to Mestizo culture.

Explicitly racist constructions of blacks, though carefully avoided in the articles specifically concerning the Atlantic Coast's black population, slipped into *La Prensa*'s discourse almost subliminally. For example, in a description of looting after one of Bluefields' periodic fires, Creoles are referred to in the diminutive: "Los negritos [the little darkies] immediately got drunk"; the distribution of aid after the fire is described figuratively and literally as a "merienda de negros" (blacks' free-for-all).[20]

As noted earlier, there were many similarities between the Somocistas and their emerging opposition in terms of how they viewed the problematic and inferior character of the Coast and Costeños; however, there were important differences as well. The transformist Somocista discourse emanating from the group that ruled by controlling the state constructed the nation as a seamless intersection of political, economic, and cultural community within a clearly delimited territory. All self-consciously culturally and racially different communities were depicted as either subnational, uncultured primitives (e.g., Miskitu marginal to the nation but with national potential through assimilation) or invisible, irredeemably non-national others (e.g., Creoles).

The alternative discourse produced by the emerging alternative bloc engaged in a war of position had an inclusive validating (expansive) quality. The contradictions the Atlantic Coast presented at the intersection of Nicaraguan territorial and cultural nationalisms were partially mitigated and negotiated as a strategy in their struggle. These intellectuals recognized the possibility of cultural difference within the nation. For them the territorial national community was now commensurate with a dominant national cultural community and a number of historically related cultural and racial subnational communities. They no longer saw these subnational cultures as unevolved precursors of the national culture but as the latter's historically related and independently valid variants, each with its own redeeming positive characteristics. These subnational cultures, however, did not have equal standing with the dominant national culture; the opposition's intellectuals clearly saw them as inferior. Radical and high-prestige cultural heterogeneity, such as that exhibited by the Creoles, with its potential as the basis for competing national claims, remained too threatening even for the alternative bourgeoisie.

That the opposition's incipient expansive hegemony was incomplete, contradictory, and permeated by racialist ideologies was exemplified by the manner in which its intellectuals represented the Creoles. For important elements of the alternative bloc, Creoles remained invisible. Those prepared to consider them as part of the national community constructed them as inferior, racializing them as "*negro*" and "*africano.*" The latter signified a fragmentary culture, at best folkloric, but in the main libidinal, instinctual, and biological.

The Proliferation of Alternative Hegemonic Discourse about the Coast

As time went on and the repression and corruption of the Somoza regime deepened, the reformist alternative bloc consolidated. In 1974 it formed the Democratic Union for Liberation (Unión Democrática para la Liberación—UDEL), a broad-based anti-Somocista political coalition. Led by P. J. Chamorro, *La Prensa* spearheaded the growing opposition to the Somoza regime and significantly reduced its social base. Also in 1974, the FSLN further contested the crumbling authority of the Somoza regime by undertaking its first armed operations in Managua.

The Somoza state responded to the widening threat to its domination with massive repression; it declared martial law, censured the press, and intensified its counterinsurgency activities. During and after a thirty-three-month state of siege, P. J. Chamorro and *La Prensa* led a national wave of political discontent with the regime. Though *La Prensa* championed a liberal democratic agenda aimed at promoting a bourgeois alternative to Somoza, it became increasingly radicalized during this period and supported strikes and other working-class moves against the regime. It even championed the Sandinista forces in their armed efforts against the Somozas. By the time of his assassination in 1978, P. J. Chamorro and *La Prensa* headed a pluralistic alliance that had wrested control of civil society from the Somoza regime for the bourgeois opposition (Chamorro Z. 1982, 1983; Hodges 1986). Concurrently, this emerging bloc consolidated a level of national consensus around sets of alternative hegemonic ideas, including those discussed earlier concerning the Atlantic Coast. The power of these ideas and realpolitik responses to more militant Costeño politics prompted modifications even in the Somoza regime's discourse concerning the Atlantic Coast and Costeños.

In a speech inaugurating his 1974 presidential election campaign in Bluefields, Tachito addressed the crowd in English, Miskitu, and Sumu. He characterized the Coast's resources as "the patrimony of the Nicaraguans of the Department of Zelaya" rather than as strictly national. This passage also clearly designates Costeños as nationals—"nicaragüenses." Somoza also had discovered the existence of Nicaragua's African forbears and even downplayed the negative aspects of Creole association with Anglo culture by advocating the continued teaching of English in the schools. Overall, the tone of his discourse about the Atlantic Coast was much different from his speeches of five years earlier. There was much less lamenting of the underdeveloped nature of the area and the primitiveness of the people and more emphasis on specific programs aimed at helping Costeños develop the region rather than at developing the "primitive" Costeños.[21]

The increasingly hegemonic nature of alternative bloc representations of the Coast was also evident in the discourse of the group on the opposite end of the political spectrum from the Somoza regime—the Sandinistas. The Atlantic Coast of Nicaragua and its population were not a major focus of Sandinista intellectual inquiry or political work in the twenty years before the Triumph; therefore, there is very little textual evidence of their ideas about the area. The Sandinistas were, however, loosely allied with the *Prensa*-led alternative bloc, whose leadership they assumed in the last years before the Triumph. Though sketchy, the available evidence indicates that they shared important aspects of the alternative bloc's expansive hegemonic discourse about the Coast.

El programa histórico del FSLN (The FSLN's Historical Program), originally published in 1969, is the only document I have come across that makes sustained reference to the Atlantic Coast during the protracted struggle against the Somoza regime. The section of this document entitled "Reincorporación de la Costa Atlántica" (Reincorporation of the Atlantic Coast) is not very detailed but does provide insight into how the Sandinistas thought of the region. As were Somocistas and alternative bloc intellectuals, the Sandinistas were preeminently concerned with what they saw as the nationally unincorporated character of a resource-rich area. Like the alternative bloc intellectuals, the Sandinista blamed the Coast's poverty and unintegrated character not on Costeños but on the neglect of past regimes and the exploitation of "foreign monopolies, particularly by Yankee imperialism" (FSLN 1981). Similar to Mestizo discourse in general on these matters, Sandinista discourse proposed to resolve the Coast problem by developing its material and human resources.

Sandinista concern about the cultural penetration of Atlantic Coast cultures by foreigners was shared by both the Somocistas and the alternative bloc; however, unlike the Somocistas, the Sandinistas recognized the existence of independently valid cultures on the Coast and thought that their continued existence should be supported. They were, though, uneasy with what they saw as the contaminated nature of Coast culture. Therefore, they supported the rescue and promotion of only "authentic" Coast culture: "Stimulate the flowering of the local cultural values of this region that arise form the original aspects of their historical tradition" (FSLN 1981). This interest in the promotion of "original" cultural features is clearly linked to the Sandinistas' advocacy of the construction of a "pure," unsullied Nicaraguan culture and, ultimately, to their anti-imperialism (FSLN 1981).

The most distinctive aspect of pre-Triumph Sandinista discourse about the Coast is their strong stand in opposition to discrimination against Costeño members of racial and ethnic minorities: "Destroy the hated discrimination of which the Miskitu, Sumu, Zambo, and blacks of this region have been the objects" (FSLN 1981). Somocista and alternative bloc discourse held that discrimination, for all intents and purposes, did not exist in Nicaragua; the Sandinistas were very clear about its existence and their opposition to it.

Sandinista use of the words *zambo* and *negro* indicates that they, like most Pacific Mestizos of the era, had a racialized concept of at least those portions of the Atlantic Coast population who were of African ancestry. By this period, "Zambo" was no longer utilized to designate Miskitu who seemed to be of African heritage. On the Atlantic Coast, all Miskitu, regardless of phenotype, were referred to culturally as "Miskitu." Similarly, as I have mentioned, *negro* was not used by Creoles to designate members of their group during this period.

Sandinista Discourse about the Coast

At the time of Chamorro's assassination, the reformist elite's leadership of the alternative bloc had reached its apex. In the absence of Chamorro, control of UDEL passed to the heads of national business associations, which had been galvanized into action by the assassination. From this point on, effective leadership of the alternative bloc gradually slipped out of the grasp of the reformist elites, whose discourse was increasingly out of step with that of the radicalized popular forces. They had no military wing and therefore had no response to the power of the Somoza regime, which, now based almost exclusively on the coercive power of the National Guard, had undermined the Nicaraguan citizenry's confidence in electoral strategies for change. The intellectual elites were therefore forced to rely on the unpopular possibility of the intervention of U.S. forces or, worse, negotiations with Somoza for the resolution of the crisis (Bulmer-Thomas 1987; Chamorro Z. 1982, 1983).

The spontaneous popular insurrection and national strike that followed Chamorro's death created a favorable conjuncture within which the Sandinistas gradually assumed leadership of the oppositional bloc. The FSLN consolidated this position by engaging in strategic armed operations that galvanized the Nicaraguan populace and by shifting from a class-based strategy to one of pluralist alliance against the Somocistas. The armed operations demonstrated the viability of the FSLN as a military alternative to the National Guard. They also precipitated an unprecedented wave of repression against the Nicaraguan population, which further radicalized the latter.

The FSLN's strategy of broad anti-Somoza alliance inside and outside the country included downplaying the discourse of class struggle previously central to its program; however, it presented a more radical agenda than that of the reformist bourgeoisie. This appealed to the radicalized popular sectors of the country but was broad enough to facilitate continued bourgeoisie and middle-class participation. This broad-based political agenda included such elements as the redistribution of material resources, a mixed economy, national reconstruction, social justice, and participatory democracy.

Key to the growing hegemonic leadership of the FSLN was its historical identification with Sandino and the anti-imperialist anti-Somocista tradition this embodied. The Sandinistas were able to utilize Somoza's close identification with the United States and U.S. culture as the basis for the forging of the key counterhegemonic nationalist idea of "the identification of the Nicaraguan as anti-imperialist" (Chamorro Z. 1983:20).

As we have seen, the Sandinistas' meager discourse about the Atlantic Coast that developed in the late 1960's was more or less consistent with the sets of ideas associated with expansive hegemony that underpinned the anti-Somocista alternative bloc, whose leadership the Sandinistas had assumed in the late 1970's. The Sandinistas' anti-imperialist emphasis on Nicaraguan cultural authenticity, however, as well as their class-based agendas, would have important repercussions for the development of their discursive treatments of the Coast in later years.

Post-Triumph Sandinista Discourse: The Transformist Turn

Once the Sandinistas were in power, their war of position focused on consolidating the alliances that had brought them to power—the FSLN's hegemony over the alternative bloc, and the legitimization of Sandinista state rule. They were faced with a number of daunting obstacles, including the physical and social devastation of years of war, the need to rebuild and transform the state apparatus, a pluralistic historical bloc rife with contradiction whose central organizing anti-Somoza theme had been removed, competition from their bourgeois anti-Somoza allies for control of the state and leadership of the historical bloc, and increasing interference and opposition from the United States.

Under these circumstances, the FSLN's position hardened. In particular, the expansive strategy of broad anti-Somoza alliances was replaced by one in which the workers and peasants constituted the engines of the Revolution. This led to increasing opposition from important sectors of the reformist bourgeoisie, including those directing *La Prensa* (Bulmer-Thomas 1987:232; Vanden 1982:57–58).

The achievement of power over the state and the accompanying changes in its strategic alliances had important implications for the FSLN's perceptions of the Atlantic Coast. The FSLN, which had previously been antagonistic to the Nicaraguan state, was now essentially synonymous with it. Before the Triumph any movement with a basis for claims against the state or the ruling regime had been a potential ally. Concessions were often made in the discourse of the alternative bloc to include diverse and frequently contradictory positions in the anti-Somocista alliance. After the Triumph, any group that continued to have a basis for claims against the state was a potential threat to Sandinista rule. The historically marginalized and exploited Costeños now turned from being candidates for coalition into sources of potential conflict for the Sandinistas and their ruling alliance.

Furthermore, this shift in the relationship between the FSLN, the state, and the Atlantic Coast served to revive the perceived national ambivalence of Costeños. This became particularly problematic because the Sandinista Revolution's domination and transformation of the Nicaraguan state facilitated the construction of a conflation between the Revolution and the nation. The identification of the Revolution with the nation became a critically important aspect of the FSLN's efforts to maintain the viability of its multiclass historical bloc and to consolidate its hegemony over it. The discourse of *national* unity and liberation from imperialism became even more important as a unifying theme, as the FSLN attempted to retain important sectors of the bourgeoisie and middle classes as allies while simultaneously increasing the centrality of class struggle within the revolutionary process (Wheelock 1981:7).

As the Revolution sought to make itself indistinguishable from the nation, a threat to the nation became a threat to the Revolution and vice-versa. The revival of the representation of Costeños as nationally ambivalent and hence a potential threat to the Revolution marks an important shift from the expansive alternative hegemonic discourse about the Atlantic Coast to a transformist revolutionary hegemonic discourse about the area.

In the immediate post-Triumph era, the Sandinistas shared many of the same ideas about the Atlantic Coast held by other groups of Nicaraguan Mestizos. For them it was a vast, almost uninhabited, area rich in natural resources (Anonymous 1979a; Anonymous 1979b:4).

Similarly, the Sandinistas represented the Coast as unintegrated, underdeveloped, and marginal to the nation/Revolution: "Slowly but surely
our brothers of the Atlantic Coast are beginning to fully join the new
Nicaragua" (Anonymous 1979c). Much as the pre-Triumph alternative
bloc intellectuals had, the Sandinistas viewed the Coast's marginal and
underdeveloped status as the result of the "abandonment" of previous
regimes and the "exploitation" of foreign companies. The Sandinista
revolutionary state proposed to attack these problems immediately and
to awaken the "sleeping giant" by improving the means of communication with the Coast and by developing it economically (Anonymous
1979d). From a position similar to that of Somocista discourse, much was
now made of the potential economic contribution to the nation of the
large quantities of *divisas* (foreign exchange) that could be garnered for
the benefit of the nation/Revolution.

In keeping with time-honored Nicaraguan Mestizo ideas about
Costeños, the Sandinistas represented them as backward and undeveloped: "the people of the Coast have great hopes that the Revolution will
help them escape the backwardness in which they find themselves."[22]
They developed a dual position, however, with regard to Costeño
cultures. To an extent much greater than in Somocista or alternative
bloc discourse, the Sandinistas expressed public concern about the
nationally divisive potential of Costeño cultural difference. Two weeks
after the Triumph, Commandant Carlos Núñez, member of the national
directorate of the FSLN, claimed: "The Atlantic Coast will be fully
integrated into the Nicaraguan revolutionary process . . . We know that
work will be hard in this sector, above all on account of the people's wish
for independence . . . the spearhead of the counterrevolution could
happen there, due to circumstances already mentioned . . . there are
problems there of ethnicity and autonomy"(in Rediske and Schneider
1983:36–37).

Though the perceived cultural difference of Costeños was problematic for the Sandinistas, it was the tainted character of these cultures that
was most onerous. This was clearly articulated with the centrality of
anti-imperialist nationalism in the FSLN's hegemonic discourse. According to Commandant Daniel Ortega, there was "the problem of
cultural disintegration . . . In the case of the Miskitos we find that their
religious music is influenced from abroad. Their language has many
words taken from English" (Anonymous 1979b:4). Costeños, because of
their long history of exploitation by Anglo foreigners, had become at
least partially culturally assimilated. From the Sandinista perspective,
the sharing of cultural features with members of imperial nations
signified a weakening of identification with autochthonous Nicaraguan
culture, the Nicaraguan nation, and the Revolution.

The idea of cultural "purity" and the superiority of historical cultures was in many ways reminiscent of the ultranationalism of many alternative bloc intellectuals (e.g., Pablo Antonio Cuadra). For the Sandinistas, one of the most important steps in the process of integrating Costeños into the nation/Revolution was the reversal of their "cultural degeneration": "It is necessary to rescue our cultural values, music customs, and Miskito and Sumu languages now that they have been degenerating and deforming their culture."[23]

The emphasis placed by the Sandinistas on the historically dependent relationship between Coast peoples and imperial powers created an image of Costeños devoid of agency and revealed a paternalistic attitude toward them: "they have been manipulated by the English, who created the pantomime of creating a Fly [Mosco, derisive word for Miskitu] King, by the imperialist monopolies, manipulated by Conservatives and Liberals, and always within the same misery that they clearly feel" (Anonymous 1979d: 4). Paternalism also lurked within the Sandinista idea that "authentic" indigenous Coast culture needed to be rescued by Mestizo Sandinistas from the irresponsible forgetfulness of the Costeños themselves. According to Father Ernesto Cardenal, minister of culture for the new government, "the Revolution will try to restore Miskitu and Sumu culture, which has been exploited and forgotten for centuries . . . It will dedicate all of its energies to rescuing this culture, support it, promote Miskitu and Sumu dance, music and crafts 'before it is lost'" (Anonymous 1979e:8).

Though the problem of Costeño "cultural disintegration" through contamination was particularly noxious because of the influence of imperial cultures, "Western cultural dependency" was considered by the Sandinistas to be a generalized problem in the country. Accordingly, the Sandinistas, much like the alternative bloc intellectuals, viewed the maintenance of what they considered to be autochthonous cultural traits in a positive light precisely because of their anti-imperial significance: "These communities, especially the Miskitu, maintain their language, their culture has managed to survive invasions, foreign influences, dictators, etc. . . . they have manifestations of primitive socialism that are no longer present in the rest of the country." As long as these cultural practices did not get in the way of national cultural practices and identification, "now it is a question of their joining the revolutionary process and rescuing their cultural values, maintaining their language, and enriching it. Learning Spanish without abandoning their mother tongue. This is what the Revolution is doing, integrating the Miskitu."[24]

Despite the endorsement of "pure" indigenous cultures, the identities that emerged from heterogeneous cultural practice were feared by the Sandinistas in their new role as guardians of the state and nation. On the

one hand, they continued their pre-Triumph discourse concerning the
existence of Mestizo racism: "the people of the Pacific carrying this
deformation of colonizer, which is transferred to the colonized, have a
tendency to discriminate against the Miskitu." On the other hand, they
denied its importance, emphasizing instead the economic nature of the
historical exploitation of Costeños: "the Atlantic Coast was marginalized
by the Somocista system and not for ethnic reasons, as large sectors of
this zone still believe . . . The discrimination against this zone is based
on economic reasons."[25] What to the Sandinistas were the similar class
origins of Costeños and important sectors of the Sandinista bloc were
seen as the basis for an identity that would draw Costeños and the FSLN
together. As a result, members of the Atlantic Coast's racial/cultural
groups were represented as members of class fragments rather than as
racial/cultural groups: "when we say campesinos we also include Sumu
and Miskitu, because they work and live off the land."[26] This position led
Daniel Ortega, in a speech on the occasion of the formation of
MISURASATA (Miskitu, Sumu, Rama y Sandinista Asla Takanka—
Miskitu, Sumu, Rama, and Sandinista Working Together), to the extraordinary position of denying the importance to the Revolution of
historical struggles against racism and placing the Revolution squarely
in favor of the reinvention of the homogeneous nation (Anonymous
1979e:1): "our Revolution does not claim to defend racial causes, but to
seek integration, identity, and unity of the people of Nicaragua."

This had obvious concrete implications for Costeños, namely, immediate cultural and material assimilation into the nation: "The immediate task that you [Miskitu and Sumu] have is to integrate into the
economic life of the country, learn the Spanish language, and, in this
manner, form a 'Kupia Kumi' [one heart]" (Anonymous 1979e:8).

As in the Somocista discourse about the Atlantic Coast, Creoles were
practically invisible to the Sandinistas, even though they claimed there
were eighty thousand Creoles living in the area. In a brief aside in an
interview, Ortega refers to Creoles as "*negros*" and said they were a
reality that deserved the attention of the Sandinistas. He stated that
"black power and other manifestations . . . [were] far from their reality"
and made it clear that, from his perspective, black racial politics was not
of importance to the Creoles and had no place in Nicaragua (Anonymous
1979c:4).

Conclusions

In Nicaragua during the 1970's, intellectuals associated with the broad-
based opposition to the Somoza regime transformed hegemonic notions
of the nation and the race, class, and culture conflation on which it was

grounded and, accordingly, dominant Mestizo discourses of race. Certain aspects of racial/cultural heterogeneity were tolerated or even encouraged to facilitate the formation of a valued oppositional social identity and to incorporate it into an emerging alternative historical bloc engaged in the struggle against Somoza. The cultural and racial difference of Creoles and Miskitu was used not as a mechanism of exclusion but, rather, for inclusion in the reformist national project.

Despite these transformations, a number of aspects of Mestizo discourse about the Atlantic Coast remained relatively constant over the twenty years treated in this chapter. The Coast as geographic space was seen as an important potential source of wealth for the nation but, simultaneously, as nationally ambivalent: physically isolated, unintegrated economically, under tenuous government control, and as an area whose sovereignty was disputed with foreign powers. Costeños were uniformly seen as racially inferior primitives and stereotypically represented in international terms as aboriginal "noble savages" or African tropical bodies. Creoles in particular were constructed as barely national, even when consciously included in the national mix. Often, their racialization as "*negros*" combined with their association with the "English," a competing international culture, to construct them as so inferior and non-national as to be transparent to the national gaze.

Through the twenty-year process of imagining the nation, Atlantic Coast cultures remained potentially dangerous. They were feared as capable of bursting out of their subnational subordinate cages and into national contention if they were able to gain enough social capital on which to base the organization of independent political unity. Following the logic of their construction by Mestizos, the radically non-national Creoles were particularly threatening in this regard. After the Triumph of the Revolution, when the impetus to control and national consolidation outweighed the forging of alliances against the state, racial/cultural heterogeneity became a potential liability for the ruling revolutionaries and had to be muted, its targets homogenized or remarginalized. Under this pressure, once again, dominant Mestizo discourses of race changed. As we shall see, Mestizo discourses of race, culture, and place regarding Costeños influenced Creole political common sense and in many ways were the foil for Creole identities and politics.

6.

Ambiguous Militancy
on the Threshold of Revolution

Oh, idolized giant, when will you awake to enjoy the luminous rays
that flirt with the restless waters of the Atlantic, reservoir of faith
and hope?
                                                    —Roberto Hodgson

ATLANTIC COAST, AN AWAKENING GIANT . . .
Today we can confirm the mobilization realized by the [revolution-
ary] state's organisms in close coordination with the [Sandinista]
army to rescue from oblivion and degradation the Department of
Zelaya . . . [and] to put an end to the barrier of backwardness and the
exploitation of our brothers.
                                          —*Barricada* (November 12, 1979)

When I arrived in Bluefields in late 1981, one of the most pervasive
Sandinista ideas about the Creoles was that they were politically
inactive and submissive. Indeed, this was an idea that many Creoles held
about themselves. This idea persisted despite memories of Gen. George
Hodgson and the Twenty–five Brave and despite demonstrations and
strikes against the revolutionary government in the preceding months.
The notion of Creole submissiveness can also be found in Creole
pronouncements about themselves made during the 1970's. It is especially evident in the metaphor of the Atlantic Coast as "sleeping giant"
—being asleep and needing to open its eyes to wake up to its political
reality—found in so much of the Creole political writing of the 1970's.
    Yet other sources offer a markedly different impression of Creole
politics. According to these sources, during the 1970's Bluefields was a
hotbed of political ideas and activity. As the 1960's and 1970's led up to
the Triumph of the Sandinista Revolution in 1979, it was a time of great
socioeconomic change and political struggle throughout Nicaragua. In
Bluefields the level of political turmoil was not nearly as high as else-

where in the country; however, while constraining influences, particularly the Somocista PLN—representing national capital and the state—and the Moravian Church—representing international capital and the U.S. imperial state—remained strong, a number of important Creole reformist political movements and discourses developed from within these very institutions. Creoles led these movements, which had the empowerment of the Creole people as a goal. Despite this shared objective, the aspect of Creole identity emphasized by each movement and the specific issues around which they mobilized varied considerably.

This chapter brings together much of the work done in previous chapters. In it I describe and analyze Creole political common sense as it existed during the late 1970's and the early 1980's. To do so, I rely on oral histories and archival materials from Creole political movements that emerged during the late 1960's and the 1970's in Bluefields. I also illustrate the manner in which Creole political common sense was forged through the diverse historical social processes described in previous chapters. I place special emphasis on the disparate, ambiguous, multiple, and contradictory character of Creole political common sense, which is an effect of that diversity; however, I also argue that, despite the polyvalent character of the group's politics, Creole politics was not endlessly contingent, and I map the specific forms of Creole identity and politics generated from common sense and experienced by Creoles as salient in particular historical moments.

The first half of the chapter describes and analyzes five Creole social movements active during the 1970's. These movements included the efforts by a small group of Creole pastors to gain control of and reform the Nicaraguan Moravian Church; the much-larger social and economic developmentalist movement of Creole intellectuals organized by the Organización Progresista Costeña (OPROCO—Progressive Costeña Organization); the intellectual movement led by Creole scholar Donovan Brautigam Beer, which struggled to establish Creole cultural difference and a space for it within the Nicaraguan nation; a small group of Creole students loosely organized as Sandinistas; and the powerful SICC, originally organized around issues of cultural politics and local power.

The ethnographic analysis of these movements along with materials from previous chapters and my own experiences provide the elements for the synopsis of Creole political common sense presented in the second half of the chapter. The result is a description of Creole political common sense, politics, and identity in the ethnographic present of the late 1970's and the early 1980's. This prepares the way for the culminating discussion of Creole political common sense and Creole politics in the early Sandinista era, which is the work of chapter 7.

Nationalist Modernizing Creole Pastors

From its inception through the 1960's, the Moravian mission in Nicaragua was controlled by foreign missionaries. One of the long-term objectives of the Moravian Board of World Missions, however, was to create self-sustaining churches in the areas they missionized. Therefore, an important part of their activity was to train "natives" for leadership positions in the field.

The Moravian High School in Bluefields played an important role in this strategy in Nicaragua. A high percentage of the leaders and participants in the social movements I describe in this chapter were educated by the Moravians in this facility during the early to mid-1950's. Moravian High School yearbooks from this era present a "Who's Who" of Creole ecclesiastical and secular leadership of the late 1970's.

The Moravians also set up a Bible Institute in Bilwaskarma to provide religious instruction for students whom they identified as having the potential for leadership positions in the church and who would thereby eventually increase the number of "native" clergy. In the early 1960's, a group of young Creole divinity students recently graduated from the Moravian High School engaged the all-powerful white missionaries of the Bible Institute in a relatively obscure struggle over church doctrine; their aim was to make the church more egalitarian, open, and responsive to the specific needs of Costeños. These students were concerned with the way in which infant baptism was performed and Eucharist was given. They thought that the refusal to baptize infants of unmarried parents in the church was unjust. They also thought that the giving of the Eucharist should be more public and that the practice of "speaking" (public informing on those who strayed from the church's rules) and church discipline, which regulated who was able to receive the Eucharist, should be reformed. When the students threatened to withdraw from seminary if these changes were not made, the missionaries gave in.

After this first victory, the Creole-led movement to "modernize" church doctrine gathered momentum. It was greatly strengthened by the Moravian Board of World Missions' decision to send these same Creole students outside the country for further training. In the past, divinity students had been sent to seminary either in Jamaica or the United States. Unfortunately, many of those who were sent abroad found life in these places more appealing and never returned to Nicaragua. Therefore, in the early 1960's the decision was made to send students to the Seminario Bíblico Latinoamericano in San José, Costa Rica, for more advanced theological training. Here they came into contact with other students and faculty from all over Latin America. They were also exposed to Liberation Theology, which was sweeping through Latin

American Christian circles during this period. Well-known figures such as Pablo Freire, Emilio Castro, James Cone, Samuel Escobar, Gustavo Gutiérrez, and Quince Duncan gave classes there.

As a result, these young students became more worldly and politicized.[1] As they became pastors and advanced through the church hierarchy in Nicaragua, what they had begun as a movement to modernize church doctrine expanded into a movement to force the church to hasten the process of "nationalization." They began to press for the change from mission to local control of the church.

Simultaneously, these young Creole pastors also pushed the church to become more active in the Coast's socioeconomic affairs and the material well-being of its people. According to Norman Bent, one of these Creole pastors (interview, 1988), "There was more questioning of missionary administration by six to eight pastors who came back from seminary with a degree and began to question the role of the [foreign white] missionary more severely. And I guess missionaries began to complain to the Board of World Missions that 'We cannot keep up with this pressure any more.'"

There was considerable resistance on the part of many of the white missionaries. One missionary who had strongly advocated making the church more socially active was forced by his colleagues to leave. The Creole pastors who favored this kind of work had to look outside the church, mostly to nongovernmental organizations (NGOs), for funding and support. These pastors also began to use their position to stake out cautious political stances regarding the exploitation of Coast resources by foreign and Pacific capital and the mistreatment of Costeño workers. The missionaries reacted to these developments negatively. They were loath to see the church "dragged" into "politics." They frowned on the ideas and activities of their newly educated Creole subordinates. "The missionaries believed that we were coming back too liberal" (Norman Bent interview, 1988).

After 1967, however, when the Unity Synod (the general synod of Moravian churches worldwide) came out in favor of local control of missionary churches, the missionaries in Nicaragua gradually decided to accede to the nationalization of the Nicaraguan church.[2] According to Norman Bent, one of the most active of the Creole pastors, by the mid-1970's this had as much to do with the fear among the missionaries of the emerging Sandinista insurgency as it did with Creole pressure. The U.S. missionaries remembered with great apprehension the death of a missionary at the hands of Sandino's forces in the 1930's and were anxious to get out of harm's way. Due to a combination of factors, the Creole pastors' push for nationalization proceeded at a much more rapid pace than planned. By 1973 the first Nicaraguans had been appointed to the positions of superintendent and secretary-treasurer of the mission. In 1974, the 125th anniversary of the Moravian presence in Nicaragua, the first all-Nicaraguan Provincial Board was elected. Additionally, both the Moravian schools and the church's many medical facilities were handed over to Nicaraguans. In a little over a decade after their initial rumblings, the small group of Creole pastors had assumed control over the Moravian Church's operations in the country: "A few of our coworkers from the U.S. seeing how happy and proud we were might have thought that we had gone overboard on emotional nationalism" (Kelly 1975:14). One of their first moves was immediately to set up CASIM (Comité de Acción Social de la Iglesia Morava—Moravian Church Committee for Social Action) to consolidate the church's new emphasis on social action (Keely 1974:19).

There was resistance to the new leadership and direction of the Moravian Church from two quarters. The first was from the remaining missionaries. Four of the five left by the following year (Kelly 1976:20). The one remaining missionary headed the church in Managua, where he could be relatively independent. According to Norman Bent, the white missionaries felt that they could not work under the direction of Nicaraguans (interview, 1988): "I remember talking to some of the younger missionaries with whom we had some good rapport, whom we thought were very liberal and progressive. They said to us, 'You know we have to leave because we cannot take orders from Nicaraguans.' By the end of the year they were gone." The missionaries also feared that they would lose the privileges they had enjoyed when the mission was under their control (Norman Bent interview, 1988: "They felt that they could not spend their weekends on Corn Island anymore, that there would have to be a boss and they would have to ask permission to do so." The departure of these missionaries also meant the forfeiture of their salaries from the church's budget. This unplanned financial shock was resented by the Costeño pastors.

Even though many Creoles supported the nationalization of the church and the liberal positions of their pastors, there were others, especially older members of the community, who were very critical of these moves. Race played a factor, especially, according to the Rev. Stedman Bent, in Bluefields, where the white missionaries remained pastors of the church the longest (interview, 1991):

> When it comes to the congregation and Bluefields, there were lots of pastors who always said—black pastors—that Bluefields would be the last place that they would want to come to serve simply because people were used to the white man being there, being in the pulpit and in the office and week after week, month after

month, year after year, and so there was a crash within the life of the church when people didn't relish this idea of the white man moving out.

Outside of the small group of Creole pastors who were directly involved and who took over the leadership of the church from the foreign missionaries, the modernization, nationalization, and politicization of the Moravian Church during the 1960's and the 1970's is not generally recognized by Costeños as a political movement. Nevertheless, it had far-ranging political consequences for Creoles in Bluefields. It forced them to question the hegemonic role of U.S. whites, not only in the churches but also in other economic and social institutions. In this manner, it undermined the complex of commonsense ideas I refer to later as "Anglo ideology," though these ideas continued to be reinforced by the Creole pastors' reverent adherence to most aspects of the received doctrine and rituals of this Anglo church. Simultaneously, the movement stirred regionalist feelings and the recognition that Creoles could and should handle their own institutions. It rekindled a sense of Creole pride and self-worth and opened Creole eyes to questions of social justice and communal action for themselves as a people. In this manner, the movement lent legitimacy to commonsense ideas I refer to later as "Creole populism." As we shall see, control of the Moravian Church as an institution also facilitated the mobilization of institutional support for other, more overtly political, institutions.

OPROCO and the Politics of Regional Development

The longest-lived and most important social movement of the 1960's and 1970's was OPROCO. This was a secular group formed by Creole professionals (teachers, dentists, doctors, and so on) most of whom in the 1950's had been Moravian High School classmates of the nationalist Creole pastors.

In a May 1963 circular addressed to "Señores del Margen" (Gentlemen of the Fringe), Waldo W. Hooker, renowned in the Creole community as its greatest and most-powerful politician and at the time governor of the Department of Zelaya, called a meeting of twenty Creole Liberal Party members in his offices. Members of this group organized themselves to present a series of demands to René Schick, the new president of Nicaragua. As Hugo Sujo explains this move (interview, 1991),

Even though the Creoles were the majority from the beginning, they didn't have proportional with the number of positions that they should have. And things reached to such a point that some of us couldn't stand it anymore and we started to pressure, you know, to pressure and when René Schick won the elections . . . , he and Waldo were personal friends. And through the influence of Waldo a group of Creoles—Waldo got an appointment with René Schick and a whole bunch of us got on a plane and we went to Managua. And we put the cards on the table. And we told René Schick, since the election was rigged in such a way that only Mestizos come out, now we want at least 50 percent of all the positions that was given by appointment, and that's when they started to appoint some of the Creoles to outstanding positions.

Following up on this successful initiative, the next year key members of this group organized OPROCO:

The objective of this organization is to look out for the progress and interests of the Costeño people and defend their social, cultural, and moral values, such as: . . . disseminate the principles and possibilities of the Communal Development Program so as to achieve a change in the people's attitude toward their problems . . . participate and execute in a coordinated manner activities that tend to achieve the economic and sociocultural betterment of the communities such as: training courses, promotion of small industry and artisanry, development of education, recreation, and assistance programs, formation of different types of cooperatives, etc.[3]

In 1991 Dr. Roberto Hodgson, a longtime member and one-time president of the organization, remembered the group's beginnings as being rooted in racial/cultural politics; however, as he explains, the precarious character of even reformist politics of this kind during the Somoza regime dictated organizing under the banner of Coast economic and social development (interview, 1991):

The objective is that we felt that blacks were marginated, that is, Creoles, in Bluefields and the Atlantic Coast in general. And we realized then that we would never be able to do anything unless we really got organized. Just writing a letter . . . as an individual really didn't make sense. So we thought, really, one had to be organized. I don't know if it's scared or prudence or whatever, but we never really want to call the group political, you know. It was a civic movement, but in the background we really think political rights. Well, as a matter of fact, during the Somoza regime there was just two parties anyway; you couldn't think of a third. Well, you could think of it, but you wouldn't get anywhere with it. It was more like a movement. . . . The OPROCO really was more the adults, the leaders.

In many ways, OPROCO defended the status quo as it worked to achieve its reformist racial/cultural and developmentalist goals. Though initiated by Creoles and with an overwhelmingly Creole membership, OPROCO members made the tactical decision to admit some Mestizos, including a few of the leading Liberal Party politicians (e.g., Antonio Coronado Torres, vice minister of Gobernación), "to avoid being called racist or so by the [Mestizos]. But the Mestizo had to be someone who really identified himself with the needs and the problems of the Coast" (Roberto Hodgson interview, 1991).

Nominally, OPROCO had no political affiliation; however, the organization was very closely aligned with the Liberal Party. Its public pronouncements were characterized by uncritical admiration of the current Somoza ("our Supreme Leader, the Most Excellent President of the Republic, General Don Anastasio Somoza Debayle"). Most, though not all, OPROCO members were also members of the Nationalist Liberal Party. During the 1972 national elections, a front-page editorial by Rupert Linton Whitaker in *La Información*,[4] Bluefields' weekly newspaper, which was closely aligned with OPROCO, urged

> Costeños, fellow party members, and friends of the Coast, if you
> want to continue enjoying the PEACE, PROGRESS, AND LIBERTY
> that we cherish, vote in the red box of the Nationalist Liberal
> Party, headed by the indisputable leader of the Nicaraguans,
> General Anastasio Somoza D., brilliantly seconded in this sector by
> Costeños don Pablo Rener Valle, doña Alba Rivera de Vallejos,
> Ralph Moody, and don Frank O. Hodgson M. (February 6, 1972)

Articles and editorials proclaiming loyalty to the PLN and filled with fawning praise of its leaders continued to be published by OPROCO in *La Información* into the final months of the Somoza regime in 1979. For example, on July 6, 1978, the paper congratulated Sen. Pablo Rener, the Coast's Liberal Party political boss, on his saint's day. Under a photo that showed the corpulent and bespectacled white politician stuffed uncomfortably into a tie and jacket, the editors effused:

> Sen. Don Pablo Rener Valle . . . received many messages of con-
> gratulations . . . , appreciation, and sympathy, which he has gained
> through his obliging manner as well as his valuable work in the

Senate, especially that in favor of this sector of the homeland, which he represents, and from his fellow countrymen who feel for him a personal and unvarying affection.

It is our extreme pleasure to insert a photograph of this beloved friend and eminent son of the Atlantic Coast. We send him, on wings of affection and recognition, the testimony of our effusive congratulations.

OPROCO also served as cheerleader for many of the Somoza regime's development projects on the Atlantic Coast while simultaneously seeking and receiving government support for its own projects. The most notable of the latter was the road the group was attempting to build between Bluefields and the Río Kukra south of town.[5] This road became the centerpiece of its labors and was what most Creoles remember about OPROCO's activities and positions in the 1980's.

The male members of OPROCO (the organization seems to have had few female members) were almost obsessively concerned with the relative underdevelopment of the Atlantic Coast and the overexploitation of its resources. This they understood to be the result of a negligent state and the unfettered rapine of national and international capital. They also were strongly anticommunist. In the early seventies, this meant unfavorable comments and jokes about "Communist countries," particularly the Soviet Union, East Germany, and Cuba (see, e.g., *La Información* [January 16, 28, 1969]). Cuba was used in editorial commentary as the epitome of totalitarianism, and sayings like "es solo en Cuba compadre" (only in Cuba, friend) followed some egregious example of dictatorial behavior ("La esquina de Wing Sang," *La Información* [August 12, 1971]).

By the late seventies, this anticommunism was focused on the FSLN in the pages of *La Información*. In a special report published in November 1978, the FSLN was characterized as "terrorists . . . Marxist Leninists . . . Castro Communists . . . masked monsters . . . lackeys of Fidel Castro" and accused of all manner of atrocities against defenseless Nicaraguans (Arana Mayorga 1978).

The United States was generally esteemed and praised by the members of OPROCO. Pres. John F. Kennedy was admired and the intent of the Alliance for Progress appreciated. There were close interactions between OPROCO's Creole leaders and the U.S. missionaries who ran both the Moravian and the Catholic churches and schools. In a speech inaugurating the Moravian High School's new gymnasium, OPROCO leader Lindolfo Campbell expressed admiration for the missionaries (*La Información* [April 29, 1972]): "the Moravian mission, an essentially Christian and educating mission, once again is presenting us with something that should be a prestigious honor for this city. Since the first missionaries arrived on these beaches 123 years ago, their mission has been to comply with the mandate of the Divine Master, who said: 'Go preach and teach.'" OPROCO also interacted extensively with U.S.-based aid agencies, particularly the Hermanos de Wisconsin program, which participated in development projects in conjunction with the organization (*La Información* [February 29, 1972; January 22, 1971; December 21, 1978]; Hodgson 1971). Over the years a number of articles were published in *La Información* that recalled with nostalgia a flourishing economy in the 1920's dominated by U.S. capital (Reyes Campos 1978; Mena Solórzano 1975).

OPROCO enthusiastically embraced the dominance and basic tenets of Western capitalism, U.S. imperial economic and political interests in the Atlantic Coast, and Somocista nationalist internal colonialism. This embrace was part of a reformist tactic the group used in an attempt to advance the interests of Costeños, and Creoles in particular, by occupying and working to expand the oppositional spaces left them within the terms of these dominant discourses and practices. For example, OPROCO often publicly accepted the Reincorporation as a glorious and beneficial circumstance. Dr. Roberto Hodgson's obsequious statement published in *La Información* on March 4, 1969, lauding the Reincorporation and two of the most hated Mestizos in Coast history is exemplary of this approach:

Finally the day came when a man of firm determination and valiant character named Don José Santos Zelaya occupied Nicaragua's presidency. He entrusted Gen. Rigoberto Cabezas with the task of occupying the Mosquitia, which was accomplished. General Cabezas holds the honor of having been the first in 392 years to establish a national government that definitively hoisted in Costeño lands the blue and white flag under whose shadow all of us children are proudly sheltered. His heroic exploit . . . places him among the greatest national heroes.

Nevertheless, article after article in *La Información* lamented that the "real" reincorporation had not been accomplished and would be only if the Coast were assisted to develop on its own terms. The tension in OPROCO discourse, generated by seeking autonomy within integration, is clearly evident in an article by OPROCO leader Lindolfo Campbell in which he deplores the fact that no national television channels reached the Coast: "Not only in this, but in many other aspects, we see our department marginalized and excluded from national life. This makes us ponder whether the Atlantic Coast is really reincorporated into the rest of the country. Theoretically, we can affirm it as so, but in practice the reality is negative, and the citizens who demonstrate their resentment and disagreement by one means or another cannot be blamed."[6]

Similarly, OPROCO never questioned the rule of the Nicaraguan state; however, article after article protested the domination of government posts by Pacific Mestizos and demanded that more Costeños occupy positions of political power. In 1971, for example, OPROCO discreetly championed a number of Costeño candidates for the position of vice-minister of public works in charge of development of the Atlantic Coast. The position was ultimately won by Remy Rener, Pablo Rener's son. This appointment generated a high level of resentment because important sectors of OPROCO felt that Remy was not an "authentic" Costeño (*La Información* [June 22, 1971]; Roberto Hodgson interview, 1991). In 1973 OPROCO fought to save the job of the Creole head nurse at the municipal hospital. In 1978 *La Información* editorials demanded that a Costeño be appointed magistrate of the Bluefields Court of Appeals.

While always careful to praise the party leadership (principally Somoza and Rener), OPROCO was willing to confront the local PLN party structure in its battle for a share of state power for Creoles and governmental assistance for the Coast.[7] The foremost example of this disposition was OPROCO's public fight with the Mestizo-dominated local leadership of the PLN over the choice of the party's candidate for mayor of Bluefields in the 1972 elections. The Mestizo leadership wanted to make Pedro Bustamante, the son of the departmental party president and a Mestizo, its candidate. OPROCO, on the other hand, championed the candidature of Frank Hodgson, the founding president of the group (Hugo Sujo interview, 1991). In an article in *La Información* that came perilously close to criticism not only of the Bustamantes, whom he referred to as "nuestros altos electores indirectos" (our high indirect electors), but also of the Somozas and the Reners, who ruled the national and departmental PLN structures, respectively, through family alliances, Hugo Sujo Wilson, a one-time OPROCO president, commented: "There is currently in the local liberal ranks too much resentment caused by some small groups and families who carry on as if the Nationalist Liberation Party were their personal patrimony" (Sujo Wilson 1971). An anonymously written editorial/gossip column published on June 18, 1971, "En la Esquina de Wing Sang," summed up OPROCO's general position in these matters:

> The parents of Costeño families are now thinking that it is better not to send their children to the university, that it is not worth it because when they receive their professional degrees to work in

their own town, the public posts have been given to professionals from the interior, leaving them out in the cold. If in the Supreme Court of Justice there were a Costeño, another rooster would crow in the judicial branch.

OPROCO's integrationist politics precluded the adoption of historical Creole demands for a return of the Atlantic Coast to the semi–independent status it had held before the Reincorporation. One of its members' most cherished positions, however, was the demand that Nicaragua comply with its treaty obligations in relation to the Coast. The most important of these was the agreement that the state's share of income from the exploitation of the area's natural resources be reinvested in the region. In a note from the editors following a February 28, 1974, *La Información* article reporting on the substantial earnings of the seafood industry in 1973, this position was forcefully stated:

> As can be seen, the highest production in the seafood category, by a factor of three, is that of our Atlantic Coast. If they complied even minimally with the clause of the Harrison-Altamirano Treaty promulgated more than EIGHTY years ago, which has never been complied with by the central government and which clearly specifies that "the taxes deriving from the products of the Atlantic Coast will be strictly invested in the same Atlantic Coast," imagine for yourself, Costeño reader, how much our departmental institutions would receive from taxes on this handsome quantity of dollars that only in 1973 were produced by Costeño shellfish? The commentary we will leave to your healthy, honest and patriotic criteria! (Original emphasis)

Much ire in this regard was directed toward INFONAC (Instituto de Fomento Nacional—National Development Institute), the institution principally responsible for the regulation and taxation of resource exploitation on the Atlantic Coast. The "detective" writing in the weekly "La esquina de Wing Sang" on June 9, 1970, commented in this regard: "Bluefields residents are not uncomfortable with paying the Declaración de Bienes Inmuebles (real estate taxes), but they would like the taxes they pay to go not just to beautifying Managua, as happens with the taxes on shrimp that INFONAC consumes without belching or spitting."

The OPROCO crowd was not concerned only about the lack of regional income from the exploitation of its natural resources; they were outraged by what seemed to them to be the extreme avarice of Pacific Mestizos, who thought of the Atlantic Coast as their patrimony and insisted on representing it as only a rich and inexhaustible natural resource reserve for the nation (Campbell 1975): "For many years the celebrated phrase 'the Atlantic Coast is the economic future of Nicaragua' has been heard. For conscious Costeños this constitutes an offense to their dignity. The former seems consistent with the characteristic marginalization and oblivion that the Department of Zelaya has been the object of since its Reincorporation."

There was also deep concern in the ranks of OPROCO about the perceived overexploitation and exhaustion of these natural resources by both national and international capital. In article after article throughout the 1970's, OPROCO members decried the historical and contemporary abuse of the Coast's resource base. In a particularly polemical article published on July 31, 1971, and entitled, presciently, "Oh Gigante Idolatrado, Cuando Te Despertarás!" (O Adored Giant, When Will You Awaken!), Roberto Hodgson made precisely these points:

> There are many who advocate the idea of the Atlantic Coast as a NATIONAL RESERVE. Others assure us that it is "the promised land." However, as long as the ANACHRONISTIC MENTALITY of those who boast of their wisdom but who suffer from an INEXPLICABLE FEAR of expressing their convictions (going along with the political current but blushing in embarrassment because they have sacrificed their dignity) remains in force, "the promised land" will remain on the distant horizon while the "reserve" is rapidly exhausted, enriching, instead, extracommunal merchants and the foreign octopi. (Original emphasis)

Hodgson's article also indicates the manner in which preoccupation with the overexploitation of the Coast's resources for the benefit of outsiders became the springboard for more radical assertions linking the social injustice and economic oppression of Costeños with international postcolonial struggles: "when equal opportunity and social justice are proclaimed to the four winds, . . . in our society economic servitude predominates. It is really disgraceful that, because of an unacknowledged fear, an intellectual servitude also coexists in our 'Modern Democracy,' with disastrous consequences for our situation."

During the 1970's there were a number of specific moments when Creole discontent around these issues of marginalization and exploitation of Costeños and their resources intensified. During these moments, the most important of which were in 1972 and 1976, the voices of the Creole intellectual elites clustered in OPROCO became more radical. This was clearly reflected in the pages of *La Información*. In 1972 there was a sharp wave of Creole nonconformity precipitated by a short-term downturn in the local economy accompanied by the closing of a local sawmill amid generally rising economic expectations based on the seafood industry boom of the late 1960's and the 1970's. The immediate trigger, however, was the rise in rates implemented by the electrical monopoly ENALUF (Empresa Nacional de Luz y Fuerza—National Light and Power Company), which was centrally controlled by the state from Managua. Creole and other residents of Bluefields responded with mass demonstrations against the rate hikes. The political discourse that this situation provoked on the part of OPROCO's Creoles in the pages of *La Información* was surprisingly radical. They decried the passivity of Costeños in the face of their oppression. Interestingly, in many of their essays, they used a metaphor, that of Costeños awakening and opening their eyes, that would become quite controversial in the future:

> All of the above [exploitation and economic depression] has fallen on top of us because the Costeño people characteristically have been submissive, quiet, and passive. The Costeños have characteristically accepted their luck as it has come to them. Nevertheless, the Costeños are waking up to the reality of their circumstances and demanding justice.
>
> The great nonviolent demonstration against the ignominious imposition on May 23 was a clear example of this. This will be an unforgettable day in the history of the Coast. . . . The people said: "Enough now!" The people said: "We are not willing to continue suffering abuses . . . we think its time that those on high come down to the plain and listen to the clamor of the people who have been humiliated, abused, and exploited so many times."[8]

The pages of *La Información* were opened to Creole youth such as Enrique Campbell, who used the opportunity to insinuate the need for radical solutions to Coast problems:

> With the problem that arose around the electric utility, it is plain to see that the people want a change in the structures.
>
> The civic conscience of this people has been killed by unscrupulous politicians who seek only their own welfare and have no interest in the welfare of the city—a bunch of outsiders who have no interest in the condition of the city; but the people are now fed up with this situation and have begun hollering to the four winds. I want to be accepted as someone and not as something. I want my dignity to be respected. I want most of all to be a man.[9]

Campbell's condemnation of the active underdevelopment of the

Coast echoed the position of the older Creole professionals in OPROCO; however, he went further than the latter in a number of ways, including directly criticizing the antidemocratic character of Nicaraguan party politics. The article was an early salvo of the radicalized Creole youth whose movement becomes central to my narrative later. There were no subsequent articles by Campbell or others with his perspective in *La Información*.

Though in subsequent years Campbell's statement must have seemed to some of the Liberal OPROCO members to have been extremist, aspects of it clearly resonated in the heady political moment that was 1972. The earthquake at the end of the year served to suppress some of the political passions raised by the ENALUF crisis in the Creole community; however, beginning in late 1972 and continuing into 1973, Hugo Sujo, a longtime OPROCO leader, wrote a series of commentaries arguing against exploitation by outsiders and for a strong "localism" on the Coast. In these articles he epitomized the regionalist Costeño position from which OPROCO's Creoles waged their politics (*La Información* [December 20, 1972]; Sujo Wilson 1973):

> There was also in Bluefields a regression back to something that we thought we had risen above: the cruel exploiters from other parts of Nicaragua and the world with the complicity of local traitors and through "might makes right," thinking of the Coast as conquered territory, have sought to enrich themselves at the expense of the humble and peaceful Costeño native. . . . we must never sacrifice or renounce our patrimony, our rights and duties as natives and exalt any immigrant element over our own local values because of an inferiority complex, discriminatory prejudice, rancor, or conflicting interests. To proceed in this manner is censurable because it is treason and prostitution.

In 1973 *La Información* also served as a forum for one of the touchiest of all political topics during the Somoza era—criticism of the powerful National Guard. In March of that year and again in August, the pages of *La Información* carried commentary denouncing the "brutality" of the National Guard (L. Campbell 1973; El Detective 1973). The paper even went as far as to denounce Tachito's mistress's brother, who was a particularly abusive National Guard member "who so cruelly, inhumanly, and bloodily mistreat negrito Cuabná [a black street person]" (El Detective 1973). This unusual public criticism of the National Guard could only have taken place in the aftermath of the Managua earthquake. Following this disaster, the Guard had been discredited for its corruption and its failure to provide adequate emergency relief; this momentarily reduced its coercive efficiency. Nevertheless, these commentaries provide an unguarded indication that Creoles resented the coercive arm of the Nicaraguan state.

OPROCO's members were the Creole community's leading teachers, politicians, professionals, and business leaders, and as such their ideas were very influential in that community. As a reform movement, the group produced and held a rich amalgam of ideas simultaneously deferent to and subversive of the status quo. All of these ideas were constituent ideas of Creole common sense.

On the side of deference to dominant power, a central set of these ideas revolved around very high regard for the United States as a beneficent power. This involved such notions as the adoration of the memory of John F. Kennedy, the soundness of ideas about hemispheric development and the U.S. role in it symbolized by the Alliance for Progress, and the normality of the Costeños' role as clients of U.S. programs, agencies, and NGOs specializing in "aid." OPROCO's message also strongly endorsed political ideas championed by the United States, as leader of the "Free World," in relation to Latin America. These included anticommunism, Western capitalism as engine of development and universal prosperity, and human rights as embodied in the idea and trappings of representative democracy.

OPROCO members also staunchly supported the idea of a strong allegiance to Nicaraguan nationality and the Nicaraguan state. Moreover, the idea of the state was embodied in the figure of a strong central authority and paternalistic leader. This also translated into an allegiance to party politics and, especially, to the Nationalist Liberal Party as the party of democracy, religious freedom, economic development, and progress.

Simultaneously, central to the OPROCO members' images of Creoles and Costeños in general was the idea of their collective poverty, backwardness, and overall lack of progress. Accordingly, at the core of OPROCO's understanding of the Creole community's most urgent needs were notions of economic and social development, which would bring Costeños up to the level of the metropole (Managua and the United States). OPROCO understood the Nicaraguan and U.S. states as the sources of the assistance and leadership needed for such development; this assistance was thought to be the responsibility of the former and the beneficence of the latter.

On the side of subversion of dominant power, OPROCO members believed the notions of the past irresponsibility of the Nicaraguan state as a source of the Coast's backwardness as well as the complicity of greedy foreign entrepreneurs in the overexploitation of Coast resources. The idea of the need to protect regional natural resources from rampant exploitation by outsiders was very strong. Equally strong was the idea that Costeños had the historical right to be the beneficiaries of the exploitation of the region's resources.

Similar views were held concerning the political arena. The idea of the right to local political control by historically marginalized Creoles was preeminent. There were strong feelings against clientelism in both the political and the professional realms, which favored Mestizos over Creoles in the local arena. In short, OPROCO championed the idea that politics and the economy should be under local control.

Donovan Brautigam Beer and Creole Culturism

In the OPROCO Creoles' public discourse, their tactical regionalist orientation and preoccupation with socioeconomic matters overshadowed questions of cultural and racial marginalization and exploitation. In the early 1970's, however, there were a few cryptic references in *La Información* to Creole racial identity and the existence of racism directed at them. All appear in the satirical "La esquina de Wing Sang" or " La esquina de Erasmo" columns signed with pseudonyms such as "the Detective" or "Sherlock Holmes."[10] This was a case of the unspeakable being placed in the mouth of the nameless and farcical. These statements indicate that, although for tactical reasons OPROCO chose to ignore racial and cultural matters, these issues were of some significance for Creoles.

In 1970 the Detective lamented the reluctance of local authorities to appoint blacks (here synonymous with Creoles) as jury members. This snippet published on October 6, 1970, includes a racial epithet against Mestizos and is unprecedented in its Creole chauvinism: "only 15 *negritos* were involved, even though here they are the majority and the most suitable elements and of greater intelligence than many *pañas* [Spaniards], who hardly know how to scratch out their innocuous scribblings." The meaning of blackness in this jocular but biting discourse was equivocal, however. In an "Esquina de Erasmo" column (August 16, 1972, original emphasis), the racist attitude of the head of the Nicaraguan baseball federation, FENIBA, was decried by the Detective in the following terms: "[he] spewed denigrating phrases about our *negrito* players . . . ; these procedures and insults are what makes one feel *British*."

The idea of Creoles being simultaneously black racially and Anglo culturally and nationally was a recurrent, albeit veiled, theme in *La Información* during the early seventies. It would become an explicit element of cultural politics among some sectors of the community in the coming years.

From the discussion in chapter 5 we know that there was a simmering national dialogue concerning race, culture, national identity, and the place of Costeños in the nation throughout the second half of the twentieth century. Outside of Brautigam Beer's articles on history, however, Creoles had not publicly taken part in this discussion. In the mid-1970's Creole voices began to be heard on these issues, and three explicitly articulated Creole positions emerged: the culturalists, the black Sandinistas, and the antiracists. *La Información* provided the venue for some of the original Creole statements in this debate, but serious Creole-Mestizo interchange took off in the pages of *La Prensa*, reaching a crescendo in 1976.

Just why this debate came to a head in 1976 is unclear. These were volatile times in Nicaragua. There was growing opposition to the Somoza regime and increasingly radical discourse being bandied about in the Pacific by those associated both with UDEL and the FSLN. This was also a period of Mestizo rediscovery and fascination with the exotic Atlantic Coast and its cultures. Coast music and dance, especially the May Pole, became the rage in the Pacific. The Atlantic Coast became the destination of the adventurous for their Holy Week excursions.

In the northern portion of the Coast, the formation of ALPROMISU (Alianza para el Progreso de los Pueblos Miskitos y Sumos—Alliance for the Progress of the Miskitu and Sumu Peoples) in 1974 to promote the rights of the Coast's indigenous population and the economic development of their communities focused Mestizo attention on the region (see, e.g., *La Prensa* [Managua] [June 15, 1974]). The response to the news of ALPROMISU's formation was immediate and hysterical (*La Prensa* [June 9, 1974]):

> THREAT OF MISKITU REBELLION
> The Miskitu . . . of Puerto Cabezas are organizing a genuine rebel-
> lion against the Nicaraguan authorities . . . they organized a march
> that culminated with the raising on the Coast of an English flag
> and speeches threatening that, if there are no Miskitu mayors, they
> will rise up in protest and ask for help from foreign governments.

In the South the splintering of OPROCO facilitated the emergence of more radical dissident positions that included questions of race and culture. It is difficult to judge their numbers, but some key OPROCO members resented the close identification of the organization with the PLN and the occupation by Mestizos of key government positions at the behest of the party hierarchy. A few resigned from the organization over these issues. In some cases, these persons were prepared to disregard the taboo against public discussion of the sensitive issues of race and culture; however, in general, during the late 1970's OPROCO remained extremely supportive of the Somoza regime and increasingly reluctant to level criticism at the regime's handling of Coast issues and reticent to join the emerging debate on race and class. This no doubt goes a long way in explaining OPROCO's waning influence on popular Creole politics from the mid-1970's onward, especially among the young.

The central Creole figure in the emerging national debate on race and culture was Donovan Brautigam Beer. Through the 1960's and the 1970's, he published a number of articles, mostly on Coast history, in *La Información*. Though he was not a member of OPROCO or of the PLN, he was of the same status and age group as the OPROCO members and had been educated in the same institutions. He was highly respected by them as *the* Coast historian and held political ideas that in general were very similar to theirs.

On January 31 and February 27, 1973, *La Información* published a number of articles by Brautigam Beer. In most respects, these represented a continuation of the impressive body of scholarly production that had made him, by the late 1960's, the outstanding national authority on Coast history and culture. In the articles, which were addressed to Costeños, he argued explicitly that their culture distinguished Atlantic Coast identity from that of Pacific Nicaraguans. He also strongly urged Costeños to take pride in their cultural traditions and to organize to preserve them: "We think that the time and the circumstances demonstrate the need to preserve, perpetuate, and disseminate what gives depth and form to the Coast . . . What has distinguished and will distinguish the Coast? Folkloric traditions" (Brautigam Beer 1973). In these articles Brautigam Beer also traced the folkloric aspects of Creole culture to European origins.[11] This, in part, was the basis for his assertion that the maintenance of these traditions would make Bluefields attractive to "cultured people" internationally.

Three years later, in a series of articles published in *La Prensa*, Brautigam Beer considerably elaborated these ideas into a coherent theory of Nicaraguan/Costeño racial/cultural relations. These articles were part of an unprecedented barrage of articles in *La Prensa* over the course of 1976, that expressed opinions about the Coast. Brautigam Beer himself, by far the most productive and knowledgeable contributor, wrote more than twenty. In this body of work he clearly outlined what I refer to as his "culturalist" perspective. In 1976 only a handful of Creoles were capable of laying out this perspective as extensively and skillfully as he was; however, my reading of the available Creole literature of the time and my experiences in the Creole community beginning five years later lead me to believe that many other Creoles, especially those who were older and relatively well educated, including most of the members of OPROCO, shared Brautigam Beer's perspective. Therefore, this 1976 body of work merits close attention.

In contrast to most of the Creole intellectuals writing during the seventies, Brautigam Beer in this period was not centrally concerned with the economic and political exploitation of the Coast. When he directly addressed these issues, as he did in an article published toward the end of 1976, he coincided with most Creole intellectuals in recognizing the foreign and national sources of exploitation and with the more radical in naming these forms of exploitation as colonialism: "From English colonialism to today's internal colonialism, the attention conceded to the region has been determined by the political and economic interests of the metropole" (*La Información* [December 17, 1976]). He also connected these issues of political and economic power directly to struggles over racial/cultural identity and status, however. In the same article, Brautigam Beer states that the politico-economic underdevelopment of the Atlantic Coast had been maintained by an attitude "determined in part by the class system, in particular, the prejudices of the metropole." For him a "class system" was akin to what I would call "status": "an arrangement of internal and external relations, constituted by the concession of 'deference' to individuals, roles, and institutions and taking into account the place they occupy in the systems of power, property, occupation, etc." This key element, deference, for him was an act of respect or honor associated with the sentiment of equality or inferiority. Sentiments of disrespect, deprecation, subestimation, or superiority were also part of this concept. The political and economic subordination of the Coast by the foreigners and, more important for Brautigam Beer, Pacific Nicaraguans was a product of the deprecating attitudes that the latter held toward Costeños. A major thrust of his work was challenging these attitudes.

One of Brautigam Beer's most important priorities was to challenge what he believed to be the Nicaraguan Mestizos' erroneous assumption that Costeños were backward and uncivilized. "Was the Coast backward and living in darkness before 1894? Some believe so" (*La Prensa* [September 23, 1976]). As we shall see, Brautigam Beer insisted that Nicaraguans were not racist. Nevertheless, he was particularly concerned to counter Mestizo assertions that Costeños and especially Creoles were racially black and of African descent. For him, such a racial designation signaled uncivilized primitiveness and inferiority and had to be denied. His counterassertion was that racial admixture had eliminated the racial specificity of Costeños.

He railed against the irrationality of the "one-drop rule" as it operates in the constitution of U.S. racial identities: "This mental illness [racism] has penetrated as far as North American sociology . . . A blonde white man with one drop of black blood for these sociologists belongs to the Negro race as if his blood had another color than red" (*La Prensa* [May 26, 1976]). He stated clearly in this article the idea that racial identity was socially constructed and implied that application of the one-drop rule in Nicaragua was equally ridiculous.

In "Errores sobre la Costa Atlántica" he points out what to him are the contradictions involved in the Mestizo racialization of Creoles as blacks (*La Prensa* [September 4, 1976]):

> Let's bring together two identical specimens, one from the Pacific and the other from the Atlantic (the Costeño could be blond). The latter is accepted as a Spanish Mestizo, as is the first. But upon learning that he is from the Coast and that he speaks English, now he [the latter] is black. . . . the descendants of the surnames indicated [mostly German] . . . were considered to be of mixed European ancestry; on the other hand, the Creoles were those of Scottish ancestry and the blacks were blacks. However, around 1894, they [blacks] were denominated by Migration [the branch of the Nicaraguan state concerned with immigration status] to be black Jamaicans, and after 1910 they are now black Creoles, though in the Coast a differentiation has always been made.

Brautigam Beer believed that, although some of their ancestors were black, the Creoles were in fact a very racially mixed group as a result of the high level of miscegenation among Europeans, Amerindians, and Africans that had taken place over the course of Coast history (*La Prensa* [September 23, 1976]). To identify Costeños in general as belonging to one or another race would be incorrect. Though he did refer to some Coast groups as Indians, he never referred to Costeños as black. In general, identity as a "Costeño," the only word he consistently used to name the Coast population, was for him not racialized.[12] Lest Mestizos try to use the Costeños' multiracial ancestry as the basis for claims to racial superiority, Brautigam Beer pointed out that "Nicaraguan culture is not Hispanic, as you claim, but Indio-Afro-Hispana" (*La Información* [October 21, 1976]).

For Brautigam Beer, Costeños were not only racially but also culturally mixed and heterogeneous, a point he makes over and over again in his work. For example, in his study of the element of Creole culture best known to Mestizos, the May Pole dance and music, he stated (*La Información* [May 8, 1976]): "Costeño culture is totally heterogeneous and its May Pole is the result of the confluence of various cultures." Despite this hybridity, however, he emphasized in a number of articles that Coast culture was preeminently European in origin: "Costeño culture, being hybrid, has influences that are now well known. In the first place, we have the English influence, next the North American, the Miskitu, the Spanish. The Costeño people themselves have also forged their own ideas" (*La Prensa* [April 20, 1976]), and more specifically in the case of Creoles, English (*La Prensa* [May 8, 1976]): "A critical revision of the oral and literary testimony . . . indicates that the May Pole of the extinct Mosquitia is a relic of universal culture, in general, of European culture and, in particular, that of Great Britain." He continues this theme in another article (*La Prensa* [August 4, 1976]): "The majority of the 'English' Costeños have some English blood. Their parents, who in many cases were English, transmitted to them English culture with some modifications determined by the time and the distance." Brautigam Beer's emphasis on the English roots of Costeño culture and the ethnographic descriptions of the culture he provides make it clear that, in general, when he wrote about Costeño culture, he was referring to that of the Creoles, not the indigenous population.

In some of his writings, Brautigam Beer admitted that many Creoles, though certainly not all, had some African ancestry. Consequently, to sustain his argument about the European character of Costeño culture, he had to explain away possible African contributions. This he was able to do, despite his scathing criticisms of U.S. sociologists, by using outdated, but still commonly accepted, U.S. sociological theory (e.g., Frazier [1939] 1951). In his article on the May Pole dance and music, Brautigam Beer argued convincingly that African culture had had no influence on Costeño culture (*La Prensa* [May 8, 1976], emphasis added):

> Africans, once in the New World, separated from their brothers who spoke the same language and shared the same culture, were inevitably obligated to forget the major portion of their culture. In Jamaica and other regions, they produced a subculture that was, in part, an imitation of the culture of their masters . . . With the growth of the colored population, the subculture became the popular culture. The *natural* creativity, inventiveness, and musicality of this population created a new style for the May Pole celebration.

Brautigam Beer was prepared to accept that "Afro-Creole Jamaicans" had made a contribution to aspects of Creole culture that ranked second only to that of the British; however, he claimed that what they had contributed was corporeal, innate, stereotypically black, and only an amendment to what was fundamentally British.

Through this series of arguments, Brautigam Beer went about establishing the European pedigree of Coast culture with the aim of disproving Pacific Mestizo claims of its debased and primitive nature. Simultaneously, he developed a related set of arguments that challenged Mestizo national cultural chauvinism and specifically the idea that there should be one homogeneous Nicaraguan culture that was the basis for national unity and identity. For him this national cultural chauvinism was an equally important basis for the marginalization and exploitation of the Atlantic Coast by the Pacific.

In his argument for a culturally pluralistic Nicaraguan national identity, Brautigam Beer was careful to point out that, unlike the intractable problems being experienced by the United States, the problem in Nicaragua was one of ethnocentrism and not racism. In his principal article on the subject of racism, he constructs an exceptionalist argument by recounting how a North American resident in Nicaragua had gone back to the United States for a visit and was not allowed to get on a bus in the South "because it was for colored people. He had forgotten that he was not in Central America, where discrimination is immaterial" (*La Prensa* [May 26, 1976]). In explaining this difference he claimed that, "as there were few Spaniards who came to Latin America, and almost only them, there has been no noticeable discrimination."

According to Brautigam Beer the problem in Nicaragua, then, was not racism but the less-intractable ethnocentrism (*La Prensa* [July 7, 1976]): "an ex-schoolteacher was sent to Bluefields as commander [of the National Guard]. He was full of an ethnocentrism that still has not disappeared." His accusations of Mestizo ethnocentrism were based on the Mestizos' unwillingness to accept the civilized (i.e., European) status of Costeño culture. For him Mestizos were ethnocentric because, from their racialized view of Costeños, they mistakenly believed that Costeño culture was principally derived from its Amerindian and African cultural roots. His argument, however, was one of cultural relativism only in the sense that he thought that the Costeños' European heritage was at least the equal of the Mestizos'. He did not argue for the independent validity of the Costeños' non-European cultural background.

For Brautigam Beer, Mestizo ethnocentrism was also evident in their refusal to embrace Costeño culture as legitimately Nicaraguan. He argued strongly against the idea that there was only one Nicaraguan culture. He presented ethnographic data proving that Coast culture was worthy of recognition as a legitimate Nicaraguan culture and he championed the benefits of a multicultural nation: "Costeño culture is an agreeable variation in the multiform national culture" (*La Prensa* [June 29, 1976]):

The living poetry of this Coast, the May Pole, reestablished in its ideal form, will enrich the cultural wealth of the country, maintaining diversity in unity, inasmuch as variety is the fragrance of life, the immense poetry of God, the supreme art, and the supreme science. Those who argue for uniformity, for cultural homogeneity, contradict nature's testimony, the intrinsic being of humankind, and do not recognize the character and power of God. (*La Prensa* [May 8, 1976])

A geographic people that does not include all of its historical roots will perish for lack of vision. (*La Prensa* [July 29, 1976])

Brautigam Beer's pleas for national cultural pluralism called for an egalitarian relationship between the nation's cultures, and his writings clearly reflected his awareness of and selective utilization of the concept of cultural relativism.

His articles about the Atlantic Coast during the period in question contained yet another paradoxical theme. He never explicitly stated but nevertheless continually implied the idea that Costeño culture was actually more civilized than and therefore superior to Mestizo culture. This idea is presented in a number of forms. He maintained, for example, that Coast culture, because it was heterogeneous, from diverse origins, and in constant contact with foreign cultures, was more cosmopolitan than Mestizo culture (*La Prensa* [April 20, 1976]): "The man from the Coast is not as ethnocentric as those from other parts . . . He is cosmopolitan, considers himself a citizen of the world." He also claimed that Coast culture was very close to its European roots (*La Prensa* [June 29, 1976]): "A friend from Corn Island relates that arriving on the docks of London he could not understand what language was being spoken (it was Cockney), but when he entered the British Museum he felt right at home." There was an implication in his work that Coast culture was closer to English culture than Nicaraguan Mestizo culture was to that of Spain.

Finally, Brautigam Beer's insistence that Coast culture had its roots in English culture and not in African or Amerindian cultures established for it a higher rank in the international hierarchy of nations and cultures.

Brautigam Beer's writings distilled, refined, and simultaneously generated the dominant counterhegemonic Creole discourse on identity during this period. That discourse's constituting ideas were key elements of Creole political common sense. As elaborated into a philosophy by Brautigam Beer and other leading Creole intellectuals, it took from and skillfully utilized a number of influential international discourses. These included its adroit manipulation of the dominant international notions of the hierarchy of nations and cultures, emerging Third World ideas of dependency and anticolonialism, as well as liberal democratic notions of cultural pluralism.

In essence this position maintained that the Coast was an exploited internal colony of the Pacific portion of Nicaragua. This historical relationship of Mestizo oppression was preserved in part because the people of the Pacific held a series of erroneous ideas about the Atlantic Coast. The most problematic were Mestizo notions that Costeños were backward, uncivilized, and non-Nicaraguan culturally because they were racially black and Indian. On the contrary, the central ideas of the "culturalist" position were that Costeños were indeed different, but that this difference was culturally and not racially constituted and that in the comparison of cultural differences, Costeños actually came out ahead. The "culturalist" view was that Costeños were Creoles who were urban, educated, and predominantly Anglo culturally. In other words, they practiced a culture derived from that of their British ancestors, which, if the Mestizos insisted, could be shown to be more civilized than their own.

According to the culturalists, Mestizo racialized (not racist) assumptions of Costeños' blackness were also mistaken. The idea was that Mestizos, while they had no history of racist practice of the sort found in the United States, mistakenly believed Costeños to be black—of African descent. The culturalists' counter position held that Creoles were not black but racially mixed (as were Nicaraguan Mestizos) and therefore racially neutral. The most positive formulation of this idea understood black/African culture to have been erased by slavery; therefore, Creole people were a cultural blank slate on which their English ancestors wrote. At its most negative, this formulation suggested the idea of black culture as primitive—nothing more than the instinctual and libidinal urges of black bodies leaving the way open for the Anglo portion of Creole heritage to fill that cultural void.

The culturalist position as argued by Brautigam Beer exposes a key element of Creole political common sense, that is, the idea of the Creoles' Anglo cultural identity, not black racial identity, as the standpoint from which to resist Mestizo oppression. Moreover, through Brautigam Beer's skillful rhetorical moves, he connected a series of commonsense Creole ideas in a unique way with powerful potential for the future of Creole politics. As we have seen, he argued that the political and economic subordination of the Atlantic Coast by Mestizo Nicaraguans—which Creoles in general believed was their lot—was the product of the Mestizos' deprecating opinion of Creole culture—which

Creoles in general believed the former held. This created a commonsense relationship between a set of ideas in which the lack of Mestizo appreciation of the Creoles' Anglo cultural heritage was understood to be the source of all forms of the group's marginality. The commonsense resolution of this problem, from the culturalist perspective, was the construction of a culturally plural Nicaraguan nation in which the Creoles and their Anglo culture would have equal standing with the Mestizos.

As might be expected, these Creole opinions printed in *La Prensa* over the course of a year of intense debate drew impassioned opposition from many Mestizo intellectuals. This served only to reinforce these crucial elements of Creole common sense. Some of the most impassioned rebuttal came from the intellectuals of Chontales, the Nicaraguan department that forms the interior frontier between the Pacific and Atlantic zones (Eli Tablada Solís, *La Prensa* [October 8, 1976]):

> In my opinion, the ideas of Mr. Brautigam Beer should not be disseminated by *La Prensa,* which is a newspaper much read by Nicaraguans, inasmuch as such ideas are contrary to Nicaraguanness, which, as you well know, is based in our Hispanic roots. What unites the Nicaraguans is their Spanish culture and Catholic religion. . . . Mr. Brautigam Beer opposes the Hispanicization or the Nicaraguanness of our country, . . . [Spanish] must be spoken in the entire Nicaraguan territory because it is the language of our forbears who have conquered and colonized these lands, to pray to Jesus Christ and speak Spanish, as our great poet Sir Rubén Darío said.

The Black Sandinistas' Focus on Imperialism and Racism

Though the most prevalent and by far the most highly elaborated, the culturalist position was not the only Creole position on these issues. It was not even the most controversial. In December 1975 David McField, a nationally known Creole poet, was interviewed about the Atlantic Coast by Rosario Murrillo.[13] McField had moved to Managua from Bluefields to attend university twenty years earlier and stayed on. He was by this time a member of Gradas, a group associated with the arts and closely aligned with the FSLN. He presented a perspective on Creole politics and identity later characteristic of a group I call the "black Sandinistas." These were Creoles, mostly young and male, affiliated with the Sandinistas. I have already referred to Enrique Campbell's article published in the June 29, 1972, issue of *La Información* after the

ENALUF demonstration as an initial statement of this group's evolving viewpoint. In 1972 Campbell's perspective blended Sandinista political discourse with an emphasis on the specific problems of the Coast:

Liberty is a right given by God to each man and therefore must be respected. Here they take freedom of speech from us; to speak in honor of the truth is a mortal sin. This community is a slave to fear and therefore does not have the right to act and express its ideas. A community is what its citizens make of it. As soon as we begin to open our eyes, the community will begin to develop.

We must start to open our eyes so that we can see more clearly: Puerto Cabezas, a town almost extinct for the lack of resources; the rich resources of the mines of Rosita and Bonanza have been exploited with no benefit remaining for the people; Bluefields is on the road to the extermination of its natural resources; the wood has already been finished; the bananas are already finished; the shrimp are about to be finished; the city has received no benefit because up until now we have been unable to protest with valor and virility and distancing ourselves for partisanship. WITH OUR SILENCE WE ARE DIGGING OUR OWN GRAVES. I think it is much better to struggle for our rights than to die of hunger because we are cowards. The earth is only a transitory stage, sooner or later we will have to leave it, but while we are here we have to live with dignity.

In 1972 a number of elements of Campbell's position represented a new radicalism in Coast politics clearly influenced by international national liberation movements and, closer to home, by the positions of the FSLN. He emphasized the role of youth in political struggle while criticizing the cowardly, compromised position of their elders. He denounced the Liberal and Conservative hold on Nicaraguan political processes. He indirectly condemned the authoritarianism of the Somoza regime. He emphatically pointed out the consequences of the exploitation of Atlantic Coast peoples and natural resources by international capitalists. He advocated a radical "patria libre o morir" (free homeland or die) sensibility. He also explicitly referenced, for the first time in *La Información*, the Theology of Liberation.[14]

In 1975, McField's article added racial politics as a key focus of this emerging discourse. In his interview McField referred to the Creoles as blacks (*negros*) and stated that they were descendants of Jamaicans and Caymanians. His major theme was that most of the negative circumstances of Coast blacks were the result of "the years of exploitation by

North American companies, . . . [and] the decisive influence of the English first through direct control and later through their Caribbean colonies" (Murrillo 1975:10, 24).

McField claimed that Costeños thought themselves superior culturally to the Mestizos of the Pacific and, unfortunately, lacked a Nicaraguan national identity. He also stated that, because of the "years and years of colonization and servitude," Coast blacks were submissive to their former English and American exploiters and had acculturated toward the Anglo cultural standards of their oppressors. For McField this process, positively valued in the culturalist paradigm, was clearly negative. He also asserted that Coast blacks had internalized the racist conceptions of them held by these foreign exploiters and "creat[ed] our own image in the form in which these people want to see us." He stated that only in recent years, with the appearance of black power, the Black Panthers, and Muhammad Ali, had these submissive attitudes begun to change. He declared that this series of problems could be remedied only by profound structural and economic change on the national level because, according to the model he derived from dependency theory, the Coast had all the problems of "the Latin American peasantry." He did not mention the possible role of Mestizo ethnocentrism or internal colonialism raised by the culturalists.

From the black Sandinista perspective as presented by McField, the problems of the Coast were seen as stemming from the economic exploitation of international capital supported by the U.S. and British states. Racism against Costeños was principally the legacy of the activities of racist imperialists on the Coast. In this set of ideas, there was a clear disjuncture between Costeños and the foreign exploiters who came to take advantage of the Coast's resources and the labor of Costeños and then left.

This is the only expression of the black Sandinista paradigm in *La Prensa* or *La Información* during this period. I consider it to be a successor to the Enrique Campbell article published three years earlier in *La Información*; however, there were differences in the two arguments, most notably the emphasis on race, culture, and racism and the absence of a criticism of Pacific Mestizos in McField's presentation. These differences had to do with the increasing impact of Sandinista antiimperialism and the heightened level of national discourse about race and culture during this period.

My interactions with Creole Sandinistas five years later lead me to believe that the black Sandinista position, as exemplified by Enrique Campbell and especially David McField, was held by many young Creole university students during the late 1970's. They, like Campbell and

McField, had been radicalized by their experiences attending university in the Pacific and by 1976 were involved in political organizations aligned with the FSLN. Most, if they did not already belong, would become members of the party in the future. Members of the group would take control of Bluefields in the name of the FSLN in mid-1979, and many played a central role in Creole politics during the 1980's.

SICC and the Struggle against Internal Colonialism and Racism

The split in OPROCO opened space for the fifth Creole social movement. In early 1976 Roberto Hodgson, a former president of OPROCO who would soon resign from the organization, wrote a stinging editorial in *La Información,* now OPROCO's official organ, denouncing the Somoza government's key Coast development project—the intercoastal canal. He claimed that the development efforts of the state did not take into account the interests of Costeños but instead "only personal interests" (Hodgson 1976). This criticism was seconded two months later by Rollin B. Tobie F., a leading Creole member of OPROCO's Managua chapter. His editorial in *La Información* also represented an initial published statement of an emerging Creole paradigm that linked racism against the group with the internal colonialism suffered by the Coast at the hands of Mestizos from the Pacific. This perspective was so incendiary that the paper's OPROCO editorial board felt compelled to place a disclaimer at the foot of the column.

Tobie's editorial is noteworthy from a number of perspectives. First, he places the struggle of Costeños in international and African diasporic perspective by citing Kwame Nkrumah and the struggle for African independence and arguing that the Coast existed in a state of neocolonialism in relation to the Pacific portion of the country (1976b): "The dichotomous word 'neocolonialism' was coined by the deceased pan-African leader Kwame Nkrumah of Ghana, and its meaning in essence is applicable to our condition as postcolonials of the British." This was an extremely radical statement because it not only characterized the relationship between the Coast and the rest of the Nicaraguan nation as one of purposeful exploitation by the latter rather than neglect, but also constructed the Coast as occupying a position similar to that of the previously colonized nations of Africa and the Caribbean.

Tobie goes beyond territory-based economic exploitation and raises the specter of ethnocentrism and racism (1976b): "the ridiculously low number of compatriots suffering under the egotistic illusion that they as individuals have progressed should think about the fact that not even one Creole element has been outstanding, neither in the political field nor in the social hierarchy nor in the economic world. The forces that manipulate our destinies want only the illusion of progress, not the essence of our economic and political improvement."

The response from less-radical members of OPROCO based in Bluefields, who now controlled *La Información,* was swift. In a front page editorial in the next edition, Hugo Sujo asserted that the canal project did indeed represent progress for the Coast, that "a strong and stable government like ours . . . cannot go around consulting the people of every region of the country each time that they plan a project," and that, while there were problems concerning the exploitation of the Coast's resources, they were trying to solve them through the system. Sujo, adopting a position that was very different from that of OPROCO only a few years earlier, went on to write that Creoles were represented in positions of power in a manner commensurate with the size of their population. Accusing Tobie of overplaying Creole racial victimization, he added (1976, emphasis added): "in *the system* without *discrimination* in which we now live, to lament and to worry too much, opening past wounds that are now being healed, constitutes ethnic masochism."

Tobie's article implying Mestizo racism, Sujo's response denying it, and Brautigam Beer's *La Prensa* article also dismissing the possibility of Mestizo racism were published within three weeks of each other in May and June of 1976. Undoubtedly influenced by the McField article published six months before, which opened up the national discussion of race, these Creole essayists were clearly in conversation. Sujo and Brautigam Beer staked out the reformist criticism of the Coast's relation to the nation while simultaneously insisting on Nicaraguan racial democracy. As we have seen, these were key aspects of the culturalist perspective held by most of the well-educated Creole elite during this period.

Eleven days after Sujo's response appeared in *La Información, La Prensa* published the key germinal piece in the Creole paradigm linking Mestizo racism with internal colonialism. Robert L. Johnson's "¿Es nicaragüense nuestra Costa Atlántica?" (Is Our Atlantic Coast Nicaraguan?) (1976:2) dropped like a bomb on the Nicaraguan intellectual scene. What seemed to many Mestizo intellectuals to be its treasonous content provoked a wave of articles and commentary about the Coast published in *La Prensa* over the remainder of the year.

Johnson stated that there was a racial problem in Nicaragua that pitted the small portion of the population that was white (the *criollos*) against Nicaraguans of color (*La Prensa* [June 23, 1976]):

> . . . the whites, descendants of the Spaniards . . .
> . . . do the *criollos* [whites] intend that the country be their exclusive property?

. . . the national budget is totally for the benefit of the white
race, nothing is left for the Mestizos, Indians, blacks, and Miskitu
of the country?

He also claimed that Costeño blacks in particular were suffering at the
hands of those from the Pacific: "As we are human beings equal to you,
we the Costeños feel that we have over us Nicaragua's boot." Much like
the culturalists, he stated that the Pacific *criollos* were denying Atlantic
Coast Creoles the right to practice their culture: "It is necessary that the
government of the republic take Bluefields into account and give it the
place that it deserves within the Nicaraguan reality, beginning with
respect for our religions, our languages, and all our traditions."

Like the culturalists, he also claimed that the culture of the blacks was
English culture and that it was actually purer than the Spanish culture,
which those from the Pacific claimed to be practicing. This was a clear
insinuation of black-English cultural superiority similar to that found in
Brautigam Beer's work: "We blacks of the Atlantic Coast, although
humble and poor, received from the English the culture of that country.
. . . the *criollos* have not been capable of giving the Spanish culture to the
other races, reserving it as an exclusive privilege of those who have the
capital, the politics, and the religion."

For Johnson the result of the cultural colonialism of those from the
Pacific was a series of other abuses: "the authorities do not speak our
language and we have to resort to interpreters to make ourselves
understood in our own country." He departed totally from the culturalist
paradigm in his assertion that the problems between Costeño blacks and
the people of the Pacific were based on racism. He went on to claim that
this racist situation was actually worse than that afflicting U.S. blacks,
because in the United States the phenomenon was recognized and steps
were being taken to do something about it:

As much as they talk about the U.S., I am pleased to say that with
all the bad things that are happening to blacks there, things are
going much better than here; at least they are looking for solutions
to the problems. Meanwhile, in our situation there is slavery
without chains. A hypocritical slavery that drowns those who have
the double misfortune of being born black and, worse yet, Nicaraguan "citizens" where a white minority exploits like a wrung rag
our wretched humanities.

In what was perhaps the most shocking aspect of the article for
nationalist Mestizos, Johnson compared the situation of the Atlantic

Coast with that of Belize. With this maneuver he managed not only to criticize the relationship between the Coast and the Pacific portion of Nicaragua but also to imply the desirability of independence for the former. He stated that visiting Belizeans were horrified when they saw in the Coast an example of what was likely to happen if they were absorbed by Guatemala. They would have to "abandon their language, their religious freedom, and their English civilization full of rich and healthy customs that make [them] feel very proud of having inherited them."

He took the analogy one step further by reaching back into the annals of Creole protest and stating that

> it was those of us from Bluefields who were the ones who made a testimonial document recounting all that had happened to us since President Zelaya incorporated the Coast into Nicaragua: the commission obtained similar documents from Colón, Panama; Puerto Limón, Costa Rica; and altogether they were presented to the English government to save Belize from falling into the claws of Guatemala.

This was read in Managua, as Johnson surely knew it would be, as a treasonable act. An unprecedented companion editorial by *La Prensa's* editorial board refuting Johnson's article and published alongside it characterized the statement as "calling for . . . the subjugation of our Coast, Puerto Limón, Colón, etc., like Belize to the British Empire, which is an outrage."[15]

I have been unable to locate anyone who admits to knowing who the author of this extremely controversial and provocative article was; Robert Johnson was undoubtedly a pseudonym. As we shall see, however, the positions the article adopted and the seeming contradictions it contained were so characteristic of those of an emerging sector of Nicaragua's Creole community that I have no doubt that it was written by someone closely associated with it.

As I have already pointed out, the article shared much with the hegemonic culturalist position through its identification with the English and its simultaneous claims of cultural marginality and superiority. In other ways, however, it was very different. There was an identification with diasporic blackness, and, in fact, the loaded name "Creole" was never used to refer to Costeño blacks; only *negros* was used. There was a clear invocation of the communal black experience of racial terror, that is, slavery and contemporary racism in Nicaragua. There was a call not only for cultural pluralism but also for the recognition of the

Nicaraguan nation's racial pluralism and the demand for an end to racism. Johnson's solutions were black cultural autonomy and equity in a racially and culturally plural nation.

I have been unable to find Creoles willing to defend completely Johnson's position in the pages of either *La Información* or *La Prensa* during this period. Tobie's piece on neocolonialism and racism was reprinted in *La Prensa* later in the year, as well as his commentary about an infamous poem by Fernando Silva about Bluefields blacks, which he condemned for "hate of the black race."[16] Other Creoles, however, played off the radical quality of Johnson's statement to lend credibility to their more reformist positions. In an example of this tactic, Conservative representative to the National Assembly from the Coast Stanford Cash, a Creole from Bluefields, addressed that body as follows (1976):

> An article was published in the newspaper *La Prensa* . . . with the signature of a respected citizen of the Department of Zelaya . . . that I consider to be a clear and authentic reflection of the resentment and bitterness of this preoccupied citizen. As a natural reaction, other articles in turn have been written . . . on the basis of the criteria of the first article, with which I am in complete disaccord. . . . However, if we do not take rapid and effective measures, it is not a remote possibility that one or more other Mr. Johnsons expounding on problems will emerge, which will not be healthy for the country.

Indeed, there was a growing movement in Bluefields composed principally of young Creoles who shared many of Mr. Johnson's opinions. The paradigm of Mestizo internal colonialism and racism had maximum expression in this social movement of the mid- to late 1970's, which culminated in the organization of the famous SICC (Southern Indigenous Creole Community).

SICC members did not publish their political ideas in the local or national newspapers. The organization was aimed much more at Creole self-improvement than at publicly lobbying the power structure for change. Therefore, there are few materials available to give us an idea of the organization's political discourse. Thus, the brevity of my presentation of the ideas of the Creoles involved in the group is not an accurate indication of the group's importance.

The primary moving force behind SICC from its beginnings in 1975 to its demise in exile in Costa Rica and Miami in the late 1980's was the organization's longtime president, Miss Jenelee Hodgson. Miss Jenelee was perhaps the outstanding Creole charismatic figure of her time. She attended the Seminario Bíblico Latinoamericano from 1970 through

1974, where she overlapped with some of the Creole pastors who were involved in nationalizing the Moravian Church. She credits her experiences there, especially reading black figures like Fanon and Martin Luther King, Jr., and a course on black culture given by noted black Costa Rican writer and activist Quince Duncan, with radicalizing her views on Creole racial identity. On her return to Bluefields in 1975, she began teaching at the Moravian High School, newly under Creole control, and working with the young people's group at the Baptist church of which she was a member (interview, 1995): "I went home all pumped up. I felt sure of myself. I knew who I was. I wasn't ashamed of myself. I was proud to be black. I was wearing an Afro just as big as Angela Davis'." When she got back to Bluefields, Miss Jenelee claims, she found people ashamed to be Creoles and of their blackness and afraid to publicly remember their history:

> We formed UCCOD [United Committee for Community Development] for that reason—the Spanish people did look on us like we were nothing . . . And when I came back then I was with this black push. I said, No, No, No, No! We are not no minors here. Get this thing off! You are important! You are who you are! And afterwards they said I was racist. We had to build the confidence in the young people that they were important. And I used a phrase that I learned in Costa Rica . . . "Black is beautiful and if you doubt it just look at me." That was one of my phrases. . . . That was a movement in the United States also. "Black is beautiful." That stuff was catching and we were right in—we got in the spirit of the times.

Working first with the Baptist Young People to make the Sunday school classes the latter taught to younger children more relevant to the Creole experience, Miss Jenelee soon led them in other directions. The Young People's meetings became a kind of Christian political reading group. They began reading about and discussing such things as black history, Coast history, and Liberation Theology. Sometime in 1976 Miss Jenelee and a number of her young followers organized UCCOD. This enabled them to begin working with young members of the Creole community from other religious denominations and age groups. Miss Jenelee in her position as a teacher at the Moravian High School was able to influence and bring into the group Moravian young people as well.

The focus of the group quickly became the recompilation of Creole and Coast history. They began interviewing Creole elders about the group's history. Memory of the heroic exploits of Gen. George Hodgson and the Twenty-five Brave was revived. These personages and events became symbolic of the emerging process of revitalization of Creole pride and identity (Gray n.d.). Miss Jenelee also made an effort to recruit young people she refers to as "bad boys." They were not affiliated with the established churches, but she tried to engage them in the work of gathering oral history. These young men were involved in the beginnings of the rasta movement on the Coast. They were listening to reggae, beginning to "dread up," and learning the culture from album covers and the few Jamaicans resident in the region. They became actively engaged in recovering history, especially that of the UNIA in Bluefields.

UCCOD also put on a Caribbean Festival as part of the 1977 celebration of Bluefields' birthday. The idea was a cultural event that would explicitly invoke and celebrate the Caribbean (black) roots of Creoles and their history in general. Group members contacted a large number of Creole organizations, including the Helping Sisters, Pink Tea Party, Rose Girls, Harlem Brothers, baseball clubs, the committees from the four Creole barrios, the Anglican School, and the Moravian High School (Jenelee Hodgson interview, 1995; SICC 1983). The cooperation of these elements of Creole civil society was unprecedented and of immense symbolic importance in forging a collective Creole identity. All Spanish speakers were excluded, as was the integrated, state-supported Colón High School. Mestizo Mayor Pedro Bustamante was deliberately not consulted (Jenelee Hodgson interview, 1995):

> We said, "Okay, we are going to have this historical event to wake up the town. . . ." We did not allow not a Spanish person to sing and they were mad! I said no Spanish songs, no Spanish people; this is a Caribbean Festival. . . . It was done for an awareness of the people . . . that we had something to be proud of. We had beautiful girls. We had beautiful people. We had beautiful talent. We didn't have to always depend on having a queen as representative that had to be from a Spanish side.

There were several days of cultural and historical activities, including a calypso contest, dance presentations, poetry readings, traditional games and contests, to celebrate Creole identity. The proceedings culminated on the final day with a parade that wound through all of Bluefields and in which each group had a float. The high point of the parade was a float representing the personage and exploits of General George and on which the ten remaining members of the Twenty-five Brave were driven. This float was a presentation of persons and events purposefully enacted to elicit social memory of the organizational and military prowess of the Creole community on behalf of an implicitly separatist cause. Given the repressive nature of the Somoza regime, this previously hidden memory could perhaps only have been presented publicly in the carnivalesque context of a parade.

This public enactment of the previously unspeakable was precisely the reason for staging the festival and for its great popularity and success. UCCOD was engaged in the uncovering and dragging into public discourse of the previously unspeakable—the history of an oppressed people. This is brought out by Miss Jenelee's recounting of the recovery of a historical document from an older Creole woman: "was a lady had it hidden between her mattress. I said why are you hiding it? She told me a long story that they were always afraid because Spanish people always . . . saying that they wanted to separate the Coast. So there was a repression, and I remember that there was time when you couldn't mention General George's name in Bluefields. People were still too afraid to mention it. They were scared" (interview 1995).

The overwhelming success of the Caribbean Festival and its oppositional character immediately positioned the organization as a political force. The Mestizo politicians interpreted this event and the group's other historical and cultural activities as political and threatening (Gray n.d.; Jenelee Hodgson interview, 1995). UCCOD took advantage of this to begin to push an explicitly political agenda:

> I personally went to Bustamante [the mayor] and I told him, I said, "Look now, Bustamante, our situation is this. We are reading the Altamirano [Harrison-Altamirano treaty]. Because we feel like every person on the East Coast should know what is stipulated in that document. . . . look at number 2. You want to tell me that you can't even leave two cents out of the money that you are collecting [from the seafood companies] . . . for us to have some development in this place?" I said, "No, man! See what this says." Well, he said, "That is not for me. That is for the Central Government." Oh, so it fall right in the same. By this time I had read in the book about General George that the same thing he questioned and fought about. (Jenelee Hodgson interview, 1995)

In 1977 a Young People's retreat organized by CASIM, the Moravian social action group, was held in Pearl Lagoon. Miss Jenelee and top members of UCCOD participated actively in this event and returned to Bluefields even more focused on the task of "discovering who they were." This meeting is mentioned by many of those involved in the early years of this movement as being central in its consolidation. It allowed the group to make contact with young people from throughout the region and to disseminate their ideas much more broadly. The UCCOD participants left determined to create a more formal organization. The retreat also seems to have been important in gaining the support of important sectors of the Moravian leadership (Gray n.d.).

In 1978 SICC was formed from UCCOD. Ivan Cassanova and Hernan Savery, the latter a new teacher at the Moravian High School, had arrived from Managua and convinced the members of UCCOD that to create a more broad-based and effective organization that could attract funding from NGOs, they would have to model themselves after indigenous organizations like the enormously successful ALPROMISU. The young UCCOD members reluctantly agreed to do so, reforming themselves as SICC. The new group nominally included the Rama Indians, and a new board of directors was formed to include a majority of older and more well established Creole men. The major part of the new organization's funding came from CEPAD (Centro Evangélico por Asistencia y Desarrollo—Evangelical Center for Aid and Development), a national ecumenical social action organization that also funded ALPROMISU. Savery claims that SICC was in contact with a number of international indigenous and black organizations including Operation PUSH, the Organization of Black City Mayors, and Cultural Survival in the United States; the World Council of Indigenous People; the Costa Rican Indian Council; the Panama Indian Council; and the World Black Council based in Brazil (Hernan Savery interview, 1986).

The newly nationalized Moravian Church also heavily supported the new group. In fact, Bishop John Wilson and the first "native" superintendent of the Moravian Church in Nicaragua, Joe Kelly, were members of the original SICC board of directors. Many of the group's meetings were held in Moravian High School classrooms. CASIM provided the funding for many of the group's seminars and other projects. Some Moravian clergy were members of the organization, and they and other Moravian clergy took active part in the organization's events.

Surviving SICC documents are vague about the organization's goals. There seem to have been two areas of concern. The first was the promotion of self-knowledge of the cultures and history of the racial and cultural groups of the Southern Atlantic Coast in general; however, in practice, the group remained almost exclusively Creole in membership and focus. The second set of goals had to do with the development of the Coast's human and natural resources for the benefit of Costeños. In an effort to carry out these goals, a series of seminars were organized. For example, sometime in late 1978 or early 1979 a seminar on cultural survival was held by SICC and presided over by Miss Jenelee and two of the nationalizing Creole pastors. Amid the singing of hymns, praying, and bible reading, the three main sessions were entitled "Leadership," "Black Leaders," and "Historical Background of the Creole" (SICC n.d.).

Additionally, Miss Jenelee had a daily radio program through which the group's message was disseminated. SICC also strongly supported Ray Hodgson's (Jenelee's brother) mayoral bid in 1978, which was run partly on a black pride platform.

SICC also branched out into economic development projects. The group was particularly interested in encouraging agricultural self-sufficiency in the region and had projects in Pearl Lagoon and on an island in Bluefields Lagoon. In addition, they were interested in the forming of Creole leadership and sought funding for students to study outside Nicaragua. They hoped that the resulting group of well-prepared professionals would then be able to return and take over the leadership of the southern Coast: "there was a real feeling for us to be in control, so that is why we had this program of twenty-five. Each year twenty-five young people go away. By the time they get back here, they are ready to take this thing over, man" (Jenelee Hodgson interview, 1995).

SICC also began to make a concerted effort to organize older Creoles. This was accomplished by dividing the group in two by age. The older folks who joined SICC were relatively well educated and economically comfortable but not of the same status in the Creole community as those still organized in OPROCO. SICC's emphasis on Creole culture and history raised in them much higher levels of "national feeling and the desire to regain cultural values and historic recognition" than it had in the younger members (SICC 1983). These "feelings" would have explosive repercussions in the 1980's.

Almost from the beginning, SICC drew the attention of the state at the local and national levels and of the FSLN: "It is noteworthy that at the local level the group began to be suspected, given the national crisis of the moment: the continual progress of the FSLN in the war. Besides, there was an emphasis on auto-determination and the dignity and identity as black people. This frightened the local politicians" (Gray n.d.). The FSLN members who were familiar with SICC evidently also were concerned with some SICC elements' flirtation with separatist rhetoric and the group's seeming hostility toward Mestizos (Hernan Savery interview, 1986). By late 1978 the national political crisis had gotten so severe that many of SICC's activities were curtailed. Nevertheless, the organization survived the triumph of the Revolution and continued to operate in Bluefields through the early 1980's.

The Creoles of Bluefields, rather than being submissive in the decade immediately prior to the Triumph of the Sandinista Revolution, had actually been quite politically active. SICC's organization and activities were in many ways the culmination of these activities. The ideas of the members of this group provide important insight into the composition of Creole political common sense in the late 1970's and the early 1980's.

SICC's members were attentive to the issues of regional development and exploitation raised by other Creoles and were strong proponents of the concept of internal colonialism as a means of understanding the Coast's marginalized relationship to the rest of Nicaragua. They were strong advocates of social and economic development of the Coast to counteract the region's marginalized and underdeveloped position; however, strongly influenced by the anticolonial, civil rights, and cultural nationalist struggles of blacks elsewhere in the Diaspora, they had other concerns as well: "We respected OPROCO . . . a highway or a road to join Kukra Hill was necessary, but, my God, I mean there were other things to be focusing about" (Jenelee Hodgson interview, 1995).

The idea of Mestizo racism was central to SICC's analysis. Indeed, Mestizo racism was seen as the engine of the internal colonialism the Coast suffered. In response, SICC's principal focus was on the revitalization and repositioning of the Creole groups' cultural and racial identity as Caribbean and black—as fundamentally different kinds of Nicaraguans and proud of it. The idea of a glorious Creole past of black struggle against Mestizos and the Mestizo-dominated Nicaraguan state was a particularly strong aspect of the SICC paradigm. This in combination with the influence of black cultural and political movements outside Nicaragua was the basis for an incipient black nationalist perspective that activated the idea of Atlantic Coast independence. This in turn was reinforced by the suggestive idea of the Creoles' indigenous status and black identity. Finally, unlike the four other Creole social movements, SICC was much more a grassroots movement championing the idea of mass participation of the Creole community in the cultural reorientation of Coast society.

On the other hand, in many ways SICC defended the status quo. It was very closely associated with the dominant Protestant churches and therefore, despite its championing of Creole culture, firmly tied to basic precepts of Anglo culture. It was also a reformist movement in many ways. It launched no attack on such basic ideas as representative democracy and Western capitalism. In fact, it made no general criticism of the Somoza regime. The group was concerned with the general relationship between the Coast and the rest of the country. Somocista leadership was even embraced by many SICC members, especially as it was increasingly threatened by the Sandinistas. Moreover, because of its close ties to the Protestant churches, the SICC leadership was strongly anticommunist and therefore hostile to the icons of "communism," the Soviet Union and Cuba, as well as to the increasingly influential FSLN. This position emanated from the idea that communism was intrinsically antireligion. These sets of ideas would play a central role in Creole interaction with the Sandinistas in the coming years.

Creole Political Common Sense, Politics, and Identities

I turn now to the task of constructing an ethnographic description of Creole political common sense in the early 1980's. It is drawn from Creole historical processes, structural relationships, and contemporary political practices I have presented in this and previous chapters and from my own experiences during the latter part of this period.

My conception of "political common sense" is taken from Gramsci. It is a historically produced reservoir/repertoire of political practices and ideas that agents draw on in the generation of conjunctural political attitudes and activities. It is composed of (a) ideas and practices that are the production, past and present, of a group involved in struggles over political power relations and/or social transformation; and (b) ideas and practices appropriated from other groups as tactical maneuvers in that group's struggles or "for reasons of submission and intellectual subordination" (Gramsci in Forgacs 1988:328, 333). As a result, political "common sense is ambiguous, contradictory and multiform" (Gramsci in Forgacs 1988:346).

The content of political common sense is both tacit and expressed. Elements may shift from one level to another over time or may occupy both levels simultaneously among different sectors of the group of whose political common sense they are a part. In any given moment, a community's politics is generated from its political common sense. Specific conjunctures of economic, political, and other social relations stimulate the expression of sets of elements of political common sense. These elements tend to be arranged into some form of internal coherence (Gramsci's "philosophy"), usually by the community's organic intellectuals, and thereby can be recognized as related sets of ideas and serve as organizing ideas through which people understand their world and around which they formulate explicit political practices.

Creole political common sense, then, is an amalgam of related and contradictory, similar and disparate historically produced ideas and practices concerning the "natural" order of political relationships and practices. Creole politics is the conjuncturally expressed elements generated from the reservoir of Creole political common sense. Creole politics is in general also multiple, disparate, and contradictory. This is because (a) different sets of the elements of political common sense may be expressed as organizing frames simultaneously by differently situated sectors of the Creole community; and (b) as economic, political, and other social conjunctures change, different sets of the elements of political common sense are evoked as organizing frames for the formulation of Creole politics so that from one moment to the next the group's politics transforms.

Multiple, contradictory, and disparate historically produced ideas about Creole group identity also reside in common sense. Specific expressions of Creole racial/cultural identity emerge to salience from common sense as actors collectively attempt to locate themselves and are placed by others within international, national, and regional social/ cultural orders in changing political, economic, and other social conjunctures. Expressed Creole identities and Creole politics are not necessarily coterminous; however, the former may constitute an identity politics when they become the mediating ideas among the organizing ideas of the politics of a particular moment.

Creole Racial and Cultural Identity

A key aspect of Creole identity formation is group boundary formation—the everyday marking of difference from members of other groups and similarity to other Creoles. In the early 1980's there existed in Creole common sense a historically produced complex of racial (phenotypic), cultural, social, and economic elements that were used by both themselves and others as markers to identify them as Creoles—members of a social unit distinct from other Nicaraguan racial and ethnic groups. These traits were by no means unitary or internally consistent; they exhibited the multiple and often contradictory character of Creole common sense in general.

Judging from the social movements of the late 1970's and my experiences in the early 1980's, Creole identity as expressed at that historical moment was constituted by three central markers: language, kinship, and racial phenotype. The most important index of Creole identity for both Creole and non-Creole Nicaraguans was the Miskitu Coast Creole language as first language. Miskitu Coast Creole exhibited a post-Creole continuum, and most Creoles could and did move easily between the basilect (farthest from standard English), the mesolect, and even the acrolect (closest to standard English) levels of Miskitu Coast Creole. As we shall see, the acrolect had a high status value for Creoles because they associated it with British and North American English. The basilect form of Miskitu Coast Creole was publicly denigrated by many Creoles; however, its use was recognized as the highest expression of group solidarity. It was the principal grounds on which Creoles distinguished themselves as a group even from English speakers. In my day, Creoles who had been away from Bluefields and living in the United States and who returned affecting some form of U.S. English were said derisively to *gringar* (speak like a gringo). They stood accused of trying to separate themselves from and elevate themselves over the rest of the Creole community. Despite the centrality of Creole language to Creole identity, there were persons born in Managua who could not speak Miskitu Coast Creole but who were considered by most Creoles to be members of the group. These persons, however, were black phenotypically and had surnames that placed them as members of historically Creole families.

In general, Creoles recognized the "black/African" phenotype as an attribute of their group, though almost all would claim that they were racially mixed. Blackness had been the central feature of Creole identity during the height of the UNIA movement on the Coast and became so again in the late 1970's for Creoles associated with SICC. The racialization of Creoles by Mestizos created a Mestizo stereotype of Creole blackness. The ability to speak Creole English and "black" phenotype were the determinant markers in the construction of Creole identity from outside the group, especially by Mestizos. There were many other Nicaraguans, however—Miskitu, Garifunas, and even some Mestizos—who shared this same phenotype and a substantial number of Creoles who did not.

For Creoles, group membership was determined in large part by kinship relations. They imagined the group as a web of interrelated families with core families rooted in each of three geographical areas: Bluefields, Pearl Lagoon, and Corn Island. All of these families were understood to be connected. Creoles were people who were members of or otherwise could demonstrate relatedness to historically Creole families. In my experience, one of the first sets of issues discussed when a Creole met a stranger who exhibited Creole potential either through language or phenotype was that person's family ties. I was continually asked if I was from the Bluefields or the Corn Island Gordons or was I from Mr. Tom's or Mr. Leo's side of the Bluefields Gordons. Since I was neither, my Creoleness was suspect.

As important as family relations were in determining Creole identity, alone they were not enough to establish that identity. For example, large sections of the Jackson family were not Creoles, even though Jackson was a Creole surname. The "Spanish" Jacksons were light skinned, spoke Spanish, and had Mestizo ancestry. For most Creoles they were Mestizos.

Within Creole common sense, there were additional sets of features used by Creoles to differentiate themselves from other Nicaraguan racial-cultural groups. Many had been more central to the marking of Creole identity in the past. The salience of each varied with the social context in which group identity was enacted.

Religion played a central role in Creole social life and identity. Historically, Creole Protestantism, especially membership in the Moravian Church, was a key oppositional symbol to Mestizo Catholicism and conferred high status through its association with "Anglo" culture. By the early 1980's, however, many Creoles were not Protestant and many were flocking to evangelical Protestant churches, which were racially and ethnically mixed.

There were other cultural features in Creole common sense used at different moments by Creoles to differentiate themselves from other Nicaraguan racial-cultural groups. These included Creole clothing and housing styles, distinctive cuisine, and musical style and listening preferences. Apart from these racial, cultural, and linguistic categories, there were also socioeconomic indices of group identity in Creole common sense. Creoles continued to see themselves as the "civilized" elite of the Atlantic Coast's racial-cultural hierarchy. They took pride in the urban "middle-class" status they felt characterized them as a group, even though by most other standards they were poor—but genteel poor.[17]

Despite a strong process of identity formation as Creoles, members of the group also identified as Nicaraguan. The increasing strength of national hegemony over the preceding fifty years had enhanced their feelings of belonging to the nation. Thus, as we have seen, in the era leading up to the period under analysis, most demands for political rights were made by Creoles as a minority group within the Nicaraguan nation and to the Nicaraguan state.

Processes of racial and cultural identity formation create meaning beyond that associated with the drawing of boundaries and delimitation of groups. They are also fundamentally about the negotiation of position or status—the assignation of value to identities in national sociocultural orders. This suggests a process parallel to that of group boundary formation within the process of Creole identity formation. An important aspect of Creole identity politics has been the battle to position themselves against the competing, and often-disparaging, claims about them of contending racial, ethnic, and national groups in the ideologically constructed international orders of cultures, races, and national identities.[18] This was accomplished through Creole ascription by others to and group identification with a set of crosscutting macro or transnational identities. These transnational identities have also allowed Creoles to position themselves against the constricting boundaries of the Nicaraguan nation.

Creoles historically inhabited three transnational identities simultaneously, with the popularity and salience of each varying historically. These three can be identified by the names that Creoles have called themselves. In this book I refer to the group mainly as Creoles, but it should be clear from the copious Creole political discourse I have presented that Creoles also refer to themselves as Costeños and blacks (*negros*). The elements of Creole identity I have presented are also used by Creoles as indices of these macro identities.

Creole black Caribbean diasporic identity is signified by their calling themselves blacks (*negros*). It is also signified by their production, appropriation, and identification with Afro-Caribbean and U.S. black music, their collective memory of racial abuse and violence, and their association with black diasporic political figures and movements (e.g., the UNIA, Kwame Nkrumah, and Martin Luther King, Jr.). Creole social memory of the group's origins continually names Jamaica and other areas in the Afro-Caribbean as a source of the group's ancestors. Creole recognition of their condition of economic exploitation and its similarity to the colonial and neocolonial positions of other blacks is the basis of a class component of black Caribbean diasporic identity. In the late 1970's and early 1980's, this black diasporic identity was the basis for the Creole social movement exemplified by SICC.

Creole Anglo diasporic identity was signified by their calling themselves Creole. This name historically connoted an affiliation with the British. Anglo diasporic identity was also evinced by Creole appropriation of and identification with metropolitan English and Anglo missionary Protestantism, with their appropriation of country and western music, and in general by their assertions of the Anglo roots of their culture. Creole social memory names England as a key origin source of the Creole people. The Creoles' relatively advantaged economic position in comparison with other Coast groups and the historical association of this privilege with Anglo capital is the basis of the class component of Anglo diasporic identity. Brautigam Beer's writings in the 1970's and the culturalist positions of some members of OPROCO are exemplary of this identity.

Creole indigenous identity is signified by their calling themselves Costeños. By the 1970's this name had taken the place of the politically taboo Mosquitian identity. Creoles were the people "indigenous" to the territory located in southern Zelaya, which included Bluefields, Pearl Lagoon, Corn Island, and the southern Coast to San Juan del Norte. From the Creole perspective, they were indigenous in the sense that they were the ruling native population before the arrival of the colonizing Mestizo Nicaraguan nation in 1894.

In addition to its regional referent, the name "Costeño" denoted Creole affiliation with indigenous Indian groups on the Coast, especially the Rama and the Miskitu. It further symbolized Creole claims to continuity of inhabitation from before the establishment of Nicaraguan national claims to their region. Costeño indigenous identity was transnational in that by the mid-1970's it was used by Creoles to identify themselves with the international "Fourth World" movement of indigenous peoples. Here again, Brautigam Beer's writings and the regionalist positions of OPROCO are based in this indigenous Costeño positioning.

Affiliation with the international indigenous movement was an important objective in the formation of the Southern Indigenous Creole Community from UCCOD.

Creole group identity and its disparate diasporic correlate identities— black Caribbean diasporic, Creole Anglo diasporic, and Costeño indigenous—when expressed often helped organize, legitimate, and make natural other sets of practices and ideas as they emerged to salience from the reservoir of Creole political common sense. The movement in and out of political salience of these sets of practices and ideas, however, which constituted Creole politics in a particular historical moment, was not necessarily isomorphic with the process of identity formation.

Creole Identity and Populism

For analytical purposes, I have separated these other areas of Creole political common sense into two ideal type sets of component ideas and practices. These do not exhaust the range of ideas and practices that composed Creole political common sense during the period in question, but they, along with the varying and associated modalities of Creole identity, were the dominant motivators of Creole political expression. Though the ideal type model used here for heuristic purposes may seem to imply duration and stability and hence an essentialized notion of Creole political common sense, Creole common sense is multiple, ambiguous, contradictory, and mutable.

Historically, Creoles developed a tradition of resistance to what they perceived as their oppression as a group. Their perception of oppression and development of attitudes and behaviors of resistance were based on a set of political ideas whose expression during the early 1980's I call "Creole populism." This set of ideas emanated from the historical specifics of the Creole experience. Creole populism was preeminently the political assertion of Creole identity and racial, ethnic, and class solidarity in the face of oppression by and competition with other ethnic groups—that is, Creole identity politics.

Most of the components of Creole identity set forth in the previous section were important markers of that identity because they were exclusionary. As possessors of these elements of identity, Creoles had a strong positive sense of belonging to the Creole ethnic group as distinct from other Nicaraguan ethnic groups, and especially Mestizos. This differentiation was politicized as Creoles resisted perceived threats to their identity by other, "opposing" ethnic groups. Creole populism, then, was based in resistance: group advocacy and protection of Creole culture and position in the Coast's and the nation's social, political, and class structures. Since Nicaraguan Mestizos historically had been the

Coast ethnic group that was the most different from, and most threatening to, the Creoles' position, the latter's identity-related political ideas
and practices were preeminently concerned with power and rights vis-
à-vis Mestizos.

Creoles believed that, by virtue of their historical position of sociocultural and economic superiority, they should play a leading role in the
determination of the affairs of the Atlantic Coast. They further believed
that they had the right to be *the* dominant ethnic group (socially,
politically, and economically) in their indigenous area, where they
traditionally had been the majority population: southern Zelaya and
particularly Bluefields, Pearl Lagoon, Corn Island, and the southern
Coast to San Juan del Norte. This thirst for political power stemmed not
only from the perception that such power was "justly" theirs, but also
from the belief that such power was necessary to preserve their right to
live as Creoles (i.e., to worship in the religion they wanted, to speak their
own language, and so on). These rights, they believed, were threatened
by a nation dominated by a different and unsympathetic ethnic group.

Creoles felt that, because they had not been able to exercise political
control in these areas since the Reincorporation, they had been discriminated against and oppressed by the Pacific-based, Mestizo-dominated
national government. They saw this situation as a consequence of
Mestizo internal colonialism and ethnocentrism or racism. Creoles also
did not fully accept the political aspirations of any of the other Coast
ethnic groups. Such aspirations were considered invalid because Creoles
saw other ethnic groups as inferior competitors who discriminated
against them.

There was also some resentment toward U.S. whites. This stemmed
principally from the irrational exploitation of the Coast's nonrenewable
resources by a string of large U.S. corporations. Also, adult Creoles had
surprisingly common personal experiences with racism on the part of
North Americans living on the Coast. In contrast to the response to
Nicaraguan Mestizo oppression, however, resentment toward North
American whites was usually aimed at individuals rather than at the
group as a whole. The identification of U.S. corporations with economic
opportunities, the U.S. government with charity and development
money, and white missionaries with Christian good works and social
services kept the negative perceptions of U.S. whites from becoming
generalized.

Creole populism also exhibited a strong class content. Creoles were
very concerned about the economic viability of the Coast and about
maintaining or enhancing their position in it. Politically, this was
manifested in strong Creole sentiment against what they believed was
the Coast's status as a Nicaraguan internal colony. They claimed that

traditional national government policy was to appropriate the income from Atlantic Coast economic activities. There was deep resentment of Mestizo economic power on the Coast in the form of both business and government patronage. There was also despair over the chronically depressed condition of the local economy, a by-product, as Creoles saw it, of Mestizo mismanagement and parasitism. Many Creoles, especially those from the rural areas, championed local control by medium-sized producers, business owners, and professionals in opposition to the large-scale economic enterprises of North Americans, Cuban exiles, and Pacific Mestizos favored by the national government.

Creole populism was reinforced in important ways by other aspects of Creole culture. For example, Creole culinary practice, with its emphasis on root crops rather than corn, coconut oil rather than lard, and so on, was a constant source of Creole pride as well as derision aimed at Mestizos.

The account of Creole political history contained in chapters 2 and 3 demonstrates that forms of Creole identity politics that were the precursors of the construction of Creole populism in the 1970's and the early 1980's have been extremely important historically. Creole resistance to the Reincorporation, participation in the Garvey movement of the early twentieth century, continuous rejection of Nicaraguan Mestizo rule over the Coast, periodic armed uprisings, and insistence on the teaching of English in the schools were all proof of their historical appeal. In the period immediately prior to and after the Triumph of the Sandinista Revolution in 1979, the Creole social movements of the time—the Creole pastors, OPROCO, black Sandinistas, and SICC—as well as Creole political writings demonstrate that Creole populism was the most consistently articulated element of the group's political common sense. Each of the three forms of Creole macroidentity was integral to different ones of the Creole social movements of the 1970's. Each of the former in different ways helped rationalize and legitimize different combinations of the sets of political practices and ideas that compose Creole populism.

Hegemony and Anglo Ideology

I have already noted the perception within Nicaragua during the 1970's and the 1980's that Creoles as a group were politically apathetic and inactive, blind to issues of their own oppression and that of those around them. I have also speculated that this perception stemmed from the fact that, during the thirty years prior to the 1970's, Creoles, for the most part, supported the Coast's political and economic status quo. During this period, most Creoles did not directly challenge the dominant political and economic structures. Though they agitated against some aspects of their oppression, mostly through the Mestizo-dominated labor movement, this was generally done from within the system and without challenging its basic tenets.

This apparent anomaly can best be understood as a product of the role of precursor forms of Anglo ideology. In the early 1980's, Anglo ideology was a powerful facet of Creole common sense whose components Creoles acceded to and tactically appropriated for their own ends as a by-product of their historical insertion in a social formation dominated by Anglo others. As we have seen, in the century preceding the Triumph of the Revolution, the Coast was a North American imperial enclave of U.S. capital and a Nicaraguan internal colony. The agents and associates of these social forces (i.e., the missionary churches, the U.S. media, expatriate elites, comprador bourgeoisie, the Somoza regime, and so on), through their domination of the Coast's social processes, created the conditions under which Creoles internalized many of the political ideologies that legitimized that domination while simultaneously providing them the means to optimize their position within those power structures.

Chief among these hegemonic ideologies was that of "democracy." The particular version of it held by Creoles was similar to that favored by moderates and liberals in the United States and Europe. Its main components included liberal democratic principles such as freedom of religion, political pluralism, "democratic" electoral politics, "human rights," and limits to violence in the enforcement of sociopolitical norms. These were all assumed to operate within the context of capitalist rather than socialist economic systems. Individual property rights were emphasized, as was the possibility of upward mobility through personal effort. Material wealth was seen as one of the most important measures of personal well-being. Other related ideas included the absolute superiority of Western civilization, in particular, its "Anglo" version, and the assumed racial superiority of whites.

Creoles had also come to strongly subscribe to "anticommunism." "Communism" was understood by Creoles to be atheistic, antichurch, totalitarian, a threat to individual economic independence and viability, as well as economically irrational. Thus communism for Creoles was more than just a mistaken politico-economic theory; it was a moral abomination. Creoles were very hostile to movements and countries that were defined by U.S. whites as communist. This affected Creole opinions of popular movements in other parts of the Americas and the possible applicability of these to the Coast. Socialist Cuba and its leaders were particularly disdained.

Concrete manifestations of the hegemony of Anglo ideology within

Creole political common sense abound. Most important for our purposes, in the decade before the revolutionary triumph, the majority of
Creoles backed the Liberal Party and the Somoza regimes. For them the
Somoza governments were legitimate because they fit the Creole image
of a democracy. Moreover, the U.S. government, U.S. representatives of
businesses operating on the Coast, and the U.S. missionaries—the
experts on such things—subscribed to that conception and backed the
government. Creoles might have been pushed aside socially, politically,
and economically by the representatives of these regimes, but they
tended not to question overtly the legitimacy of their rule.

Creoles accepted U.S. white influence and presence on the Coast in its
military, economic, and cultural manifestations. The U.S. government
was seen as the outstanding proponent and defender of democracy. The
United States was also seen as a paternalistic benefactor and savior of last
resort in any serious crisis. The assumed superiority of U.S. whites
meant that U.S. political positions were defended as correct whether or
not Creoles could rationalize that correctness. Creoles resented being
called "nigger," being paid less for comparable work than a white person,
or even having the U.S. Marines support governments that they were
actively fighting against; however, they seldom questioned the "right"
of the United States and its white nationals to be on the Coast and do as
they pleased.

Historically, Anglo dominance played a decisive role in the development of all aspects of Creole culture. Anglo ideologies permeated all
cultural domains.[19] To give just two small examples of this broad and
extremely important phenomenon: Creole ideas of their language (Miskitu
Coast Creole) as an inferior corruption of "good" (i.e., British) English
reinforced in important ways hegemonic ideologies about Anglos that
existed within Creole political common sense and vice versa. As we have
seen, from the Creole perspective, the high status of their ethnic identity
derived from its close relationship to Anglo cultures. Creole Anglo
diasporic identity, while it lent support to Creole populism in the early
1980's, obviously also held the potential to reinforce and legitimize
Anglo ideology.

Adoption of hegemonic Anglo ideology can be understood as a coherent tactical response on the part of Creoles. It explained and justified, and
thus made acceptable, a system of power relations that lower-class
Creoles as individuals felt powerless to change and from which Creoles,
especially the elite, received considerable benefit. There were positive
rewards for accepting it and the status quo it legitimized (jobs, social
acceptance, higher status, admission to heaven, and so on) and punishment (jail, social ostracism, going to hell, and so on) for not accepting it.
The inculcation of Anglo ideology was by no means an easy process. The

historical sources reviewed in this book bear witness to the protracted struggle by missionaries, educators, public officials, "civilized whites," and so on, to get Coast people to think and act in a "moral," "reasoned," "modern," "civilized," and "correct" (i.e., Anglo) fashion.

Creole political common sense, then, was a complex amalgam of ideas and practices that sprang from the specifics of Creole history and culture, Creole class and sociopolitical positions, and the hegemonic ideas of non-Creole ruling elites. Both Creole populism and Anglo ideology existed as ideal types within Creole political common sense.

There were congruences and reciprocal ideas between Creole populism and Anglo ideology. For example, the ideas of the superiority of Anglo culture and the Creoles' Anglo diasporic identity played important roles in each. There were, however, also a host of dissonances between them. For example, at the highest level of abstraction, Creole populism advocated the assistance and protection of small local capital, whereas Anglo ideology supported free enterprise, including large extranational capital. The first insisted on the rights and value of Creoles as black people; the second posited the superiority and justified the domination of whites as well as Creoles as cultural whites. The first emphasized the need for popular, ethnically sensitive political control; the second was based on elitist power and party-dominated democracy. These dissonances manifested themselves concretely and became conscious in myriad ways.[20] The potency and transparency of Anglo ideology, however, as well as its congruence with Creole Anglo diasporic identity, kept the potential dissonances between the two sets of ideas from developing into conscious contradictions at a level of intensity that would force Creoles to seriously question Anglo ideology.

This is clearly demonstrated in the Creole social movements of the 1970's and the early 1980's in which the resistant elements of populism can be clearly identified. Their salience in this historical moment was the basis for Creole politics of resistance. Simultaneously, however, each of the elements of Anglo ideology was also demonstrably present in the discourse and practices of these social movements. Although in this particular moment they were not the organizing ideas of Creole politics, they were, nevertheless, as commonsense political notions of the community, sufficiently powerful to impede a transformational Creole politics. Consequently, during the 1970's Creole resistance proceeded within the confines of Mestizo and Anglo power structures. As we shall see in chapter 7, this would change momentarily after the Triumph of the Sandinista Revolution in 1979.

The Moravian Sunday School Hall and Central Church (*left*) and the Moravian High School (*right*) looking south along central Calle Comercial during the 1980's, Bluefields. (CIDCA-Managua Library)

The controversial "Sandino Sun" mural, commissioned by the Sandinistas, on the *palacio*, Bluefields' seat of municipal government, early 1980's. (CIDCA-Managua Library)

Sandinistas campaign in Barrio Beholden, the largest of the town's black neighborhoods, early 1980's. (CIDCA-Managua Library)

Near Wing Sang's corner in downtown Bluefields, early 1980's, a famous spot for socializing and the interchange of community news and viewpoints. (CIDCA-Managua Library)

CIDCA-Bluefields Library with librarians Azalee Hodgson and Helen Fenton. It has become the center for the housing and dissemination of knowledge about Nicaragua's Atlantic Coast. (Edmund Gordon)

7.

Creole Politics and the Sandinista Revolution: Contradictions

[After the Triumph of the Revolution] the Creole element was feeling out to get a position that sure is due the Creole . . . they [Creoles] figured . . . at the Overthrow, they would be the ones to be on the scene because . . . it's a longing then . . . we feel like we deserved to be on the first page of a situation . . . right after the Overthrow, because they are longing for that possibility.
—Loyd Forbes interview, 1983

It is time to get tough. It is time for a real change . . . Organized as the "Floyd Wilson Task Force" we are inspired with the motivation for an anti-communist fight. We do not share separatism and express our repudance [sic] to an autonomy project issued by the Sandinista government. In a multi-ethnic region like the Atlantic Coast, the autonomy idea is only an infusion [sic] for ethnic contradictions . . . Communism is false, monstrous and malicious. It is the main cause for war, it is the father of dictatorship; the communists are masters of slavery and extermination of classes.
—FDN-UNO 1986

Most observers of the interaction between the Creoles and the Sandinista regime in the early 1980's alluded only to the tensions between the two parties and emphasized one or the other of two standard explanations of these difficulties. The few scholars who made reference to Nicaragua's Creole population during this period (1979–1985) ignored initial Creole enthusiasm for the Revolution. Moreover, they seemed unaware that this enthusiasm was based on the Creole community's perception that the Triumph of the Revolution would lead to the recognitions of their long-held racially and culturally based demands. These scholars, instead, asserted that the ensuing problems between Sandinistas and Creoles sprang from the latter's historical identification with Anglo oppressors and their position as the Atlantic Coast's middle class

(Adams 1981a, 1981b; Bourgois 1981, 1985; Dennis 1981; Rediske and Schneider 1983).[1] For their part, many Sandinista thinkers in the early post-Triumph years concluded from their own class analysis and anti-imperialist perspective that Creole opposition was based on the intrinsically pro–United States and "reactionary" nature of Creole political consciousness.[2]

Subsequently, the escalating racially/culturally based demands of the Miskitu and exposure to the racial/cultural problems and solutions of other "socialist" societies forced the Sandinistas to reassess their analysis of the difficulties on the Coast. By early 1985 the FSLN's understanding of its rocky relationship with the Creole community had shifted. The Creoles' culturally oriented political consciousness became the official Sandinista explanation of the problems they encountered in securing Creole participation in the revolutionary process. Internationally, the media and political activists on both the Right and the Left reached similar conclusions.[3]

All these observers of the troubled Creole involvement with the Sandinista Revolution were partially correct in their assessments of its dynamics. The elements cited as problematic in each of the two modes of explanation—the Creoles' "culturally" based demands and their "reactionary" political consciousness—were indeed troublesome. Taken individually, however, these analyses fail to provide a full understanding of the variability and complexity of Creole politics and, by extension, the Creole/Sandinista relationship.

First, these accounts were chronologically out of synch with the predominant modes of political expression in the Creole community. As I shall illustrate, in the early post-Triumph years, when Creole assessment of the Revolution could plausibly have been considered racially/culturally based, these observers employed the "Creole reactionary" explanation. Similarly, by the mid-1980's, when these observers utilized the "ethnic" explanation, so-called reactionary politics would have more accurately described the basis of the Creole response. The Sandinistas' misconceptions in this regard became a self-fulfilling prophecy. From the outset their handling of Creoles as "reactionaries" and their inattention to Creole racially/culturally-based desires created the conditions for the emergence of the very pro–United States, "anticommunist" politics of which they had erroneously accused the Creoles.

Second, and perhaps more important, such explanations, with their emphasis on monomorphic forms of Creole political consciousness, did not recognize the shifts in the elements of Creole common sense that served as the organizing ideas through which Creoles understood and formed attitudes toward the Revolution. The inadequacy of these observers' explanations was the product of their superficial understanding of the ambiguous, multiple, and contradictory character of Creole political common sense and its generative relationship to Creole politics and identity. The scant consideration given to Creoles' concrete experiences of the social transformations triggered by the revolutionary process only deepened the shortcomings of their explanations.

In this chapter I argue that close analysis of Creole politics during the period from 1979 through 1985 reveals that both Creole interpretations of and attitudes regarding the Revolution were not static but changed rapidly and markedly. The majority of Creoles initially favored revolutionary change and only later viewed it unfavorably. Their interpretations were not based on a single internally consistent political consciousness. Instead, they explicitly articulated and employed both Creole populism and Anglo ideology in their interpretations of the revolutionary process. The interpretive significance (salience) for the Creole community of each of these sets of elements shifted over time in response to the dynamics of economic, political, and other social conjunctures, including modifications in the revolutionary process itself.

I have found that immediately after the Triumph, Creoles organized an identity politics around the ideas of Creole populism in which their black Caribbean diasporic identity was central. In this politics Creoles enthusiastically accepted the Revolution as the key to realizing their utopian vision of a return to Creole dominance in southern Coast society. Subsequently, a social conjuncture formed in which Creole hopes for achieving their group aspirations were frustrated, the country's military and economic crisis deepened, the United States opposed the FSLN and labeled it "communist," and Creoles experienced the Sandinistas' mistrust. In this conjuncture, Anglo ideology emerged from common sense and eclipsed Creole populism as the predominant set of ideas around which Creoles organized their politics. In this new politics Creoles rejected the Revolution as "communist" and longed for a past when U.S. power assured the "stability" and "prosperity" of the region. Though Creole Anglo diasporic identity played a role in this new politics, in general, it was not an identity politics inasmuch as the ideas of Creole identity were peripheral to it.

My analysis indicates that at the height of their predominance, each of these sets of organizing ideas was *experienced* by a majority of Creoles as standpoints from which to mobilize their politics. Lived as centered politics, these ideas had real material effects as such. Nevertheless, during the period when one of the two sets of organizing ideas was predominant, the other set did not disappear but remained a part of Creole common sense. At any particular moment, the tacit ideas of the majority of the Creole community were the expressed organizing ideas of a smaller, differently positioned sector of the Creole population. Just as important, many of the same (often contradictory) ideas, though with different emphases, were utilized in the politics organized by both Creole populism and Anglo ideology. Consequently, despite in particular moments being experienced by many Creoles as monolithic and centered, Creole politics remained multiple and shifting.

This characteristic simultaneity of Creole political common sense provides a possible explanation for other observers' chronologically out-of-synch postulations regarding the basis for Creole perceptions of the Revolution. Ideas from the organizing frame (Creole populism or Anglo ideology) that were not salient at a given moment bobbed between the expressed and the tacit as they were mediated by the predominant frame; they thereby remained identifiable to those observers predisposed by their own interests and experiences to identify them. Hence the Sandinistas, influenced by dominant Mestizo representations of Creoles, saw reactionaries when Creoles themselves thought they were revolutionaries.

To substantiate these assertions, I have organized the chapter in the following manner. First I present a narrative of Creole politics from just before to a few months after the Triumph of the Revolution. This period marks the pinnacle of Creole enthusiasm for the revolutionary process and the predominance of Creole populism as the organizing frame for Creole politics.

Next, I describe the beginnings of the shift away from populism as the Sandinistas' policies frustrated Creole aspirations. This period of political transition is particularly illustrative of the multivalent and simultaneous character of Creole politics.

In the next section, I document the growing predominance of Anglo ideology in the Creole community after the civil disturbances of "Black September" and in the context of the economic and military crisis sweeping Nicaragua in the mid-1980's.

The chapter ends with a summary of the political transformations undergone by the Creole community during the first half of the 1980's and reviews the utility of my paradigm for their explication.

Populism and the Racial Struggle for Power in Bluefields

The Revolution Draws Near

In the final two years of the 1970's, racial tensions in Bluefields increased.[4] Events unfolded that, when interpreted by Creoles through the dominant lens of Creole populism, smacked of Mestizo racism. First there was the bitter campaign for the presidency of the local chapter of the Red Cross. The position was important, as the Red Cross was one of the few civil institutions that was relatively independent of either PLN or Moravian Church control. The two candidates were well-known Bluefields professionals. Cyril Omier was a Creole dentist, a Liberal, and a member of OPROCO; Moisés Arana, his Mestizo opponent, was a pharmacist and president of the local UDEL. At other historical moments, this contest might have been viewed in political party terms; however, the Creole community felt racially abused when its candidate lost.

A second series of racially tinged events revolved around the 1978 election of Ray Hooker, the son of powerful Creole caudillo Waldo Hooker, as dean of humanities at the Universidad Nacional Autónoma de Nicaragua (UNAN) in Managua. This selection was opposed by the Frente Estudiantil Revolucionario (FER—Student Revolutionary Front), which was closely affiliated with the FSLN and favored a more "progressive" candidate. The controversy grew violent and the appointment was annulled. The Creole community, led by the faculty of the Moravian High School and SICC, saw the conflict in racial/cultural terms. To them a distinguished Creole had been denied a position of national importance because of Mestizo racism within the student movement. By association, the FSLN was implicated as well.

In response, the rejected dean withdrew from the UNAN and started a project for the development of a university on the Atlantic Coast. The Creole population, again led by the Moravian High School faculty, supported this initiative, which was financed and supported by the Somoza regime. Mestizo leaders and members of UDEL, the bourgeois opposition to Somoza in Bluefields, opposed the project as pro-Somocista. The struggle immediately acquired an interracial dimension: Mestizos opposed, Creoles in favor. The association of the local UDEL movement with Mestizo identity and against Creoles was strengthened as well.

Racial tensions rose during the following year, when a young Mestizo UDEL member addressed a student assembly in Bluefields (Eustace Wilshire interview, 1983): "While in the country the people are fighting and dying, the people of Bluefields are dancing like monkeys." The Creole community assumed that the monkey reference was to them and considered it a grave racial offense. The statement was widely recounted throughout the community and added to the growing feeling that Bluefields Mestizos in general, and those associated with UDEL in particular, were racists.

Though race relations deteriorated in Bluefields, the increasing political instability of the country and repression by the Somocista state during the late 1970's inhibited Creole political activity. By late 1978, SICC, which had been the most active Creole group, was cutting back on its activities; however, during this period another group of Creoles that would play a major, though unlikely, role in the struggle for Creole empowerment began to emerge.

From the mid-1970's on, many of the increasing number of Costeño students attending university in the Pacific were radicalized through their involvement with the FER. These students also established a series of Costeño student organizations in Managua that were mostly social in character but that also aimed to promote the interests of the Atlantic Coast. In 1978 many of the more politically active decided to form the Asociación de Trabajadores, Estudiantes y Profesionales de la Costa Atlántica (ATEPCA—Association of Workers, Students, and Professionals of the Atlantic Coast). They planned for this group to be clearly political in its anti-Somoza objectives and broader in its membership than previous organizations. ATEPCA's membership grew to around forty-five, most of whom were Creoles. Miskitu students had a separate organization, which was affiliated with ALPROMISU. According to former members, ATEPCA's activities in Managua were severely handicapped by National Guard repression, which some have since claimed was brought down on them by a Miskitu informer from ALPROMISU. Nevertheless, during this period about fifteen loosely organized, mostly Creole ATEPCA members operated intermittently in Bluefields and traveled back and forth to the Coast from school and jobs in the Pacific.

While in Bluefields they agitated against Somoza and in favor of the FSLN in the Creole population. They planned a number of operations aimed at disrupting the everyday life of the town. Their objective was to foment the sense of instability and crisis being experienced in the rest of the country during that period. Most of their planned maneuvers were not realized; however, they were able to paint the town with the red and black of the FSLN in early 1978, burn part of the stands in the baseball stadium and paint the FSLN's initials on the outfield wall for opening day of the season, and turn an UDEL-sponsored mass for Pedro Joaquín Chamorro into a mass demonstration against the Somoza regime (Eustace Wilshire interview, 1983).

In the months before the Triumph, Bluefields was tense. Much of the city nightly watched the warfare raging on the Pacific Coast on Costa Rican television. Many nights young Creoles organized by those affiliated with ATEPCA exacerbated these tensions by randomly detonating contact bombs. Fears grew in the Creole community that the warfare in the Pacific would soon spread to the Atlantic Coast. These fears were heightened by the rumor that Somoza had authorized the bombing of Bluefields. Many young Creole men whose parents could afford it were sent out of the country in fear that they would be conscripted into the

National Guard. Simultaneously, Bluefields filled with former residents fleeing the unrest and warfare in the Pacific.

The ATEPCA members made considerable headway in their efforts to politicize Bluefields' population, especially among the Creole youth (Dexter Hooker Kaine interview, 1986):

> At night we used to start meet up, basically in the black neighbor-hood with a lot of the guys them, but that would sit down and listen to you. Maybe possible that you don't have the spirit nor-mally but with [unintelligible] you can discuss and you could teach a lot then . . . But those are the guys them that I start seeing that in the long run going answer. You know start doing. Okay, we start cutting all the wire up in the poles. You know, start doing like that. That some of them get even bored off it and switch off. And you know some more come in. But then we start classifying and seeing which one, even being [marijuana] smoker, which one going respond militarily in a moment.

Dexter Hooker Kaine (whose nom de guerre was Comandante Abel) was particularly adept at this kind of organizing. He had traveled to Costa Rica to meet with leaders of the FSLN, including Jaime Wheelock, and returned to Bluefields entrusted with specific political objectives. Abel seems to have been the only Creole activist operating in Bluefields who received direct orders from the FSLN. Working on the Coast during early 1979, however, he was isolated from the accelerating pace of the revolutionary process in the rest of the country and was unable to receive direct orders from his FSLN superiors. Abel and the largely Creole group of young men he was organizing decided to initiate their own military operations in the name of the FSLN. On June 28, 1979, after weeks of careful preparation, they attacked the U.S.- and Nicaraguan-owned PESCANICA seafood-processing plant situated on an island in the Río Escondido delta just outside of Bluefields.

The operation was carried out by sixteen men and without casualties. It was undertaken in part to assist the hundreds of refugees, Bluefields natives who had been stranded in Rama without food or medicine while fleeing the Pacific. After successfully taking over PESCANICA, Abel's group loaded liberated food, medicine, money, hostages, and heavy arms onto three company fishing boats already laden with shrimp, took three other speedboats, and headed up the Río Escondido to Rama. While making their escape, a National Guard boat arrived and fired on them; the attack quickly ceased when Abel informed the National Guard by radio that hostages, including the manager of the plant and several

foreigners, were on the escaping boats. A number of workers also decided
to accompany the group on the trip to Rama. In fact, the company
workers, many of whom were acquaintances of members of the rebel
group, assisted the latter in their activities.

When the group reached Rama early the next morning, their reception
was mixed. In Abel's words (Dexter Hooker interview, 1986):

> The reception wasn't the best. . . . the same little fellows them
> [Sandinistas from Rama] wasn't the best because they was like a
> little envious. All Sandinistas there mostly, they who live in the
> town . . . a little enviousness about our weapons. We with M16 and
> they with 22 guns.
>
> We spend the day and by night they took me up by up Cuapa to
> the *cuartel general* [the regional Sandinista headquarters]. I met
> Pancho [Luis Carrión] there. . . . When we saw each other it was
> different then. But when I get back to Rama all the guy them in
> jail. Seem like the Rama fellah assault them the night because they
> had dollars. Because what we did with the dollars just before I left,
> we left a little pusha [distributed some of the money] because we
> were planning to leave in a next two days for guerrilla fighting and
> it's not one man have that. We give a pusha. But then when they
> broke them they even find some grass on them. . . . Our guy was
> very mature . . . when they went after them the night there was a
> lot of shooting up and, well, they didn't answer the gun them
> because it was 22. And good say they didn't answer. It was a real
> mature act. And they spend the night in jail. Well, when we reach
> back the next day, well, we put everything back under control.

During the entire time the group spent in Rama, however, there was
considerable tension between group members and the Rama Sandinistas
(Eustace Wilshire interview, 1983). This tension was interpreted by
Abel's group in racial terms (Dexter Hooker interview, 1986): "We had
some kind of a little contradiction with that same feeling of Spanish and
black . . . that is mostly the same Rama people . . . so what I was trying
to do then was just don't get nobody's ill-feelings. . . . in Rama we had
serious problems because racial problems arose between the people of
Rama and those from Bluefields."

These racial problems challenged the "black Sandinista" position
held by Hooker and the other ATEPCA leaders, that U.S. imperialism
was the principal source of the racism Creoles experienced in Nicaragua.
Such experiences of racial/cultural conflict between Creoles and Mestizos aligned with the FSLN continued and intensified over the course of
the following months of social conflict and change. They had an

important impact on these Creole leaders' politics and the politics of their followers and of other members of the Creole community.

On the other hand, the Costeño refugees stuck in Rama greeted the group as conquering heroes. Word quickly spread downriver to Bluefields and surrounding communities of the operation's success, and boatloads of both Creoles and Mestizos eager to join the coming insurrection began arriving at Rama. By the time Abel and his troop were ready to go back to Bluefields, more than seven hundred mostly unarmed volunteers had joined them.

The original idea had been to stay in Rama only a couple of days then proceed downriver and form a base in the Pearl Lagoon area and from there prepare the liberation of Bluefields. This was never carried out. The group needed ammunition and antiaircraft weapons, which they were unable to obtain in a timely manner. Abel thought his raw troops needed two or three days of military training. He was promised some instructors from the *cuartel general,* but they never arrived. Time went by and the swelling group remained in Rama, although they became restive. Conditions were uncomfortable for the neophyte revolutionaries (Dexter Hooker interview, 1986): "it wasn't too soft, too good. A lot of contradiction. And then the same fellow them start get frustrated because, well, they need a toothbrush, then need a pretty clothes, they need a new pants. And you know those guys them just not doing nothing up there." Small patrols undertook a few missions, during one of which a member of the original fifteen blew off his big toe. The racial tensions with the Rama Sandinistas continued. Then just as they were getting ready to mount their move downriver, the *cuartel* in Rama burned to the ground, destroying all the group's weapons.

During the more than three weeks they remained in Rama, Abel formed an *estado mayor* (staff). This consisted of himself as head and Eustace Wilshire (whose nom de guerre was Shaft), another Creole ATEPCA activist who had joined them at Rama, as *político* (chief of political affairs). They also selected leaders from the Asociación de Estudiantes Secundarias (AES—Association of High School Students), a group composed mostly of students from the Colón school in Bluefields who had organized in opposition to the Somoza regime. This group was mainly led by Mestizos, but a number of Creole students were active members. They had carried out a series of strikes at the Colón school since 1977 and were engaged in other politicizing activities as well. They had made contact with the FSLN in the mines (commanded by Comandantes Henry Ruiz and René Vivas) but had lost that connection. After the success of the PESCANICA operation became known, they sent representatives to Rama to make contact with the Bluefields group there who were known to be operating under orders of the FSLN. From this group, Charles Wilshire, Eustace's brother, Francisco López, Rubén López, and a third Mestizo were added to the *estado mayor.*

With the arrival and integration of members of this second group into Abel's group, this Bluefields revolutionary force became racially integrated at the level of both leadership and troops. It was clear to most, however, that Creoles were the dominant group within it.

In early July, Moisés Arana, the president of Bluefields' UDEL, and Gregory Smutko, an American missionary Catholic priest, arrived in Rama (Dexter Hooker interview, 1986): "a commission I think went up [to Rama] from here with Smutko and Arana, went up talking about we mustn't come war down here [Bluefields]. That the Guardia them want peace and so and so."

The contradictions, tensions, and jockeying for power that immediately emerged with this commission exacerbated the growing racial tensions in Bluefields. The Creole-led group in Rama, as the military force designated by the FSLN's National Directorate to take control of the Atlantic Coast, saw itself as the area's legitimate vanguard group. They suspected that Arana was trying to obtain this position for himself and the UDEL faction by negotiating the surrender of the Bluefields National Guard directly with the FSLN's leaders (Dexter Hooker interview, 1986): "He [Arana] basically claim mostly like he did wanted not to talk to us. [He wanted] to talk to Pancho [Luis Carrión] . . . Up there we done organize . . . an *estado mayor.* But Arana was more insisting to talk with a next level." Arana had in fact been in communication with the National Guard general and was planning to arrange their surrender directly to the FSLN National Directorate in Costa Rica.

Abel's group kept Arana in Rama against his will for two weeks, greatly exacerbating the enmity between the two groups. They told Arana that he was being held for his own protection. He may have been held to keep him from providing the National Guard general details about the FSLN forces in Rama; however, his interpretation was that "there was a desire for power, an ambition for power on the part of many persons who were interested that I stay in Rama" (Moisés Arana interview with Ray Hooker and Alicia Slate, 1983).

Then on July 18, the day after Somoza left the country, Abel and his group left Rama for Bluefields (Dexter Hooker interview, 1986): "in the morning before day a next Christian group went up there but with a next conception headed by Brother Ray, I think Thomas Kelly . . . and I think about three or four of them and say, well, you know, told us the situation were needed that we come down immediately and that's when we come down back." The members of this commission sent to facilitate Abel's group's takeover of Bluefields represented a number of important constituencies in the town's Creole community. Brother Ray Hodgson was a Creole Pentecostal pastor, former mayoral candidate, future mayor of Bluefields and governor of the region, and Jenelee Hodgson's brother. Thomas Kelly became an important Creole leader of the FSLN. Erica Hodgson, an important local leader of the Conservative Party, was a part of the commission, as was Gayland Vance, a leader of the adult chapter of SICC. The participation of representatives of these constituencies in support of Abel's group had important implications for Creole politics in the immediate post-Triumph period.

Abel, the rest of the *estado mayor,* and about a dozen others left immediately for Bluefields to assume control of the town. Moisés Arana was allowed to leave Rama only after they had departed. They arrived in Bluefields that same day, a day before the FSLN took over the national government.

The situation in Bluefields at the time of the Triumph was indeed propitious for the arrival of the group from Rama. As the legitimacy of the Somoza government waned and the social order disintegrated under attack from forces inside and outside Nicaragua, so did Creole support for the regime. Most Bluefields Creoles thought that it was time for an end to the Somozas' rule. By mid-July the town's schools, state offices, and some businesses were closed. Supplies of food and other essentials were getting low. The town was overflowing with refugees from the Pacific. Creoles had grown tired of the uncertainty and tensions. Formerly repressed historical resentments against the Somoza regime and its functionaries as the embodiment of the colonizing Mestizo state gathered force.

On the other hand, many Creoles, influenced by the events described earlier, by the attitude of the churches, and by anticommunist propaganda (e.g., the Voice of America), were afraid that an FSLN victory would mean "Cuban-style communism" in Nicaragua and discrimination against them as a group from that quarter. Despite these concerns, by July 1979, the majority of the Creole community was optimistic about the possibility that a new government would aid the Atlantic Coast in general and Creoles in particular (Roberto Hodgson interview, 1991):[5]

> People was just so enthusiastic. The seventeenth of July, when they heard that Somoza had turned over power and left the country, people were just crazy. Walked the streets and some piece of red and black flags are all over the place. Just a few minutes after when people heard that the vice-president [Urcuyo Maliaño] said but "I am going to stay." Ahhh! they tore down all the flags. They had even started pulling down the statue [of Somoza García] in the

park there and everybody just scattered. But of course two days after, when the vice-president really left for Guatemala, then things began again. The first days it was really chaotic, confusion.

Events of the following two months, however, had a lasting effect on Creole perceptions of the revolutionary process. The National Guard at Bluff and Bluefields had agreed before the Triumph to give up peacefully. After July 17, the day Somoza left the country, they remained in their barracks, as there was no constituted power in Bluefields to whom they could surrender. During these days of uncertainty, most of the top officials in the former PLN-dominated local government and a good part of the town's social and economic elite rapidly left the country by boat. Interestingly, all of the Mestizos in these categories left, whereas a good number of the Creoles remained, though they maintained a very low profile.

Who Are the Real Revolutionaries?

A power vacuum ensued. In most barrios, lightly armed civilian patrols were mounted to keep the peace. In the months before the Triumph a group of Mestizos led by a National Guard deserter and the Aragón twins (two local toughs) had engaged in a series of small military skirmishes with the National Guard in the famous Lara Swamp, a huge swamp outside of Bluefields. On July 17 this group occupied the Palacio, the major seat of civil, municipal, and departmental government in the zone, in the name of the FSLN. Members of the AES and a large number of unaffiliated individuals joined them there. These and other Mestizo leaders, including members of the UDEL such as Moisés Arana's brother Alfredo, met at the *casa cural* (rectory) and organized a *comité de defensa civil* (CDC—civil defense committee). This group and the National Guard, mediated by the Catholic bishop, entered into negotiations to take control of Bluefields (Wong López 1979).

Before the group from Rama arrived on the eighteenth, racial conflict had already broken out. Loyd Forbes, a longtime Creole union activist and an affiliate of the ATEPCA group, recalled what happened (interview with Ray Hooker and Alicia Slate, 1983):

> I can remember when I . . . went into the Palacio . . . the Spanish element there didn't permit me to go into the Palacio, so I questioned them there on the spot . . . 'cause I was well known [as an activist] . . . so right on the spot I told them, "All right, if I can't come into this Palacio, I'm going to Beholden [the largest Creole

barrio] and organize a *cuartel* with some of the Creole people," and I did that. . . . I organized the *cuartel* in which I had the boys . . . we gave them some guns when we could get them . . . [those in the Palacio] were like, say a group of boys controlled by the Arana brothers . . . they had a movement that was . . . like only Spanish people involved . . . already I knew . . . like a racial conflict was getting shaped up.

When the Creole-led group arrived from Rama, it was joined by many of the radical Colón students who had been in the *palacio*, the Creoles from the Beholden commando, and other sympathizers; however, they evidently rejected the aid of some of the CDC and sent them back to the *palacio*. The National Guard surrendered to the group led by Abel, which then occupied the former National Guard headquarters and barracks in Bluefields (the *cuartel*). On July 19, the FSLN took control of Nicaragua. The *cuartel* group under the direction of the *estado mayor* created in Rama and led by Abel moved immediately to establish control of much of the Coast in the name of the FSLN. Delegations were sent to key locations such as the Bluff, Corn Island, and Pearl Lagoon to assume control. In Bluefields the group moved to take control of the various command posts; however, as Dexter Hooker relates, they immediately ran into problems (interview, 1986):

[We] found a little commando up there like for the black people in Beholden. . . . then the Spanish people them—but without no political idea more like *maliant* [bad guys]—some [were] guarding COPESNICA [a fishing company]. The Spanish people commando [was] up in the *palacio* and I think one was up by San Mateo by the graveyard and then the Guardia them down here [*cuartel*]. Nobody touch nobody.

So we had to come in now to broke that. But we don't even know what kind of situation. So what we did we march down to the *cuartel* to see reaction. Okay. The reaction was peaceful . . . and we come and officially review and we take over . . .

I went up to the fellow [those in the commandos], "Okay, now we don't have any commando. This is one structure." But I think there is where the biggest feelings came in—we came in traditionally. I feel like is the same, you know, that, well, *the black now throw off the Spanish. I feel like there is the . . . essence of the problem . . . I mean they* [Mestizos] *had a lot of control now and these other people* [Creoles] *just going to come over them . . .* I mean the situation wasn't the best. (Emphasis added)

The group in the *palacio* left the building but soon returned, angered that they had not been called on to form part of the military leadership represented by those in the *cuartel*. They accused the *cuartel* group of improperly instigating tensions in Bluefields for the sole purpose of grabbing power (Moisés Arana interview with Ray Hooker and Alicia Slate, 1983):

> [After the fall of Somoza] . . . everything was tranquil, production
> continued tranquilly, the Guardia did not leave the *cuartel* . . .
> civilians guarded the town; frankly, there was tranquillity. . . . the
> problem arose when the *compañeros* who had carried out the
> operation at PESCANICA arrived. That is when the uneasiness
> started . . . then different positions were taken . . . That is when a
> strange process of struggle. I maintain that it was a struggle for
> power more than anything else; the process of enmity . . . and the
> group that came from Rama grabbed the power.

The *palacio* group further accused those in the *cuartel* of fomenting racial division by advocating "black power" (Eustace Wilshire interview, 1983). They refused to leave the *palacio* and claimed that they were the legitimate representatives of the FSLN in Bluefields. This claim was reinforced by the arrival of a young woman and man from Chontales with the FSLN representative from Rama. They claimed to represent the Estado Mayor del Frente Oriental Roberto Huembes. This group was nominally in control of Chontales and Zelaya Sur for the FSLN and was commanded by Luis Carrión (Moisés Arana interview with Ray Hooker and Alicia Slate, 1983):

> In a few days an FSLN delegation from Chontales appeared with a
> *compañera* and *compañero* whom I know. They told me that they
> had brought a list of eight persons to form the Regional Govern-
> ment of Bluefields, the Junta de Reconstrucción, . . . they came and
> told me that it was very important that I read this list and tell
> them which persons on it I was interested in or not and what we
> could change. I said I was grateful, I headed the list . . . I said . . . it's
> preferable that you place on it a pastor from the Moravian Church
> so that you have variety and not only racial but religious.

The *cuartel* group claims to have not been consulted about the Junta's composition nor were any of its leaders placed on it. They denied its legitimacy and did not allow it to exercise power. Moisés Arana recalls the racial character of this conflict (interview with Ray Hooker and Alicia Slate, 1983):

Then began one of the saddest things that I have had happen in my life. They began to say that it was Moisés Arana who is making the Junta and that it is Moisés Arana who is racist and that he is against the blacks and then something arose . . . something against . . . to the extreme that they . . . raised, I remember, a placard which said *"Arana and Somoza are the same thing"*. . . .
     After this . . . I couldn't, for fifteen days, do anything in the Junta. They blocked me totally. There were problems with Abel. There were problems with other *compañeros* who were with Abel . . . and then the famous Kalalú appeared. (Emphasis added)

A report from the ill-fated Junta to the national *estado mayor* of the FSLN written in the midst of crisis over Creole opposition to its formation described "a meeting in the Old Bank barrio where militiamen associated with Abel and colored politicians . . . cried and swore that they would struggle against what they interpreted as a continuation of white domination over blacks, almost like Somocismo without Somoza" (Wong López 1979).

Both the *cuartel* and the *palacio* groups claimed to represent the FSLN. In some sense, both probably did, since each was in contact with and sponsored by a different tendency in the FSLN's politico-military organization. At this early date, the provisional central government was not fully operational and coordination was deficient.
     Power struggles between politico-military factions in other areas of Nicaragua during this chaotic moment were not uncommon. Unfortunately, the particular history of racial/cultural social divisions on the Atlantic Coast transformed this struggle for local power into a full-scale racial/cultural confrontation. Many Creoles in Bluefields believed at the time of the Triumph that they would be the ones to take political control of the area. By the time of the Triumph, most Creoles supported the Sandinistas' efforts to end the Somozas' rule and had begun to resonate to portions of the former's political discourse. Moreover, during this period of social dysfunction, a "utopian project" based in Creole populism had begun to take form in the Creole community. The emerging social movement that embodied this project was articulated by Creoles with the Sandinista movement.
     As the Creoles understood it, the Revolution had been fought to return power to the people. To their minds, they *were* the people of Bluefields and by rights should govern it, thereby returning to their deserved positions of local political power and socioeconomic prominence. As Moisés Arana's and William Wong's (a Chinese/Mestizo member of the *palacio* group) statements indicate, the perceived racism of the Mestizos

was read by Creoles in that moment as antirevolutionary, the reincarnation of Somocismo.

The *cuartel* group, as the champion of the Creole community's utopian project, had its overwhelming support. Dexter Hooker, Eustace Wilshire, and other black Sandinistas who were the leaders of this group actively recruited Creoles to their cause and their vision of the Revolution on the basis of racial/cultural identity and rights. A Creole former OPROCO member and Somoza supporter in a 1985 conversation told me that while he was lying low in his house during the unstable period just after the Triumph, he remembered Wilshire walking through the streets of Cotton Tree with a rifle over his shoulder and rallying the Creole community. He called for them to come out of their houses: "Creoles of Bluefields, this is your chance. Come out and defend your rights."

The community recognized the black Sandinistas as their leaders and their ideology as the leading ideas in the broad social movement that coalesced around the struggle to consolidate Creole power; however, individuals who were members of other political groupings of Creoles were active in this social movement as well. Key roles were played by Creoles who were associated with SICC, such as Ray Hodgson, Gayland Vance, and Hernan Savery. They saw in the movement a response to the internal colonial racism of Mestizos, which had been the object of their ire.

The bulk of the *cuartel's* military personnel, however, were very loosely organized young men from the Creole barrios. They were generally from families of lower economic status and not well educated. Some, like Berto Archibald, who became the *cuartel* group's commander at the Bluff, were from families closely associated with SICC. Some of these youth were associated with the emerging rasta group that would become known as Culture for I.

In general, the members of the *cuartel* troop were stereotyped by the bulk of Bluefields' population as low-status "*vagos*," or "bad boys." This slightly disreputable status was most often symbolized by their reputation as marijuana smokers. Many of them did in fact smoke the drug, which had become quite popular among Creole youth during the mid-1970's; however, the smoking of ganja was only one aspect of an oppositional cultural identity that was emerging among this sector of the Creole community.

The consumption of and identification with commodified black diasporic culture on the part of Creole youth played an important role in the emergence of an oppositional racial politics during this moment. Percy González, one of the leaders of Bluefields' rasta community, remembers how reggae and rasta entered Bluefields and became popular as a mode of cultural expression for Creole youth (interview, 1991):

Well, round in '77, '78, a lot of Jamaican fisherman used to be around here fishing up Tasbapaunie and they used to come here to Bluefields, some of them did even living at Bada house, and the same time the music start come in, the reggae music, . . . well, we first start check out the dancing because when they used to have them house party and one or two of the fellow used to go and dance, he dance in a way that nobody used to dance round here, . . . everybody still used to dance soul music, . . . but we see them man them, so we ourselves start picking up the style and dancing when we go party . . . from there then it start popular.

Ganja smoking by Creole youth as part of this cultural complex had begun a few years before the Triumph; however, the wearing of dreadlocks, the icon of rasta and its black nationalist cultural politics, began only after the Triumph at precisely this moment of racialized identification and conflict. Most of the young Creole men identified closely with the newly popular "dread" culture of Jamaica and the Anglophone Caribbean. An important aspect of this identification was a growing pride in blackness and a firm rhetorical stance against racism. Their attempt to consolidate Creole control of the Coast under the auspices of the Revolution fit well with this emerging cultural politics.

Kalalú, Black Power, and Conflict

As the power struggle between the *palacio* and *cuartel* groups intensified, an African Costa Rican, Marvin Wrights, locally known as "Kalalú," arrived in Bluefields. He had entered Nicaragua with the Brigada Simón Bolívar, a military contingent of international supporters of the Revolution. Kalalú was a gifted orator and charismatic leader. He soon became an adviser to the *cuartel* group. He brought with him a brand of Trotskyist black nationalism new to the city and was instrumental in inciting the Creole population to demand what they believed to be their rights (Dexter Hooker interview, 1986):

Most of the people mixed up in those moment were black people, as I said before. So then it's like a feeling of identification through being black towards the Revolution. And they get a next bigger shove from the moment that the Simón Bolívar came down and they has a guy that in history we didn't know a guy black could talk and talk politics to them like Kalalú. . . .

Kalalú call the black workers and start organizing unions and syndicates and with this pretty way of talking, you know, the black people really started.

On the other side, the Bluefields Mestizo community came to the support of those headquartered in the *palacio*. In the face of *cuartel* group accusations that they were racists, those associated with the Palacio claimed that "we do not have anything against blacks, only against a particular group." They accused Abel of being incapable of managing the military affairs of the region. They also were enraged by what they saw as Creole racism and high-handedness expressed as favoritism toward blacks at the expense of Mestizos in the distribution of food and weapons. And in the gravest accusation, they claimed that the *cuartel*'s Creole youth reproduced the authoritarian practices of the National Guard they had replaced.[6]

Rasta leader Percy González remembered the tenure of one of his friends as commander of the Bluff (interview, 1991):

> Well, I did went gone visit Archie one of the time. You know he did—I laugh because we is brethren . . . I see some time his atti-tude, how he act. He come back different. Not different, well, he the same. But toward next people he act like he want to show, well, demand respect or something. For instance he used to—a black guy have a lot of beard, he had a big beard, strapping. People come want to talk to him. He got a sitting table and he got a lamp flashing down in the visitor face and him behind there and talking to you rough—all under pressure then.

The most fundamental criticism had to do with what Mestizo leaders felt was the low intellectual and moral standing of the Creole group. The fact that many of these Creole youth smoked marijuana was the basis of the most vociferous and long-lasting Mestizo criticisms of this group.[7] Concern with groups' intellectual and moral capacity clearly was asso-ciated with Mestizo commonsense assumptions about the natural character of blacks, especially poor ones.

As the situation deteriorated, interracial-cultural animosity became the order of the day in Bluefields. Members of the opposing groups were afraid to venture into each other's barrio. Racial tensions in the local high schools, particularly the Moravian High School, became acute. Various juntas organized along racial/cultural lines and failed. In frustra-tion, most of the members of the biracial group of radical Colón students separated from the *cuartel* group and began to organize the Juventud Sandinista (Sandinista Youth) and the *comités de defensa civil*.

The conflicts finally came to a head. Sectors of the *cuartel* group organized what they intended to be a peaceful demonstration of the Creole community in the town park facing the *palacio* to demand that the *palacio* group give up its pretensions. The latter got wind of the plans, assumed it was a military attack, and took up defensive positions. That same afternoon, the Brigada Simón Bolívar convinced leaders of the *cuartel* group that those in the *palacio* should be evacuated by force if necessary. The *cuartel* leaders led an armed contingent to the *palacio* to carry this out.[8] Family members and others in the Mestizo community turned out to support the *palacio* group. A chaotic scene ensued in which the large civilian presence precluded military action (Dexter Hooker interview, 1986):

> That first concentration . . . Kalalú then even turn it. Because the thing with the Palacio then it start take a taste of like, black. The black commando down here and the Spanish commando there.
> . . . I think were one of the biggest manifestation we ever had in Bluefields and worse black people. And not coming out to say let's inquire. You know, hollering and talking. But, basically, it was a manifestation of the racism.

The crowd milled about from 5:00 to 9:00 or 10:00 PM, freely exchanging slogans, threats, epithets, and fists. What happened next is not clear. Apparently, one of the armed *cuartel* Creoles became overexcited and shot himself accidentally. There are, however, many people who still insist that the two sides exchanged gunfire that resulted in deaths. The shooting scattered the crowd, which was then kept out of the area by the combined *cuartel*/Brigada Simón Bolívar troops. An ultimatum was given to the poorly armed *palacio* group. By 11:00 PM the latter had abandoned the *palacio* and were dispersed. Creoles were, however briefly, the rulers of Bluefields.

Again, at this point, during the first weeks after the Triumph, most sectors of the Creole community were solidly behind the Revolution as locally led by black Sandinistas. They acted according to their understanding of how revolutionaries were supposed to act: they called each other *compañero*; they initiated worker control in the local sugar mill; young Creole men joined the militia and their families supported them by providing food and moral support. Creoles began collectively to rebuild their neighborhoods. They participated in the local Comités de la Defensa Sandinista, organizations designed for communal self-help and defense of the Revolution.

Managua Descends

It was inevitable, however, that the conflicts in Bluefields would bring a response from the FSLN in Managua. In fact, before the *palacio* group was disbanded, it sent a delegation of five to Managua to denounce those in the *cuartel* as undisciplined separatists and to ask for assistance. Shortly after the *palacio* group was forcibly disbanded, the FSLN's national *estado mayor* dispatched a high-level military commander, Comandante René Vivas, and a contingent of inexperienced troops from Puerto Cabezas to Bluefields to restore order. They immediately assumed military and political control of the town, disarmed the *cuartel* group, and deported Kalalú (Dexter Hooker interview, 1986):

> And then René Vivas came down . . . he came down and immediately brought some people down from Cabezas and now basically the black people what was in the commando was taken out of it . . . by the time I get back, well, all the conception of the commando— when we reach, you know, where all the black people—you know the commando was something popular. By the time we reach back it was all changed then. But it changed because essentially all the black man was out of it and then the Mestizos them took over completely . . . And I think where there were a lot of feelings come back to these fellows that, you know, were recognized as marijuana smokers or, you know, let's say, socially low level and then these other guys them that had, let's say, a little intellectual capacity just take away the gun and say, okay, thank you, you go home now and now you come you take this because your moral status is different and I didn't believe in that then . . .
>
> With the taking out of Kalalú and taking out all the structure [the *cuartel* group's *estado mayor*]. I think then the black spirit then just turn right back. Because . . . the first days them in the black neighborhoods the people them was working.

Most Creole leaders of the *cuartel* group were either sent to Managua or out of the country for further education. A Bluefields Junta for Municipal Reconstruction was formed and its membership approved at a public meeting held in the town park. The junta included representatives of the two ethnic groups and the major religious denominations.

The Creole community, however, was not satisfied. Creoles had not gotten the power they thought they deserved. The fact that Mestizo representatives from Managua came to Bluefields and imposed a solution that, in their eyes, denied them that power was not appreciated. Some of the members of the *cuartel* group declined to turn in their arms. Secret meetings were held to plan action. The Creole barrios, which had briefly burst into action for community uplift, turned sullen and restive. The *cuartel*, which had been a center of Creole social activity but was now in the hands of troops from outside Bluefields, was shunned.

In response to these developments, the national Sandinista *estado mayor* sent a contingent of battle-hardened special troops headed by Comandante William Ramírez from Managua. They rapidly brought the situation under control by totally disbanding the *cuartel* group. They became the first non-Creole military contingent to undertake an operation in the black barrios.

Though there were no clashes, the operation had a negative impact on the community. Subsequently, the Government Junta for National Reconstruction asked Comandante Ramírez officially to oversee Atlantic Coast affairs, relieving Comandante Vivas.

Just prior to this, the FSLN had appointed Comandante Lumberto Campbell as military commander under Comandante Vivas. The people of Bluefields thought that Campbell, a Creole born in Bluefields, had been killed in combat during the revolutionary struggle. On his arrival, he was emotionally received by the Creole community, which hoped that through him their cultural aspirations would be realized. Their enthusiasm was dampened, however, by the fact that Vivas and then Ramírez, Mestizos from the Pacific, were his superiors and the supreme authorities on the Atlantic Coast.

The foregoing events occurred within the space of about five weeks (July 17 to approximately August 24, 1979). This short period of time was crucial in the formation of Creole perceptions of the Revolution. At the Triumph of the Revolution, Creoles were swept away by a utopian vision of Creole autonomy, and Creole populism became even more central to the organization of Creole political ideas and practices. Initial Creole optimism that the Revolution would restore their rights as a group waned, though, as intercultural tensions heightened and Mestizo Sandinistas from the central government seemed to support other Mestizos in local, racialized power struggles. Basing their evaluation of the Revolution on the organizing ideas of Creole populism, many Creoles began to see the Revolution as a Mestizo project that could not serve their community's interests.

The failure of the social movement led by the black Sandinistas to consolidate control of the local state apparatus had negative implications for their ideological leadership of the larger Creole community. These leaders clearly understood the racial character of their struggle for power with local Mestizo Sandinistas. For a brief moment, they had been able to forge a new popular politics by articulating the revolutionary politics of the FSLN with Creole populism.

Most of the black Sandinista leaders, however, remained loyal to the FSLN, even after having lost their bid for local power. To align their politics with the Sandinistas, for whom the problems of racial and

cultural difference within the nation were considered divisive, and to
rationalize their continued loyalty to the Revolution, struggles around
racial/cultural issues internal to Nicaragua had to be subordinated to
those centering on national liberation and class struggle. "Black Is
Beautiful but . . .," a poem written in the early 1980's by Carl Rigby, the
preeminent Creole poet of the period and a longtime black Sandinista, is
exemplary of this repositioning:

> black is beautiful—but . . .
>   not this de kind a way:
>   in the *back*
>   they still put you to bed
>   with their diversionist talk about black:
>   that there is neither white yellow nor red
>   :the *ones* who do us this is because they handle the bread
>   . . . but it's time to wake-up now
>   :and *we* know why and *we* know how . . .
>   after all—who the hell you think built the color-wall!?
>   :black is no class—
>   let's not be an ass!
>   :there is no time to stare at the clock
>   ...:come on! :find your flock
>   and you will see that the poor and working class a people
>   can only be as high as a steeple
>   if we take-down those who are setting us back
>   :and this goes for white yellow red and black—

In a 1983 interview with me, Eustace Wilshire, who had been *político*
of the *cuartel* group, also clearly emphasized class issues over those of
race and culture: "speak of demands not of Miskitu, nor of Sumu, nor
Rama, nor Creole, nor Mestizo . . . we speak of a general revolution of
poor people." He went on to state that Creoles who claimed that the
Revolution was racist did so because they did not understand their own
history of racist oppression by foreign whites and were in other ways
beholden to them:

> There are some blacks who are saying that this struggle [the
> Revolution] is racist. They are taking up the customs of outsiders.
> I can agree that blacks are black no matter where you take them,
> but I can assure you that there are black reactionaries. . . . Here in
> Bluefields the blacks do not know their history . . . they do not
> know their roots, they do not even know why they were slaves,
> there are those who do not want to accept this theory and who

do not know why they have to defend the victory [of the Revolution] . . . the black still does not know how he got here to Nicaragua . . .

What is more, if we look at the black sector, 80 percent have family members in the U.S. Therefore, they cannot be against the United States because monthly the dollars come.

The rejection of a political discourse and practice that articulated with Creole populism—the set of ideas that dominated Creole political perspectives during this moment—cost the black Sandinistas their leadership role in the social movement they had initiated and led. It also meant that their political ideas and those of the FSLN in general were increasingly seen by the Creole community as marginal to the latter's interests as a community.

Despite this growing unease, many Creoles continued to be active in revolutionary work such as neighborhood cleanup and improvement, child vaccination drives, civilian militia, and, later, the literacy campaign. As an example, even after the arrival of René Vivas, Hernan Savery led a number of SICC members (a group that would soon become very critical of the Revolution) who had volunteered to travel to Honduras to recover stolen fishing boats for the Revolution. The rapid expansion of the revolutionary state meant that many Creoles, who were the best-educated Costeños, were able to obtain jobs in the expanded bureaucracy. The Revolution also promoted a number of popular initiatives that seemed to promise rapid economic expansion. Percy González, remembering this period, commented (interview 1991): "For the beginning, it did really look bright round in the '80's, '82, things did look bright. 'Cause, for instance, I did get on a job little—round in '80. Used to go buy grains, rice in hull up the communities. The bank did lending money to the farmers them. Things did working on." Subsequent events, however, many of which were associated with the newly consolidated revolutionary government's efforts to transform the nation's political and economic institutions, slowly fed the Creoles' growing disillusionment.

The Beginnings of a Shift

Sandinista Policies Have Their Effect

Immediately after the Triumph, the public sector expanded rapidly in Bluefields as the revolutionary government created new institutions to implement its programs. The domination of the economy by foreign capital and the Somoza family had been far more complete on the

Atlantic Coast than in any other region of Nicaragua. As a consequence, confiscations of these interests' properties created a state sector on the Coast far larger than anywhere else in the country. The central government, fearing the Costeños' lack of revolutionary consciousness and desire for autonomy, sent a trusted Mestizo cadre from Managua to take over top positions.

Three instances of this practice were especially controversial. The national government appointed Comandante Ramírez minister of INNICA, an institution created in 1980 to coordinate all government activities on the Atlantic Coast. He also took responsibility for the regional FSLN party structure. Creoles thought that Comandante Campbell was the appropriate choice for these positions.

The new central government placed the fishing industry, the economic backbone of southern Zelaya and a traditional Coast activity, under the control of Mestizos from Managua who had little practical experience to recommend their appointment. Creoles took pride in being the experienced originators of this industry, and this snub was deeply resented.

In a particularly undiplomatic move, in 1979 the revolutionary government replaced a highly respected Creole medical doctor, Roberto Hodgson, with a young Mestiza doctor from Managua as head of the region's Department of Health. The Creole doctor had been appointed to the position only months before and was not notified of the change before it occurred. This move had a strongly negative impact on Creole participation in government-sponsored health campaigns. Roberto Hodgson described these events and their effect on the community to me in 1991:

> Just two months after, a group of younger people [Ramírez and Campbell] came in from the Pacific . . . and I was removed . . . They sent a letter naming Martha Medina. . . . She came from León. She was doing her social service, and she took over. . . . She was sent down, and I was in Managua . . . getting off materials . . . It was a move from Managua. . . . That happened in September of '79.
> . . . most of people started making a big noise about it. . . . most of the young leaders . . . they made up a letter with signatures.

The government also assigned many Mestizos from the Coast, whom they considered more supportive of the Revolution than Creoles, to positions of responsibility. In 1978, the year before the Triumph, Mestizos held 62 percent of the leadership positions in state institutions, major political parties, and large privately owned companies in southern Zelaya, while 31 percent were held by Creoles. By 1980 the FSLN had moved to consolidate its hold on local political and economic power. There were no longer opposition political parties openly operating in the area, and all the large private companies had been nationalized. As part of this process, the percentage of Mestizos in leadership positions in the area (state institutions and mass organizations) rose to 78 percent while Creoles held only 22 percent of these positions. In 1985, at the end of the period covered in this book, despite the FSLN's policy at that time of involving more Creoles in the leadership of the region, 70 percent of the top leadership positions were held by Mestizos and 30 percent by Creoles.[9]

Overall, then, the rising expectations created by Creole identification of their utopian project (based on Creole populism) with that of the Revolution became increasingly incongruent with the realities of Sandinista policy. Creoles resented Mestizo occupation of politically and economically important posts. They could not understand how Mestizos from the Pacific with little or no knowledge of the Atlantic Coast could be hired instead of Creoles equally or more qualified for state jobs. What the Creole community considered to be extravagant and discriminatory salaries and social benefits received by these interlopers only exacerbated the situation.

Relations between the Protestant Creole churches and the Sandinistas were also problematic during this period. Church leaders felt threatened by large-scale Creole participation in revolutionary activities. In particular, Creole participation in the Sandinistas' organized health and neighborhood cleanup campaigns on Saturdays and Sundays significantly reduced church attendance in the period immediately after the Triumph. Church leaders saw their power over the Creole community beginning to slip away. As a result, some church leaders were among the first and most influential critics of the Revolution.

The ethnic tensions brewing in the Moravian High School in the weeks following the Triumph worsened this situation. The school became an institutional focal point for Creole dissatisfaction with the revolutionary process. Many of the Creole teachers and students held, and voiced, sentiments critical of the Revolution. Two of the leaders of SICC, which had not been publicly active since before the Triumph but was nevertheless viewed with trepidation by the Sandinistas, taught at the high school. The school was also a place of employment and, to a certain extent, refuge for former OPROCO members who had also been PLN members and who would not or could not leave the country, as the Somocista Mestizo elite had.

As a result, the Moravian High School was a target of Sandinista suspicion. This was greatly resented by Creoles and cast by them in racial terms. For many years, Creole memory of this hostility was symbolized by a statement attributed to Miss Angélica Brown, a member of SICC and at that time a teacher in the Moravian High School. During an open meeting between local Sandinista representatives and the Creole community in the Moravian High School gym, she is reported to have asked Sandinista representatives: "Why when the blacks have meetings do you worry and when the Mestizos have meetings you do not?" For Creoles the statement neatly summed up Sandinista identification with Mestizos in an atmosphere of racial/cultural antipathy as well as Sandinista opposition to Creole political organization.

In the final months of 1979, the Creole pastor and director of the Moravian High School was denounced by the revolutionary government as having been an informer for the Somoza regime. Shortly thereafter he left Nicaragua. The Creole community alleged that he was not given an opportunity to defend himself, and the government never presented public proof of the charges. Bishop John Wilson recalled this series of events and their impact on the Creole community in the following terms (interview with R. Hooker and Alicia Slate, 1983):

> Well, William [Ramírez] was really upset. He didn't even take Rev. Miller [the alleged informer] into account. And I pleaded. I said, "Well, William, give the man a chance to defend himself" and he said no he wouldn't. So, well, Rev. Miller got very upset and I guess a little nervous because this thing was a shock . . . So, well, the verdict was that he have to leave the country between so many days. Well, he came home, told his wife, and they all broke down. Then they packed their things and tried to get out the country; they went the Monday. I accompanied them to Managua and ever since the Moravian community has been pressuring me to do something about Rev. Miller . . . So up to the present there is this sort of ill-feeling towards, I guess, the government for not having clarified and not having met the demands of our people . . . because the proofs have not been shown to the people, they sort of have lost confidence and, well, they sort of blame me, too.

Bishop Wilson's memory of the Miller episode points up another crucial aspect of the deteriorating relationship between the Sandinistas and the Moravian Church. A number of the nationalist and modernizing Creole pastors were relatively sympathetic to the revolutionary process and attempted to play a mediating role between the Sandinistas and the Creole community; however, as these relations worsened, they were caught between these forces. Because the Sandinistas were unyielding in their demands for the recognition of revolutionary power, the conciliatory moves of these pastors were registered as capitulation by the Creole community. This greatly reduced their influence within the Nicaraguan Moravian Church structures and with their congregations. This in turn undermined attempts at reconciliation between the church, the Creole community it represented, and the revolutionary state.

During this same period, the pastor of Bluefields' Baptist church was jailed when his refusal to participate in a neighborhood cleanup campaign degenerated into a heated oral exchange between him and some overzealous soldiers. Though he was released as soon as Comandante Campbell got word of his arrest, sectors of the Creole community were outraged that one of their religious leaders should suffer such an indignity.

The Sandinistas' major concern, though, was with the Moravian Church. They saw it as a competing power on the Coast, one that disposed Costeños to the divisiveness of racial/cultural identity and politics and identification with imperialist forces. In a secret memorandum written by the vice-minister of INNICA probably in early 1982, this comes out clearly: "The structure of the Moravian Church, its form of organization and pastoral activity, fertilizes the terrain of separatism and by its own character and historical antecedents deepens the indigenous communities' ethnic problem. . . . the training of its cadre and its international links are related to this objective" (Samarriba n.d.).

These and other problems between the Creole churches and the revolutionary government contrasted with the good relationship that existed between the latter and the Catholic Church in the region. In the same internal policy memo, Comandante Samarriba recommended that the Sandinistas work to "take away the social base of the Moravian Church and pass it over to the control of the Catholic Church," where, from his perspective, the Sandinistas had "more political control." The contrast between the positive Catholic Church/Sandinista relations and the latter's problematic relations with the Moravians further fueled the growing Creole belief that the Revolution had little respect for them as a people or for their institutions.

There were other aspects of the troubled interaction between the Protestant Creole churches and the revolutionary government that had negative implications for Creole/Sandinista relations. One of the guiding principles of the Revolution was the state's responsibility to provide its citizenry with basic social services (i.e., health, education, and welfare). After the Triumph, the revolutionary government rapidly moved to assume this responsibility, which had previously been in the hands of the churches. In fact, in the half decade before the Triumph and in the years immediately following it, the newly nationalized Moravian Church had significantly stepped up the scope of its social program through CASIM. The revolutionary state's increasing arrogation of control in these areas effectively reduced church power. Comandante Samarriba recommended the elimination of CASIM and measures that would "prohibit the development of economic social activities by churches and limit them to religious activities." Members of the Creole community began to feel that the Revolution was attempting to eliminate the church or at least to limit its power.

In sum, the Protestant churches, and particularly the Moravians, were one of the few venues where Creoles could exercise political and economic power in the region. Weakening or eliminating them implied loss of power as a racial/cultural group. The Sandinistas recognized the centrality of the Protestant churches, and particularly the Moravian Church, to the exercise of local racial/cultural power and worked to undermine it. In the words of Comandante Samarriba, "It is impossible to resolve the ethnic political problems and the maneuvers of the counterrevolution without dismembering and controlling the Moravian Church in all of its dimensions." The Sandinistas, to my knowledge, never embarked on a policy as radical as Samarriba's recommendations; however, Sandinista policy and practice weakened the power of the Protestant churches and, as a consequence, Creoles felt power slipping from their grasp.

To these woes were added a continual series of circumstances and events that seemed to reconfirm Sandinista racial/cultural insensitivity and eroded Creole support for the Revolution. For example, the Sandinistas under the direction of INNICA, which was established in 1980, began a national campaign to publicize their goal of modernizing and incorporating the Atlantic Coast. In newspaper articles, on murals and placards, and in advertisements across the country, they referred to the Coast as the "Awakening Giant." This infuriated Creoles, even though the metaphor seems to have originated in the Creole community in the 1970's. Creoles felt that they were already awake, already more advanced than the Mestizos, and that the phrase as used by the Sandinistas was denigrating. A huge mural painted on the face of the Palacio by the revolutionary government depicted a black man seeming to worship the rising sun painted in the likeness of Sandino. This not only invoked the awakening metaphor but also seemed to Creoles both anti-Christian and to advocate black subservience to the Mestizo Sandinistas.

SICC began to reemerge in late 1979 and stepped into the leadership position in Creole politics left vacant by the abdication of the black Sandinistas. As those who had been involved in the Creole community's post-Triumph effort to seize power disengaged or were pushed out of their positions, they and those leaders who had remained inactive began to meet privately at the Moravian High School. In November CEPAD invited four SICC leaders to attend the meeting in Puerto Cabezas between Daniel Ortega and indigenous leaders from which MISU-RASATA emerged. Jenelee Hodgson, Hernan Savery, Angélica Brown, and Iván Cassanova attended. For a variety of reasons, some of which I discussed in chapter 5, Ortega and the Sandinistas were not interested in having the Creoles participate in the indigenous organization he helped form (Jenelee Hodgson interview, 1995): "We saw then that the Sandinistas had no intention of ever taking us into account. . . . No, he [Ortega] never did recognize us. And when we claim him . . . 'what about us?' . . . he said, 'Don't even mention the Creoles' . . . We were very insulted." Ortega even went as far as to state that black racial politics had no place in the revolutionary process (Anonymous 1979b).

By early 1980 SICC began to meet again publicly, organizing seminars and festivals and renewing plans for the education and development of the Creole community. Its members soon became embroiled in the divisive controversy over the Revolutionary Government's literacy campaign. Some of its leaders were centrally involved in agitating for and then planning the campaign in English. According to Hernan Savery, most of the SICC members were enrolled in the original campaign in Spanish as teachers; however, most resented the initial Sandinista position that all Nicaraguans should be taught to read and write only in Spanish. They were further incensed by the Sandinistas' reluctance to initiate a literacy campaign in English and were infuriated when it was canceled before it had reached its goals. SICC's Creoles viewed this as racial discrimination.

Creole political positions, led by SICC, regarding their inclusion in MISURASATA and the literacy campaign indicate a continuing preoccupation with racial/cultural issues correlated with Creole populism through late 1980. The organization was simultaneously beginning to focus on issues more closely articulated with elements of Anglo ideology, however (Jenelee Hodgson interview, 1995): "Gayland Vance was coming down from Old Bank and he said to Erica Hodgson, 'Erica, how this thing look like it going left.' Erica said, 'Damn if it gone left' . . . it not going, it gone."

Some SICC leaders, like Jenelee Hodgson, seem never to have been sympathetic toward the Sandinistas. Her reservations, and probably those of others who were deeply involved in the life of the Coast's churches, had much to do with their association of the FSLN with communism and what they understood to be communism's opposition to religion.

Creoles in general were also very uneasy about the confiscations of private property that the Sandinistas initiated after they stabilized the revolutionary state's control over Bluefields. Before the Triumph, the story circulated in the Creole community that in Castro's Cuba if you had a pair of shoes one shoe would be taken away and given to someone else. In addition to the fishing plants and other large enterprises, some of the property of former Somocistas, particularly those who had left the country was confiscated.

The idea that socializing property was a mandate of the revolutionary state was so strong that some Creoles redistributed their wealth without being directed to do so. Renowned boat captain Alan Stephenson (interview, 1991):

> If you had four boats you had to get rid of three. Well, it really wasn't official. But it was some kind of a decree they had here, and if you had a taxi you couldn't have a store and whatever business you had. If you had a truck besides, you had to sell that truck to the driver . . . And we start to have a little bit of timidity and you know we didn't argue the point. And, really, it didn't sound too bad at the time.

Not everyone was as open as Mr. Alan. George Berger (interview, 1991): "What did make them [Creoles] mad from the beginning is the same thing. Taking way people's things, people property, people house. That was the main, main, main thing that about what everybody was vexed about. . . . Those are the things . . . that make the people them get against them."

There was a large demonstration in Bluefields in early 1980 to protest the confiscation of a pawnshop and the practice of state appropriation in general. Most of the confiscated property, however, belonged to Mestizos or foreigners, and the bulk of the leaders of and participants in the demonstration were Mestizos. Nevertheless, the idea that the FSLN was moving toward communism was gaining currency and was viewed as a threat by sectors of the Creole community. The community's commonsense ideas that I have grouped under the rubric "Anglo ideology," though not the predominant organizing ideas of Creole politics during this period, influenced their thinking about the Revolution.

In 1980 the revolutionary government asked the Cuban government for aid in the reconstruction of the country. The Cubans sent technicians, medical workers, teachers, and so on, a number of whom came to the Atlantic Coast. They were to fill the positions left vacant by technical personnel who had left the country after the Triumph, particularly in the local hospital and fishing plants. Some were also to teach in rural communities, where there was a severe shortage of qualified teachers. The Creole community reacted negatively to the Cuban presence.

Many Creoles worried that the Cuban teachers would give their children a communist rather than a Christian education. Others feared that the aid workers threatened their economic position: they thought Cuban teachers would take the jobs of Creole teachers; Cuban medical personnel, those of Creole medical personnel; Cuban technicians and boat captains, those of Creole captains and technicians in the fishing industry; and so on. Workers in the fishing industry and teachers were particularly vocal. A number of their leaders went to Comandante Ramírez to protest the situation but either left dissatisfied with his response or were turned away. The situation became very tense. Miss Jenelee remembered (interview, 1995) that "things were getting hot now, the unrest is rising . . . August, September [1980], and whew! it was rising. The people were talking. People were up and down. People were commenting they couldn't stand it. So many were getting information about the Cuban captains and losing their jobs. The teachers were going to be substituted for Cuban teachers." SICC played a key role in the mobilization of the Creole population (Jenelee Hodgson interview, 1995):

> We [SICC] were meeting. Then is when we started. We had the barrios who started to bring in the ideas of the possibility that the government was not going to last and that we—since we had representation from every barrio and had representatives from every social group—we were the ones responsible to make it known, to make a public manifestation as to what the Sandinistas were doing.

For some time, key members of SICC had been meeting with representatives of a variety of forces interested in destabilizing the revolutionary government. In 1986 Hernan Savery told me that he had met on a number of occasions with a North American who was promoting a drive to have the United Nations recognize the independence of the Atlantic Coast. According to Savery, a small group of adult male SICC members met on a number of occasions to discuss this option. Savery added that the North American had offered money for organizing and had discussed the possibility of mercenary troop support in exchange for rights to exploit Coast resources after independence. According to Savery (interview, 1986), he personally was skeptical about these plans, for they would mean "war with Nicaragua and the rest of Central America"; however, "the older men in SICC loved the idea."

By mid-1980 others of the older male members of SICC, including Savery, were also in conversation with representatives of political parties in opposition to the Sandinistas and other Mestizos in Managua who were dissatisfied with the Revolution. Savery mentioned Bernardino Larios, Eden Pastora, and Roberto Pineda as people he personally met with to discuss their mutual discontent with the Sandinistas. Miss Jenelee remembers this crucial period with some bitterness (interview, 1995):

> I didn't know that Savery was talking to someone outside . . . until afterwards when we had several of these gringos come down and one by one they were asking questions. By this time we didn't know. I personally did not know what the men were doing, but they were in something else. They began to use SICC at that moment as a front . . . All I knew was that the people were being supplanted. The people were losing their jobs to the Cubans and I was completely against that. . . . They all had their other interests but SICC was the only organized group. . . . Dickie Jackson, he was talking to some of the Somoza people that had left. And Gayland [Vance] was talking to the Conservatives. Fire Fire [Archibald] was talking to the Conservative people. And here I am with this cultural group. . . . Savery was talking to the . . . we call them Blue Eyes . . . So here I am. They are not talking to me, they are talking to these guys. So when we had the last meeting and they voted and they said the only way to let the people in Managua to know what is happening is to have a manifestation.

Although it is not clear exactly who was involved or the precise nature of the varied interests they were serving, a demonstration was planned by a small group of Creoles associated with SICC. Ostensibly, its focus was to demand the removal of the Cubans; however, almost all the Creoles I have spoken to who participated affirm that the Cuban issue was only a catalyst for the three days of disturbances that followed. More than two-thirds of Creoles interviewed in a 1984 CIDCA survey said that they did not believe that the Cubans were a threat.

In fact, there was a host of other demands. These included demands for more Creole representation in the government, the dismissal of the manager (a Pacific Coast Mestizo) from one of the fishing plants, free marketing of consumer goods, and so on. As we have seen, some of the SICC leaders who helped organize the demonstration favored the separation of the Atlantic Coast from the rest of Nicaragua. These persons evidently planned to use the demonstration toward this end. Indeed, in our survey a third of the Creoles interviewed said they supported these separatist plans at that time (Gordon 1987).

Black September

On September 28, 1980, the series of events now referred to as "Black September," or the "Manifestación," began with a demonstration in Beholden, the largest of Bluefields' Creole barrios. It quickly gathered momentum. Demonstrators marched through Bluefields' Creole neighborhoods, picking up participants as they went along. Emotions ran high as people vented their accumulated frustrations (Jenelee Hodgson interview, 1995): "When the group got so big and church was over, all of the young people from Baptist, we came out to the front of the church. Ahhhhi! They say now, well, 'Miss Jenelee, this thing is so big!' They say, 'Come on!' So, well, they going to the park. So we went along to hear."

On the first day, the march ended in the town park, where all gathered to hear speeches denouncing the Cubans and the Sandinista government. The demonstration then took on a spontaneous quality lasting for three days. Businesses and government offices closed. Supporters arrived from most of the Creole settlements in South Zelaya. For three days the streets were filled with people. At one point the demonstrators marched to the *cuartel*, where they became a huge, jeering, stick-waving, stone- and bottle-throwing crowd. In the crowd were a few former members of the *cuartel* group armed with automatic weapons. The crowd threatened to enter and take control from the soldiers, who had been confined to quarters during the demonstrations. Shots were fired in the air and the crowd dispersed, but not before at least one person was injured by gunfire and several soldiers by hurled debris.

Crowds formed in front of government officials' houses. There they demanded that the officials come out and hear the crowd's complaints. When the officials appeared, the crowd shouted them down and threatened them. Creoles identified with the Revolution were beaten and threatened with death by the demonstrators. The protesters took over the government-controlled radio station and broadcast messages supporting the rebellion. They barricaded the streets in all the Creole barrios. The town's seafood-packing plant was broken into and a number of automatic weapons taken from the security guards' stock.

The third day the government called in the POI (Policía de Orden Interno—Internal Order Police) from Managua to restore order. The people of Bluefields were told that members of the Government Junta for National Reconstruction were coming to negotiate with them; they gathered at the municipal wharf on the lagoon to await them. Instead of the Junta, the POI arrived in helicopters at the airport in full battle dress. From the moment they arrived, they began firing their weapons in an effort to intimidate the people. They were immediately trucked to the center of town, where they set up barricades and took battle positions. These troops dispersed the demonstrators at the wharf with gunfire and by roughing them up. They made arrests and a few people were injured, some by stray bullets.

Black September is one of the central events in contemporary Creole history. Leading Creole historian Hugo Sujo told me (interview, 1988) that he believed that, had the Creoles been able to obtain sufficient weapons, they would have used them on that occasion to "free" the Coast. He also said that another Creole leader had stated that he had never been so proud to be a Creole as he was on the day the Manifestación began.

During my time in Bluefields, many Creoles recounted for me their experiences over these three days. Their accounts were invariably detailed and fresh in the minds of the tellers, despite the fact that some, like the one by Percy González recounted below, were narrated more than a decade after the events. I include a long portion of Percy's account to give the reader a better feel for the events, their spontaneity, the heavy-handed Sandinista response, and the demonstration's lasting effects on the Creole community:

> Yes, I was in that rush—for the manifestation. . . . Yes, well, I watching because that month was the San Jerónimo and a lot of people in the street. Everybody in the street. And the manifestation. I remember I come walk up here and the whole street did full up. But the day before, even some old people and things did marching going against the Cuban them. I wasn't in that. I watch it pass. But the days them passed and they have meeting in the Moravian, public meeting where this one accuse the next one. Plenty stiff pulling . . . During the manifestation I come around here—them did gone with Brother Gayland [Vance] jail. And the people them, "We want Brother Gayland. We want Brother Gayland." They down to did shoot one old man around there. Just they didn't kill him. The people them like breaking down the jail door and stoning rock. A little after that I see they bring out Brother Gayland. They lift him up and just people, people. . . .
>
> So after that the following day, no, that night they did had a meeting in the Moravian with Lumberto. My brother did in there, too, John. People them get kind of aggressive. They nearly down to beat him up with a umbrella. The people them was upstir. They say, well, today in the Moravian again. And like them did send get the POI them from Managua.
>
> That day we did standing up by Stanford Cash house, up in

Beholden front of the Baptist school. Was Alan, one guy name Earl, next one Alvin Downs, Rat did out there, too. Talking out there from one thing to the other. And we hear bullet fire down street. There they shoot off some women foot. And people running up, coming up from by the *depósito* come here. I tell them, "Boy, let's we make a move." And the people them coming. You know, and by we talking to one of Stanford son, he say, "Well, let we go in, right in the house till the people them pass." So his mother say, "No, no, no, none of that here! Not here!" She lock the door. But we still yet got time to move. Them boys them say we not doing anything. We going stay right here. I say things no look good and I went behind one house, by Stanford house, one little board house.

I standing up behind. And we hear when the captain come and get everybody spread down on the ground. Yes, got them with their hands kissing the ground . . . on the street man . . . on the pavement, kicking their foot open and telling them rough words. Ten, fifteen minutes pass, I only hear silence. I say, "Well, I going take a peep and see what." And as I peep to the door one was looking direct. "Hey you! . . . Come on here to the ground." They carry we down and make we get up. One of the guy did got on a military boots, one of my buddy. "Where you get this boots from?" roughing him up. And then tell we stand up and running so with we hand behind we reach by Ertell Brown house. The curve down. When we reaching by Chinese Club, a next guy what is *panguero* [boatman] here, he coming laughing and watching. But they no studying the women them. When I look, they ask him, "And you, where you going? Come on here in the line."

Man and boys. They carry we to Zelaya corner, gone move some big bricks and rocks and stump and tree. Because the people did have it block off. We move the thing them, no. One of them with one big-mouth gun so—just so the gun mouth big, his mouth big, too. Rain coming and we done move the thing them so we rushing by one barber shop . . . and he say "Get out here, you all SOB! You all not out butter [You will not melt from the rain]! You SOB! You all don't know what the Revolution means." And they start pick out you, you, you, you, you. No going. The balance could go. But by I's one of the shortest one in the crowd, I stay behind. And I coming by Burti Smith. That time I just begin growing my hair, got on a blue shade. One of them say, "Pay attention to this one here." And them boys start laugh. They say, "You salt boy [You have bad luck], Percy." But when it picking out time, now one of the guy want answer the fellow. I tell him, "Cool down, man. Them man will hurt you right now. You know and he stay behind. The tall one them gone up ahead and I stay in the back. When he say "uno [you all] could go." . . . gone.

I didn't come out for nothing . . . Scraping up everybody. . . . No question, no question, you know. Them feel like you want— because them say we want separate here from back yonder. Them man come in with strict orders. They did carry Alan Managua, too. Same woman, too, Puna. They did carry Puna Managua. I hear they make she shove some of the cardboard [from placards] down her mouth and all them things. One priest they make help back [carry] one wooden beam here in town. That did up Beholden. . . . It did really look dread. From there is where the people start get—I feel like from there is where the people get more and more against what did going on then.

In the early morning of the following day, the troops entered the black barrios searching for the *cuartel* boys who had taken the weapons from the seafood plant and for the SICC leaders who had organized the demonstration. Some witnesses reported that the soldiers were initially met with sporadic automatic weapons fire. Searching and occasionally firing under houses, calling people from their beds, breaking down doors, the troops traumatized the neighborhoods as they arrested the presumed leaders of the disturbance. Creoles claim that the troops treated prisoners roughly, randomly threatened community members, and frequently used racial insults: "All the blacks who want to govern come out!"; "Black son of a whore!"; "Dance now, monkeys!"

Order was restored.

In the ensuing days, Comandante Jaime Wheelock of the National Directorate of the FSLN arrived to talk to the Creole community and to apologize for the POI's excesses. Government and FSLN representatives held meetings with community representatives to discuss possible solutions to the community's grievances.

The demonstration was a watershed in Creole opposition to the revolutionary government. It served to unify the Creole community in its criticisms of the Revolution. The community concluded from the handling of the incident that the FSLN was insensitive to its needs and desires and was its enemy.

The Manifestación also marked the suspension of overt Creole political activity. The arrest, detention, and subsequent exile of SICC's adult leadership smashed the only remaining Creole popular organization. From that point on, most Creoles were afraid to organize independent of the FSLN's party structures. State Security and the Sandinista police did a good job of suppressing any attempts to do so.[10]

All that was left of pre-Triumph Creole political forces were the discredited black Sandinistas and the disorganized remnants of the old OPROCO Creole elite. The former were largely integrated into the lower echelons of the FSLN's local party structure;[11] the latter maintained a low profile but clustered in the Moravian High School and remained influential in the community. The elimination of SICC as an organization and the exile of its leadership as well as the black Sandinistas' forced abdication of racial cultural politics closed the space for effective racially and culturally based organization in Bluefields' Creole community. In general, over the next five years the Creole community bore its complaints, problems, and differences silently.

Creole Populism to Anglo Ideology

The Reaction

The importance of the Cuban question as a rallying point during Black September indicates that the latter was a turning point in another sense as well. By late 1980 the focus of the Creole criticism of the Revolution was changing. During the next five years, Creoles kept their counsel and grew increasingly alienated from the revolutionary process. The set of organizing ideas behind their politics changed from Creole populism—from what they saw as the Revolution's racism, ethnocentrism, and perpetuation of internal colonialism—to Anglo ideology, essentially a rejection of the Revolution's "communistic" (i.e., antireligion, anticapital, antidemocratic, anti-U.S.) character. Once this latter set of ideas became predominant in organizing ideas for Creole politics, all problems, both real and imagined, were ultimately reducible to it.

This transformation was influenced by Creole relations with other oppositional forces. The growing militancy of the Miskitu and other indigenous groups organized in MISURASATA played an important role in this regard. The potential for racial/cultural and/or regional alliance with the Miskitu, who by 1981 were also having serious problems with the Sandinistas, was negated by Creole feelings of superiority and Miskitu denial of Creole indigenous status. I was told by Creoles on a number of occasions that the Coast's Indian leaders had publicly stated that all Mestizos would have to leave the region when Indians took their rightful positions. Creoles, on the other hand, would be allowed to stay, but only under Indian authority. Creoles resented this mightily and also began to reflect on the possible threat of others' racial/cultural politics to their position. The Creole commonsense notion of relations between

Creoles and Miskitu and their respective politics during this period was summed up by Miss Azalee Hodgson, a Creole, as follows: "The Miskitu don't give a rip about niggers."[12]

The transformation in Creole politics was also influenced by alliances forged by influential sectors of the community. As we have seen, by late 1980, for a number of SICC leaders the Sandinistas had become the central representatives of Mestizo power and the Nicaraguan nation. Paradoxically, while at the forefront of the Creoles' racial/cultural social movement, they simultaneously sought support for their struggle against the revolutionary state from conservative Mestizos and U.S. whites. Alliance with these political forces could only be forged on anticommunist, anti-Sandinista grounds and not on racial or even cultural grounds. Anticommunism, therefore, became an important element of this militant Creole group's politics in ways that it had not been when many of these same leaders embraced the Trotskyite "race man," Kalalú.

Organic leadership for the emergence of this new politics was provided by Moravian High School teachers. The departure of those teachers who had been SICC leaders left a faculty that, because of its strong support of organized religion, was very anticommunist and, because of its historical affiliation with the U.S. missionaries, pro-U.S. These teachers, some of whom, as we have seen, were former members of OPROCO, were generally supporters of the culturalist perspective and had strong Anglo diasporic identities. This reinforced their identification with the United States and weakened their penchant for the race-based politics associated with Creole populism and black Caribbean diasporic identity.

Creole Politics in Times of Crisis

The political transformation of the Creole community, however, had much to do with the evolving political, economic, military, and social conjuncture and the everyday mobilization of elements of Creole political common sense by Creoles as they struggled to make sense of these conjunctures and developed politics to confront them. From late 1981 onward, I was a close observer and participant in this process.

The period between 1982 and 1985 was one of great turmoil of all kinds in Bluefields. The Creole community entered this era in a funk, its high expectations for the recovery of its once-preeminent local position dashed and apprehensive about the future. At the end of this era, just before the easing of military tensions and the beginning of the implementation of partial political autonomy for the Atlantic Coast, the community had sunk into a state of despair and disgust with the "communistic" Revolution. The Creole economy had collapsed. The community's cultural continuity and influence in the region had plunged into a downward spiral from which it will, perhaps, never recover.

Warfare raged during much of the era, with Creoles participating as combatants on the opposing sides but mostly as civilians caught between them. My family and I lived through these times.

My direct introduction to terror and the awesome responsibility for the effects of my own intellectual practice came in 1983, when I was working with fishing cooperatives in the Creole and Miskitu communities north of Bluefields. We had successfully helped a group of fishermen in Tasbapaunie get organized and distributed some fishing gear to them. I had worked particularly closely with Thomas Hunter, a Creole fisherman and father of five, who was vice–president of the cooperative. This particular day, while he and others were out fishing shrimp, a group of Contras composed of both Miskitu and Creoles had entered Tasbapaunie. Word was sent to the fishing grounds of their arrival.

Most of the other fishermen decided not to go back to the village that evening. Thomas, claiming that he had done nothing wrong and therefore had nothing to fear, came home to his family. The Contra group captured him and took him across the Lagoon to Gun Point. There they tied him to a coconut palm. After four days of intermittent torture, they cut off his ears and penis and stuffed them in his mouth. Then they killed him.

Placing Thomas Hunter's ears in his mouth was a symbolic message that even a child could read. He died accused of being an informant for the Sandinistas. This accusation was undoubtedly based on his work with me and others identified with the revolutionary state in the establishment of the cooperative.

In my memory, war and violence were the defining reality of this era. They pervade the meager field notes I began taking toward its end, as can seen from the following textual extracts:

Miss Alva's boy just died. He was hurt in action about a month ago. He was carried back to base camp and died in his hammock. The cook for the group saw him buried. She [Miss Alva] went to Tasba, but came back because she was afraid someone would denounce her there. 8/29/85

Sylvia Fox's brother and sister were killed in an attack on their panga [speedboat] yesterday while on their way to Pearl Lagoon. One other from Lagoon was injured. . . . The Haulover people told me that the Contra were sorry for the incident. It was raining and everyone was huddled under military raincoats. The Contra thought the Foxes were military and attacked. 9/23/85

Two weeks ago on a trip to Sandy Bay a boat carrying medicine, fishing materials, food, a light plant, cement, and other goods from the government to the community was held up by the "bush boys" just north of Tasbapaunie on the inside. Alfonso Smith, the new head of MISURASATA in the zone (Makantaka), gave orders to let traffic go through, but the boat was attacked anyway. Fishing materials, three-fourths of the medicine, and food were taken by the boys, many of whom were from Bluefields and Tasba. Half Creole and other half Miskitu. Now everyone is afraid to travel through the canal. 9/23/85

The "Express" was fired upon at Kisuta, just outside of Tasba, by the Contras on Sun. 13th Oct. The Contras in the area are said to be new people and wearing masks. 10/21/85

Fighting up by Le Fe. One Orinoco man was killed. An attack on Pearl Lagoon was repulsed. 10/28/85

A member of the EPS [Ejército Popular Sandinista—Popular Sandinista Army] came home drunk and blew off his foot while trying to shoot his mother last night at 1:30 AM in the Seminario behind our house. From our beds we listened to his shouts of anger and later his screams of agony for what seemed like an hour. 1/24/86

Over the years the tension and terror became almost normal; their impact was, however, revealed in our dreams:

Wyatt [my son] is sick with fever. I'm hoping it is just a cold. I had two dreams that I remember last night. One had to do with a renegade boat that later turned out to be Contra. It came into the harbor at full speed, belching black smoke. It was wooden in dilapidated condition with half-gone white paint job. It rammed several boats and they rammed a panga with an old man standing in it. It crumpled the panga and the man was left standing to the side of the boat, half hanging on. Then it went back for another shot and wrecked up some other boats. I was watching from on the top of a grassy hill with some houses on it near the water. As I was going away from the hill I saw two Hind helicopters hovering over the boat and people were cheering. I came down to CIDCA. There was a middle-aged man riding a motorcycle. Then things got serious. The people in the militia house were getting armed up. I saw a bunch of them to what was [near] a wide door ready to fight, one was naked. At the last instant, Orlando with a gun scrambled to be with them. I think some shooting started. I woke up.

In the next dream I was in a classroom or meeting when Dwight Narciso came up to me to tell me in confidence that Daisy [my wife] had been wounded in an attack on the "Express" and had been taken by the Contras to some hospital in the Chontales bush. She had a gaping slash in the front part of her body from chest to abdomen.

I woke up. I didn't get much sleep tending to Wyatt. I am scared, feel sick, and am tired. 11/7/86

What follows must be read with a soundtrack of AK-47 bursts, rocket launchers, helicopter engines, and army boots in the mud, the rancid cooking-oil and old-sweat smell of tropical armies, and a constant, throbbing undercurrent of absence, deprivation, tension, fear, and nostalgia for simpler, less-dangerous times. Such was the backdrop of Creole lives and politics during the early 1980's.

When I first started traveling regularly to Bluefields in late 1981, there was a fairly high level of discontent with the revolutionary process in the Creole community; however, although many people told me that Bluefields had changed for the worse in the two years since the Triumph, it was hard to see how. I had arrived during what turned out to be a two-year lull between the unstable period of insurrection and consolidation of revolutionary state power and the outbreak of war in the region. At that time, despite the extreme bitterness over the political dynamics of the recent past, there was an atmosphere of normalcy to the place. The patterns of daily life seemed well established and regularized. The level of discontent seemed no higher than in subaltern communities I was familiar with in the United States: there was no overwhelming joy, but neither was there insufferable pain or sorrow. Events, though, were already under way that would substantially undercut this normalcy and usher in an era of almost continual crisis and transform Creole politics.

By mid-1980 small groups of Creoles and Miskitu from communities north of Bluefields had taken up arms against the Revolution. Many were armed by the Sandinistas in the early days after the Triumph as the latter had taken control of the Coast. The activities of these young men had no perceptible impact on Bluefields in 1981. I remember being impressed by how few military personnel and equipment were visible in Bluefields compared with what I had experienced in the rest of the country.

Nevertheless, the growing threat of "counterrevolutionary" activity prompted the formation of militia battalions from Bluefields' population. The first was mobilized in 1980 and included a fairly large number of Creoles. Initially, the realities of war were brought to Bluefields' Creole community through the experiences of these young men.

By 1983 large portions of Bluefields' hinterland were a battlefield, and the Creole community experienced the warfare directly when people traveled anywhere outside of town. Boats were regularly fired on and hijacked, and transportation throughout the region was disrupted. Out-lying communities unsympathetic to the counterrevolutionary forces were attacked. People were kidnapped and forced to join the opposition forces; many more joined of their own accord. Fishing boats were robbed, hijacked, and sabotaged. The Sandinista army fought skirmishes with opposing forces throughout the region. In a 1985 predawn raid, Bluefields itself was attacked. By afternoon the battle was over. Twenty-two bodies of dead Contras, including sons of Bluefields residents, were dumped in the town park for public display. The so-called low-intensity war af-fected every aspect of Creole life.

Many Creoles, accepting the Reagan administration's position that the Sandinistas were waging an unnecessary war as agents of the Cubans and Soviets, blamed the Revolution for the warfare. After another of the seemingly continuous attacks on an outlying Creole community by opposition forces, I had a conversation with the Whitikers. It was similar in many ways to others I had with Creoles during this period. The Whitikers were convinced the warfare was mostly the Sandinistas' fault, even though opposition forces had attacked Creole civilians and com-munities and the whole region was suffering from their terrorism. They repeated the Reagan administration line that they had heard on the Voice of America and in the streets of Bluefields: the Sandinistas were sending arms to the illegitimate revolutionaries in El Salvador and therefore irresponsibly provoking the United States. The Whitikers' position was that the Sandinistas should stop sending arms so that the war would end. What the Whitikers hoped the government would do was to become less "communist" and stop fighting as the way to make "Reagan stop the war." The intricacies of how this was to be done and still maintain a Revolution were not of much concern to them. Perhaps this was the whole point: for the Whitikers and many other Creoles in the mid-1980's, it was the Sandinistas, not the United States, who were foment-ing the senseless conflict.

To this situation of seemingly endless uncertainty and tension was added material deprivation. Few problems generated more Creole ani-mosity toward the Revolution in the post-Manifestación era than the growing economic crisis. After the Triumph, most of the major mer-chants of Bluefields left, reducing the availability of consumer goods. Imported consumer goods all but disappeared as a consequence of the U.S. economic blockade and Nicaraguan government policy designed to terminate economic dependence. It became hard for Creoles to find many of their "decencies," especially goods imported from the United States. Creoles were not comfortable with the government rationing of basic consumer items initiated to assure their availability to all Nicaraguans; they were accustomed to buying as much as they wanted (or could afford) whenever they desired.

Economic conditions on the Atlantic Coast grew steadily worse after early 1982 as a result of the grave national military situation. As warfare and terrorism engulfed the countryside, agricultural production on the Coast plummeted, causing shortages of some traditional foodstuffs. War-related inflation ate away at Creole buying power.

To add to these problems, production in the fishing industry flagged. Fleet size shrank dramatically because of owner flight and boat hijackings. The efficiency of the packing plants diminished, undermined by anti-quated machinery, lack of spare parts, and shortages of technically qualified personnel. Two of the five fishing companies in the area had to be closed, eliminating close to a thousand jobs.

Under the strain of the general crisis, basic services in Bluefields deteriorated. Repair parts and, at times, fuel for the generators at the municipal power plant were difficult to obtain. Most nights, sections of Bluefields were without light for four or five hours. The already-limited phone system connecting Bluefields to the Pacific was often inoperable. In general, transportation and communications connecting Bluefields with the rest of the nation and the Coast were often disrupted and, in general, uncertain.

Creoles became obsessed with the economic crisis. For years it was nearly the only topic of conversation on the street and in homes. The irregular supply and outright scarcity of basic consumer items was particularly destabilizing. People spent inordinate amounts of time searching for goods that previously had been readily available. At various times, there was no hand soap, no toilet paper, no white sugar, no sanitary pads, no meat, no light bulbs, no bottled gas, no clothing, and on and on. For a while we and our neighbors had to take the light bulbs on our front porches in at night because, since you could not buy light bulbs, people were stealing and reselling them. The loudest complaints were heard on the occasions when there was no beer in town.

Hyperinflation had set in by the mid-1980's and profoundly under-mined the Creole standard of living. You had to either spend your monthly pay check in the first days after receiving it, change it for dollars on the black market, or risk having it be practically worthless by the end of the month. At one point, we had one-million-córdoba bills in which the new number designations were merely stamped over the original number on one-thousand-córdoba bills.

In CIDCA's 1984 survey, almost two-thirds of those Creoles inter-viewed pointed to economic problems as the basis of their disillusion-ment with the Revolution (Gordon 1987). "For Creoles the economic crisis was an ethnic crisis as well."[13] They were losing their status as an economic elite. The types of jobs that defined their identity were disappearing. The imported components of their material culture were not available. They yearned for Kraft American cheese and Tang and Levi's, but these were not to be found. In response, many Creoles left the country. Their group identity and cohesiveness were therefore threatened, along with their economic power.

Creoles accepted, to a point, the Sandinista claim that the war was a major cause of the crisis. As we have seen, however, they blamed the Revolution for that warfare. From the perspective of Anglo ideology, most believed that the ills of the economy stemmed from a combination of the Sandinistas' unjust war and the economic irrationality of the communistic system that the revolutionary government had instituted. They pointed especially to government control of prices, the distribution of basic products, external trade, the movement of foreign exchange, and the confiscation of private property as basic problems and proof of this ideological tendency.

Post-Manifestación problems between the Creole community and the revolutionary government over the role of the Creole church were now seen not so much as indications of Mestizo ethnocentrism as of more proof of Sandinista communism. By 1982 it was evident that the Sandinistas were running into problems with non-Creole sectors of the religious community. In the northern portions of the Atlantic Coast, as the situation between the revolutionary government and the Miskitu disintegrated, local Miskitu leaders of the Moravian Church took prominent roles in antigovernment activities, including military actions. This further soured the relationship between that church and the Sandinistas.

Later attempts at reconciliation eased tensions between the Moravian Church hierarchy and the revolutionary government; however, toward the end of the period in question, many of those in church leadership positions who had been conciliatory toward the government were marginalized. In 1985 the national synod voted into power leaders who were relatively sympathetic to the Miskitu resistance and hostile to the Sandinistas.

The intensifying problems with the Moravian Church occurred simultaneously with increasing problems on a national level between the Sandinistas and the hierarchy of the Catholic Church. These tensions grew to the point that the Sandinistas considered the Catholic Church hierarchy to be the internal front of the counterrevolution. This hierarchy, based in the Pacific, withdrew key Catholic clergy sympathetic to the Revolution from their positions on the Atlantic Coast. As a result, the Catholic Church on the Coast became much less enthusiastic about the revolutionary process.

These events coincided with the advent of U.S. propaganda that pictured the Sandinistas as communists and therefore antireligion. Creoles began to see the problems of their churches as stemming not so much from ethnic conflicts as from the antireligious communism of the Sandinistas.

Once Creoles judged the Revolution to be communistic, a host of other "proofs" of this judgment were not hard to come by. The Sandinistas' strong stand against imperialism, the strongest force tying together the FSLN's post-Triumph alliance, was unpopular among Creoles and, for them, yet another indication of its communist leanings. The United States and North Americans, following Anglo ideology and Anglo diasporic identity, were viewed in a sympathetic light by Creoles. In one of many conversations I had with James Fenton in 1988 on the subject, he told me that the Sandinistas were wrong to go against the United States. It was the United States that had put the FSLN in power and then the ungrateful FSLN hadn't wanted to have anything to do with it. He went on to say that no nation could get along without the help of the United States, the most powerful country in the World: "The U.S. is the mother of the world." In his view, Nicaragua could not get ahead without U.S. help and sooner or later would have to go to the United States for aid. Instead of fighting the United States, the Sandinistas should be getting help from it. One of his most fervent hopes was that the FSLN would be taken out of power and normal relations reestablished with the United States.

The Sandinista embrace of the Soviet Union and Cuba and rejection of the United States in 1988 was seen by Creoles as another clear indication of Sandinista communism and rubbed against the grain of Creole common sense. The strength of Creoles' association of the FSLN with nations of the "Communist bloc" is brought out by the following anecdote.

In 1982, when groups of North American tourist supporters of the Revolution first began arriving in Bluefields, much of the Creole community was convinced that they were Soviets. After all, they had been convinced by propaganda that North Americans were against the Revolution and would not come to Nicaragua. They also had heard and believed that there was a large Soviet presence in Nicaragua, though they had never seen anyone. To Creoles, then, these white people, as supporters of the Revolution, must be Soviets.

In 1983 and again in 1984, the Sandinistas accused some leaders of the Creole community of trying to revive SICC and plotting with the counterrevolution. They were picked up and jailed for varying periods of time. In the outlying Creole communities, security forces arrested villagers for collaboration with the Contras. In 1985 the Sandinista government declared a nationwide state of emergency, which led to the closing of the national opposition newspaper, *La Prensa*. These events and the anti-Sandinista propaganda that accompanied them verified in the Creole mind the accusations of Sandinista totalitarianism.

By 1984 the accumulation of events and experiences over five years of revolution had crystallized in many Creole minds into a negative association of the Revolution and communism. Alan Stephenson's statement of this thinking is perhaps more eloquent than the average but in many ways typical of the Creole laments I heard during these times (interview, 1991):

> What really hurt me was when they start arresting people—midnight—innocent people locking them up. . . . around that time or a little after [the Manifestación] when they start picking up people that used to work for Somoza and was in partnership with Somoza just lock them up in jail. . . . there was Fred Copeland, Amos Hodgson, . . . They didn't take everybody one day . . . Anyway, there was dozens of people . . . had them locked up in the Variedades Theater. Some of the people were sent to Managua, like Charles Notice and Fire Fire.
>
> . . . When they start picking people up, taking away their business, confiscating their property . . . having people spy on you, reporting lies—that's when I really started thinking differently about them. . . . That was the reason why we couldn't have any meeting in the home, any private meeting, and they even had some of the neighbors watching me. . . . You couldn't go out in the night on a boat and you still have that law. If you want to go to the Bluff you have to get out a *zarpe* [travel authorization]. . . . right here in town they went too far to suit me . . . They were exploiting the fishermen. When the devaluation start to go crazy, they didn't change the price of the lobster to correspond with the dollar price we were making. So I started out in 1980 at U.S.$4.20 a pound and around the middle 1980's that C$42 was worth U.S.$0.42 . . . So we just couldn't survive. I figure, well, they meant to crush all private enterprise and that was one of the way to do it. . . . That was when I change my mind about Sandino.
>
> . . . they turn radical communists. They call it socialist, but they took away everybody business and then they had these *expendios* [expenditures]. If you want to buy a pound of rice, you had to get in a line, and when they get to you they say they don't have any more. Things like that. And spying and—I don't know, the control in general over the people. Nobody could do anything unless you were Sandino. . . . So I see where you would not survive with them unless you joined up with them.

The gravest blow to Creole/Sandinista relations was the recruitment of Creole youth into the Servicio Militar Patriótico (SMP—Patriotic Military Service). The revolutionary government implemented compulsory military service in 1983 in response to the worsening national crisis. Recruitment was not begun in Bluefields until 1984. Creoles, who did not favor the Revolution to begin with, were particularly incensed that their sons would have to serve in the army. This was viewed as the ultimate invasion of individual rights and further proof of the nefarious and communistic nature of the government. The initial community response was to hide their young men in their houses or to send them to outlying communities.

At first, most recruits were in fact volunteers. After a while, young men of draft age were picked up at school, off the streets, in the movie theaters, at parties, and the like. A decision was made not to invade homes in search of draft evaders, but young men in public spaces were fair game.

In 1984 a group of mostly Mestizo students organized a protest movement against the SMP in Bluefields in which some Creole students participated. Demonstrations organized in the streets were confronted by *"turbas"* (FSLN cadres) mobilized against them instead of by the police or military, and stick, stone, and fist fighting broke out.[14] The movement was crushed in this manner (Tito Marino interview notes, 1989). Subsequently, wave after wave of Creole youth left the country. Most walked to Costa Rica; many ended up in the refugee camps there; many others, however, were recruited into the counterrevolutionary military groups that operated in the southern Atlantic Coast and were headquartered in the neighboring country. Not only did the SMP provide further evidence to the Creole community of the FSLN's communist totalitarianism, but, by facilitating the recruitment of Creole youth into the forces of the counterrevolution, it provided a positive basis of identification for them and their families with forces whose principal criticism was the leftist positioning of the government.

Taking Stock

The shift, then, from a criticism of the Revolution based on issues of ethnopolitical power to one based on the Revolution's supposed communistic nature was the result of a number of interrelated factors. The Sandinistas made the ethnopolitical struggle untenable for Creoles. They smashed Creole social movements forged first by the black Sandinistas and then by SICC and forced many of the important Creole leaders of these movements to join them unconditionally or to leave the Atlantic Coast. The Creole community was demoralized and intimidated. After the Manifestación, Creoles realized that the revolutionary state was willing to use coercive power, to which they had no response, to maintain order and, by default, the racial/cultural status quo. Creoles realized that their struggle for racial/cultural rights was an isolated one and that they could expect little support on this issue from other of the growing oppositional forces (Miskitu, Mestizo, or U.S. white) inside or outside the country. As a consequence, Creoles deemphasized demands and criticism based on Creole populism.

For Creoles, the initial legitimacy of the Sandinista government was based on the latter's promise of popular representation; however, Creoles blamed the defeat of their ethnopolitical project on the Sandinistas and believed that they had betrayed the terms of their own revolution. Creoles did not feel empowered or in control of their destinies under the government dominated by the FSLN. This meant that from the perspective of Creole populism the Sandinistas did not and could not represent their interests. During the year and a half immediately following the Triumph, the revolutionary government lost its legitimacy in Creole eyes.

Correspondingly, the FSLN and, in particular, the black Sandinistas lost their potential as the political leadership of the Creole community. After the undermining of the black Sandinista project and the FSLN's initial loss of legitimacy, the Sandinista political project was increasingly rejected by Creoles. There was no other agency or group within or outside the Creole community with politics and strong enough influence to shape the development of a counterhegemonic organization of Creole political common sense that could offset Anglo ideology, the heritage of an oppressive and exploitative colonial past.

Had the Sandinistas been able to establish their legitimacy with the Creole community through a combination of Creole empowerment and the creation of a vision of a better future for Creoles in collaboration with the Revolution, they might have been able to cement a political alliance with them, as they had done with other segments of Nicaraguan society. More important, on this basis, it would have been possible to assist Creoles in the creation of a distinctively Creole liberating counterhegemony that, in theory, could have facilitated coordinated FSLN and Creole opposition to imperialism and other forms of oppression. The dissonances between Creole populism and Anglo ideology offered a basis for the organization of such a counterhegemony based on Creole populism. This agenda would have been all the more possible during the first years after the Triumph, when opposing ideological forces such as those of U.S. capitalism and the Central American bourgeoisie, were inactive and confused in their response to the Revolution. The social movement that began to coalesce around the black Sandinistas in the months after the Triumph seemed to contain the grounds for such an opportunity; however, it was not to be.[15]

SICC, whose leaders' racial/cultural stand focused almost exclusively on the racist internal colonialism of the Mestizo-dominated state and not on racial imperialism, compromised their racial/cultural politics to form anti-Sandinista alliances with Mestizos and U.S. whites. When this move was smashed, Creoles, disillusioned by their inability to make headway on the racial/cultural front and already nudged in this direction by sectors of the SICC leadership, downplayed their "utopian project" based on populism. Lacking any alternative organization of commonsense criteria and never fully convinced by the new political ideas of the Revolution, Creoles roused hegemonic Anglo ideology as a basis for judging the Revolution. In this politics they were led by important elements of the remaining group of Creole leaders and intellectuals who were clustered around the Moravian High School.

The resultant Creole criticisms both dovetailed with and were educed by those of the Reagan administration and the Nicaraguan bourgeois opposition who depicted the revolutionary government as Marxist-Leninist or communist. By 1981 increasingly virulent anti-Sandinista propaganda was being disseminated throughout the Atlantic Coast by the North American media, the U.S. government (through the Voice of America and two CIA-supported radio stations), and other important U.S. clients, especially the bourgeois media in Costa Rica (television and radio), Honduras (radio), and Nicaragua (newspaper and radio).

Creoles, well versed in cold war ideology, understood that this meant that the Sandinistas stood accused of being totalitarian, antireligion, war mongering, economically irrational, and the like. The characterization of the Revolution in these terms evoked an almost Pavlovian response in the Creole community based on the hegemonic role of Anglo ideology. Henceforth any practical problems that the Creole community experienced within the Revolution were understood to be the consequence of Sandinista communism. Even the denial of ethnic rights, while still important for most Creoles, could now be seen as just another aspect of a totalitarian state's denial of popular democracy.

Anglo diasporic identity played an important role in this regard. The anti-U.S. posture of the Revolution was read by Creoles as anti-Anglo and therefore anti-Creole. Additionally, Anglo diasporic identity facilitated the expression of commonsense elements of Anglo ideology as natural components of a Creole politics.

Creole populism never totally faded away as a basis for understanding the Revolution. There were members of the community for whom the racial/cultural question remained the most important basis for criticism. In part this was based on the continued salience of black Caribbean identity. The rasta boys and those associated with them and the huge popularity of reggae music among Creoles were the outstanding examples of this tendency. Their politics was closely related to trans-

Caribbean currents of black nationalism and racial transgression as the
Soul Vibes lyrics in the epigraph in the preface indicate. For the majority
of Creoles, however, Creole populism became secondary to Anglo
ideology as the salient position from which to evaluate the Sandinista
project.

By 1985 Anglo ideology had so far overshadowed Creole populism that
some Creoles were denying the validity of the previously all-important
racial/cultural struggle. By this time, the national government, admit-
ting that it had made a number of mistakes in its handling of the Atlantic
Coast and its racial/cultural minorities, instituted a process that led to
the eventual establishment of regionally autonomous governments for
the area. In a propaganda pamphlet prepared by the Creole counterrevolution based in Costa Rica for distribution by their guerrilla bands in
Nicaragua's Creole communities (extracted in the epigraph at the
beginning of this chapter), however, the communism of the Sandinistas
and its threat to religion and so on was decried at the same time that
racial/cultural demands for separation of the Atlantic Coast and "autonomy" were explicitly rejected.

The authors of the pamphlet were Creole leaders who had left
Nicaragua after the Manifestación. The ideas found in their pamphlet
represent the most commonly articulated Creole political positions at
the end of the period under analysis. Comparison of this tract with one
authored just prior to the Revolution by a leader of OPROCO, whose
anti-internal colonialism represented the most consistently enunciated
Creole political position of that time, indicates the shift in emphasis and
articulation of Creole political common sense (Tobie 1976):

> Our gradual relegation or displacement is nothing new, it is but a
> trend that has been taking place over the past 3/4 of a century. This
> policy of acculturation, which culminated in the closure of our
> schools during the Zelaya era, continued with the assignment of
> practically all government posts, from messengers upward, to
> emigrants from the Interior. The dire effects in the psyche of the
> Coast people is evident up to this day. The consequences were not
> only your confinement to a lower economic strata, and emigration
> looking for a better life due to the restriction to our sources of
> income; but, as a natural outcome, the instilling of a sense of
> purposelessness in all our endeavors.
>
> What say do we have in our own affairs? . . . we should be
> masters in our own house; . . . we should be the determining factor
> in our own destiny!

8.

Conclusion

This book is a narrative of a vibrant and complex people; thus it cannot be simply summarized, and it certainly cannot end. Nevertheless, every book needs a conclusion and I have reached that point in this one. My intimate relationship with Creole everyday politics has ended and my place in the Bluefields community has changed over the decade this book has gestated. Since in important ways the book is as much about my relationship with the community and its politics as it is about the community itself, I will conclude with the changes in that relationship and how they affect the book's status.

I was awakened by a phone call from my mother, a dyed-in-the-wool Frente supporter, at around 5 AM on a January day in 1990. It was still dark in Austin, and cold. She told me that the Sandinistas had lost the national elections held the previous day in Nicaragua. This was unimaginable. When I finally got in touch with Daisy in Bluefields hours later, she described the disbelief of the population. Even though they and their friends and families had not voted for the FSLN, Bluefields' Creole community expected almost everyone else in Nicaragua to vote for the Frente and for Daniel Ortega.

No one in Bluefields expected the outcome, but none were more shocked than the Sandinistas themselves. They seemed not even to have entertained the possibility of losing. Months before the election I remember being startled by the self-assured conviction with which a Creole Frente member told me that they would win "sin lugar a duda" (without a doubt). They had spent plenty to get elected. Frente hats, t-shirts, belts, key chains were all over the place on the Atlantic Coast. There had been last-minute pork barrel projects like an extravagant push in providing infrastructure for the small-scale fishing activities so important to smaller Creole and Miskitu communities of the region. The Frente had even brought in reggae icon Jimmy Cliff for a special campaign performance in Bluefields. (Jimmy evidently thought the

Creole crowd was the deadest group of black folks he had ever seen. Inexperienced in the protocol for such spectacles, they had stood gaping rather than joining in.)

Well, they *had* lost and nobody in Bluefields was ready for it. There was no public celebration. No one in the streets. Everyone seemed to be waiting to see what would happen next. Seven years later it is still not clear "what happens next"; everyone seems still to be waiting.

The elections of 1990 changed many things for my family and me. At the time I was starting my second semester teaching in the Anthropology Department at the University of Texas at Austin. Affirmative action was still an acceptable notion in some circles and, as a valuable racial commodity, I had worked out a two-year deal with UT under which I taught one semester a school year and spent the rest of my time in Nicaragua. In the previous three or four years, things had gotten kind of rough for me on the Atlantic Coast. Due to the suspicions of State Security and other complications, I was no longer able to play the kind of role in local affairs I had gotten accustomed to. With the UT deal I could maintain my commitments and connections in Bluefields and still explore different intellectual relationships, earn enough money to maintain my family in middle-class style, and travel a bit.

But spring 1990 was my last year with the part-time deal and we had to decide whether I would begin teaching full time at UT or go back home to Nicaragua. The elections forced our hand. It was clear that things were going to change, that the revolutionary experiment was going to end. What would be the consequences for our kind of politics? for our friends? for our projects? for CIDCA? We had two children. It was not a time for further experimentation. We went for the sure thing and moved to Austin, Texas. That's right—Texas. Who would have believed it—from Harlem to Philly to the Bay Area to revolutionary Nicaragua to . . . *Texas.*

A tenure-track job is a great thing to have. It is also a curse before you get tenure. The carrots of lifetime employment, family security, and prestige are held out before you, but the path is blocked by a number of formidable hurdles. One of the largest is the book that must be produced. In our department it is almost a direct trade-off—a book published by a "prestigious" press in exchange for tenure. Immediately, it was made clear to me that regardless of whatever else I did, I *had* to produce one.

This did not seem like too much of a problem. In Bluefields I had been a participant and observer for an extended period and had accumulated all sorts of knowledge that surely could be translated into a scholarly product that could be traded for tenure. For years I had been doing intellectual work: research, writing and thinking about Creoles, work for the Creole community to be used by a particular sector of that community in its struggle on the community's behalf. The book would be the same thing, expanding on the core of work already produced with these objectives.

So little by little I began transferring almost ten years of accumulated information detritus—books, pamphlets, tapes, notebooks, papers—to Austin. Finding that even with all the junk I had accumulated I had very little of the kind of data anthropologists usually emerge with from the field, I spent the summer of 1991 in Bluefields interviewing a bunch of folks about Creole history and the like and toted the tapes back to my office in Texas. I also hit the archives and libraries in the United States with vigor. The interlibrary loan folks and I got close.

There were problems with this formulation, however. In this new phase, Bluefields and its Creole community remained the object of my intellectual curiosity and production but I was no longer there, no longer directly involved in the day-to-day life and politics of the community. More important, given my distance, my loss of contact with my Creole reference group, and the changes that had taken place in the political scene in Nicaragua, it was no longer clear that my intellectual work had any direct relationship to what was going on there. My years of work in Bluefields and the book project itself had been transformed from "home-work" to fieldwork.

What was this book for? Tenure. Who was this book speaking to? A limited number of elite North American scholars. Who were the Creoles whose perspective my work shared? Was I now speaking on my authority as an expert alone? It was a contradictory and paralyzing circumstance. I began working on other projects.

The early 1990's was the era of the "crisis of the black male." I am one, I practice a version of our culture, and I am part of a number of communities of black women and men. There was analytical work to be done. I had something to say that could contribute to an important politics around gender and race in black communities. I got involved with a group working on issues of African American men under the auspices of the Children's Defense Fund; I worked with black students on campus; I tried to organize a black fathers' group at my children's elementary school; I lectured groups in the community; and I marched to Washington to "atone" with the rest of us. I began teaching courses about the politics of race, culture, and gender and even published some articles about black men. I tried to re-create the model of activist scholarship developed at CIDCA during the 1980's and now in large part lost to me.

The Creole work got pushed to the background and the tenure clock ticked. I began to get prodded from a number of quarters: my father and mother, my wife, my close friend and mentor James in the department, Charles, other colleagues, even black students. "How did tenure look? What about the book?" So I went back to it. But what had started out as a political project as I describe it in chapter 1 was now a commodity to be traded in for career advancement. The ultimate irony for me was that for a number of years I was too busy writing a book about Bluefields to visit Bluefields.

My increasing inability to see the relevance of my Creole work was a serious impediment. Partial salvation came from the Atlantic Coast. In the early 1990's two new universities opened in Bluefields. This was an exciting new development. Professor Sujo was teaching history at one of them and at the Moravian High School. He had told me how for the first time Coast history was being taught in Nicaragua—and about students' enthusiastic reception of it. During my few visits back, I had seen the numbers of mostly Creole students who daily crowded into CIDCA's tiny library seeking documentary information on a host of issues having to do with the Coast. Among the increasing numbers of Creoles concerned with these matters there was concern about the general lack of written materials available and the absence of Creole history in particular. I built these observations into a motivation for completing the book. It would focus on Creole ethnohistory and there-fore respond to Creole desires and political needs for an authenticating history of the community.

I sent drafts of the history chapters to Professor Sujo, who used information from them in his classes. This and the omnipresent threat of failure, of not being a successful academic or responsible (read *employed*) husband and parent are what enabled—no—forced me to complete the manuscript and submit it for review.

The reviews came back generally favorable but agreeing that the manuscript had to be cut. After being afraid that I would have too little to say to write a book, I had produced a monstrosity of over five hundred pages. A book of this length is no longer feasible, given the current economics of academic publishing, so something had to be cut. The reviewers suggested, for a number of reasons, that it be the Creole history. So the history it was. Sitting in the hard drive of my computer and in messy piles on my office floor are pages and pages of Creole history that I thought Creoles wanted and should have access to.

So what is left of this grand political project that I regaled you, the reader, with in my introduction? Where is the homework and local group of affiliation that resolve my "crisis of authority"? In what ways is this work of use to the subjects of my investigation? What is the work's politics?

Since completing a draft of this book almost two years ago, I have been able to reconnect with Nicaragua. Former colleagues at CIDCA and I have initiated a new "activist" research project in which we are participating with the indigenous and Creole communities of the Atlantic Coast in the "ethnomapping" of their communal lands. This is to be the first stage in a process of legalizing their historical and deeply contested claims to these lands.

In connection with the project I have made a number of visits and spent two months during the summer of 1997 in my house in Bluefields. As one might expect, Bluefields has continued to change since I wrote the introduction to this book. It has gotten bigger and poorer. There are few jobs. Unemployment officially hovers around 80 percent, though this seems impossible. There are more consumer items than I remember as retail enterprises continue their rebound from almost total elimination during the 1980's. People, especially Creoles, are spending money, although it comes mainly from remittances. Bluefields continues to become more and more Mestizo as Mestizos continue to enter from the interior and Creoles continue to move to the "States." Creoles could not possibly account for more than 30 percent of the population and are probably closer to 20 percent.

Capital from the Pacific is moving into the area as well. With only one major exception, the fishing companies that are not owned by shady U.S. capital are owned by equally shady business cartels from the Pacific. There is a land rush going on in the southern Coast, with both campesinos and Pacific elites staking out claims to huge tracts of land for subsistence, on the one hand, and speculation, on the other. The Regional Autonomous Governments institutionalized in the Sandinistas' final years to grant Costeños a measure of power over their own lives are under attack from the new national government after years of not-so-benign neglect from the previous one. The Autonomous Governments themselves have become the field for political wrangling by the local representatives of national parties and are largely dysfunctional.

In these circumstances, many Creoles feel deeply threatened. They feel that the pace at which they have been losing control of what they see as their lands, resources, and lives has been accelerating. Many feel that they are disappearing as a people, that the influence of their culture on the region is rapidly decreasing and that their culture itself is threatened. Most are deeply disillusioned by the autonomy process; many are ready to give up on it totally.

Nevertheless, there are important sectors of the Creole community committed to continuing their struggle for what they believe are their rights and for their vision of a more just future. Some of these Creoles are persons I worked with and struggled alongside when I lived in Bluefields; however, many of these persons are younger professionals who were high school or university students in my day. They are Creoles who took advantage of the educational opportunities made available by the Revolution and who returned to Bluefields to make lives for themselves and contribute to their community. For a number of reasons, many of these "organic" intellectuals are women. Many are also the children of mixed marriages between Mestizos and Creoles. Some of them are able to speak only a little Creole, but most identify strongly as both Creole and black. Much to my delight, I found that many of the ideas and much of the information in this book speaks strongly to this group of people.

There is a demand for Creole history. I was asked on numerous occasions when the book (which Creoles understood would be a history—what else could it be about?) would be out and whether copies would be available on the Atlantic Coast. With Creoles increasingly dispersed and Creoleness seemingly slipping away, there is real interest in a canonical history that projects the group back in time, grounds it, authenticates it, and, with the work of Creole historians and educators, provides a past around which Creoles can rally. Though not without trepidation at such presumption on my part and at the risk of being gauche (at least from a postmodern perspective), I offer up what is left of the Creole history in this book to that project.

There are concerns among the young intellectuals that Creoles as a group are too passive and that there is no basis on which the community can be politically mobilized. This work indicates, first of all, that Creoles as a community have been very active politically on their own behalf over the course of their history, often heroically so. One need only recall the Creoles' Maroon ancestors resisting re-enslavement, the community's uprising against the Overthrow, General George and the Twenty-five Brave, or Abel and the black Sandinistas to realize that there is basis for optimism in this regard. This work also demonstrates, though, that there can be no facile assumptions concerning the central political concerns or tendencies of the community or on what basis it might be mobilized. Only concrete ethnographic analysis of Creole political common sense and careful analysis of the political, social, and economic conjuncture combined with political praxis can provide the basis for developing successful mobilizing strategies. Through its ethnography/ethnohistory of Creole common sense and analysis of Creole interaction with the Revolution, the work of this book speaks directly to this observation. I think it will be useful to my Creole friends in this regard.

The shift in emphasis from Creole populism to Anglo ideology as the criterion on which the Revolution was judged by Creoles described in chapter 7 goes against the grain of conventional wisdom in these matters. For activists or social scientists steeped in the politics of cultural and racial difference in Nicaragua or elsewhere, racial/cultural identity are generally assumed to be *the* crucial determining factors in the politics of subaltern racial/cultural groups. This is certainly what the Sandinistas came to believe after their experiences with the intractable problems on the Coast forced them to drop their class-based analysis of their problems there.

This ethnohistory/ethnography of Creole politics and political common sense casts Creole politics in a different light. The Sandinistas' and their advisers' conclusions were based on the erroneous assumption that there was a single internally consistent element in Creole political consciousness. They reasoned that if the essential core was not politically reactionary pro-Americanism, then it must be racially/culturally based identity and demands instead. As we have seen, however, there has never been a single set of central political ideas or identities in Creole political common sense; it has always been multiple, multifaceted, and contradictory.

In the last decade the political expressions of the Creole community have once again taken a number of seemingly erratic and incomprehensible twists and turns; these have been unsettling for those Creoles attempting to foment progressive social change. For example, in the national elections of 1990 and 1996, the community showed little interest in the formation of local race- or culture-based political organizations and voted en masse for Managua-based political parties, which did not support autonomy or "ethnic" rights for Costeños. On the other hand, during the 1990's Creoles have manifested universal and sustained anger over what they consider to be the Nicaraguan state's racist and internal-colonialist control over and exploitation of the region's natural resources. Of course, as all Creoles are aware, the same Managua-based parties that most have supported vociferously and with their votes at election time have controlled the government during this period.

Only detailed ethnohistorical and ethnographic work with other groups will indicate whether the complex character of Creole political common sense is unique and whether the manner of conceptualizing political consciousness adopted in this book is more generally useful. It is clear to me that, in the case of Nicaragua's Creole community, understanding the complex transformations of the group's political expression is difficult without it. I offer this book to interested Creoles as a starting point for this kind of work in Bluefields.

This book also speaks to the contemporary Creole activist and intellectual fears about Creole loss of influence and possible extinction as a group as a result of out-migration and being overwhelmed by Mestizo immigrants. The feelings of despair in this regard are particularly intense among the younger generation of Creole intellectuals, who strongly associate Creoleness with black Caribbean diasporic identity. For them, people of African descent, and therefore Creoles, are being squeezed out of the Coast.

In conversations with my Creole friends, I have argued, on the basis of my work for this book, that Creole identity is not stable but complex and multiple. It has incorporated disparate peoples in the past and forged alliances with others through the adoption of disparate transnational identities. It seems to me that therein lies the strategic basis for strengthening Creole influence in Nicaragua.

In this book I claim that, historically, Creole identity formation has been a tactical and negotiated process structured by uneven power relations. The cultural and racial content of Creole identity changed over time. The core ancestral group started out in the 1790–1820 period as Maroons—formerly enslaved Africans, European Africans, Zambo, Miskitu, and Rama Indians, and combinations thereof. They had a strongly "African" *identified* culture; however, it was not African in the formal sense, but a new creation laced with African, Amerindian, and European elements.

By the 1830's, Creoles were slaveholding coloreds born on the Coast and identified with the British. In large part their identity was constructed in contrast to that of the largely African-born slaves whom they held and the Amerindian communities they subjected. From the 1850's through the 1870's, Creoles were African-descended English speakers (no matter their racial and cultural mix) who included the Creole elite's former slaves and immigrants from the West Indies. Their culture still had an "African" feel but was also acculturating toward a German/British cultural standard set by the Moravians as Anglo hegemony consolidated.

From the 1870's through the 1930's, Creoles were peoples of color who were English speakers born on the Coast and Anglo acculturated by missionaries. The group included a large contingent of Anglo-acculturated colored and economically comfortable British West Indian immigrants. In Pearl Lagoon a significant portion of the group consisted of acculturated or intermarried Miskitu Indians and their progeny. In Bluefields the group's ranks were further swelled by the progeny of U.S. and other whites and Creole women. In part this Creole identity was constructed in contrast to darker, more working-class, more "African" cultured, "Negro" immigrants and took as its "European" acculturative standard U.S. white culture. From the 1930's onward the progeny of these *"negros"* became Creoles as well.

In sum, the genesis of Creole identity was not primordial, or monogenic. There is no monolithic historical set of Creole cultural traits or a single Creole identity. Creole identity formation was and is a multifaceted process critically mediated by shifting relations of power, the specifics of the community's history, and its social memory. Nevertheless, while highly multiple and even contradictory Creole identities are not endlessly contingent, their range is limited by these same forces.

Similarly, historically, Creoles did not wage identity politics from a stable subjectivity but instead from a variety of crosscutting subject positions. Creoles tactically dressed their group identity in more encompassing subject positions. This often lent the group greater legitimacy or became a means of creating alliances with other powerful interests.

At times, Creoles cast themselves as modern and civilized and constructed a diasporic "Anglo" identity for themselves. This recurring subject position was especially invoked in the wake of the Overthrow, when it seemed that British or possibly U.S. assistance on their behalf might be mobilized. Creoles mobilized around issues of class under the banner of planters during the planters' strike. They also played on their indigenous identifications, especially in the 1920's, with the advent of the various indigenous leagues. Here the appeal was to their autochthonous rights as an original people of the Atlantic Coast. They simultaneously strongly identified as black, subscribing to a black Caribbean diasporic identity that gained considerable international notoriety and influence during the 1910's and 1920's. They shifted over time and under the influence of Nicaraguan national hegemony from a strong Mosquitian national identity to identify as Nicaraguan nationals after the 1930's and simultaneously invoked both Costeño regional identity and became partisans of the Liberal Party.

From these manifold shifting and crosscutting subject positions, Creoles waged political struggle around a complex of conjuncturally mediated and interconnected issues and using a large variety of political practices and discourses generated from their political common sense. The residues of these subject positions, issues, practices, and discourses are important components of contemporary Creole political common sense.

As an African American strongly identified with blackness over the years, I have been overjoyed with the tendency for Creoles again to become more and more black identified. In fact, I worked hard toward that end. Now it seems to me, however, that Creoles might be better served to excavate alternative residual identity processes residing in Creole political common sense. I have two in mind; one is a stretch; the other is already under way.

Given Creoles' historical capacity as a group to assimilate peoples of widely different cultural, racial, and class origins, why could they not assimilate Mestizos? If a concerted effort were made while Creoles still manage to hold on to many of the positions of authority in the local government, could not all children be taught English at school, English be used in the region's churches, Creole holidays be observed, Creole food be featured in restaurants, Creole place names be preserved, and so on? Maybe not. Creole identity is not endlessly contingent; it is limited by the historical experiences of Creoles as a people and their resultant common sense. Historically, Creole identity has been and continues to be produced in opposition to Mestizos. More important, the power of Nicaraguan nationalism and its intrinsic articulation with Mestizo culture and identity make this an untenable strategy. Perhaps if the effort were limited to Mestizos who are Costeños, it would succeed.

As part of our project to map and ethnographically substantiate the communal land claims of indigenous and Creole peoples of the Atlantic Coast, I was assigned to write a section analyzing the land claims of Creole communities. Since Creoles are understood to be of African descent, they cannot claim to have occupied their lands previous to the colonial claims of the Spanish, from which the claims of the Nicaraguan state derive.

I went to the Creole villages of Haulover and Pearl Lagoon, about an hour and a half north of Bluefields by speedboat, to talk to the people there about how they rationalized their claims to communal lands. I expected to participate in the development of complex rationalizations based on Creole residence prior to the establishment of the Nicaraguan state or contesting the existence of Spanish control over the area or claiming rights based on reparations for the horrors of slavery. I hoped to be able to use these as a basis not only for contributing to the securing of Creole land rights but also for contributing to discussion of blacks' right to land throughout the African Diaspora in the Americas.

You would think that after sixteen years I would know better than to make assumptions about Creole identity. The first time I went to Haulover in the summer of 1997, I sought out some of my friends who now occupy positions of influence in the community. In the 1980's, when I spent considerable time in Haulover, the villagers told me that they were Creoles but that their old people had been Indians. This time one of my friends told me that Haulover's claims to land were based solely on the fact that their ancestors had been Indians, even if the present inhabitants were not. My other friend told me that everyone in Haulover was actually Miskitu and so they clearly had rights to all the land in the area. The next time I went to Haulover, both my friends again told me everyone in the village was Miskitu. They also said that the people in Bluefields and Pearl Lagoon were all Creoles and that they had no rights to communal lands.

I also went to Pearl Lagoon on these trips. It is a half-hour walk from Haulover, and the two villages, although antagonistic, have a long history of interaction and there are many familial ties between the two. Pearl Lagoon is, with Bluefields, the birthplace of Creole culture and identity. In the 1980's there was no question of the Creole identity of the people of this village; in fact, they were something of a bulwark against the incursions of the Miskitu resistance in the area.

On this visit, one of my friends told me that he claimed to be Creole only because he looked black; however, his ancestors were Miskitu. This, then, was the basis for his and the rest of the village's land claim. He went on to say that the Creoles of Bluefields had no claim because they were not there when the indigenous communities of the region were established. Another longtime friend and co-worker who vaguely resembles the movie character Putney Swope and whom I always thought of as Creole claimed that the entire community of Pearl Lagoon was descended from the "Sulira" Miskitu. Yet another stated that Pearl Lagoon people were "Indian by blood and Creole by custom." There are evidently now no real Creoles in the lower Pearl Lagoon Basin—just Miskitu who have legitimate land claims as the indigenous inhabitants of this area.

Over the last thirty years, Creole emphasis on either their Anglo diasporic or black diasporic identity has separated them from the much more numerous Miskitu populations who reside predominantly in the northern Atlantic Coast. In part because Creoles were afraid of being overwhelmed by the Miskitu, they pushed to divide the Coast in half when the Autonomous Governments were institutionalized. This has separated them from an important and much more powerful ally. The trend that has already begun, of Creole identification as Miskitu, has strong grounding in Creole common sense and seems to me a potentially important strategic move.

In addition to the political work that this book proposes to do in Bluefields, its critical analysis of Creole processes of identity formation and politics addresses a number of complex intellectual issues with political implications of interest elsewhere in the African Diaspora. Since this is not the primary objective of the work, I mention them only briefly in closing.

First, I demonstrate that Creole identity formation and politics are strategic and negotiated processes that are structured by uneven power relations (Bourgois 1989; Hale 1994; B. Williams 1991). This suggests that essentialist constructions of identity as primordial, monogenic, and monolithic (e.g., by Asante 1988; Thompson 1983) need to be reconsidered. It also calls into question the assumptions of scholars who maintain that racial and "ethnic" identity are always (or should be) *the* crucial determining factors in the politics of subaltern racial and "ethnic" groups.

Second, I contribute to the newly emerging literature on transnational and diasporic processes of identity formation (see, e.g., Clifford 1994; Gilroy 1993; Hall 1995). My research indicates that Creoles have a shifting sense of racial identity and an ambiguous positioning vis-à-vis other peoples of African descent. This leads me to criticize scholarly notions of diasporic identity as a racially determined attribute (see, e.g., Harris 1993; Padmore 1956) or even as a necessary product of shared memory and experience (Gilroy 1993). I argue that it is best understood as a tactical positioning within a world of shifting transnational interrelationships.

Third, the Creole case challenges the work of those scholars who subsume the dynamics of race, as a mechanism of social differentiation, under ethnicity theory (Glazer and Moynihan 1975). This study demonstrates a clear disjuncture between racialized Mestizo representations of Creole identity and the Creoles' own more culturally based construction of their group. This suggests that, analytically, it is important to distinguish between these interrelated but distinct processes of identity formation. (Omi and Winant 1986 makes a similar argument.)

Fourth, the study contributes to the theoretical debates on hegemony and processes of national, racial, and cultural identity in Latin America, particularly as they relate to people of African descent (see, e.g., Hanchard 1994; Wade 1993; Wright 1993). Here I build on the work of those scholars who assert that dominant representations of subaltern racial and cultural groups are critically related to hegemonic constructions of the nation and cultural nationalism (Stutzman 1981; B. Williams 1991); however, the Creole case points up the critical role played by "racial hegemony," racialization, and transnational representations of people of African descent in the dynamics of Latin American race relations.

The objectives of this book, which were motivated by the politics of a moment now past, seem to have relevance to the struggles Creoles are currently waging and perhaps to those of others of us in the black Diaspora. Now that I have arrived at what is finally the end, I realize what I have known all along: the easy part is getting it all down; the hard part is a political engagement that takes on the tasks and responsibilities engendered by the ethnographic and analytical work without imposing the authority of a knowledgeable outsider.

Notes

Preface

1. In this regard, I see my work as part of a move by women scholars and those of color to "speak from the place one is located to specify our sites of enunciation as 'home,'" that is, as a means of decolonizing anthropology by "enact[ing] a different politics of location, one that redirects its gaze homeward rather than away" (Visweswaran 1994:104). Homework conceived in this way has a fundamentally different character from "fieldwork," whose "primary goal is . . . to create an ethnographic understanding of the 'Other.'" Homework instead is based in the effort of "fellow citizens" "to understand what must be done, why it must be done, and what the consequences are of doing it one way and not another" (Williams 1995:25).

2. Miskitu Coast Creole culture played a major role in the forging of Belizean Creole culture. It has also exerted considerable influence on the Creole cultures of Providencia; San Andrés; Boca del Toro, Panama; Caribbean, Costa Rica; the Cayman Islands; and, to an extent, Jamaica (Holm 1978). Despite their relative importance in this regard, only Holm (1982), Olien (1988), and, more recently, Freeland (1988, 1995) have made Creoles the object of study.

3. Throughout this book I use the term "racial/cultural" instead of "racial" or "ethnic" to name subjectivities and identities that are constructed "historically, culturally, [and] politically" (Hall 1988:29). In this I have departed from my previous use of the term "ethnicity" to describe Costeños (e.g., Gordon 1995). I want to emphasize "the specificity of race as an autonomous field" in the construction of "ethnic" identity, which is usually associated predominantly with culture while maintaining a sense of the importance for the latter. My use of racial/cultural also seeks to highlight the importance of race as a "fundamental access of social organization" (Omi and Winant 1986:52,13) To this end I also utilize the term "racism" to designate the exercise of power over subaltern "racial/cultural" groups on the Coast, thereby moving against the tendency to use the term "ethnicity" "as a means of disavowing the realities of racism and repression" (Hall 1988:29). Finally, I have chosen to use the term "racial/cultural" as a means of signifying the mutual interpenetration and articulation of these processes of identification on Nicaragua's Atlantic Coast.

1. Introduction: Race, Identity, and Revolution

1. The conflation of U.S. identity with whiteness is strongest among younger Creoles. Older Creoles sometimes signify their differentiation between white and black Americans by referring to the latter as "American darkies." This terminology is clearly a holdover from Anglo usage in the early-twentieth-century U.S. enclave on the Coast.

2. Obeah is an African-influenced belief system.

2. Anglo Colonialism and the Emergence of Creole Society

1. Over the last three decades, revisionist histories have highlighted both enslaved Africans' organized movements (e.g., Harding 1981; Price 1979) and everyday resistance (e.g., Blassingame 1972) against their condition. These were produced against the previous body of historical work, which was largely silent regarding the agency of the enslaved.

2. Because of the political work they are intended to do, chapters 2 and 3 are deliberately written against important recent scholarship on the history of the African Diaspora. I provide an "authoritative narrative," in contrast to Price's work (1983, 1990), whose innovative multivocal approach has been so influential in Diaspora studies. Similarly, despite David Scott's (1991) fine critique of the essentializing nationalist agenda of much of Diaspora historiography (including that of Price), my Creole history remains focused on the construction of an "authentic" past for the Creole community.

3. These historical elements, which may come to compose Creole common sense, following Raymond Williams, may be archaic or residual, the latter being the more important. The archaic is "that which is wholly recognized as an element of the past, to be observed, to be examined, or even on occasion to be consciously 'revived,' in a deliberately specializing way." The residual is that which "has been effectively formed in the past, but is still active in the cultural process, not only and often not at all as an element of the past, but as an effective element of the present" (Williams 1977:122). Both processes are important in the contemporary process of Creole common sense.

4. See Newton (1966:302), Holm (1978:179). See also Bell (1899); Conzemius (1932); Esquemeling and Dampier (1978); Hodgson (1766); letter of Robert J. Prowett, PRO (1847:30); M. W. (1732: 295–298).

5. According to Forbes (1993:233), "the terms 'mustee' and 'mestizo' as used in the British Caribbean colonies would seem to always refer to American [Amerindian]-European hybrids until perhaps the 1770's–1790's when mixed-bloods of a light color were also included, at least in some parts of the Caribbean."

6. Estimates of the size of the slave population during this period vary widely. Robert White (1789:34), the source for these data, was the legal representative of the Mosquitian slaveholders and perhaps had more complete data on the slave population than did other observers.

7. White (1793). There is conflicting evidence as to how many persons were living on the Coast before the evacuation, how many left, and how many stayed. White (1789:34) claims that at the time of the evacuation, 416 "free persons" and

1,808 slaves were living on the Coast. Elsewhere it is stated that 537 "white and free persons" and 1,677 Africans were evacuated to Belize (Burdon 1831:161–162).

8. Porta Costas (1990:54, 56, 57).

9. Porta Costas (1990:57–58). There are a number of estimates of the number of slaves held by Hodgson in Bluefields in the late 1780's (see Romero Vargas 1994:480, 490, 506, 507, 510). It may well be that this represents the fluctuations in his slave force brought on by the transfer of his site of operation to Bluefields from Black River and the initiation of cotton cultivation on Corn Island. Hodgson's wife, Elizabeth Pitt, inherited one hundred of her father's slaves from Black River (Romero Vargas 1994:490). These were evidently combined with those already owned by Hodgson.

10. In 1790 Colonel Caesar protected the Bluefields Maroons from the Tawira Miskitu, who threatened to re-enslave them. In 1802 the Zambo Miskitu regent, Prince Stephen, imprisoned and threatened with forced labor the English captain of a trading ship "for having beaten and treated with the greatest cruelty . . . a Negro of the Coast" (O'Neille 1802 in Costa Rica 1913:585).

11. Roberts (1965:103); FO 53/15, fol. 76 in Olien (1988:11).

12. Bell (1899:20); Bell to Fancourt, North Bluefields, November 18, 1843, CO 123/67.

13. Samboes are people of African and Amerindian heritage. They were probably Zambo-Miskitu in Pearl Lagoon and an African/Rama Indian mixture in Bluefields.

14. Walker to the Earl of Aberdeen, August 1, 1844, FO 53/1 78568; Christie to Palmerston, May 15, 1849, FO 53/49 73305.

15. Miskitu Coast English Creole is a linguistic system clearly distinct from standard English. Its lexicon has evolved largely from English. Syntactically, it is a compromise between English and African languages. It is closely related to Belizean English Creole (Holm 1978).

16. Mintz and Price (1985:6) state that "the term 'Creole' (which probably came from the Portuguese 'crioulo') refers, on a general level, to something that comes from the Old World but is raised in the New." In different areas of the New World during different times, the term "Creole" (or *criollo* [Sp.], *crèole* [Fr.]) has had different meanings. On the Miskitu Coast it probably had the same meaning as in Jamaica and Belize during this period, as the Mosquitia had strong historical connections with these colonies (Codd in Bolland 1977:95; also Long 1970:351). According to Brathwaite (1971:xv), in Jamaica between 1770 and 1820, the word *Creole* "was [used] in its original Spanish sense of criollo: born in, native to, committed to the area of living, and it was used in relation to both whites and slaves."

17. Interestingly, according to Le Page and Tabouret-Keller (1985:63), "Belize and Miskito Coast Creoles are in the minority among Caribbean settlements in referring to themselves as Creoles and to their language as Creole." The English Creole-speaking communities of San Andrés and Providencia also refer to themselves as Creoles (Parsons 1956:66). This should come as no surprise, given their close historical connection with the Mosquitia.

18. In the mid-1840's, Alexander Hodgson had been a magistrate for nineteen

years: "Mosquito Land Grants 1844 to 1848," FO 53/44, p. 65. William and
George Hodgson, mixed-race descendants of Col. Robert Hodgson, had been the
acknowledged authorities in Bluefields from the 1820's (Roberts 1965:103). In
1842 George Hodgson was the governor of the Bluefields district and later
became the governor of Greytown ("Deposition of George Hodgson and William
Halstead," October 27, 1842, CO 123/65; Christie to Palmerston, September 5,
1848, Consular Letters, CIDCA-Bluefields Archives).

19. Bell to Fancourt, October 21, 1843, CO 123/67; Christie to Palmerston,
September 5, 1848, Consular Letters, CIDCA-Bluefields Archives.

20. The Creoles were members of the elite and two of them were direct
descendants of Robert Hodgson: George Hodgson, Sr., and Alexander Hodgson.
The other members were William Halstead Ingram, James Porter, and John
Dixon ("Minutes of the Council of State," September 10, 1846, FO 53/5, in
Oertzen et al. 1990).

21. Ibid.

22. Ibid.

23. Over the decades this process evolved to the extent that in 1874, when a
new chief was sworn in, his speech was delivered in English and simultaneously
interpreted into Miskitu by a Moravian missionary for the benefit of visiting
Miskitu headmen (Lundberg 1875:308).

24. Martin (1870:407); Lundberg (1874:218); De Kalb (1893):275. For almost
three decades two sets of Creole fathers and sons from Pearl Lagoon were among
the most influential political figures in the Mosquito Reserve. Charles Patterson
succeeded his father, Henry, as vice-president of the reserve in 1874, holding that
position or the presidency of the Executive Council until 1894. James W.
Cuthbert was attorney general during much of this period, while his son James
served as secretary of the council (Lundberg 1874:307; Renkewitz 1874:222; De
Kalb 1893:237).

25. "Minutes of a meeting held on the subject of slavery and compensation for
slaves at Bluefields, Mosquito Shore the 10th August 1841," CO 123/67, fols. 1–
2, p. 5, fols. 3–4, p. 6; Christie and Venables to the Earl of Clarendon, September
18, 1855, FO 53/49, fol. 1; Bell to Walker, November 12, 1842, CO 123/65;
Bowden to Walker, September 5, 1844, CO 123/62, fol. 1. Slave owners on the
island, many of whom came from San Andrés, were both white and colored. The
slaves at Corn Island had provided the labor for a small but thriving plantation
economy based on sea island cotton, which rapidly withered following emancipation (Parsons 1956:19).

26. Estimates of the population of Bluefields and Pearl Lagoon vary, hence the
uncertainty in the percentage of the populations that were slaves. In 1844 Walker
claimed that "in this Village [Bluefields] there is a population of upwards of three
hundred souls, all of whom are descendants of British settlers or slaves. At Pearl
Cay Lagoon . . . there are about two hundred and at Boca del Toro nearly three
hundred of the same description" (Walker to Lord Bishop of London, September
11, 1844, FO 53/1 in Oertzen, Rossbach, and Wunderich 1990:xx). In 1841,
however, the Miskitu king granted land to a Bluefields population of about four
hundred persons (Mosquito Land Grants 1844–1848, FO 53/44, pp. 123–124). In
1848 Consul Christie reported five hundred residents at Bluefields plus one
hundred newly arrived Prussian immigrants (Christie to Palmerston, no. 7,

September, 5 1848, CIDCA-Bluefields Archives).

27. Chatfield to Palmerston, April 19, 1848, CIDCA-Bluefields Archives; Bell (1899:26); Parsons (1956).

28. Christie to Palmerston, May 15, 1849, FO 53/49 73305, fol. 5; Walker to the Earl of Aberdeen, August 1, 1844, FO 53/1 78568, fols. 3–4; Pfeiffer, Lundberg, and Jurgensen (1857:243); De Kalb (1893:283); Bell to Walker, November 12, 1842, CO 123/65; Martin (1990:134); Christie to Palmerston, May 15, 1849, in "Papers Respecting Mosquito Land Claims: 1849–51," 1860, FO 53/49, fol. 5; Smith (1872:314).

29. According to a visiting member of the Moravian Mission Board, more than three hundred thousand coconuts were exported from Bluefields to New York annually (Wullschlagel 1990:130).

30. Sieborger (1884:175); Renkewitz (1867:470). It is probable that most Creole "dealers in Indian-rubber" operated on a very small scale; however, a few of the elite, like Henry Patterson, became "very wealthy, having made a good deal of money in the Indian rubber-trade" (Renkewitz 1874:218–224, quotation on 222).

31. Walker to the Earl of Aberdeen, August 1, 1844, FO 53/1 78568; Clarence in Lundberg (1875: 309). According to a British observer in the 1840's, the Creole elite magistrates were "disposed to make any exertion of power, only in the punishment and the oppression of the class of freed slaves and of the Indians, while greater malefaction of their own class, especially those who have good family connexions . . . enjoy entire immunity" (Bell to Fancourt, North Bluefields, October 21, 1843, CO 123/67).

32. Wullschlagel (1856:34–35).

33. Traders Peter and Samuel Shepherd were particularly influential: Bell to Fancourt, North Bluefields, October 21, 1843, CO 123/67.

34. Christie to Palmerston, September 5, 1848, Consular Letters, fols. 136–137, CIDCA-Bluefields Archive; Feurig (1862:309).

35. Anonymous (1882:285).

36. Kandler (1851:526); Wullschlagel (1856:34); Mueller (1932:94).

37. See, e.g., Pfeiffer (1849:202); Grunewald (1863:56); Grunewald (1872:198).

38. Wullschlagel (1856:35); Anonymous (1882:280).

39. M.C.M.A. (1895:563–564).

40. See, e.g., Lundberg (1866:53); Peper (1879:263).

41. Martin (1872:363).

42. See, e.g., Roberts (1965:108); Blair (1873:433); Ziock (1882:310).

43. Bell to the Earl of Elgin, North Bluefields, April 19, 1843, CO 123/65. For discussion of a similar situation that developed in Belize, see Bolland (1977) and Ashdown (1979: esp. pp. 17–19).

44. Feurig (1857b:349).

45. Bell to Fancourt, North Bluefields, October 21 and November 18 1843, CO 123/67.

46. Bell to the Earl of Elgin, North Bluefields, April 19, 1843, CO 123/65.

47. Pfeiffer, Lundberg, and Jurgensen (1857:243).

48. Bell to Governor Sir Charles Grey, Bluefields, February 25, 1848, Consular Letters, fol. 8, CIDCA-Bluefields Archives; Bell (1899:19); Christie to Palmerston, September 5, 1848, Consular Letters, fol. 136, CIDCA-Bluefields Archives.

49. Christie to Palmerston, September 5, 1848, Consular Letters, fols. 136–

137, CIDCA-Bluefields Archives.

50. Circular letter of Synodal Committee (1851:164). See Comaroff (1985:131) for a discussion of the similar relationship between missionary activity, acculturation to British Protestant culture, and the articulation between a local society and the global forces of European political economy in southern Africa.

3. Negotiating Modernity: Disparate Racial Politics in the Twentieth Century

1. Rule is domination by a group or groups over others by means of coercion. Hegemony is domination by a group or groups over others through persuasion, negotiation, and the organization of consent. Relations of domination in any social formation are achieved through the complex interplay of rule and hegemony.

2. In 1855 Bluefields had a population of between six hundred and seven hundred, of which one hundred were Indians. The total Creole population in the Mosquitia was about twelve hundred (Wullschlagel 1856:34–35).

3. The Moravian mission on the Coast was originally established by the Moravian Mission Board, headquartered in Herrenhut, Germany. Until World War I most of the missionaries were Germans; however, there were missionaries of other nationalities, particularly black Jamaicans. A number of the German missionaries had also spent considerable time involved in mission work in Jamaica. The missionaries used English or, later, Miskitu in their mission work, and in response to what they understood to be the British colonial status of the Mosquitia did their best to inculcate British culture and allegiances.

4. In 1874 the Moravians changed the spelling of Mosquito to Moskito; since then they have called the area the Moskito Coast or Moskito.

5. Martin (1882:254). This process of acculturation was by no means complete. Over the years, the Moravians were often distressed by the absence of orthodoxy and constancy in the conversion of Coast people.

6. Michael J. Clancy to Thomas O'Hara, Bluefields, August 27, 1897, no. 99, BCPR.

7. *"Negros"* (Cabezas in Pérez-Valle 1978:156, 158, 159); *"negros de Jamaica"* (Zelaya in Pérez-Valle 1978:149, 214); *"jamaiqueños"* and *"extranjeros"* (Madriz in Pérez-Valle 1978:169, 190, 193).

8. There was a substantial population of blacks among the "foreign born" composed of persons from Jamaica, Grand Cayman, Roatán, and Belize, in order of numerical importance. U.S. blacks, though less important numerically than any of the foregoing, probably made up two-thirds of the U.S. residents of the reserve during this period. There were also sixty-three white and one hundred Mestizo residents (*Bluefields Messenger* 1890).

9. *La Gaceta Oficial* 32, no. 28 (April 21, 1894) in Pérez-Valle (1978):183.

10. For example, a U.S. man-of-war was stationed off of Bluefields in 1909 when a strike by Creole planters threatened the stability of U.S. enterprise in the area (Clancy to State Department, May 22, 1909, no. 68, BCPR; Clancy to Secretary of State, May 14, 1909, BCPR). U.S. troops occupied Bluefields in 1894, 1910, and 1926.

11. Clancy to William Merry, San José, Costa Rica, February 1905, no. 25, BCPR.

12. Clancy to State Department, August 16, 1909, no. 78, BCPR; Dozier (1985:157–158).

13. Clancy to John T. King, Mobile, Alabama, September 24, 1897, no. 126, BCPR; Clancy to State Department, June 3, 1909, no. 71, BCPR.

14. Moravian Church and Mission Agency (1896: 96); Clancy to Hill, November 24, 1904, no. 43, BCPR; Clancy to Merry, March 29, 1909, no. 43, BCPR.

15. Clancy to Secretary of State, February 29, 1909, BCPR; Clancy to Secretary of State, February 26, 1909, no. 43, BCPR; Clancy to Merry, August 28, 1905, no. 36, BCPR.

16. Clancy to Hill, November 2, 1904, no. 32, BCPR. The concession was made to Charles Weinberger in return for a guaranteed loan of one million dollars made to the Nicaraguan government (Clancy to Asst. Secretary of State, August 21, 1908, no. 5, BCPR). Anyone could purchase bananas, but they could not use the river to transport them.

17. Clancy to Asst. Secretary of State, May 15, 1909, no. 67, BCPR; Clancy to State Department, June 3, 1909, no. 71, BCPR.

18. Chalkley to Young, no. 15, November 10, 1915, Crowdell Papers, CIDCA-Bluefields.

19. McCoy, Pearl Lagoon to British Consul, Bluefields, April 16, 1911, Crowdell Papers, CIDCA-Bluefields; "Signed Depositions made before the British Titles Commissioner H. I. Chalkley, Bluefields," June 17, 1905, no. 33, Crowdell Papers, CIDCA-Bluefields; Chalkley to Young 1915, H. C. Chalkley, Special Commissioner of H.B.M. Government, to C. Alban Young, His Majesty's Envoy Extraordinary and Minister Plenipotentiary, Guatemala, no. 18, November 23, 1915. Some of the choicest tracts went to president Zelaya himself and his family. T. López and Zelaya owned eight thousand hectares between Bluefields and the Río Cukra, which they then traded for land farther to the south at the anticipated construction site of a transisthmus railroad (H. C. Chalkley, Special Commissioner of H.B.M. Government, to C. Alban Young, His Majesty's Envoy Extraordinary and Minister Plenipotentiary, Guatemala, no. 18, November 23, 1915).

20. See, e.g., Fred Thomas to Charles Patterson, Representative of the Mosquito Indians, Bluefields, May 3, 1911; Patterson et al. to Chalkley, 1911, Crowdell Papers, CIDCA-Bluefields.

21. For more on the process of land distribution under the terms of this treaty, see Hale (1991, 1994). Hale argues that the allotments were inadequate to the agricultural needs of Coast communities.

22. People of Bluefields and Rama Indians to H. O. Chalkley, British Consul, Bluefields, April 22, 1911, Crowdell Papers, CIDCA-Bluefields Archives.

23. Some few members of the Bluefields Creole elite, generally those most closely associated with U.S. economic interests, were willing and able to join the new governmental structures almost immediately. H. C. Ingram was acting mayor of Bluefields in 1895 (Harrison to Kimberley, 1895 in Oertzen, Rossbach, and Wunderich 1990:402, 407–408). Stephen A. Hodgson was elected mayor in 1898, as was John Taylor, with the support of the Union Club, in 1904 (Clancy to Sorsby, January 7, 1898, no. 2, BCPR; Clancy to Hill, December 5, 1904, no. 2, BCPR). Alfred W. Hooker held an array of positions in both the local and the national governments.

24. Lee to Secretary of State, March 19, 1911, BCPR.

25. Clancy to State Department, December 18, 1908, no. 31, BCPR; Clancy to Asst. Secretary of State, November 6, 1908, no. 23, BCPR; Moffat to State Department, November 17, 1909, no. 34, BCPR.

26. H. Chafmt to Bingham 1909; H. chafmt, Actg. British Vice Consul Bluefields, to H. F. Bingham, British Consul, San Juan del Norte, Nicaragua.

27. Mission Board (1900: 351–353). Later that same year, during a fire in Bluefields, Nicaraguan police threatened and beat church members and compelled them to destroy the Moravian elementary school building (Brethren's Society for the Furtherance of the Gospel 1900: 406).

28. Clancy to Merry, August 16, 1905, no. 35, BCPR; Moffat to State Department, October 21, 1909, no. 17, BCPR.

29. In 1879 the Moravians reported fewer than half of their 227-member Pearl Lagoon congregation as being Creole (98); the rest were Miskitu (Anonymous 1880:338). By 1894 the Pearl Lagoon congregation had more than doubled, to 484 members, and was now described by the missionaries as being "mostly Creole" (Anonymous 1894:402).

30. "Coloreds" is a term used to designate people who are mixed race (white and black) and generally "middle class." It is a third racial category in the Anglophone Caribbean.

31. Clancy to King, October 4, 1897, no. 135, BCPR; Lawder to Young, June 22, 1916, no. 1/16, Crowdell Papers, CIDCA-Bluefields.

32. Over time Creoles evidently lost many of these jobs to Mestizos from the Pacific. In 1927 Ruiz y Ruiz characterized the latter, not the former, as, typically, state employees, lower-level employees of foreign companies, and professionals (1927:73).

33. As late as the 1930s outside observers commented on this phenomenon (Conzemius 1932:7; Mueller 1921:57).

34. There were also two hundred whites, fifteen hundred Mestizos, five hundred Chinese, and three hundred Amerindians (Ruiz y Ruiz 1927:72).

35. Guido Grossman, "Annual Report of the Province of Nicaragua," Moravian Archives, Bethlehem, Pa., 1918.

36. Clancy to Hill, February 11, 1905, no. 97, BCPR.

37. Clancy to Sorsby, March 14 1898, no. 54, BCPR.

38. Clipping from *The Recorder* (Bluefields), August 21, 1897, in Clancy to O'Hara, August 20, 1897, no. 93, BCPR.

39. Clancy to O'Hara, August 10, 1897, no. 110, BCPR.

40. Citizens of Bluefields to Samuel T. Lee, Bluefields, April 7, 1911, BCPR.

41. British Colonial Secretary's Office to Consul, Bluefields, October 5, 1912, Crowdell Papers, CIDCA-Bluefields.

42. Grossman, "Annual Report of the Province of Nicaragua," Moravian Archives, Bethlehem, Pa., 1926; Society for Propagating the Gospel (1927:61).

43. Lee to Secretary of State, March 19, 1911, BCPR.

44. Miskito Indian Patriotic League, Bluefields, 1926, CIDCA-Bluefields.

45. J. O. Thomas to Chalkley, Bluefields, October 22, 1915, Crowdell Papers, CIDCA-Bluefields.

46. Petitioners to J. O. Sanders, Bluefields, April 2, 1919, BCPR.

47. Grossman, "Annual Report of the Superintendent for 1919" (1920), p. 438.

48. Clancy to Hill, December 5, 1904, no. 50, BCPR; Clancy to State Department, December 18, 1908, no. 31, BCPR.

49. Clancy to Merry, December 24, 1904, no. 13, BCPR; Clancy to Hill, November 14, 1904, no. 37, BCPR; Clancy to Hill, November 15, 1904, no. 38, BCPR; Clancy to Hill, December 7, 1904, no. 51, BCPR; Clancy to Hill, December 12, 1904, nos. 56 and 57, BCPR; Clancy to Hill, December 19, 1904, no. 68, BCPR; and Clancy to State Department, June 12, 1909, no. 74, BCPR.

50. Clancy to Merry, January 16, 1905, no. 19, BCPR.

51. Clancy to Asst. Secretary of State, May 15, 1909, no. 67, BCPR; Clancy to Merry, July 19, 1909, no. 8, BCPR.

52. Clancy to State Department, May 22, 1909, no. 68, BCPR; Clancy to State Department, June 3, 1909, no. 71, BCPR.

53. Clancy to Asst. Secretary of State, May 15, 1909, no. 67, BCPR.

54. Moffat to State Department, October 16, 1909, no. 12, BCPR.

55. Moffat to State Department, October 16, 1909, no. 11, BCPR.

56. Moffat to State Department, November 7, 1909, no. 29, BCPR. According to Consul Moffat, "The unequivocal desire of the leaders of this movement and the people generally is for a declaration of their independence and the establishment of a separate republic."

57. Moffat to State Department, October 11, 1909, no. 7, BCPR.

58. Moffat to State Department, October 16, 1909, no. 12; November 18, 1909, no. 35, BCPR.

59. Deverall in "Mass Meeting at the Union Club," *The American*, Bluefields, March 19, 1911; clipping in Lee to Secretary of State, March 19, 1911, unnumbered, BCPR.

60. Moffat to State Department, April 12, 1910, no. 124, BCPR.

61. Moffat to State Department, June 12, 1910, no. 178, BCPR; Teplitz (1973: 385–387, 405–408).

62. Moffat to State Department, June 12, 1910, no. 178, BCPR.

63. Moffat to State Department, May 19, 1910, no. 146, BCPR.

64. Moffat to State Department, April 12, 1910, no. 124, BCPR.

65. The Inhabitants of Pearl Lagoon Mosquito Coast to his Britannic Majesty's Government, Bluefields, February 23, 1911, Crowdell Papers, CIDCA-Bluefields.

66. The Conservative government was generally unpopular in Nicaragua and would not have stood without U.S. support. Opposition was spearheaded by the agro-export bourgeoisie and urban petty bourgeoisie. Important segments of these class fragments were to be found in Bluefields, center of the most advanced capitalist sector in the country (Araya Pochet and Peña 1979:5).

67. The Moravian mission had very strained relations with the Conservative governments (Society for Propagating the Gospel 1911:105; 1929:57).

68. Petitioners to J. O. Sanders, Bluefields, April 2, 1919, BCPR.

69. Memorialist Committee, 1919; Memorial to the President, Bluefields, October 11, 1919, Crowdell Papers, CIDCA-Bluefields Archive..

70. UNIA Foreign Divisions 1926, UNIA Central Division Files, Schomburg Collection, New York Public Library.

71. Grossman, "Annual Report of the Province of Nicaragua, 1920," Moravian Archives, Bethlehem, Pa., 1920.

72. Ibid.

73. G. A. Heidenreich, "Annual Report of the Bluefields Congregation for 1924," Moravian Archives, Bethlehem, Pa., 1924.

74. Grossman, "Annual Report of the Province of Nicaragua, 1920," Moravian Archives, Bethlehem, Pa., 1920; Society for Propagating the Gospel (1930:8; 1931:96).

75. Heath in Grossman, "Annual Report of the Province of Nicaragua," Moravian Archives, Bethlehem, Pa., 1920.

76. Solórzano was elected in 1924 with Vice-President Juan Bautista Sacasa as a Liberal.

77. Miskito Indian Patriotic League to U.S. Secretary of State, February 10, 1926, Richard Stephenson private collection.

78. Hodgson et al. to McConnico, Bluefields, May 4, 1926, Crowdell Papers, CIDCA-Bluefields.

79. J. O. Thomas to Anna Crowdell, February 4, 1927, Crowdell Papers, CIDCA-Bluefields.

80. Samuel Howell, "General George Hodgson: His Life and Achievements," pamphlet, CIDCA-Bluefields Archives, n.d.

81. Grossman, "Annual Report of the Province of Nicaragua," Moravian Archives, Bethlehem, Pa., 1926.

82. Ibid.

83. "Creoles, Indians etc of Pearl Lagoon to Owen Reese, British Consul," Bluefields, 1927, Crowdell Papers, CIDCA-Bluefields.

84. J. O. Thomas to Anna Crowdell, February 4, 1927, Crowdell Papers, CIDCA-Bluefields.

85. "Indians and Creoles to E. Owen Reese British Consul," February 1, 1928, Crowdell Papers, CIDCA-Bluefields.

86. Alfred W. Hooker was one of the most influential politicians in Atlantic Coast history. In a career that spanned more than thirty years, he held such local positions as secretary to Juan Pablo Reyes, one of the first governors of the Coast; president of the Union Club; Bluefields' mayor, tax collector for the Department of Zelaya. On the national level, he served as minister of education, minister of development, deputy of the National Assembly, and senator.

87. Creoles of Bluefields to Alfred W. Hooker, "La Voz del Atlántico," June 1930, Crowdell Papers, CIDCA-Bluefields.

88. Horatio Hodgson, "Memorial of the People of the Department of Zelaya to That Just and Honorable Assembly, Our National Congress," 1935, CIDCA-Bluefields Archives.

89. In 1914, responsibility for the mission was shifted from the Moravian Mission Board, headquartered in Herrenhut, Germany, to the North American Synod, headquartered in Bethlehem, Pennsylvania.

90. See, e.g., Society for Propagating the Gospel (1925:77); Grossman, "Annual Report of the Province of Nicaragua," Moravian Archives, Bethlehem, Pa., 1926.

4. Creole History and Social Memory

1. For more than 150 years, the liberation of the island's enslaved community has been celebrated on August 27.

2. All interviews in this section were conducted in English Creole. I have

transcribed them in standard English orthography. While much of the grammatical difference between standard English and English Creole is maintained, the significant differences in pronunciation are lost. The names of all the Creoles I interviewed whose accounts I use in this section have been replaced with pseudonyms. (All Spanish/English translations are my own.)

Terry García was one of the original Bluefields rastas and a leader of the group that was active throughout the revolutionary period. Terry was extremely interested in the politics of the Diaspora and organized a number of events in Bluefields, including an annual commemoration of the death of Bob Marley and one protesting apartheid in South Africa. Thoughtful and intellectually curious, he had graduated from high school and in the early 1980's worked for a while for the government. He was also a talented graphic artist. Toward the end of the 1980's and in 1991, when this interview was conducted, he began to support himself by painting signs.

3. Here I have in mind Richard Price's representation of Saramakan oral historical knowledge. A close reading of Price's description of his methodology, however, makes it clear that the historical knowledge he collected was also fragmentary and contradictory. Though transparent in the constructed account, the ethnographer had to work hard and authoritatively to produce an internally consistent and chronological narrative of Saramaka history that, though he uses Saramaka voices, he admits "would amaze (and be new to) any single living Saramaka" (1983:25).

4. A number of renditions of the history of the Atlantic Coast have been published in Nicaragua. Most are narratives of conflicting colonial powers and nationalisms rather than histories of Coast peoples. The most important of these works include Gámez (1939), Robert M. Hooker (1945), and Brautigam Beer (1970a and b).

5. These recurring themes are also present in the historical narrative I presented in chapters 2 and 3; however, many specific events that I include in my "academic" account were not significant enough to Creoles at the time they spoke with me about Creole history for them to recount or to have kept them from fading, at least for the moment, from their memories. Forgotten or deemphasized memories can, however, also be read for their contemporary significance.

6. Herman Dixon is my wife's third cousin. At the time of my interview with him in 1991, he was in his mid-thirties. He was one of the original Creole counterrevolutionaries and spent time in Costa Rica and the "bush" south of Bluefields with the Contras. He was not very well educated and had worked as a fisherman. After the change in government in 1990, in which the UNO (Unión Nacional Opositora, United National Opposition) coalition of political parties in opposition to the Sandinistas took power, he served as regional governor Alvin Guthrie's bodyguard.

7. In 1991 Lucy Williams was in her late sixties or early seventies. She was well respected in the community and worked as a teacher at the Moravian High School. She was known nationally for her dance troupes, which presented "dignified" versions of a number of Creole dance styles. She was also known as a keeper of the traditions and history of Creole dance and music. She was a friend and intellectual collaborator of Donovan Brautigam Beer.

8. Burt Hodgson had been a schoolteacher before he left Bluefields for Costa Rica a few years after the Triumph. There he was active as a leader with the Southern Indigenous and Creole Community (SICC, after the Triumph of the Sandinistas, the organized Creole counterrevolution) during the mid- to late-1980's. He did not serve in a military capacity with SICC. At the time of my interview with him in 1991, he was working as an adviser to the Regional Assembly of the Autonomous Government.

9. René Hodgson at the time of this discussion with him was in his early forties. René was the son of a very famous Creole boat owner and captain and therefore had standing in the community. Fairly well educated, he had held a number of civil service positions with the revolutionary government. We worked together for a number of years on fishing development projects. He was anti-Sandinista and held a high position in local government after the elections of 1990.

10. Berta Blanford was a well-educated, middle-aged schoolteacher and administrator in the bilingual and bicultural program instituted during the revolutionary era for Creole-speaking children. She attended the Seminario Bíblico Latinoamericano in San José, Costa Rica, in the early 1970's and on her return worked for nationalist pastor Rev. Joe Kelly. She subsequently taught at the Moravian High School until the triumph of the Revolution. She was an early member of SICC, a group dedicated to Creole cultural preservation and social uplift before the Triumph of the Sandinista Revolution.

11. Thomas Jackson was in his mid-twenties at the time of my interview with him in 1991. He had gone through the first years of high school and worked as a fisherman. One of a number of Creole youth who had run away from the SMP (Servicio Militar Patriótico, Patriotic Military Service), he joined the Contras and operated for a time with them in the Pearl Lagoon area before becoming disillusioned and returning to Bluefields.

12. Kevin Whitiker was introduced in chapter 1. I lived with him and his wife for a number of years in the early 1980's. Kevin at the time of this discussion in 1991 was in his seventies. He had been a cook for the senior Somoza and was anti-Sandinista.

13. James Johnson was in his mid-thirties during this 1991 conversation. He was born on Corn Island to an elite Creole father who later abandoned his family. James managed to get a good education, including a couple of years of university-level training in economics in Managua. He was the original FSLN commandant in charge of Corn Island. He became a critical member of the FSLN and had many run-ins with the party hierarchy. He and I worked together on fisheries projects for many years. After the elections of 1990, he became a successful lobster boat owner and captain. He is one of my best friends and one of those whose political position this book shares.

14. Frank Parsons, a light-skinned Creole from Pearl Lagoon, was in his sixties or seventies when we had this discussion in 1991. He was the "outside" (illegitimate) son of an elite white Creole businessman. His mother was a member of a Creole elite family from Pearl Lagoon. Mr. Frank was a fine but slow carpenter who spent years working intermittently on my house in Bluefields. Although he was avidly pro-American and anti-Sandinista, we were close friends.

15. Francis Sui Williams was one of the most respected and influential members of Bluefields' Creole community. Before the Triumph of the Revolution, he had served as *jefe político* (governor) of the Department of Zelaya. He was also a longtime professor of history at the Moravian High School. In the late 1980's he became director of CIDCA in Bluefields. He was also a winning candidate on the FSLN regional ticket in the 1990 elections and served as a member of the Regional Assembly of the Autonomous Government. In his fifties, Sui was an avid Creole historian and had published a number of articles on Creole oral history. We also had a good deal of intellectual interchange. I asked him to read and comment on numerous historical and ethnographic pieces I produced, and we engaged in hours of discussion on Creole history.

16. Herman Wilson, in his early seventies at the time of this discussion in 1991, was the preeminent Creole sea captain and had experience captaining boats around the globe. He had been the owner of four fishing boats before the Revolution. He was married to the daughter of the first "native" bishop of the Moravian Church, who herself was a longtime teacher at the Moravian High School. This was an important and respected Creole family. Mr. Herman was extremely well read and enjoyed American mystery novels. We spent a great deal of time sitting on his front verandah talking about Creoles and Bluefields in previous times, and about fishing. He often read and commented on my written work on fishing and Creole history.

17. May East died in the early 1990's. She was in her eighties when this interview was conducted by Azalee Hodgson, the CIDCA-Bluefields librarian. Ms. East had been a member of the Beholden branch of the UNIA.

18. Ronny Green was a former member of the EEBI (Escuela de Entrenamiento Básico de la Infantería, Infantry Basic Training School), an elite anti-insurgency wing of the National Guard. He was for many years a commandant in the counterrevolution and operated in the area south of Bluefields. In his mid- to late twenties, he worked as a fisherman and farmer, but when I spoke to him in 1991, he was having a hard time settling back down into civilian life.

19. The historiographical work of Robert Montgomery Hooker (1945), Donovan Brautigam Beer (1970a and b), and John Wilson (1975) clearly indicates that if any of these persons had desired to do so they could have written a credible scholarly account of Creole history. Francis Sui's oral narration of Creole history during a taped discussion in 1991 has all the elements of a scholarly narrative. His published and unpublished written historical work from the late 1980's clearly demonstrates the ability to produce a comprehensive Creole history, though he has not attempted to do so.

5. The Discursive Struggle over Race and Nation

1. Brazil and Cuba, where elites have appropriated forms of "African" expressive culture in their constructions of national identity, are exceptions to this rule.

2. A. Somoza D. quoted in Anonymous (1969c:4). All translations are the author's unless otherwise noted.

3. A. Somoza D. quoted in ibid., p. 8. Somoza is referring here to two large-scale projects. The first, the Proyecto Piloto de Castellanización (Hispanicization

Pilot Project, sponsored by UNESCO, was a literacy project that also had as objectives the Hispanicization, civilization, and nationalization of the Miskitu. This speech also announced the beginning of the Francia Sirpi Project, which would resettle a number of Miskitu communities that had lost access to their agricultural zone across the Río Coco with the settlement of the territorial dispute with Honduras. These Miskitu were to be resettled, financed, and taught to be Mestizo peasant producers.

4. A. Somoza D. quoted in Anonymous (1969e:8).

5. "Cultural underdevelopment" from A. Somoza D. quoted in ibid.; "cultural progress" from Anonymous (1969b:1).

6. Bluefields was reportedly 70 percent Creole in 1964 (Incer in Pérez-Valle 1978:364).

7. The Somoza regime was in general strongly supported by the U.S. government throughout this period. The relationship was at its shakiest during the Kennedy administration, which played a role in keeping Tachito, whom Kennedy once referred to as the "co-dictator of Nicaragua," from succeeding his brother Luis as president. Tachito was particularly close to conservative Republicans, especially Richard Nixon, to whom the Somoza family reportedly donated one million dollars for the 1972 re-election campaign (Diederich 1981:64, 67–68, 88–89). Chamorro C., on the other hand, was linked to U.S. liberals such as columnist Jack Anderson of the *Washington Post* and was a great admirer of the Kennedys (Chamorro Z. 1982:168).

8. See, e.g., Anonymous (1970a:17).

9. Chamorro C. (1970c:1b). They are not, however, of the two groups believed by nationalists to be the principal "civilized" ancestor cultures: the Chorotega and the Nicaragua (Cuadra 1971). We can assume that these latter are the groups alluded to in the quotation as having displaced the ancestral Miskitu.

10. This preoccupation with the "racially" mixed Miskitu heritage is clearly in dialogue with the historical construction of the "Miskitu" as hated and feared "Zambo" (African Amerindian mix), which emerged during the Spanish colonial period and remains an important component of some Mestizo images of the Miskitu (see Helms 1977).

11. Chamorro C. paraphrased in Ruiz (1970:2b).

12. Chamorro C. (1970c:3).

13. These alleged deficiencies were a central theme of the nationalist literature of the period (see, e.g., Cuadra 1971). They were prominently elaborated in a series of articles on the Nicaraguan national character published in *La Prensa* a month after the final installment of Chamorro's Miskitu series (see, e.g., Peña 1970:3b).

14. See, e.g., Munguía Novoa (1970); Pérez-Estrada (1970:1b, 5b).

15. Pérez-Estrada (1970:1b, 5b). This article bears quoting at length because its representation of Nicaraguans of African descent and their place in the nation is echoed in much of the alternative discourse about Creoles. Francisco Pérez-Estrada, however, called "el indio" by his peers, was one of the most progressive of the alternative bloc intellectuals. He also was dark skinned and traced his roots to the town of Nandaime, a population with clear African roots. His interest in Nicaraguans of African descent was clearly personal and more intense than that of others in this group.

16. This transformation is by no means complete. For example, in one article, the Creoles' English Creole language is still described as a degenerate form of English: "el destartalado 'creole,' mezcla de inglés y de espontáneas ocurrencias" (the rambling "Creole" mix of English and spontaneous utterances) (Velásquez 1972:6).

17. In 1970 alone, *La Prensa* published numerous essays by Donovan Brautigam Beer, the poetry of Carl Rigby and David McField, photographs of June Beer's paintings, and articles about the music of Brautigam Beer and the members of the musical group Bárbaros del Ritmo, all leading Creole artists.

18. The name "*negros*" (blacks) had a pejorative connotation for most Creoles during this period. Most referred to themselves and their group as "Creoles" or "Costeños" and more rarely as "*morenos.*" "Negro" in popular usage also has pejorative connotations for Mestizo Nicaraguans. *Moreno* translated literally means "brown." In Nicaragua it is also a polite term for people of African descent.

19. Alemán Ocampo (1969:2b); Velásquez (1972:6). These travel descriptions clearly derive from the Latin American "negritude" literary movement. Articles in *La Prensa* about literary "negritude" indicate that members of the alternative bloc's intellectual circle were very familiar with the works of Guillén, Palés Matos, Guirao, and even Senghor (Arellano 1970:3b; Pallais 1970:1b; Bertocci 1971:1b).

20. Alemán (1970:10); Anonymous (1970b:1). Referring to someone as "*negrito*" is equivalent to calling a black adult "boy" in the United States. It should also be remembered that for Creoles during this period, "*negro*" had a connotation akin to "nigger." A "merienda de negros," literally, a "blacks' snack," is a racist metaphor with carnivalesque and cannibalistic undertones. Traditionally, the saying connotes an act of cannibalism in which whites are dismembered and eaten with great gusto by black heathens amid a celebratory scene of dancing, drumming, and general disorder. In this particular case, it connotes a free-for-all in which black primitives rush and fight each other to grab whatever they can.

21. Somoza D. (1974:5, 28). The programs proposed by Somoza in his speech demonstrate an impressive practical command of the Coast's needs. It is interesting to note that many of these programs were carried out or attempted by the Sandinista government during the 1980's.

22. Daniel Ortega quoted in Anonymous (1979b:4).

23. Daniel Ortega quoted in Anonymous (1979e:8).

24. Daniel Ortega quoted in Anonymous (1979d:4).

25. Daniel Ortega quoted in Anonymous (1979d:4, 1).

26. Daniel Ortega quoted in Anonymous (1979e:8).

6. Ambiguous Militancy on the Threshold of Revolution

1. The core group of Creole pastors involved in pushing for changes in the Moravian Church included the Revs. Stedman Bent, Leroy Miller, Norman Bent, Joseph Kelly, and Bishop John Wilson. They were largely supported in their positions by the older longtime Bishop Hedley Wilson and at various times by some of the Miskitu pastors.

2. The inclusion of Costeños in the leadership of the Moravian Church in

Nicaragua was a very slow process. It was not until 1952 that the first Nicaraguan, Hedley Wilson, was elected to the Provincial Board of the Moravian
Mission. In 1962 Wilson was consecrated bishop and the name of the Moravian
mission in Nicaragua was changed to the Moravian Church in Nicaragua. In
1969 John Wilson was the first national to be director of the Bible Institute in
Bilwaskarma. In his generally laudatory thesis on the history of the Moravian
presence in Nicaragua, John Wilson's understated opinion on these matters was
that "the autochthonization should have been implemented much earlier.
Perhaps lack of confidence in the national workers was one of the factors which
most impeded a rapid autochthonization" (1975:281–283).

3. "Estatutos de la Organización Progresista Costeña (OPROCO) de la
Ciudad de Bluefields, Departamento de Zelaya, República de Nicaragua," CIDCA–
Bluefields Archives.

4. In 1975 *La Información* was sold by the Bluefields vicariate to OPROCO;
however, it had been a strong supporter and outlet for OPROCO opinion since
the latter's inception. *La Información*'s obsequiously partisan position was at
least in part due to the fact that during the 1970's Rupert Linton Whitaker, the
newspaper's principal voice, simultaneously held executive positions with the
Nationalist Liberal Party, OPROCO, and *La Información* both before and after
it was sold to OPROCO. He was at various times vice-secretary and secretary of
propaganda for the PLN in the Department of Zelaya, editorial and advertising
chief and director of *La Información*, and secretary and vice-secretary of
OPROCO.

5. The economic development and welfare of the general Bluefields community was not the only reason OPROCO members and other elite Creoles had an
interest in the road to Kukra. As the roadway was pushed south from Bluefields
toward the river, many members of the group legalized claims to national lands
abutting it in hopes of reaping economic benefits from the opening up of this area.

6. Lindolfo Campbell, *La Información* (June 29, 1975). Campbell served in a
number of executive positions, including president of the group, during the
1970's.

7. L. Campbell, *La Información* (September 13, 1971).

8. L. Campbell, *La Información* (May 31, 1972).

9. E. Campbell (1972). Campbell's article is remarkable in that it presages the
FSLN-flavored discourse of the young Creoles who, like himself, would become
Sandinistas by the end of the decade. Enrique Campbell, the elder brother of the
only Creole Sandinista commandant, Lumberto Campbell, was Nicaragua's
only professionally trained geologist who specialized in thermoelectric power.
Tragically, he was killed in action against Contra forces while serving with the
civilian militias during the mid-1980's.

10. Most of these columns were written by Rupert Linton Whitaker.

11. Brautigam Beer (1973). This tendency in Brautigam Beer's work was
already evident in his seminal work on Coast history published in installments
in *La Prensa* beginning on March 18, 1970. See particularly June 12, 1970, p. 2.

12. After having gone to such lengths to debunk Mestizo racial essentialism,
Brautigam Beer slipped into some of his own by suggesting that the racial
problems of the United States would eventually be solved through a process of
"whitening": "With time will come changes. This period of racial discrimina-

tion will be overcome, perhaps through interracial marriage, inasmuch as history indicates that the black race tends to disappear when mixed with the white" (*La Información* [May 26, 1976]).

13. Murrillo (1975). Rosario Murrillo was the president of the Sandinista artists' union during the revolutionary government and Daniel Ortega's wife. David McField was a member of the FSLN and ambassador to several African nations for the Revolutionary Government.

14. Liberation Theology, so important in the growing radicalization of Nicaraguan society in the 1970's, was subsequently the focus of a number of favorable *La Información* articles. See, e.g., August 16, 1972, and January 26, 1976.

15. *La Prensa* (June 23, 1976:2). This unsigned editorial was probably written by P. J. Chamorro. It answers directly most of Johnson's charges and sums up most of the subsequent Mestizo objections to the article. The editorial states that "good" English is not spoken on the Coast. It also claims that all of the Costeño blacks have their origins in slavery and Africa and are not descendants of the English but in fact were enslaved by them. The editorial states that to make racial distinctions between Nicaraguans, as Johnson does, is racist. The implications here are that Johnson and the British are racist while Mestizo Nicaraguans are not. The editorial also states that Nicaragua has its own autochthonous culture, which is Mestizo, Indio-Hispano, and, by implication, Catholic and Spanish speaking. It does allow for the possibility of room for the cultures of minorities that have been "inculcated by the British dominators."

16. Rollin Tobie quoted in *La Información* (July 22, 1976). Silva's poem was published in *La Prensa* four days before Johnson's article.

17. I use "middle class" here to mean people who have an intermediate position between large-scale owners of means of production and holders of political power, on the one hand, and politically powerless proletarianized workers and subsistence producers, on the other. Middle-class people on the Coast in this sense are characteristically professionals, white-collar workers, artisans, small landowners, small business owners, and so on, with incomes that allow them to live comfortably by Coast standards. Urban location and relative affluence within the Coast's enclave economy traditionally facilitated Creole community access to imported consumer goods, products available only to those of the highest classes in the rest of Nicaragua. Consumption of these commodities, now a part of Creole material culture and felt by them to be necessities, is further basis for Creole self-ascription to middle-class status.

18. This order is a remnant of an ideological field created by Europeans in their struggles with other Europeans, then utilized by them in the domination of the colonized; it is now used by "the strata of colonized colonizer who have taken charge of the civilizing process in . . . [postcolonial] nations" (B. Williams 1991:28).

19. This is similar to the manner in which elements of other cultural domains reinforce Creole populism, as demonstrated earlier. For more on the role of culture in the formation of Creole hegemonic political consciousness, see Gordon (1991).

20. To give but one example, the large fishing companies owned by the Somoza clique and North American capital paid Creole fishermen only a fraction of what fishermen in other areas of the Caribbean received for comparable

product. Most were never able to own any of the major means of production in fishing. Only a favored few were ever able to acquire an industrial-sized fishing boat during this period. The fishermen resented the companies and tried to play them off against each other.

7. Creole Politics and the Sandinista Revolution: Contradictions

1. For example, Rediske and Schneider (1983:15) in the introduction to their book, written in June 1982, claim that what lay behind Sandinista problems with the Creole population was "the fear of the relatively well-off Creoles of the urban petite bourgeoisie, . . . that they would lose their privileges."

2. Daniel Ortega visited Bluefields in October 1979, in the wake of disturbances that were the result of racial/cultural conflict. In the *Barricada* article describing his trip (October 21, 1979), the racial/cultural source of these conflicts was ignored. Instead, the disaffected—presumably Creoles—although the article never mentions racial/cultural identity, are described as "counterrevolutionaries." Ortega was reported as claiming that "these cowards and traitors of the Left and the Right attempt to confuse our people, saying that the Revolution is being betrayed." He also spoke of "the bourgeois 'who sell out their country' of the rich, who were ready to hand over our country to foreign forces and who for a few cents would pawn our territory." This position fits well with the Mestizo representations of Creoles popular at the time and discussed in chapter 5.

Yet another example of the conflation of Creole identity and interests with those of Anglo imperialism is the description of the group in the first academic Sandinista treatment published in 1981 by CIERA (Centro de Investigación y Estudios de la Reforma Agraria—Center for the Investigation and Study of the Agrarian Reform): "These Creole groups . . . penetrated by Protestant religion . . . and in part adapted to British culture; formed the structure or the power base that . . . guaranteed British first and then North American neocolonialism. The culture, language and religion were plainly identified with the Anglo-Saxons" (CIERA 1981:28).

3. In late 1984 the revolutionary government publicly recognized the racial-cultural demands of Costeños and expressed the need to respect their right to autonomy for the first time. This ultimately led to the creation of two autonomous regions on the Atlantic Coast in the late 1980's. I address the subject of Creole/Sandinista tensions in a series of working papers. Some of these were published, generally a year or two after their completion and circulation in Nicaragua (Gordon 1984, 1985, 1987).

4. The narrative contained in this section is based on numerous and extensive interviews with Bluefields Creoles and Mestizos for and against the Revolution, as well as with persons from the Pacific who participated in all or some of the events recorded. Co-workers in CIDCA's Bluefields office (most notably Ray Hooker and Alicia Slate) and I conducted these interviews over four years: 1983–1987. Materials from a series of interviews I conducted in 1991 are utilized as well. This recounting is also based on my eight years (1982–1990) of participant observation in the town and surrounding villages.

5. Almost 80 percent of those Creoles interviewed in an opinion survey taken by CIDCA in 1984 claimed that before the Triumph they saw the necessity for

such a change. In our survey, nearly 90 percent of the Creoles sampled claimed to have expected good things for themselves and their families as a result of the Triumph of the Revolution ,and almost 80 percent remembered feeling positive about the future at the time (Gordon 1987).

6. Letter to Comandante Raúl from Guillermo Aragón, Simón Manzanares, and Dennis Ingram, Bluefields, August 8, 1979.

7. Ibid.

8. There are conflicting accounts about whether the attack instigated by Kalalú on the *palacio* occurred on the same day as the demonstration or not. There are also indications that the *cuartel* attacked a commando of Mestizos in Barrio Teodor Martínez as well (Carlos Castro, personal communication).

9. Institutional power was skewed in other ways as well. Through 1989, when I stopped calculating such things, there had never been any Miskitu in a position of institutional leadership. Similarly, women had held 17 percent of these leadership positions before the Triumph in 1978; by 1989 this figure had fallen to 9 percent.

10. The heavy-handed Sandinista strategy for dealing with the Manifestación seemed to them so successful that they attempted to utilize it again in dealing with the Miskitu unrest that began in early 1981. The results were disastrous. The tactic precipitated a major armed Miskitu rebellion.

11. In the aftermath of the Manifestación, they were formed into the "Trouble-shooters." The group was set up to work in the Creole barrios and initiate a process of reconciliation between the community and the Sandinistas. Initially popular among a certain sector of the young Creole adult male population because of its social activities, the group's membership rapidly dwindled when the FSLN demanded that members engage in military activities in support of the Revolution.

12. Field notes, April 1987. Jenelee Hodgson remembers the following inter-change with MISURASATA leader Steadman Fagoth: "[He said] 'Black people must go back to Africa.' We going Africa. You going Germany. We don't belong here? You don't belong here neither. Get out! . . . The same rights you have because your grandparents are Miskitu mixed with Germany. We are black mixed with Rama, so if anybody going, you going, too. Let's get out!" (interview, 1995).

13. I believe that I coined this phrase in the mid-1980's; however, it was utilized frequently by Creoles and others in analyses of Creole disaffection with the Revolution. Freeland (1988:45) cites Comandante Lumberto Campbell as its source. At this point I am not sure if I actually used it first or picked it up in conversation.

14. Imagine my surprise when, walking through the reception room at the Regional Government House in Bluefields, I was treated to the sight of a group of friends and fellow workers, all with reasonably prestigious positions in the local government, sporting torn and soiled clothing and nursing black eyes, swollen fists, scraped knees, and assorted other cuts and bruises. They were fresh from engaging in a street fight with the anti-SMP youth.

15. This is probably overly optimistic. The Sandinistas did try to do something similar to what I have here suggested by founding MISURASATA jointly with the Miskitu. While recognition of the Miskitu's racially and culturally based

aspirations and demands delayed the onset of conflicts between them and the Sandinistas, they nevertheless eventually broke out. In the Creole case, the nationalist and separatist ideas embedded in Creole populism and the pro-U.S., anticommunist ideas of Anglo ideology would probably make any long-term incorporation of the bulk of the Creole community into the revolutionary process problematic, no matter what posture the FSLN had taken toward them. Subsequent to the era treated in this book, the revolutionary government granted modified political and economic autonomy to the Atlantic Coast. This might have mollified Creoles during the period when populism was the organizing frame for Creole politics. By the time it happened, however, Anglo ideology held sway and, while some Creoles, most significantly, those leaders of OPROCO and SICC who had remained in the country, were favorably disposed toward it, most maintained a relentlessly negative posture toward the revolutionary process.

Acronyms

AES—Asociación de Estudiantes Secundarias (Association of High School Students)

ALPROMISU—Alianza para el Progreso de los Pueblos Miskitos y Sumos (Alliance for the Progress of the Miskitu and Sumu Peoples)

APSP—African Peoples Socialist Party

ATEPCA—Asociación de Trabajadores, Estudiantes y Profesionales de la Costa Atlántica (Association of Workers, Students, and Professionals of the Atlantic Coast)

CASIM—Comité de Acción Social de la Iglesia Morava (Moravian Church Committee for Social Action)

CDC—Comité de Defensa Civil (Civil Defense Committee)

CDS—Comités de Defensa Sandinista (Sandinista Defense Committees)

CEPAD—Centro Evangélico por Asistencia y Desarrollo (Evangelical Center for Aid and Development)

CIDCA—Centro de Investigación y Documentación de la Costa Atlántica (Center for Atlantic Coast Research and Documentation)

CIERA—Centro de Investigación y Estudios de la Reforma Agraria (Center for the Investigation and Study of the Agrarian Reform)

DRI—Dirección de Relaciones Internacionales (International Relations Board)

EEBI—Escuela de Entrenamiento Básico de la Infantería (Infantry Basic Training School)

ENALUF—Empresa Nacional de Luz y Fuerza (National Light and Power Company)

EPS—Ejército Popular Sandinista (Popular Sandinista Army)

FDN—Fuerza Democrática Nicaragüense (Nicaraguan Democratic Force)

FER—Frente Estudiantil Revolucionario (Student Revolutionary Front)

FSLN—Frente Sandinista de Liberación Nacional (Sandinista National Liberation Front)

INFONAC—Instituto de Fomento Nacional (National Development Institute)

INNICA—Instituto Nicaragüense de la Costa Atlántica (Nicaraguan Atlantic Coast Institute)

INPESCA—Instituto Nicaragüense de la Pesca (Nicaraguan Fishing Institute)

MISURASATA—Miskitu, Sumu, Rama y Sandinista Asla Takanka (Miskitu, Sumu, Rama, and Sandinista Working Together)

OPROCO—Organización Progresista Costeña (Progressive Costeña Organization)

PLN—Partido Liberal Nacionalista (Nationalist Liberal Party)

POI—Policía de Orden Interna (Internal Order Police)

SICC—Southern Indigenous Creole Community

SMP—Servicio Militar Patriótico (Patriotic Military Service)

UCCOD—United Committee for Community Development

UDEL—Unión Democrática para la Liberación (Democratic Union for Liberation)

UNIA—Universal Negro Improvement Association

UNO—Unión Nacional Opositora (United National Opposition)

References

Archives

Bluefields Consular Post Records, National Archives, Washington, D.C. (BCPR)
Centro de Información y Documentación de la Costa Atlántica, Nicaragua (CIDCA), Bluefields
Great Britain, Public Record Office, Colonial Office (CO), London
Great Britain, Public Record Office, Foreign Office (FO), London
Moravian Archives, Bethlehem, Pennsylvania
Richard Stephenson private collection, Bluefields, Nicaragua
UNIA Central Division Files, Schomburg Collection, New York Public Library

Newspapers and Periodicals

Barricada (Managua)
Bluefields Messenger
Gaceta Oficial (Managua)
La Información (Bluefields)
Novedades (Managua)
Periodical Accounts Relating to the Missions of the Church of the United Brethren Established among the Heathen (London)
Periodical Accounts Relating to the Moravian Missions (Bethlehem, Pennsylvania)
La Prensa (Managua)
Proceedings of the Society for Propagating the Bible: Report of the Missions of the Moravian Church (Bethlehem, Pennsylvania)
United Brethren's Missionary Intelligencer and Religious Miscellany (Bethlehem, Pennsylvania)

Secondary Sources

Adams, Richard N.
    1981a   "The Dynamic of Societal Diversity: Notes from Nicaragua for a Sociology of Survival." *American Ethnologist* 8, no. 1:1–20.
    1981b   "The Sandinista and the Indians: The 'Problem' of the Indian in

Nicaragua." *Caribbean Review* 10, no. 1:23–25, 55–56.
Aguilar Cortés, Jerónimo
1971   "La discriminación racial en la provincia de Nicaragua." *La Prensa* (December 5):2.
Alemán, Filadelfo
1970   "Gran problema de Bluefields: La recuperación." *La Prensa* (January 7):10.
Alemán Ocampo, Carlos
1969   "Viaje a la 'Costa.'" *La Prensa* (March 9):16–26.
Alonso, Ana
1988   "The Effects of Truth: Re-representations of the Past and the Imagining of Community." *Journal of Historical Sociology* 1, no. 1:33–57.
Anonymous
1880   "Moskito Coast." *Periodical Accounts Relating to the Missions of the Church of the United Brethren Established among the Heathen* 31, no. 327:338–343.
1882   "Retrospect of the Missionary Work of the Moravian Church during the Past 150 Years." *Periodical Accounts Relating to the Missions of the Church of the United Brethren Established among the Heathen* 32, no. 336:277–287.
1892   "Moskito Coast." *Periodical Accounts Relating to the Missions of the Church of the United Brethren Established among the Heathen* 1, no. 12:638–641.
1894   "Moskito Coast." *Periodical Accounts Relating to the Missions of the Church of the United Brethren Established among the Heathen* 2, no. 20:402–419.
1895   "The Moskito Coast." *Periodical Accounts Relating to the Moravian Missions* 2, no. 23:560–565.
1966   "La Costa Atlántica: Pasado, presente y futuro." *Revista Conservadora del Pensamiento Conservadora* 14, no. 68:1.
1969a   "Reincorporación de la Mosquitia." *Novedades* (June 11):6.
1969b   "Somoza inicia importantes obras de progreso cultural y material para la Costa Atlántica." *Novedades* (August 16):1, 8.
1969c   "Presidente Somoza en los minerales "La Rosita." *Novedades* (November 12):4–5.
1969d   "Camarógrafos franceses filman vida y costumbres de Miskitos." *Novedades* (November 29):16.
1969e   "Proyecto Piloto del Río Coco será reestructurado: Algo más que enseñar a leer." *Novedades* (November 8):1, 89.
1969f   "En partido espectácular Bluefields gana torneo." *La Prensa* (November 12):13.
1970a   "Alcaldía de Bluefields en bancarrota: Somoza, siempre interfiriendo." *La Prensa* (March 7):17.
1970b   "Escandalosa repartición de ayuda en Bluefields." *La Prensa* (January 19):1, 10.
1970c   "Miskitos del Río Coco." *La Prensa* (January 11):2.

1971   "África baila." *La Prensa* (July 25):26.
1972   "Fiesta 'Palo de Mayo' en la Costa y Managua." *La Prensa* (May 22):7.
1973   "Igualdad de oportunidades." *La Prensa* (July 26):2.
1979a   "INRA desarrollará colonizaciones." *Barricada* (November 22):4.
1979b   "La Costa: Del olvido a la liberación: Entrevista con el Comandante Daniel Ortega." *Barricada* (December 1):1, 4.
1979c   "Efectiva incorporación de la Costa Atlántica." *Barricada* (October 6):6.
1979d   "Costa Atlántica un gigante que despierta." *Barricada* (November 21):5.
1979e   "155 comunidades miskitas en revolucionaria asamblea." *Barricada* (November 15):1, 8.

Arana Mayorga, Sebastián
1978   "Responsabilidad tica no puede ocultarla ni negarla." *La Información* (November 22).

Araya Pochet, Carlos, and G. T. Peña
1979   "El enclave bananero en Nicaragua." Mimeographed. Managua.

Arellano, Jorge Eduardo
1970   "El tema negro en la poesía nicaragüense." *La Prensa* (November 15):3–8.

Asante, Molefi K.
1988   *Afrocentricity.* Trenton, N.J.: Africa World Press.

Ashdown, Peter D.
1979   "Race, Class and the Unofficial Majority in British Honduras: 1890–1949." Ph.D. diss. London: The British Library.

Ayón, Tomás
1956   *Historia de Nicaragua.* 3 volumes. Madrid: Escuela Profesional de Artes Gráficas.

Balladares, Hermógenes
1969   "Pesquera cooperativista abren en la Costa Atlántica." *La Prensa* (November 24):16.

Barreto Pérez, Pablo
1972   "Frank Hodgson: Esperanza para Bluefields." *La Prensa* (April 18):12.

Bell, Charles Napier
1899   *Tangweera: Life and Adventures among Gentle Savages.* London: Eduard Arnold.

Bernard, J. E.
1926   "Bluefields, Nicaragua." *Negro World* (May 1).

Bertocci, Silvio
1971   "El alma negra e india de la vanguardia: La protesta de la poesía latinoamericana." *La Prensa* (May 9):1B, 5B.

Blair, P.
1873   "Mosquito Coast." *Periodical Accounts Relating to the Missions of the Church of the United Brethren Established among the Heathen* 28, no. 298:429–438.

Blassingame, John W.
    1972   *The Slave Community: Plantation Life in the Antebellum South.*
            New York: Oxford University Press.
Bolland, O. Nigel
    1977   *The Formation of a Colonial Society: Belize, from Conquest to
            Crown Colony.* Baltimore: Johns Hopkins University Press.
    1986   *Belize: A New Nation in Central America.* Boulder, Colo.:
            Westview Press.
Bourgois, Philippe
    1981   "Class, Ethnicity, and the State among the Miskitu Amerindians
            of Northeastern Nicaragua." *Latin American Perspectives* 8, no.
            2:22–39.
    1985   "Nicaragua's Ethnic Minorities in the Revolution." *Monthly
            Review* 36, no. 8:22–44.
    1989   *Ethnicity at Work.* Baltimore: Johns Hopkins University Press.
Brathwaite, Edward
    1971   *The Development of Creole Society in Jamaica, 1770–1820.*
            Oxford: Clarendon Press.
Brautigam Beer, Donovan
    1970a   "Apuntes para una historia de nuestra Costa Atlántica." *La
            Prensa* (April 19–June 17).
    1970b   "¿Qué Hay de la Mosquitia? Una Historia de la Costa Atlántica."
            La Prensa (May 2).
    1973   "Postdata sobre avenidas, calles y otro." *La Información* (Febru-
            ary 27).
    1976   "Errores sobre la Costa Atlántica." *La Prensa* (September 4).
    n. d.   "Historia de la Ciudad de Bluefields." MS. Bluefields.
Brethren's Society for the Furtherance of the Gospel
    1900   "Moskito Coast." *Periodical Accounts Relating to the Moravian
            Missions* 4 (December):405–406.
Bulmer-Thomas, Victor
    1987   *The Political Economy of Central America since 1920.* Cam-
            bridge: Cambridge University Press.
Burdon, John Adler
    1931   *Archives of British Honduras.* Vol. 1. London: Sifton, Praed &
            Co.
Bury, Charles E.
    1922   "Interesting News of Bluefields, Nicaragua." *Negro World* (Sep-
            tember 16):8.
Campbell, Enrique
    1972   "Con nuestro silencio estamos cavando nuestra propia tumba."
            La Información (June 29).
Campbell, Lindolfo
    1973   "¿Es la policía el amigo o verdugo del pueblo?" *La Información*
            (March 9).
    1975   "Hacia la verdadera incorporación de la Costa Atlántica." *La
            Información* (September 14).
Cash, Stanford
    1976   "Brillante exposición del diputado costeño Stanford Cash." *La

Información (August 16).

Centro de Información y Documentación de la Costa Atlántica (CIDCA)
  1982   *Demografía costeña: Notas sobre la historia demográfica y población actual de los grupos étnicos de la Costa Atlántica nicaragüense.* Managua: CIDCA.

Centro de Investigación y Estudios de la Reforma Agraria (CIERA)
  1981   *La Mosquitia en la Revolución.* Managua: Colección Blas Real Espinales.

Chamorro C., Pedro Joaquín
  1970a   "Ambiente a la semana de la Costa." *La Prensa* (November 14):2.
  1970b   "Una sugerencia a educación pública." *La Prensa* (June 18):2.
  1970c   "Pobreza y esperanza en nuestra frontera recortada." *La Prensa* (June 28):1B, 4B; (June 29:3; (June 30):2; (July 1):2; (July 2):2; (July 3):2; (July 4):2; (July 5):2.
  1973   "La política de EEUU." *La Prensa* (May 15):2.

Chamorro Z., Amalia
  1982   "The Hegemonic Content of Somocismo and the Sandinista Revolution." M.A. thesis, University of Essex.
  1983   "Algunos rasgos hegemónicos del Somocismo y la Revolución Sandinista." *Cuadernos de Pensamientos Propio* 5. Managua.

Clifford, James
  1994   "Diasporas." *Cultural Anthropology* 9, no. 3:302–338.

Comaroff, Jean
  1985   *Body of Power, Spirit of Resistance: The Culture and History of a South African People.* Chicago: University of Chicago Press.

Comisión de Desarrollo de la Costa Atlántica (CODECA)
  1966   "Monografía y proyectos a organizarse en el Departamento de Zelaya." *Revista Conservadora* 14, no. 68:7–20.

Conzemius, Eduard
  1929   "Les îles Corn du Nicaragua." *La Geographie* 2:346–362.
  1932   *Ethnographical Survey of the Miskito and Sumu Indians of Honduras and Nicaragua.* Bureau of American Ethnology, Bulletin 106. Washington, D.C.: U.S. Government Printing Office.

Costa Rica
  1913   *Costa Rica–Panama Arbitration: Argument of Costa Rica before the Arbitrator, Hon. Edward Douglass White, Chief Justice of the United States.* Vol. 1. Rosslyn, Va.: Commonwealth Co.

Crawley, Eduardo
  1979   *Dictators Never Die: A Portrait of Nicaragua and the Somoza Dynasty.* London: C. Hurst.
  1984   *Nicaragua in Perspective.* New York: St. Martin's Press.

Cuadra, Pablo Antonio
  1971   *El nicaragüense.* Managua: El Pez y la Serpiente.

De Kalb, Courtney
  1893   "Nicaragua: Studies of the Mosquito Shore in 1892." *Journal of the American Geographic Society* 25:236–288.

Dennis, Philip A.
  1981   "The Costeños and the Revolution in Nicaragua." *Journal of Interamerican Studies and World Affairs* 23, no. 3:271–296.

El Detective (pseud.)
    1973   "En la esquina de BANIC." *La Información* (August 31).
Diederich, Bernard
    1981   *Somoza and the Legacy of U.S. Involvement in Central America.*
                New York: E. P. Dutton.
Dozier, Craig L.
    1985   *Nicaragua's Mosquito Shore: The Years of British and American
                Presence.* Montgomery: University of Alabama Press.
Dunham, Jacob
    1851   *Journal of Voyages.* New York.
Elkins, Stanley
    1959   *Slavery: A Problem in American Institutional and Intellectual
                Life.* Chicago: University of Chicago Press.
Esquemeling, John, and William Dampier
    1978   *Piratas' en Centroamérica. Siglo XVII.* Managua: Colección
                Cultural Banco de América.
Feurig, G.
    1857a   "Mosquito Coast." *Periodical Accounts Relating to the Mis-
                sions of the Church of the United Brethren Established among
                the Heathen* 22, no. 234:298–299.
    1857b   "Mosquito Coast." *Periodical Accounts Relating to the Mis-
                sions of the Church of the United Brethren Established among
                the Heathen* 22, no. 237:346–351.
    1862   "Mosquito Coast." *Periodical Accounts Relating to the Mis-
                sions of the Church of the United Brethren Established among
                the Heathen* 2:308–313.
Forbes, Jack D.
    1993   *Africans and Native Americans: The Language of Race and
                Evolution of Red-Black Peoples.* Urbana: University of Illinois
                Press.
Forgacs, David, ed.
    1988   *An Antonio Gramsci Reader: Selected Writings 1916–1935.*
                New York: Schocken Books.
Frazier, E. Franklin
    1951   *The Negro Family in the United States.* (1939) New York:
                Dryden Press.
Freeland, Jane
    1988   *A Special Place in History: The Atlantic Coast in the Nicaraguan
                Revolution.* London: Nicaragua Solidarity Campaign.
    1995   *Nicaragua Is No Longer Invisible: Afro-Latin Americans Today.*
                Ed. Minority Rights Group. London: Minority Rights Publica-
                tions.
Frente Democrático Nacional (FDN-UNO)
    1986   "Echo for Liberty." Mimeographed. CIDCA-Bluefields Archives.
Frente Sandinista de Liberación Nacional (FSLN)
    1981   *El programa histórico del FSLN.* Managua: Centro de Publica-
                ciones "Silvio Mayorga."

References   293

Gámez, José Dolores
    1939   *Historia de la Costa de los Mosquitos hasta 1894.* Managua:
                Talleres Nacionales.
García, S.
    1970   "Ya no hay madera en Bluefields." *La Prensa* (February 23):1.
    1971   "Minas: Explotación al minero y al joyero." *La Prensa* (August
                26):20.
Gilroy, Paul
    1993   *The Black Atlantic: Modernity and Double Consciousness.*
                Cambridge: Harvard University Press.
Glazer, Nathan, and Daniel P. Moynihan, eds.
    1975   "Introduction." In *Ethnicity: Theory and Experience.* Cam-
                bridge: Harvard University Press.
Gordon, Edmund T.
    1984   "Explotación de clase, opresión étnica y la lucha simultánea."
                Wani 1:11–17.
    1985   "Etnicidad, conciencia y revolución: La cuestión miskitu-creole
                en Nicaragua." *Encuentro* 24–25:117–138.
    1987   "History, Identity, Consciousness and Revolution: Afro Nicara-
                guans and the Nicaraguan Revolution." In *Ethnic Groups and
                the Nation State: The Case of the Atlantic Coast of Nicaragua,*
                pp. 135–168. CIDCA Development Study Unit. Stockholm:
                University of Stockholm.
    1989   "Afro-Nicaraguans and the Revolution." Mimeographed.
    1991   "Anthropology and Liberation." In *Decolonizing Anthropology:
                Moving Further towards an Anthropology of Liberation,* ed. Faye
                Harrison, pp. 149–167. Washington, D.C.: AAA.
    1995   "Revolution, Common Sense and the Dynamics of African-
                Nicaraguan Politics, 1979–1985." *Critique of Anthropology* 15,
                no. 1:5–36.
Gould, Jeffrey L.
    1990   *To Lead as Equals: Rural Protest and Political Consciousness in
                Chinandega, Nicaragua, 1912–1979.* Chapel Hill: University of
                North Carolina Press.
    1993   "Vana Ilusión!" The Highlands Indians and the Myth of Nicara-
                gua Mestiza, 1880–1925." *Hispanic American Historical Re-
                view* 73, no. 3:393–428.
Gray, Mike
    n.d.   "¿Qué fue la SICC?" Mimeographed.
Great Britain. Foreign Office
    1894   *Further Correspondence Respecting the Mosquito Reserve.* Part
                V, January–June. London: HMSO.
Grossman, Guido
    1920   "Annual Report of the Superintendent for 1919." *Periodical
                Accounts Relating to Moravian Missions, 2nd Century* 10, no.
                122:437–442.
    1988   *La Costa Atlántica de Nicaragua.* (1940) Managua: Editorial La

Ocarina, Ministerio de Cultura.

Grunewald, E.
1863   "Mosquito Coast." *Periodical Accounts Relating to the Missions of the Church of* the *United Brethren Established among the Heathen* 25, no. 241:54–57.
1872   "Mosquito Coast." *Periodical Accounts Relating to the Missions of the Church of the United Brethren Established among the Heathen* 27, no. 294:196–198.

Hale, Charles R.
1991   "Wan Tasbaya Dukiara: Contested Notions of Land Rights in Miskitu History." Working Paper, Center for International Studies, MIT.
1994   *Resistance and Contradiction: Miskitu Indians and the Nicaraguan State: 1894–1987.* Stanford: Stanford University Press.

Hall, Stuart
1988   "New Ethnicities. Black Film/British Cinema." ICA Document 7:27–31.
1995   "Negotiating Caribbean Identities." *New Left Review* 209:3–14.

Hanchard, Michael
1994   *Orpheus and Power: The Movimiento Negro of Rio de Janeiro and São Paulo, Brazil, 1945–1988.* Princeton: Princeton University Press.

Harding, Vincent
1981   *There Is a River: The Black Struggle for Freedom in America.* New York: Harcourt Brace Jovanovich.

Harris, Joseph E.
1993   "Introduction." *Global Dimensions of the African Diaspora.* Washington, D.C.: Howard University Press.

Helms, Mary W.
1971   *Asang: Adaptations to Culture Contact in a Miskito Community.* Gainesville: University of Florida Press.
1977   "Negro or Indian?: The Changing Identity of a Frontier Population." In *Old Roots in New Lands: Historical and Anthropological Perspectives on Black Experiences in the Americas,* ed. Ann M. Pescatello, pp. 157–172. Westport, Conn.: Greenwood Press.

Hodges, Donald C.
1986   *Intellectual Foundation of the Nicaraguan Revolution.* Austin: University of Texas Press.

Hodgson, Robert
1766   "Some Account of That Part of the Continent of America Called the Mosquito Shore, as at Present Actually Both Possessed and Used by the Subjects of Great Britain." In *A View of the Mosquito Shore,* by Colonel Robert Hodgson. October 12. PRO-FO 53/10, ff 16–18.

Hodgson, Roberto
1971   "Alianza para el Progreso: ¿Una década de desarrollo?" *La Información* (August 28).

1976   "¿Progreso ó despojo: Desarrollo ó desarrollismo?" *La Información*
           (February 8).
Holloway, Joseph E.
1990   *Africanisms in American Culture.* Bloomington: Indiana Uni-
           versity Press.
Holm, John A.
1978   "The Creole English of Nicaragua's Miskitu Coast: Its Socio-
           linguistic History and a Comparative Study of Its Lexicon and
           Syntax." Ph.D. diss., University of London.
Hooker, Robert Montgomery
1945   *La reincorporación de la Mosquitia desde el punto de vista del
           derecho internacional y patrio.* León: Universidad de León.
Jenkins, Thomas
n.d.   *Serapaqui: From the Records of Some of the "Alarms" Officers:
           A Short History of an Expedition.* Steam, England: Thomas
           Jenkins.
Johnson, Robert L. (pseud.)
1976   "¿Es Nicaragüense nuestra Costa Atlántica?" *La Prensa* (June
           23):2.
Kandler, E. G.
1851   "From Br. E. G. Kandler, to the Mission Board." *Periodical
           Accounts* Relating *to the Missions of the Church of the United
           Brethren Established among the Heathen* 210:525–526.
Karnes, Thomas L.
1978   *Tropical Enterprise: The Standard Fruit and Steamship Com-
           pany in Latin America.* Baton Rouge: Louisiana State University
           Press.
Keely, Robert N.
1893   "Nicaragua and the Mosquito Coast." *Popular Science Monthly*
           55, no. 12:160–174.
Kelly, Joe
1974   "Looking Ahead." *NAM* (May):17–23.
1975   "1974, Year of Jubilee." *NAM* (May):12–17.
1976   "Struggles toward a Unity of Purpose." *NAM* (May):18–23.
Laclau, Ernesto, and Chantal Mouffe
1985   *Hegemony and Socialist Strategy: Towards a Radical Demo-
           cratic Politics.* London: Verso.
Laird, Larry
1971   "Origins of the Reincorporation of the Miskitu Coast." M.A.
           thesis, University of Kansas. Translated and published by the
           Fondo Cultural del Banco de América (Managua), 1978.
Langley, Lester D.
1983   *The Banana Wars: An Inner History of American Empire, 1900–
           1934.* Lexington: University Press of Kentucky.
Le Page, R. B., and Andree Tabouret-Keller
1985   *Acts of Identity: Creole Based Approaches to Language and
           Ethnicity.* Cambridge: Cambridge University Press.

Long, Edward
    1970   *The History of Jamaica.* London: Frank Cass & Co.
López, Lino
    1982   "La masacre de Río Grande." *Nicaráuac* 3, no. 8:180–184.
Lundberg, J. Eugene
    1854   "Mosquito Coast." *Periodical Accounts Relating to the Missions of the Church of the United Brethren Established among the Heathen* 21, no. 223:158.
    1866   "Mosquito Coast." *Periodical Accounts Relating to the Missions of the Church of the United Brethren Established among the Heathen* 26:53–55.
    1874   "Moskito Coast." *Periodical Accounts Relating to the Missions of the Church of the United Brethren Established among the Heathen* 29, no. 305:218–224.
    1875   "Moskito Coast." *Periodical Accounts Relating to the Missions of the Church of the United Brethren Established among the Heathen* 29, no. 306:306–309.
    1880   "Moskito Coast." *Periodical Accounts Relating to the Missions of the Church of the United Brethren Established among the Heathen* 31, no. 326:316–318.
    1990   "Election of William Henry Clarence." In *The Nicaraguan Mosquitia in Historical Documents, 1844–1927: The Dynamics of Ethnic and Regional History,* ed. Eleonore von Oertzen, Lioba Rossbach, and Volker Wunderich, p. 158. Berlin: Dietrich Reimer Verlag.
Martin, A.
    1870   "Mosquito Coast." *Periodical Accounts Relating to the Missions of the Church of the United Brethren Established among the Heathen* 27:404–408.
    1872   "Mosquito Coast." *Periodical Accounts Relating to the Missions of the Church of the United Brethren Established among the Heathen* 28, no. 297:363–367.
    1881   "Moskito Coast." *Periodical Accounts Relating to the Missions of the Church of the United Brethren Established among the Heathen* 32 (September):72–75.
    1882   "Moskito Coast." *Periodical Accounts Relating to the Missions of the Church of the United Brethren Established among the Heathen* 32 (June):251–255.
    1990   "Creole Life in Bluefields." In *The Nicaraguan Mosquitia in Historical Documents, 1844–1927: The Dynamics of Ethnic and Regional History,* ed. Eleonore von Oertzen, Lioba Rossbach, and Volker Wunderich. Berlin: Dietrich Reimer Verlag.
Mena Solórzano, Carlos
    1975   "Remembranzas." *La Información* (September 14).
Mercer, Kobena
    1994   *Welcome to the Jungle: New Positions in Black Cultural Studies.* New York: Routledge.

Meza Briones, Samuel
    1991   *Costa Atlántica nicaragüense: 1899–1901.* Estelí: Alcaldía Municipal.
Millett, Richard
    1977   *Guardians of the Dynasty.* Maryknoll, N. Y.: Orbis Books.
Mintz, Sidney W., and Sally Price
    1985   "Introduction." In *Caribbean Contours,* ed. Sidney W. Mintz and Sally Price, pp. 3–11. Baltimore: Johns Hopkins University Press.
Mission Board
    1900   "Moskito Coast." *Periodical Accounts Relating to the Moravian Missions* 4 (September):351–355.
Moravian, The
    1963   *A Visit to Nicaragua.* Part III. Bethlehem, Pa.: Society for Propagating the Gospel.
Moravian Church and Mission Agency
    1894a   "The Bluefields Incident." *Periodical Accounts Relating to the Moravian Missions* 2, no. 18:314–324.
    1894b   "Troublous Times at Bluefields." *Periodical Accounts Relating to the Moravian Missions* 2, no. 19: 372–374.
    1895   "The Moskito Coast." *Periodical Accounts Relating to the Moravian Missions* 2, no. 21:464–474.
    1896   "The Moskito Coast." *Periodical Accounts Relating to the Moravian Missions* 3, no. 26: 95–97.
Morrow, Rising Lake
    1930   "A Conflict between the Commercial Interest of the United States and Its Foreign Policy." *Hispanic American Historical Review* 10, no. 1:2–13.
Mueller, Karl
    1932   *Among Creoles, Miskitos and Sumu: Eastern Nicaragua and Its Moravian Missions.* Bethlehem, Pa.: Comenius Press.
Munguía Novoa, Juan
    1970   "La esclavitud—el poder negro y William Walker." *La Prensa* (October 4):3B.
Municipal Authority of the Mosquito Reserve
    1884   *Formation of the Municipal Authority for the Government of the Mosquito Reservation.* New York: Burr Printing House.
Murrillo, Rosario
    1975   "Cultura, tradición y pobreza." *La Prensa* (December 4):1, 10, 24.
Mynot, Alexander
    1925   "A Bad Preacher Busy in Nicaragua." *Negro World* (March 7).
Naylor, Robert
    1967   "The Mahogany Trade As a Factor in the British Return to the Mosquito Shore in the Second Quarter of the 19th Century." *Jamaica Historical Review* 7, no. 1–2:40–66.
Newton, Arthur Percival
    1966   *The Colonizing Activities of the English Puritans: The Last*

Phase of the Elizabethan Struggles with Spain. Port Washington, N.Y.: Kennikat Press (1914).

Nietschmann, Bernard
1973   *Between Land and Water: The Subsistence Ecology of the Miskito Indians, Eastern Nicaragua.* New York: Academic Press.

Oertzen, Eleonore von
1990   "Introduction: A. The British Protectorate Up to 1860." In *The Nicaraguan Mosquitia in Historical Documents, 1844–1927: The Dynamics of Ethnic and Regional History,* ed. Eleonore von Oertzen, Lioba Rossbach, and Volker Wunderich, pp. 18–40. Berlin: Dietrich Reimer Verlag.

Oertzen, Eleonore von, Lioba Rossbach, and Volker Wunderich (eds.)
1990   *The Nicaraguan Mosquitia in Historical Documents, 1844–1927: The Dynamics of Ethnic and Regional History.* Berlin. Dietrich Reimer Verlag.

Olien, Michael
1988   "Imperialism, Ethnogenesis and Marginality: Ethnicity and Politics on the Mosquito Coast, 1845–1964." *Journal of Ethnic Studies* 16, no. 1:1–29.

Omi, Michael, and Howard Winant
1986   *Racial Formation in the United States: From the 1960s to the 1980s.* New York: Routledge.

Organización Progresista Costeña (OPROCO)
1964   "Estatuto de la Organización Progresista de Desarrollo (Comunal) de la Ciudad de Bluefields, Departamento de Zelaya, República de Nicaragua." MS. Bluefields.

Ortega, Gustavo A.
1950   "Bluefields por dentro: la reincorporación espiritual de la Costa Atlántica." *ORBE* 86, no. 16.

P. A.
1894   "Stations of the Moravian Mission on the Moskito Coast." *Periodical Accounts Relating to the Moravian Missions* 2, no. 20:402–419.
1900   "Moskito Coast." *Periodical Accounts Relating to the Moravian Missions* 4, no. 37:351–355.

Padmore, George
1956   *Pan-Africanism or Communism.* London: Dennis Dobson.

Pallais, Raphael I.
1970   "Un poema de un poeta senegalés: Leopoldo Sedar Senghor." *La Prensa* (April 12):1B.

Parsons, James Jerome
1956   *San Andrés and Providencia: English-Speaking Island in the Western Caribbean.* Berkeley & Los Angeles: University of California Press.

Peña, Horacio
1970   "Los Nicaragüenses." *La Prensa Literaria* (August 16):1B.

Peper, W.
1879   "Moskito Coast." *Periodical Accounts Relating to the Missions*

of the Church of the United Brethren Established among the Heathen 31, no. 325:262–264.

Pérez-Estrada, Francisco
1970   "El Negro en Nicaragua." *La Prensa* (September 20):1B, 5B.

Pérez Valle, Eduardo
1978   *Expedientes de campos azules: Historia de Bluefields en sus documentos.* Managua: Eduardo Pérez-Valle.

Pfeiffer, H. G.
1849   "Extract of a Letter from Br. H. G. Pfeiffer." *Periodical Accounts Relating to the Missions of the Church of the United Brethren Established among the Heathen* 19, no. 204:201–203.
1850a   "Mosquito Coast." *Periodical Accounts Relating to the Missions of the Church of the United Brethren Established among the Heathen* 19, no. 207:360–362.
1850b   "Mosquito Coast." *Periodical Accounts Relating to the Missions of the Church of the United Brethren Established among the Heathen* 19, no. 207:404–407.

Pfeiffer, H. G., J. Eugene Lundberg, and P. Jurgensen
1857   "Mosquito Coast." *Periodical Accounts Relating to the Missions of the Church of the United Brethren Established among the Heathen* 22, no. 234:242–248.

Pfeiffer, H. G., and Amadeus Reinke
1849   "Report on an Exploratory Visit of the Mosquito-Coast, Performed in the Year 1847." *Periodical Accounts Relating to the Missions of the Church of the United Brethren Established among the Heathen* 19, no. 204:161–172.

Porta Costas, Antonio
1945   "Relación del reconocimiento geométrico y político de la Costa de Mosquitos." *Revista de la Academia de Geografía e Historia de Nicaragua* 8, no. 1:27–30.
1990   "Relación del reconocimiento geométrico y político de la Costa de Mosquitos." *Wani* 7:52–61.

Price, Richard
1983   *First-Time: The Historical Vision of an Afro-American People.* Baltimore: Johns Hopkins University Press.
1990   *Alabi's World.* Baltimore: Johns Hopkins University Press.

Price, Richard (ed.)
1979   *Maroon Societies: Rebel Slave Communities in the Americas.* Baltimore: Johns Hopkins University Press.

Ramírez, José Benito
1942   *Somoza hacia el Atlántico.* Managua: Publicaciones de la Secretaría de la Presidencia de la República.

Rediske, Michael, and Robin Schneider
1983   "National Revolution and Indigenous Identity: The Conflict between the Sandinista Government and the Miskito Indians, 1979–1982." In *National Revolution and Indigenous Identity: The Conflict between Sandinista and Miskito Indians on Nicaragua's Atlantic Coast,* ed. Klaudine Ohland and Robin

Schneider, pp. 3–27. IWGA Document 47. Copenhagen: IWGA.

Reinke, Amadeus
  1848a   "Sketch of the Country of Mosquitia Commonly Called the Mosquito Shore." *United Brethren's Missionary Intelligencer and Religious Miscellany* 9:403–414.
  1848b   "Visit to the Country of Mosquitia." *The United Brethren's Missionary Intelligencer and Religious Miscellany* 9:444–461, 521–527.
  1848c   "Central America. Mosquitia." *The United Brethren's Missionary Intelligencer and Religious Miscellany* 9:549–557.

Renkewitz, F.
  1867   "Mosquito Coast." *Periodical Accounts Relating to the Missions of the Church of the United Brethren Established among the Heathen* 26:469–473.
  1874   "Moskito Coast." *Periodical Accounts Relating to the Missions of the Church of the United Brethren Established among the Heathen* 29, no. 305:218–224.

Reyes Campos, Pedro R.
  1978   "Crímenes son del tiempo y node España." *La Información* (November 22).

Rivera de Vallejos, Alba
  1969   "Pueblo costeño reitera solidaridad a Somoza." *Novedades* (November 8):13.

Roberts, Orlando
  1965   *Narrative of Voyages and Excursions on the East Coast and Interior of Central America.* Chapel Hill: University of North Carolina Press.

Romero Vargas, Germán
  1994   "Las sociedades del Atlántico de Nicaragua en los siglos XVII y XVIII." MS. Managua.

Romig, Br.
  1892   "The Moskito Coast: Visitation by Br. Romig." *Periodical Accounts Relating to the Moravian Missions* 1, no. 9:428–450.

Ruiz, Horacio
  1970   "Los Miskitos: Único grupo indígena con unidad tribal: Exitosa conferencia de P. J. Ch." *La Prensa Literaria* (June 28):2B, 4B.

Ruiz y Ruiz, Frutos
  1927   "Costa Atlántica de Nicaragua." *Informes Oficial.* Managua.

Samarriba, Marcos
  n.d.   "Tratamiento político a la Iglesia Morava." Photocopy, Managua

Scott, David
  1991   "That Event, This Memory: Notes on the Anthropology of African Diasporas in the New World." *Diaspora* 1, no. 3:261–283.

Scott, James
  1985   *Weapons of the Weak: Everyday Forms of Peasant Resistance.* New Haven: Yale University Press.

SICC
  1983   "Southern Indigenous Creole Community." Mimeographed. San
          José, Costa Rica.
  n.d.   "SICC Seminar: Cultural Survival." Mimeographed.
Sieborger, Br.
  1884   "Mosquito Coast." *Periodical Accounts Relating to the Mis-*
          sions of the Church of the United Brethren Established among
          the Heathen 33, no. 345:174–176.
  1887   "The Moskito Coast." *Periodical Accounts Relating to the*
          Missions of the Church of the United Brethren Established
          among the Heathen 34 (December):181–182.
Smith, F.
  1872   "Mosquito Coast." *Periodical Accounts Relating to the Mis-*
          sions of the Church of the United Brethren Established among
          the Heathen 28, no. 296:311–315.
Society for Propagating the Gospel
  1911   *Proceedings of the Society for Propagating the Bible: Report on*
          the Missions of the Moravian Church, 1910. Bethlehem, Pa.
  1925   *Proceedings of the Society for Propagating the Bible: Report on*
          the Missions of the Moravian Church, 1924. Bethlehem, Pa.
  1927   *Proceedings of the Society for Propagating the Bible: Report on*
          the Missions of the Moravian Church, 1926. Bethlehem, Pa.
  1928   *Proceedings of the Society for Propagating the Bible: Report on*
          the Missions of the Moravian Church, 1927. Bethlehem, Pa.
  1929   *Proceedings of the Society for Propagating the Bible: Report on*
          the Missions of the Moravian Church, 1928. Bethlehem, Pa.
  1930   *Proceedings of the Society for Propagating the Bible: Report on*
          the Missions of the Moravian Church, 1929. Bethlehem, Pa.
  1931   *Proceedings of the Society for Propagating the Bible: Report on*
          the Missions of the Moravian Church, 1930. Bethlehem, Pa.
  1938   *Proceedings of the Society for Propagating the Bible: Report on*
          the Missions of the Moravian Church, 1937. Bethlehem, Pa.
  1943   *Proceedings of the Society for Propagating the Bible: Report on*
          the Missions of the Moravian Church, 1942. Bethlehem, Pa.
  1944   *Proceedings of the Society for Propagating the Bible: Report on*
          the Missions of the Moravian Church, 1943. Bethlehem, Pa.
  1946   *Proceedings of the Society for Propagating the Bible: Report on*
          the Missions of the Moravian Church, 1945. Bethlehem, Pa.
  1954   *Proceedings of the Society for Propagating the Bible: Report on*
          the Missions of the Moravian Church, 1953. Bethlehem, Pa.
Somoza D., Anastasio
  1974   "Somoza dará progreso a la Costa Atlántica." *Novedades* (March
          25):5, 28.
Sorsby, William S.
  1969   "The British Superintendency of the Mosquito Shore, 1749–
          1800." Ph.D. diss., University of London.
  1972   "Spanish Colonization of the Mosquito Coast, 1787–1800."

Royal Historical Association 73–74:45–153.
1989   The Mosquito Coast of Nicaragua and Honduras: 1802–1974.
         Vol. 2, chap. 3. Unpublished ms.

Stampp, Kenneth
1956   *The Peculiar Institution: Slavery in the Antebellum South.* New
         York: Vintage Books.

Stutzman, Ronald
1981   "El Mestizaje: An All-Inclusive Ideology of Exclusion." In *Cul-
         tural Transformation and Ethnicity in Modern Ecuador,* ed.
         Norman E. Whitten, Jr., pp. 45–94. Urbana: University of Illinois
         Press.

Sujo Wilson, Hugo
1971   "Ciertos 'gallos tapados' podrían ser desastrosos." *La Información*
         (November 24).
1973   "Es necesario practicar un localismo sano y viril." *La Información*
         (December 22).
1976   "El canal costero." *La Información* (June 12).

Taussig, Michael
1987   *Shamanism, Colonialism and the Wild Man: A Study in Terror
         and Healing.* Chicago: University of Chicago Press.
1993   *Mimesis and Alterity: A Particular History of the Senses.* New
         York: Routledge.

Taylor, Markland
1889   "The Reception in Honor of the Election and Inauguration of the
         Hereditary Chief of the Mosquito Reservation." Bluefields.

Teplitz, Benjamin I.
1973   "The Political and Economical Foundations of Modernization in
         Nicaragua: The Administration of José Santos Zelaya, 1893–
         1909." Ph.D. diss., Howard University.

Thompson, Robert F.
1983   *Flash of the Spirit: African and Afro-American Art and Philoso-
         phy.* New York: Vintage Books.

Tobie F., Rollin B.
1976a   "Our Problem: Dissertation by Rollin B. Tobie F." MS. Bluefields.
1976b   "El neo-colonialismo." *La Información* (May 24).

Vanden, Harry, and Gary Prevost
1992   *Democracy and Socialism in Sandinista Nicaragua.* Boulder,
         Colo.: L. Rienner.

Velásquez, Juan
1972   "Rutas nicaragüenses: Managua, Rama, Bluefields." *La Prensa*
         (October 8):6.

Vilas, Carlos M.
1990   *Del colonialismo a la autonomía: Modernización capitalista y
         revolución social en la Costa Atlántica.* Managua: Editorial
         Nueva Nicaragua.

Visweswaran, Kamala
1994   *Fictions of Feminist Ethnography.* Minneapolis: University of

Minnesota Press.

W. M.
1732   "The Mosquito Indian and His Golden River." In *A Collection of Voyages and Travels*, ed. A. Churchill, vol. 6, pp. 285–298.

Wade, Peter
1993   *Blackness and Race Mixture: The Dynamics of Racial Identity in Colombia.* Baltimore: Johns Hopkins University Press.

Wheelock, Jaime
1981   "Speech by Commander of the Revolution Jaime Wheelock, Member of the FSLN Political Commission." Mimeographed. 1st International Meeting of Solidarity with Nicaragua, January 26–31, Managua.

White, Robert
1789   *The Case of His Majesty's Subjects Having Property in and Lately Established upon the Mosquito Shore in America.* London.
1793   *The Case of the Agent to the Settlers on the Coast of Yucatan: And the Late Settlers on the Mosquito Shore.* London.

Williams, Brackette
1991   *Stains on My Name, War in My Veins: Guyana and the Politics of Cultural Struggle.* Durham: Duke University Press.
1995   "Public I/Eye: Conducting Fieldwork to Do Homework on Homeless and Begging in Two U.S. Cities." *Current Anthropology* 36, no. 1:25–52.

Williams, Raymond
1977   *Marxism and Literature.* Oxford: Oxford University Press.
1983   *Keyword: A Vocabulary of Culture and Society.* New York: Oxford University Press.

Wilson John
1975   "Obra morava en Nicaragua: Trasfondo y breve historia." Thesis, Seminario Bíblico Latinoamericano, San José, Costa Rica.

Wong López, William
1979   "Informe general de la Junta Provisional de Bluefields al estado mayor nacional conjunto de FSLN." Photocopy. CIDCA-Bluefields.

Wright, Winthrop
1993   *Café con Leche: Race, Class, and National Image in Venezuela.* Austin: University of Texas Press.

Wullschlagel, H. R.
1856   "Extract from the Report of a Visit to the Mission of the Mosquito Coast, Performed in May 1855 by Br. H. R. Wullschlagel of the Mission-Board." *Periodical Accounts Relating to the Missions of the Church of the United Brethren Established among the Heathen* 22:34–35.
1990   "Missionblatt." In *The Nicaraguan Mosquitia in Historical Documents, 1844–1927: The Dynamics of Ethnic and Regional History*, ed. Eleonore von Oertzen, Lioba Rossbach, and Volker

Wunderich, pp. 204–205. Berlin: Dietrich Reimer Verlag.
Wunderich, Volker
1990   "The Mosquito Reserve and the Aftermath of British Presence."
In *The Nicaraguan Mosquitia in Historical Documents, 1844–
1927: The Dynamics of Ethnic and Regional History*, ed. Eleonore
von Oertzen, Lioba Rossbach, and Volker Wunderich, pp. 60–87.
Berlin: Dietrich Reimer Verlag.
Ziock, H.
1882   "Mosquito Coast." *Periodical Accounts Relating to the Missions of the Church of the United Brethren Established among the Heathen* 32 (September):319–313.

Index

Abel, Comandante (Dexter Hooker Kaine): and Creole history, 258; Creoles' support of, 213; Mestizos' criticism of, 220; National Guard's surrender to, 215; and racial/cultural identity, 218; in Rama, 209–212, 216

Accommodation: and Anglo ideology, 196–197; to Anglo power, 52; and Creole culture, 49; in Creole history, ix–x; and Creole political common sense, 50; in Creole politics, x, 31, 51, 80; and Creoles' Anglo identification, 46; and Moravian Church, 84; to U.S. enclave economy, 57; zero-sum assumptions concerning, 52

AES (Asociación de Estudiantes Secondarias—Association of High School Students), 211, 214

Africa and Africans: African Amerindians, 34, 39, 40, 278n.10; and African-derived Creole culture, 48–50, 56, 67, 91, 136, 138, 171, 172, 260, 270n.5; and Creole elite, 43, 48, 269n.31; and Creole ethnogenesis, 40; and Creole identity, xi, 46, 171; European Africans, 39, 260; and *mestizaje*, 121, 277n.1; and Mestizos, 126, 135; and miscegenation, 34–35, 170; and Miskitu Indians, 33, 34, 39, 96–98, 132; Moravian missionary activity compared to

southern Africa, 270n.50; in Mosquitia, 33–35, 39; and rastas, 97; and Samboes, 267n.13; and shipwrecked slaves, 96–97; and UNIA, 76

African Diaspora: and Creole history, ix, 31, 266n.2; and Creole identity, xi, 17–18, 77, 181, 192–193; and cultural creation, 32; and García, 275n.2; historiography of, 94–95; and internal colonialism, 178; and land rights, 262; Price on, 266n.2; and slavery, 30

African Orthodox Church, 75

African Peoples Socialist Party (APSP), 4–5, 6, 7–9

Ali, Muhammad, 177

Alliance for Progress, 84, 158, 165

Allum, Michael, 40

ALPROMISU (Alianza para el Progreso de los Pueblos Miskitos y Sumos—Alliance for the Progress of Miskitu and Sumu Peoples), 167, 186, 208

Alternative bloc: and Chamorro Cardenal, 127; and Costeños, 130–131; and Creole culture, 136–140; and Creoles, 134–140; and eco-nomy, 126, 128–130; and FSLN, 142, 143, 144; and Miskitu Indians, 131–134; and music, 137; and natural resources, 128–130; and Nicaraguan nationalism, 131–132; proliferation of discourse, 141–143; racism of, 134, 140–141; and Somoza regime, 126–143. *See also La Prensa*

Amador family, 2, 7

Amerindian peoples: African Amerindians, 34, 39, 40, 278n.10; and British enslavement, ix, 33, 34; and Creole culture, 172, 260; and Creole ethnogenesis, 39–40; European Amerindians, 39, 40; and india rubber boom, 43; Mestizos' attitudes toward, 124; population of, 272n.34; and racial mixing, 100, 117, 170; and Samboes, 267n.13. *See also* Indigenous population; and specific tribal names

Anderson, Jack, 278n.7

Anglican School, 184

Anglo diasporic identity: and Anglo ideology, 198–199, 251; black diasporic identity compared to, 18, 46; and Creole culture, 177; and Creole history, 261; and Creole political common sense, 45–46; and Creole politics, xi; and Creole/Sandinista relationship, 203, 205, 247; Creoles' respect for whites, 17, 22; and European ancestors, 100–101; and former slaves, 50; and Miskitu Indians, 263; and Moravian High School teachers, 240; and neocolonialism, 282n.2; and phenotypes, 18, 266n.1; and Protestantism, 191; and racial mixing, 100, 117; and resistance, 70. *See also* Creole identity

Anglo ideology: and Anglo diasporic identity, 198–199, 251; and anticommunism, 197, 231–232, 239, 246, 251; and Creole common sense, 52, 155, 197; and Creole political common sense, 197–199, 250; and Creole populism, 250, 252, 258, 284n.15; and Creole/Sandinista relationship, 205–206, 246, 247, 250; and hegemony, 196–199, 251; and

Moravian High School, 251

Anglo population: Anglo entrepreneurs, 34, 44, 45, 52, 53, 56–60; and Anglo hegemony, 51, 53–60; attitudes toward Creoles, 46, 47; attitudes toward Mestizos, 69; black population compared to, 272n.34; British settlers as, 43–44, 45; and Creole identity, 48, 260; and Creoles' position in social hierarchy, 67–68; and Moravian Church, 84; and power relations, 52; and Reincorporation, 61; and separatist activity, 73; in social hierarchy, 45, 69; U.S. settlers as, 44, 45; and Zelaya regime, 72

Anthropology of liberation, viii, 265n.1

Anticommunism: and Anglo ideology, 197, 231–232, 239, 246, 251; and Creole politics, 204, 248; of FDN–UNO, 203; of OPROCO, 158, 165; and religion, 231, 247; of SICC, 188, 240; and SMP, 249; of Somoza regime, 84, 85; of United States, 84, 85, 247

APSP (African Peoples Socialist Party), 4–5, 6, 7–9

Aquatic Ecosystems (Ecosistemas Acuáticos), 5

Aragón twins, 214

Arana, Alfredo, 214, 215

Arana, Moisés, 207, 212–213, 215, 216–218

Archaic historical elements, 266n.3

Archibald, Berto, 218, 234, 248

Archibold, Hardy, 107

Argüello, Alexis, 2

Association of High School Students (Asociación de Estudiantes Secondarias—AES), 211, 214

ATEPCA (Asociación de Trabajadores, Estudiantes y Profesionales de la Costa Atlántica—Association of Workers, Students, and Professionals of the Atlantic Coast), 208–210, 214

Atlantic Coast: and alternative

hegemony, 128–143; autonomy for, 24, 57, 159–161, 252; Belize compared with, 181; British-dominated slave society of, ix; and Chamorro, 73; and CIDCA, 10–11; Creole ethnogenesis in, 39; and Creole populism, 195; and FSLN, 11, 12, 142, 143–148; Gordon's familiarity with, 13; history of, 275n.4; immigrants to, 38–39; independence of, 73, 74, 233; and INNICA modernization, 230; marginalization of, 148, 172, 188; military incorporation into Nicaragua, 60; Nicaraguan economic connections of, 82; power relations on, 51; and *La Prensa*, 128–129, 131; and racial/cultural identity, 265n.3; and reformist national bourgeoisie, 128; regional government of, 23–24; and regional identity, 76–77, 81, 155, 164–166, 261; and Sandinista revolutionary government, 145–46; and separatist activity, 9; sleeping giant metaphor, 150; and Somoza regime, 122–126, 128; as U.S. economic enclave, viii, 197; university in, 207; as war zone, 25, 26; World War I effects on, 74. *See also* Atlantic Coast exploitation; Economy; Internal colonialism; Mosquitia; Mosquito Reserve; Natural Resources

Atlantic Coast exploitation: and Brautigam Beer, 169; and capitalist culture, 130, 176, 177, 195; and Creole pastors, 153; economic nature of, 148; and international capital, 130; and Nicaraguan government, 72, 259; and OPROCO, 158, 161–162, 164

Bahamas, 66

Banana industry: and Bluefields Steamship Co., 63, 64; and export taxes, 79; and Jamaican immigrants, 115; and Mosquitian

national sentiments, 58; and small-scale production, 56–57, 71, 72; and United States, 56–57, 74

Baptist Young People, 183

Barricada, 150, 282n.2

Barrio Beholden, 76, 214–215, 235, 237–238

Barrio Teodor Martinez, 283n.8

Bay of Pigs invasion, 123

Beer, June, 279n.17

Belize: Atlantic Coast compared with, 181; Belizean English Creole, 267n.15; and Bluefields population, 270n.8; British in, 43; Creole culture of, 265n.2; and Creole definition, 267n.16, 267n.17; Gordon's experience in, 3; immigrants from, 101; and Miskitu Indian tributes, 34

Belize City, Belize, 14

Bell, C. N., 39, 49–50

Bell, James Stanislaus, 46

Bent, Norman, 153, 154, 279n.1

Bent, Stedman, 154, 279n.1

Berger, Alan George, 232

Bible Institute, 152, 280n.2

Bilwaskarma, 152, 280n.2

Black diasporic identity: Anglo diasporic identity compared to, 18, 46; and black Americans, 266n.1; and black Sandinistas, 176; and contemporary Creole intellectuals, 259; and Creole history, 261; and Creole politics, xi; and Creole populism, 251–252; and Creole/Sandinista relationship, 205; downplaying of, 17–18; indications of, 192–193; and Mestizos' racialized view of Creoles, 191; and Miskitu Indians, 263; as mode of identity formation, 53; and SICC, 188, 191; and slavery, 30, 37, 48. *See also* Creole identity

Black nationalism, 22, 148, 177, 188, 219, 252

Black Panthers, 177

Black River, 33, 267n.9

Black Sandinistas: and Black

September, 239; and Bluefields, 178, 218; and Enrique Campbell, 280n.9; and Creole populism, 196, 225; and FSLN, 223–224, 239, 283n.11; and imperialism, 175–178; and race, 167, 210, 223; and racial/cultural identity, 167, 218, 224; and Sandinista revolutionary government, 249; support for, 221, 250

Black September, 206, 235–239, 283n.10

Blacks: in Bluefields, 15, 82, 97, 270n.8; and Creoles, 279n.18; and depression of 1930's, 82; free people of color, 34, 35, 37, 38; and FSLN, 143; as immigrants, 66–67; in Latin America, 122, 277n.1; population of, 66–67; West Indian blacks, 67, 97. *See also* Negroes

Blanford, Berta, 98, 276n.10

Bluefields, Nicaragua: and Abel, 212; and African-derived religious practices, 49; and APSP, 6; and black Sandinistas, 178, 218; blacks in, 15, 82, 97, 270n.8; as British colonial settlement, 33; capitalist culture in, 257, 273n.66; as commercial port, 36, 38; and Contra war, 241–245; Creole barrios of, 15; Creole elite of, 59, 65; and Creole ethnogenesis, 39; and Creole history, 93; Creole politics in, 150–151, 240–241; and Creole/Sandinista relationship, 214–225; description of, 14–16; economy of, 56, 257; education in, 55; FSLN control of, 215–216, 221–222; Gordon's experiences in, vii–viii, 254–255, 257; and Hodgson, 36; Hodgson's former slaves in, 37–38; and Johnson's article, 182; and kinship relations, 191; and land rights, 65, 262–263; Mestizos in, 14, 15, 257, 259, 270n.8; Moravian Church in, 54–55; as Mosquitia capital, 40–41; natural

resources of, 176; Ortega's visit to, 282n.2; and PLN, 160; population of, 42, 53–54, 60–61, 268n.26, 270n.2, 278n.6; and property redistribution, 231–232; provisional government in, 73; racial solidarity in, 9; racial tensions in, 206–207, 210, 212, 214–215, 220–221; and railroad, 74; and Reincorporation, 60–62, 65; and Revolutions of 1909 and 1926, 114; and road to Río Kukra, 158, 188, 280n.5; Samboes of, 267n.13; and Sandinista Revolution, 208–209, 213; and Sandinista revolutionary government, 225–235; and slavery, 42, 99; and Somoza regime, 85; trade in, 59, 269n.29; and UNIA, 75–76; and U.S. capital, 53, 59, 63; U.S. settlers in, 44; and Walker, 41

Bluefields Junta for Municipal Reconstruction, 222

Bluefields Lagoon, 14, 35, 187

Bluefields Messenger, 58

Bluefields Steamship Co., 63, 64, 72

Bluff, 22, 61, 62, 215, 220

Boca del Toro, 265n.2, 268n.26

Bolt, Hilda, 9

Bragmans Bluff, 33, 35

Brathwaite, E., 267n.16

Brautigam Beer, Donovan: and Anglo diasporic identity, 193; Atlantic Coast history of, 275n.4; and British influence, 102, 103; and Creole culturism, 151, 166–175, 180; and Creole history, 95, 167, 168; and Creole origins, 98–99; and indigenous population, 193; and *La Prensa*, 96, 279n.17, 280n.11; on Miskitu kings, 103; on Moravian Church, 104; on Reincorporation, 105, 107–108, 109; and Revolutions of 1909 and 1926, 114; and Williams, 275n.7; and Zambo Miskitu, 96; on Zelaya regime, 114

Brazil, 277n.1

Bregenzer, Karl, 115
Brigada Simón Bolívar, 219, 221
British colonialism: and Anglo
    hegemony, 51, 59; and Brautigam
    Beer, 169; and Creole elite, 43;
    and Creole identity, 53; Creole
    perceptions of, 101; and evacua-
    tion, 35, 37, 266–267n.7; and
    Moravian Church, 55, 270n.3; in
    Mosquitia, 33–35; and oral
    history, 102; and slavery, 98
British West Indies, 42, 58
Brown, Angélica, 29, 228, 231
Brown, Ertell, 237
Bustamante, Pedro, 160, 184, 185

Cabezas, Rigoberto, 159
Cabo Gracias a Dios, 33, 96
Caesar, Colonel, 36, 267n.10
Campbell, Enrique, 163–164, 175–
    176, 177, 280n.9
Campbell, Lindolfo, 158–159, 280n.6
Campbell, Lumberto: and Black
    September, 236; and Creole/
    Sandinista relationship, 283n.13;
    and FSLN, 223, 226, 229, 280n.9;
    and regional government, 24
Cannibalism, 279n.20
Cape Gracias a Dios, 33, 96
Capitalist culture: and Anglo
    entrepreneurs, 60; and Anglo
    hegemony, 53–56, 60, 62, 197;
    and Anglo ideology, 199; and
    Atlantic Coast exploitation, 130,
    176, 177, 195; in Bluefields, 257,
    273n.66; and Creole pastors, 153;
    and Creole populism, 199; and
    depression of 1930's, 82; and
    india rubber boom, 54; monopo-
    listic tendencies of, 72; and
    OPROCO, 159, 165; and oral
    history, 116; and SICC, 188; and
    U.S. enclave economy, 57, 159;
    and U.S. imperialism, 63
Cardenal, Ernesto, 147
Caribbean islands, xi, 66–67, 101,
    117, 265n.2
Carrión, Luis, 210, 212, 216

Cartagena, 36
Carter administration, 3
Cash, Stanford, 182, 236
CASIM (Comité de Acción Social
    de la Iglesia Morava—Moravian
    Church Committee for Social
    Action), 154, 185, 186, 229–230
Cassanova, Brunilda, 29
Cassanova, Iván, 186, 231
Cassanova, Will, 29
Castro, Emilio, 153
Catholic Church, 127, 158, 191, 229,
    246
Cayman Islands: Creole culture of,
    265n.2; and Creole identity, 176;
    immigrants from, 38, 66, 98, 101,
    117
CDC (comité de defensa civil—civil
    defense committee), 214, 215, 220
CDS (Comités de Defensa Sandi-
    nista—Sandinista Defense
    Committees), 22, 221
Center for Atlantic Coast Research
    and Documentation. *See* CIDCA
Center for the Investigation and
    Study of the Agrarian Reform. *See*
    CIERA
Central America, 33
CEPAD (Centro Evangélico por
    Asistencia y Desarrollo—
    Evangelical Center for Aid and
    Development), 186, 230
Chalkley, Vice-Consul, 65
Chamorro, Emiliano, 73, 77–78
Chamorro Cardenal, Pedro Joaquín:
    and alternative bloc, 127; assassi-
    nation of, 141, 143; and Atlantic
    Coast, 128, 131; and Costeños,
    138; and Johnson, 281n.15; and
    Miskitu Indians, 131–134, 139;
    and *La Prensa*, 141; and UDEL,
    208; and U.S. liberals, 278n.7
Chinese population, 57, 272n.34
Chontales, Nicaragua, 216
Chontales race, 132
Chorotega, 122, 278n.9
Christian Democrats, 127
Christianity, 45, 46, 48–49, 54. *See*

also Catholic Church; Moravian Church and missionaries; Protestantism

Christie, Consul, 47, 268n.26

CIDCA (Centro de Investigación y Documentación de la Costa Atlán-tica—Center for Atlantic Coast Research and Documentation): Bluefields office of, 23–24, 27, 282n.4; and Corn Islands, 91; and critical support of FSLN, 10, 12–13, 29; and Cuban aid, 234; and economy, 245–246; and Gordon, 9–10, 16, 19, 27–29, 256–257; and INNICA, 10–11; and land rights, 256–257; and Miskitu Indian relocation, 11–12; and Williams, 277n.15

CIERA (Centro de Investigación y Estudios de al Reforma Agraria — Center for the Investigation and Study of the Agrarian Reform), 282n.2

Clarence (king of Rama Indians), 112

Class issues: and APSP, 4; Brautigam Beer on, 169; and British colonialism, 33; and color, 47; and Creole planters, 72; and Creole populism, 195; middle class, 127, 192, 203, 281n.17, 282n.1; and planters' strike, 261; and racism, 8; and slavery, 34; social hierarchy, viii, 45–50, 67, 67–69, 82, 110; and UNIA, 76; and Wilshire, 224; Wilson on, 115–116

Clientelism, 80, 166

Cliff, Jimmy, 253–254

Colombia, 122, 123

Colón, Panama, 181

Colón High School, 184, 211, 215, 220

Colonialism. *See* British colonialism; Internal colonialism; Neocolonialism

Coloreds: definition of, 272n.30; free people of color, 34, 35, 37, 38

Comaroff, Jean, 55

Communal Development Program, 156

Cone, James, 153

Conservative Party: and black Sandinistas, 176; and Chamorro, 78; and Creole politics, 74–75; and Estrada, 72–73; and Erica Hodgson, 213; and imperialism, 147; and Johnson's article, 182; and Moravian Church, 74, 273n.67; and *La Prensa*, 96; and Revolutions of 1909 and 1926, 114; United States support of, 273n.66

Consumer item distribution, viii, 244–245

Consumption patterns, 66

Contras and Contra war: and Atlantic Coast, 25; and Bluefields, 241–245; and CIDCA, 27; and economy, 244–246; and Gordon's relationship with Sandinistas, 25; and government rationing, 244–245; and Jackson, 276n.11; and Mestizo emigration to Bluefields, 14; and Sandinista revolutionary government, 247

Conzemius, Eduard, 92

Copeland, Fred, 248

COPESNICA (fishing company), 215

Corn Islands: blacks in, 82; as British colonial settlement, 33, 102; Creole elite of, 65; and Creole ethno-genesis, 40; Creoles' occupations in, 66; emancipation of slaves in, 42, 100, 268n.25; fisheries of, 91; FSLN control of, 215; Gordon's physical resemblance to Creoles of, 18; history of, 91–92; and Hodgson, 36, 267n.9; and Hodgson family, 37; and Hodgson's former slaves, 38; and kinship relations, 191; and Pearl Lagoon settlers, 39; and Reincorporation, 61, 65; and slavery, 91, 98, 274n.4

Coronado Torres, Antonio, 157

Costa Rica, 123, 209, 249, 251, 265n.2

Costa Rican Indian Council, 186
Costeños: and alternative bloc, 130–
131; and Christianity, 54; and
Creole identity, 53, 193; exploitation of, 148; FSLN's policies
toward, 10, 12; governmental
positions of, 69; and land rights,
64, 65, 74; Mestizo representations of, xiii, 69, 169; and Moravian Church leadership, 279–
280n.2; and Nicaraguan national
culture, 131; and Nicaraguan
nationalism, 127; OPROCO's
characterization of, 163; and *La
Prensa,* 129–130; racism toward,
119–120; and Sandinista revolutionary government, 145–147;
and Somoza regime, 123, 128,
141; and Spanish language, 70;
and Zelaya departmental government, 65; and Zelaya regime, 72.
See also Creoles (African Nicaraguans); Miskitu Indians
Creole, definition of, 40, 267n.16
Creole and Indian League, 110
Creole common sense: and Anglo
ideology, 52, 155, 197; and
anticommunism, 247; complexity
of, xi, 205–206; contradictions in,
31, 53, 94, 190, 194, 206; and
Creole ethnic populism, 52; and
Creole history, 32, 94, 266n.3;
and Creole identity, 53, 191–192;
and Creole politics, x, 52, 174;
and Creole/Sandinista relationship, 53, 204; and Mestizos'
attitudes, xi, 12; and Miskitu
Indians, 239–240; and OPROCO,
165
Creole culture: African influences
on, 48–50, 56, 67, 91, 136, 138,
171, 172, 260, 270n.5; and
alternative bloc, 136–140; and
Amerindian peoples, 172, 260;
and Anglo diasporic identity, 177;
and Anglo ideology, 198; and
Brautigam Beer, 151, 166–175,
180; British influences on, ix, 32,

136–137, 171, 173, 174, 180, 181;
and Creole history, 32; and
Creole identity, 48, 49–50, 168,
177; and Creole populism, 196,
198, 281n.19; European influences on, 32, 168, 171, 172, 173,
260; heterogeneous nature of,
140, 149, 170, 173; and May Pole
dance, 136, 138, 167, 170–171,
173; Mestizo opinion of, 174;
Miskitu Coast Creole culture,
265n.2; Moravian Church's
influences on, 53–56; and Nicaraguan national culture, ix, 62–63,
66, 137, 142–143, 172; and *La
Prensa,* 139–140, 167, 175; and
racism, 180; and resistance, 70;
and Sandinista revolutionary
government, 146–147; and SICC,
187; and Somoza regime, 136;
U.S. influences on, 171
Creole elite: and Africans, 43, 48,
269n.31; and Anglo diasporic
identity, 45–46; and Anglo
entrepreneurs, 56, 57; competition among, 59; and Conservative
Party, 74–75; and Council of
State, 41; economic activity of,
57; and india rubber boom, 43,
269n.30; land rights of, 64; of
Mosquitia, 40, 44, 268n.20; and
Reincorporation, 65; and slavery,
42, 260; social segregation of, 110;
and UNIA, 76; and Union Club,
71, 110; and U.S. protection, 74;
and West Indian immigrants, 67;
Wilson on, 116
Creole history: accommodation and
resistance in, ix–x, 52; and
African Diaspora, ix, 31, 266n.2;
and Brautigam Beer, 95, 167, 168;
and community problems, viii;
and Corn Islands, 91–92; and
Creole common sense, 32, 94,
266n.3; and Creole identity, 30,
53, 93, 94–95; and Creole political
common sense, xii, 31–32, 94,
120–121, 151; and Creole politics,

94–95, 258; demand for, 258; Gordon's perspectives on, 28, 256; and General Hodgson, 117–118, 183, 258; incongruities of, 52; interpretations of, xii–xiii; and SICC, 187; and social memory, xi, xiii, 93–95, 96–118, 193, 275n.5; and UCCOD, 183–185. *See also* Oral history

Creole identity: and African Diaspora, xi, 17–18, 77, 181, 192–193; and African–derived Creole culture, 49–50, 171; and Africans, xi, 46, 171; and Anglo hegemony, 56; and Bluefields Caribbean Festival, 184–185; changes in, xi, 32, 259–260, 263; and Contra war, 246; contradictions in, x, 13, 190, 260; and Creole common sense, 53, 191–192; and Creole culture, 48, 49–50, 168, 177; and Creole history, 30, 53, 93, 94–95; and Creole political common sense, xii, 94, 173, 174, 205; Creole politics' relationship to, xi, 53, 151, 190; and Creole populism, 194–196; and Creole/Sandinista relationship, 23; disparate nature of, xiii, 30, 31, 194; and English language, xi, 32, 40; formation of, vii, x–xi, 53, 260; of Gordon, 25–26, 29; group boundary formation, 190; Jenelee Hodgson on, 183; and kinship relations, 48, 191; and language, 190–191; and Mestizos, xi, 194–195, 261; and Miskitu Indians, 53, 77, 193, 262–263; and Moravian Church, 39–40, 47, 48; and populism, 194–196; and power relations, 32, 260, 263; and race, xii, 18, 32, 39–40, 47, 166; and racial/cultural identity, xi, 32, 40, 46–47, 190–194; and resistance, 70; and slavery, 30, 48; transnational identities, xi–xii, xiii, 18, 192–193, 259–260, 263–264; and UCCOD, 183–184; and U.S. economic enclave status,

viii–ix; and U.S. imperialism, 282n.2. *See also* Anglo diasporic identity; Black diasporic identity

Creole language: and Creole history, 32; and Creole identity, 190–191; and immigrant blacks, 66; Miskitu Coast English Creole, 48, 67, 190–191, 198, 267n.15, 267n.17

Creole political common sense: and Anglo diasporic identity, 45–46; and Anglo ideology, 197–199, 250; contradictory character of, 151, 205, 259; and Creole history, xii, 31–32, 94, 120–121, 151; and Creole identity, xii, 94, 173, 174, 205; and Creole politics, xii, xiii, 189, 205, 240, 261; and Creole populism, 199; ethnography of, 151, 189, 258–259; frames of reference for, 206; history of, x, xii; and internal colonialism, 252; past configurations of, xi; resistance and accommodation in, 50; and SICC, 187–188; and social memory, 118

Creole politics: and alliances, 239–240; and anticommunism, 204, 248; and Black September, 206, 235–239; in Bluefields, 150–151, 240–241; complexities of, x, 205–206; and Conservative Party, 74–75; contradictions in, x, 13, 52, 189; and Creole common sense, x, 52, 174; and Creole history, 94–95, 258; Creole identity's relationship to, xi, 53, 151, 190; and Creole political common sense, xii, xiii, 189, 205, 240, 261; and Creole/Sandinista relationship, x, 12, 23, 204; and depression of 1930's, 81–82; disparate character of, 31, 51, 150; diversity of, xiii; of Gordon, 29; identity politics, 31, 93, 190, 192, 194, 260–261; integrationist themes in, 77, 80–81, 82; Mestizos' attitude toward, x; and Moravian Church, 71, 155,

230; and Ortega, 231; and Protestantism, 230; and race, 176; and racial/cultural identity, 258; radicalism in, 176; as reactionary, 204, 206; reformist nature of, 79; role of accommodation and resistance in, x, 31, 51, 80; and Sandinista revolutionary government, 258–259; and SICC, 151, 207–208, 230–231, 233–234; and slavery, 30; and small production, 72; and social memory, 118; and Somoza regime, 83, 207, 213; tranformation of, 240; and Union Club, 71; and U.S. economic enclave status, viii–ix; and U.S. support, x, 204, 225, 240. *See also* Accommodation; Resistance

Creole populism: and Anglo ideology, 250, 252, 258, 284n.15; and black Sandinistas, 196, 225; and Creole common sense, 52; and Creole culture, 196, 198, 281n.19; and Creole identity, 194–196; and Creole pastors social movement, 155; and Creole political common sense, 199; and Creole/Sandinista relationship, 205–206, 227, 239; and Mestizo racism, 206–207; and racial/cultural identity, 231, 250, 251–252; and Sandinista Revolution, 206–214, 223; and SICC, 196, 251

Creole/Sandinista relationship: and Anglo ideology, 205–206, 246, 247, 250; and black nationalism, 219; and Black September, 206, 235–239, 283n.10; and Bluefields conflicts, 214–225; and Creole common sense, 53, 204; and Creole identity, 23; and Creole opposition, 22, 150; and Creole politics, x, 12, 23, 204; and Creole populism, 205–206, 227, 239; and Creoles' counterrevolutionary stance, x, 243–246, 282n.2, 283n.13; and Creoles' middle class status, 203, 282n.1; and

Cuban aid, 232–234; and economy, 245–246; and FSLN, 204, 250; and Gordon, 5, 23, 26; and imperialism, 18–19; and Mestizo racism, 210–211, 217–218, 220–221; and Moravian Church, 228–230, 246; and Moravian High School, 227–228; and Protestantism, 227, 229–230; and racial/cultural conflict, 204, 210–211, 228, 230, 250, 282n.2, 282n.3; and racism, 12, 224–225; and SMP, 249; tensions between, viii, 203–204, 282n.3; and Troubleshooters, 283n.11

Creoles (African Nicaraguans): and African Diaspora, 30; and alternative bloc, 134–140; attitudes toward Mestizos, 22, 23, 68–69; as autochthonous group, 105, 137, 261; and capitalism, 54; and Christianity, 54; cohesiveness of, 31; and communism, 231–232; consumption patterns of, 54, 57, 66; demographic changes in, 66, 272n.29; economy of, 42–43; ethnogenesis of, xii, 30, 32, 37, 39–40; and Gordon's political views, 24, 25–26; governmental positions of, 69, 70, 77, 155–156, 160, 179, 227, 234; identity politics of, 31, 93, 190, 192, 194, 260–261; and indigenous population, 45, 46; as jury members, 166; labor hierarchy position, viii; and labor organizations, 71; land rights of, 64–65, 106, 262; and miscegenation, 32; and MISURASATA, 231, 239; and Mosquito Convention, 64; and Mosquito Reserve, 41–42, 268n.24; nationalism of, 57–59; nationalist modernizing Creole pastors, 152–155, 183, 196, 279–280n.2; nationalization of, 82–83, 85, 137–138; and Nicaraguan nationalism, 122; occupations of, 66–67, 82, 272n.32; OPROCO's images

of, 165; population of, 43, 67, 270n.2; and *La Prensa*, 134–135, 138; role of, in Nicaraguan history, ix; and Sandinista revolutionary government, 148–149; social hierarchy position, viii, 45, 48, 67–69; and Somoza regime, 126, 141–142; and trade, 42–43; U.S. ties to, 84; wage labor of, 57; and wealth redistribution, 232; and Zelaya regime, 63–64. *See also* Mestizos' racialized view of Creoles; OPROCO; SICC
Creoles of Bluefields (political group), 80
Crowdell family, 21
Cuadra, Pablo Antonio, 138, 147
Cuba: Bay of Pigs invasion of, 123; and communism, 197, 231–232, 247; and Contra war, 244; Cuban exiles economic enterprises, 196; national identity of, 277n.1; and OPROCO, 158; and Sandinista revolutionary government, 232–233, 234, 235, 239; and SICC, 188
Cukra area, 64
Cultural pluralism, 172, 173, 174, 181
Cultural relativism, 173
Cultural Survival in the United States (black organization), 186
Culture for I (rasta group), 218
Curaçoa, 38
Cuthbert, James W., Jr., 58, 268n.24
Cuthbert, James W., Sr., 44, 57, 62, 268n.24
Cuthbert family, 52

Darío, Rubén, 175
De Kalb, Courtney, 58, 71
Dilson, Alparis, 36
Dimensión Costeño, 21
Dixon, Herman, 96, 100, 106–107, 275n.6
Dixon, John, 268n.20
Down, Newton, 40
Downs, Alvin, 237

Downs, Benjamin, 40
Drake, St. Clair, 3
DRI (Dirección de Relaciones Internacionales—International Relations Directorate), 6, 9
DuBois, W. E. B., 23
Duncan, Quince, 153, 183
Dunham, Jacob, 37

Earthquake of 1972, 122, 126, 164
East, May, 109–110, 277n.17
East Germany, 158
Economy: and alternative bloc, 126, 128–130; and banana plantations, 56–57, 64; of Bluefields, 14, 56, 257; and Brautigam Beer, 169; and capitalism, 53–56; collapse of Creole economy, 241; concessions, 64; and Conservative Party, 74; and Contra war, 244–246; and Costeños exploitation, 148; and Creole elite competition, 59; and Creole politics, 72; and Creole populism, 195–196; and Creole/Sandinista relationship, 245–246; of Creoles, 42–43; Cuban exiles economic enterprises, 196; development of, 188, 225; domination by foreign capital, 225–226; and FSLN, 146; and india rubber boom, 43–45, 53, 54, 56, 269n.30; and Moravian Church, 55; and regional development, 188; and Reincorporation, 62; and Somoza regime, 122–123; and trade, 36, 38–39, 42–44, 57, 59, 61, 269n.29; and Zelaya regime, 64. *See also* Enclave economy; Internal colonialism
Ecosistemas Acuáticos (Aquatic Ecosystems), 5
Education: and Creole elite, 57; and Creole history, 93–94; in English language, 196, 261; literacy campaign, 231; and Moravian Church, 55, 66, 70, 84, 104–105, 154, 272n.27; and resistance, 70;

and social hierarchy, 82; in Spanish language, 66, 70, 84, 272n.27

EEBI (Escula de Entrenamiento Básico de la Infantería—Infantry Basic Training School), 277n.18

Ejército Popular Sandinista (EPS— Popular Sandinista Army), 242

El Salvador, 244

ENALUF (Empresa Nacional de Luz y Fuerza—National Light and Power Company), 163, 164, 176

Enclave economy: and accommodation, 57; and Anglo ideology, 197; and capitalist culture, 57, 159; and consumption patterns, 66; and Creole elite, 59; and Creole identity, viii–ix; and indigenous population, 66; and resistance, 71; and U.S. capital, 63; and U.S. imperialism, 66, 71

English Bank, 40

English language: British English, 190, 198; and Creole elite, 45; and Creole identity, xi, 32, 40, 260; education in, 196, 261; English Creole, 274–275n.2; and Miskitu Coast English Creole, 48, 67, 190–191, 198, 267n.15, 267n.17; and Miskitu Indians, 45, 268n.23; and *La Prensa*, 279n.16; and Sandinista revolutionary government, 146; and Somoza regime, 1 42, 83; U.S. English, 190

EPS (Ejército Popular Sandinista— Popular Sandinista Army), 242

Escobar, Samuel, 153

Estrada, Juan B., 72–73

Ethnicity, and racial/cultural identity, 265n.3

Ethnography: and Creole common sense, 53, 94; of Creole political common sense, 151, 189, 258–259; and Creole politics, viii, 265n.1; of Miskitu Indians, 126; and race, 122

Europeans: and colonization, 281n.18; and Creole culture, 32, 168, 171, 172, 173, 260; and democracy, 197; European Africans, 39, 260; European Amerindians, 39, 40; and miscegenation, 170

Fagoth, Steadman, 283n.12

Fanon, F. O., 183

FDN (Fuerza Democrática Nicaragüense—Nicaraguan Democratic Force), 203

FENIBA (Nicaraguan baseball federation), 166

Fenton, James, 247

FER (Frente Estudiantil Revolucionario—Student Revolutionary Front), 207, 208

Fisheries: and Contra war, 245; and Corn Islands, 91; and Creole populism, 281–282n.20; and Cuban technicians, 233; fishing cooperatives, 241; and FSLN, 253; and Gordon, 3–4, 16, 24, 28; and INNICA, 7, 8, 16; and INPESCA, 26–27; and Johnson, 276n.13; Mestizo control of, 226; in Pearl Lagoon, 16, 24

Floyd Wilson Task Force, 203

Fonseca, Carlos, 2

Forbes, Jack D., 266n.5

Forbes, Loyd, 203, 214–215

Fox, John, 40

Fox, Sylvia, 241

Fox, Thomas, 40

Francia Sirpi Project, 278n.3

Frederick, Jonathan Charles, 57

Free people of color, 34, 35, 37, 38

Freire, Pablo, 153

French internationalists, 12

FSLN (Frente Sandinista de Liberación Nacional—Sandinista National Liberation Front): and Abel, 209, 215; and alternative bloc, 142, 143, 144; and APSP, 4–5, 7–8; and Arana, 212; and ATEPCA, 208; and Atlantic

Coast, 11, 12, 142, 143–148; and Black September, 238–239; and Bluefields, 215–216, 221–222; and communism, 231–232, 247, 249; and Costeños, 10; and Creole populism, 223, 284n.15; and Creole/Sandinista relationship, 204, 250; and Creoles in leadership positions, 227; Creoles' political distance from, 24; Creoles' working with, 22–23, 24; DRI of, 6, 9; electoral loss of, 253; and FER, 207; and imperialism, 247, 250; and Johnson, 276n.13; and Kelly, 213; and McField, 175; and Mestizo racism, 207; and Mestizos in leadership positions, 226–227; and Miskitu Indians, 5, 10, 143; and Moravian Church, 153; and OPROCO's anticommunism, 158; and racial/cultural identity, 217; and racism, 10–11, 143; radical discourse of, 167; and Ramírez, 226; and SICC, 187, 188; and Somoza regime, 141, 143–144; transformist turn in discourse, 144–148; U.S. opposition to, 205; and war of maneuver, 128. *See also* Black Sandinistas

Gámez, J. D., 275n.4
Ganja smoking, 218–219
García, Terry, 92, 275n.2
Garifunas, 107, 191
Garth, Daisy Gordon: on FSLN's electoral loss, 253; Gordon's marriage to, 19, 25–26; Gordon's meeting of, 14; Gordon's political work with, 29; on racism, 119–120
Garvey, Marcus, 75–76, 109, 196
General Council of the Reserve, 42
George (Miskitu king), 41, 103
George II (Miskitu king), 36
German ancestors, 101–102, 117, 260

González, Percy, 29, 218–219, 220, 225, 236–238
Good Neighbor Policy, 84
Gordon, Edmund T.: Bluefields experiences of, vii–viii, 254–255, 257; Creole identity of, 25–26; and Creole/Sandinista relationship, 5, 23, 26; ethnographic approach of, viii, 265n.1; as fisheries expert, 3–4; political activism of, 4–5, 6, 7–8, 27–29; racial identity of, 13, 16–18; and Sandinista revolutionary government, 7–9, 24–27, 29; on Sandinista Revolution's goals, 18–19
Gould, Jeffrey L., on myth of mestizo Nicaragua, 121
Government Junta for National Reconstruction, 223, 235
Government of National Reconciliation. *See* Sandinista revolutionary government
Gradas, 175
Gramsci, Antonio, x, 189
Grand Cayman, 270n.8
Great Awakening, 54
Great Britain: and Costeños, 147; and Creole culture formation, ix, 32, 136–137, 171, 173, 174, 180, 181; Creoles' resistance and, 73, 78–79; education in, 57; and Harrison-Altamirano Treaty, 64; Hodgson's trade with, 36; and May Pole, 171; Mosquitia dominance of, xi, 33–35, 40–41, 44, 102–103; and oral history, 115–116; and Providencia, 33; and Reincorporation, 62; and Somoza regime, 129; and trade, 43–44; treaties with Spain, 35; and Treaty of Managua, 41. *See also* British colonialism
Green, Leonard E., 83
Green, Ronny, 111–114, 277n.18
Grenada, 3–4
Greytown, 62, 268n.18
Grossman, Guido, 75–76

Gurdian, Galio, 9
Guthrie, Alvin, 275n.6
Gutiérrez, Gustavo, 153

Haggard, Merle, 18
Harlem Brothers, 184
Harrison-Altamirano Treaty, 64, 80, 81, 108, 161, 185
Haulover, 66, 241, 262
Hegemony: alternative hegemony, 127, 128–143; Anglo hegemony, 51, 53–60, 62, 84, 155, 197, 260, 270n.3; and Anglo ideology, 196–199, 251; and cultural national-ism, 264; and FSLN, 144, 145; and Moravian Church, 51, 53–56; of Nicaraguan government, 51, 62–63, 70, 82, 84–85; of Nicaraguan nationalism, 127, 192; racial hegemonies, xii; and rule, 51, 63, 270n.1; Williams on, 120
Helping Sisters, 184
Hermanos de Wisconsin program, 159
Hispanicization Pilot Project (Pro-yecto Piloto de Castellanización), 277–278n.3
Hispano-Nicaraguans. *See* Mestizos
Hodgson, Alexander, 267n.18, 268n.20
Hodgson, Amos, 248
Hodgson, Azalee, 29, 240, 277n.17
Hodgson, Burt, 97, 99, 105, 108, 114, 276n.8
Hodgson, Crepe, 110
Hodgson, Elizabeth Pitt, 36, 267n.9
Hodgson, Erica, 213
Hodgson, Frank, 130, 160
Hodgson, Gen. George Montgomery: and Bluefields Caribbean Festival, 184–185; and Creole common sense, 53; and Creole history, 117–118, 183, 258; and Creole politics, 52, 150; death of, 83, 114; Green on, 111–114; photo-graph of, 90; and social memory, 110–111

Hodgson, George, 99, 267–268n.18, 268n.20
Hodgson, Hennigston, 29
Hodgson, Horatio, 81
Hodgson, Jenelee, 182–187, 213, 231, 233–235, 283n.12
Hodgson, Ray, 187, 212–213, 218
Hodgson, René, 97–98, 111, 276n.9
Hodgson, Robert, Jr.: and Brautigam Beer, 102; death of, 37; descen-dants of, 40, 268n.18, 268n.20; Miskitu expulsion of, 98; nonin-digenous settlement led by, 35–36; slaves of, 36, 37–38, 98–99, 267n.9
Hodgson, Robert, Sr., 34, 35, 102
Hodgson, Robert III, 37
Hodgson, Roberto, 150, 156, 159, 162, 178, 226
Hodgson, Stephen A., 271n.23
Hodgson, William, 37, 267–268n.18
Hodgson M., Frank O., 157
Holm, John A., ix, 32
Honduras: anti-Sandinista propa-ganda of, 251; and British colo-nialism, 33; Honduran Mosquitia, 43, 44; and Miskitu Indians, 12; territorial disputes with, 123, 129
Hooker, Alfred W., 80, 271–272n.23, 274n.86
Hooker Kaine, Dexter. *See* Able, Comandante (Dexter Hooker Kaine)
Hooker, Ray, 207, 210, 282n.4
Hooker, Robert M., 275n.4
Hooker, Waldo W., 155–156, 207
Hotel Amy, 13–14
Hotel Bluefields, 16
Howell, Sam, 110
Howell, Tommy, 110
Huembes, Roberto, 216
Human rights, 27, 165, 197
Hunter, Thomas, 241
Hurricane Joan, 14

Identity politics: and Creole/Sandi-nista relationship, 205; of

Creoles, 31, 93, 190, 192, 194, 260–261

Les îles Corn du Nicaragua, 92

Imperialism: and black Sandinistas, 175–178; and Costeños, 147; and FSLN, 144–146, 250; and revolution, 18–19; and Sandinista revolutionary government, 247. *See also* U.S. imperialism

India rubber boom: and Anglo entrepreneurs, 44, 45; and Anglo hegemony, 53; and capital penetration, 54; and Creole elite, 43, 269n.30; and economic change, 56

Indigenous population: and British colonialism, 33; and Creole elite, 43, 269n.31; and Creole identity, 193, 261; history of, 95; international movements of, 193–194; and Latin American nationalism, 121; and Mestizo discourse, 122, 125; and miscegenation, 34–35; Miskitu Indians' subjugation of, 33–34, 36, 45; and Sandanista Revolution, 18–19; and slaves, 96; and Somoza regime, 123, 125; and U.S. enclave economy, 66; and Zelaya departmental government, 65. *See also* Amerindian peoples; and specific tribal names

INFONAC (Instituto de Fomento Nacional—National Development Institute), 161

La Información: and anticommunism, 158; and black Sandinistas, 177; and Brautigam Beer, 168; and Liberation Theology, 176, 281n.14; and OPROCO, 157, 159, 162–164, 280n.4; and racism, 166, 179; and Reincorporation, 159

Ingram, Henry Clay, 57, 271n.23

Ingram, William Halstead, 268n.20

INNICA (Instituto Nicaragüense de la Costa Atlántica—Nicaraguan Atlantic Coast Institute): and CIDCA, 10–11; dissolution of, 23; and fisheries, 7, 8, 16; and

Gordon, 9–10; and Moravian Church, 229; and Ramírez, 226

INPESCA (Instituto Nicaragüense de la Pesca—Nicaraguan Fishing Institute), 4, 5–6, 8, 26–27

Intercoastal canal, 178

Internal colonialism: and Anglo ideology, 197; and Brautigam Beer, 169; and Creole populism, 195–196; and marginalized Atlantic Coast, 188; and Mestizo racism, 178–188, 218, 251, 259; and Nicaraguan government, 63, 72, 106, 159, 164, 174; and OPROCO, 252; and Sandinista revolutionary government, 239

Interoceanic canal, 44, 52

Jackson, Dickie, 234

Jackson, Gregory, 29

Jackson, Thomas, 98, 111, 276n.11

Jamaica: and Bluefields population, 270n.8; and British colonialism in Mosquitia, 33, 34; British traders of, 43–44; and Chief Robert Henry Clarence, 62; Creole culture of, 171, 265n.2; and Creole definition, 267n.16; and Creole identity, xi, 176; dread culture of, 219; education in, 57; Green on, 111; Hodg-son's former slaves' trade with, 38; Hodgson's trade with, 36; immigrants from, 38–39, 66, 98, 101, 115, 117; missionaries of, 55, 270n.3; Moravian seminary training in, 152; and Mosquito Reserve, 59; and Pearl Lagoon settlers, 39; and shipwrecked slaves, 96–98; and social memory, 193

Johnson, James, 92, 100–101, 103, 276n.13

Johnson, Robert L., 179–182, 281n.15

Jones, Mommy, 21

Jones, Sasha Kalinda, 19, 20

Juventud Sandinista (Sandinista Youth), 220

Kalalú, 9, 217, 219–221, 222, 240, 283n.8
Kelly, Joe, 186, 276n.10, 279n.1
Kelly, Thomas, 212–213
Kennedy administration, 158, 165, 278n.7
Kerr, H. W., 130
King, Martin Luther, Jr., 183, 193
Kukra Indians, 33, 45

Labor, viii, 70, 71–72, 141
Laclau, E., 51
Lara Swamp, 214
Larios, Bernardino, 234
Las Colinas, Nicaragua, 7
Latin America: Christian Democratic movements in, 127; and Liberation Theology, 152–153; nationalism in, 121; and race, 122; and racial/cultural identity, 264; and United States, 165
Le Page, R. B., 267n.17
Lee, Samuel, 65
Liberal Party: and black Sandinistas, 176; and constitutionalist revolution, 78, 83; and Creole identity, 53, 261; Creole sympathy for, 74, 83; and imperialism, 147; and la-bor organizations, 71–72; and OPROCO, 155–156, 157; and Revolutions of 1909 and 1926, 114; and separatist activity, 73; and Somoza regime, 83
Liberation Theology, 152–153, 176, 183, 281n.14
Liga Nacional del Literol Atlántico (National League of the Atlantic Coast), 76
London, Convention of, 35
López, Francisco, 212
López, Rubén, 212
López, T., 271n.19

Malcolm X, 13
Maliaño, Urcuyo, 213
Managua, Alan, 238
Managua, Puna, 238
Managua, Nicaragua: blacks in, 82;

Gordon's experiences in, 6–7, 13; and road to Rama, 82, 84
Managua, Treaty of, 41, 58, 59, 108–109
Manifestación. *See* Black September
Marblehead, 105
Marley, Bob, 18, 275n.2
Maroon former slaves, xii, 35, 37–38, 42, 260, 267n.10
Martínez, Sergio, 5–6
Marxism, 3
Marxist-Leninism, 251
McDonald, Superintendent, 42
McField, David, 175, 176–177, 279n.17, 281n.13
Mean, Francis, 52
Medina, Martha, 226
Mercantile business, 57
Mestizaje, 121, 277n.1
Mestizo racism: assumptions concerning, 119–121; and Chamorro Carde-nal, 134; and Creole populism, 206–207, 223; and Creole/Sandinista relationship, 210–211, 217–218, 220–221; and FSLN, 148, 207, 210–211; and Hispanic civilization, 68; and internal colonialism, 178–188, 218, 251, 259; and SICC, 188
Mestizos: and Africans, 126, 135; and Amerindian peoples, 124; Anglo attitudes toward, 69; assumptions about Costeños, xiii, 69, 169; and black phenotype, 191; in Bluefields, 14, 15, 257, 259, 270n.8; and Brautigam Beer's history, 96; and capitalism, 54; and Christianity, 54; and Creole culture, 167, 172; and Creole identity, xi, 194–195, 261; and Creole politics, x, 234; Creoles' attitudes toward, 22, 23, 58, 68–69, 117; and Creoles' occupations, 82, 272n.32; and Creoles' position in social hierarchy, 67, 69; definition of, 266n.5; and economy, 196; ethnocentrism of, 172, 178; and fisheries control,

226; governmental positions of, 65, 69, 160, 167, 226–227; and indigenous population, 125; and land rights, 65, 106; and natural resources, 161–162; and Negroes, 279n.18; and Nicaraguan nationalism, 121–123, 131; and OPROCO, 157; and PLN, 160; population of, 272n.34; racial/cultural identity of, 12; and Reincorporation, 62–65, 107; and rule versus hegemony, 63; and SICC, 187, 240; and UDEL, 207. *See also* Mestizo racism; Mestizos' racialized view of Creoles

Mestizos' racialized view of Creoles: and black diasporic identity, 191; and Brautigam Beer, 169–170, 172; and Creole common sense, xi; and Creole identity, 264; and Creoles as non-national, 59, 121, 138; and culturalists, 174; and FSLN, 143; and Ortega, 282n.2; and race-based politics, 9

Middle class, 127, 192, 203, 281n.17, 282n.1

Miller, Leroy, 279n.1

Miller, Reverend, 228

Mines, 82

Mintz, S. W., 267n.16

Miscegenation, 32, 34–35, 100, 117, 169–170, 278n.10

Miskito Indian Patriotic League, 77, 110

Miskitu Indians: African ancestral group of, 33, 34, 39, 96–98, 132; and ALPROMISU, 208; and alternative bloc, 131–134; Anglos living with, 35; black phenotype of, 191; in Bluefields, 15; and British colonialism, 102–103; and Christianity, 54; and civil service, 41; and counterrevolutionary activity, 243–244; as Creole ancestors, 97, 260; and Creole common sense, 239–240; and Creole culture, 171; and Creole elite, 40; and Creole identity, 53,

77, 193, 262–263; Creolization of, 66; and FSLN, 5, 10, 143; and General Council of the Reserve, 42; and Gordon's political views, 24; Green on, 112–113; history of, 33–34, 95, 96; and Hodgson, 36, 98; indigenous peoples subjugated by, 33–34, 36, 45; and institutional leadership, 283n.9; land rights of, 64–65; language of, 126, 132, 147; leaders of, 34, 41, 42, 43, 102–103, 268n.23; and Mestizo discourse, 122, 125–126; and miscegenation, 278n.10; and Moravian Church, 44, 246, 268n.23, 279n.1; and Mosquitia government, 44; and Mosquito Convention, 108; and Mosquito Reserve, 41, 59; nationalization of, 125, 133–134, 278n.3; population of, 270n.2; and *La Prensa*, 130, 134, 139–140; racial/cultural identity of, 204; racism toward 119–120, 121, 148; and Reincorporation, 62, 64, 107; relocation of, 11–12; and resistance, 70, 77; and Sandinista revolutionary government, 147, 148, 283n.10, 283–284n.15; and slavery, 37; and social hierarchy, 45, 69; and Somoza regime, 123–126; and United States, 130. *See also* Tawira Miskitu Indians; Zambo Miskitu Indians

MISURASATA (Miskitu, Sumu, Rama y Sandinista Asla Takanka—Miskitu, Sumu, Rama, and Sandinista Working Together), 148, 231, 239, 242, 283n.12, 283–284n.15

Moody, Ralph, 157

Moravian Board of World Missions, 152

Moravian Church and missionaries: and Anglo hegemony, 51, 53–56, 60, 270n.3; Brautigam Beer on, 104; and Conservative government, 74, 273n.67; and Creole identity, 39–40, 47, 48, 191, 260; and Creole pastors, 152–155, 183, 196, 279–280n.2; and Creole politics, 71; and Creole resistance to Nicaraguan rule, 53; and Creole/Sandinista relationship, 228–230, 246; Creoles' membership in, 67; cultural colonialism of, 49–50, 54, 270n.5; description of, 15; and education, 55, 66, 70, 84, 104–105, 154, 272n.27; and FSLN, 153; history of, 95, 96; membership in, 54–55; and Miskitu Indians, 44, 246, 268n.23, 279n.1; in Mosquitia, 44; and Mosquitian nationalism, 57–58; and Mosquito Reserve, 42, 44, 54–55; and Nicaraguan national culture, 70; and Obeahism, 67; and OPROCO, 158–159; and Prinzapolka, 5; and Red Cross, 207; reform of, 151; and Sandinista revolutionary government, 115, 246; and SICC, 186; social action focus, 153–154; and social hierarchy, 47–48; and Somoza regime, 84–85, 117; southern Africa's activity compared to, 270n.50; and UNIA, 75; and United States, 84, 151, 274n.89; and Whitikers, 20–21

Moravian High School: and Anglo ideology, 251; and Caribbean Festival, 184; and Creole politics, 240; and Creole/Sandinista relationship, 227–228; description of, 15; faculty of, 207; and Jenelee Hodgson, 183; and OPROCO, 239; racial tensions in, 220; role of, 152; and SICC, 230–231; and Sujo Wilson, 256

Moravian Mission Board, 269n.29

Morenos, 279n.18

Morgan, Algren, 29

Mosquitia: Africans inhabiting, 33–35, 39; Anglo dominance in, xi; Bluefields as capital of, 40; British enslavement in, ix, 32, 34, 40; as British protectorate, 41, 44, 58, 61, 102–103; Caribbean Coast known as, ix; Council of State, 41; and Creole definition, 267n.16, 267n.17; Creole elite of, 40, 43; and Creole identity, 53; Creole population of, 270n.2; ethnographers of, 32; and Honduras, 43, 44; immigrant settlements in, 33, 34; india rubber boom of, 43; and Mestizo discourse, 122; militia of, 41; miscegenation in, 34–35; Moravian Church's power in, 44, 53; Nicaraguan sovereignty over, 41, 44; population of, 34, 35, 266n.6, 266–267n.7, 270n.2; and Zelaya regime, 63. *See also* Atlantic Coast; Mosquito Reserve

Mosquito Convention: Brautigam Beer on, 108; Creoles' attitude toward, 64, 74, 77; and integrationist themes in, 81; and Miskitu Indians, 62; and oral history, 108–109

Mosquito Kingdom, 34

Mosquito Reserve: and Anglo entrepreneurs, 60; creation of, 41; and Creole elite, 41–43, 57; Creole nationalism of, 57–59; Creoles' call for re-establishment of, 78; and land rights, 64; material resources of, 63; and Moravian Church, 44, 54–55; Nicaraguan sovereignty over, 44, 58, 64; and U.S. enclave economy, 57

Mouffe, C., 51

Mozambique, 3

Mulattoes, 34, 35, 39

Munguía Novoa, Juan, 137

Murrillo, Rosario, 175, 281n.13

Musawas, 115

Music: African influences on, 136; and alternative bloc, 137; and black diasporic identity, 192, 193; and Creole culture, 170–171; foreign influences on, 146;

Mestizo rediscovery of, 167; of
Miskitu Indians, 132–133; and
tourism, 139
Mustees, 34, 35, 39, 266n.5

Nandaime (town), 278n.15
National Guard: and Abel, 209–210,
215; and Arana, 212; and
ATEPCA, 208; and Bluefields,
214; and conscription, 209;
Creoles as members of, 83–84;
and FSLN, 143–144; and Moravian Church, 85; and OPROCO,
164–165; and U.S. military, 79
National League of the Atlantic
Coast (Liga Nacional del Literol
Atlántico), 76
Natural resources: and alternative
bloc, 128–130; of Bluefields, 176;
and Creole pastors, 153; exploitation of, 259; and FSLN, 142, 145;
and OPROCO, 158, 161–162,
165–166; and U.S. capital, 63
Negrito, 166, 279n.20
Negroes: as Creoles, 39, 67, 82, 260;
immigrant blacks as, 66–67; and
labor organizations, 71; and
Mestizos, 279n.18; slaves as, 34;
and social hierarchy, 47–48, 67.
See also Blacks
Negro World, 75
Neocolonialism, 6, 178, 182, 282n.2
NGOs (nongovernmental organizations), 24, 153, 165, 186
Nicaragua: anti-Sandinista propaganda of, 251; Atlantic Coast
economic connections of, 82;
Atlantic Coast's foreign population, 65–66; Atlantic Coast's
military incorporation into, 60;
and Creole identity, 53; and
Creole power in Mosquitia, 47;
Creoles' lack of allegiance to, 80;
Creoles missing from history of,
ix; and Creoles' social hierarchy,
67; and Harrison-Altamirano
Treaty, 64; history of, 92–93; and
internal colonialism, 63, 72, 106,

159, 164, 174; and Mestizo myth,
121–122; and Mosquito Convention, 108; and Mosquito Reserve
autonomy, 57; and Mosquito
Reserve sovereignty, 58, 64, 109;
national hegemony of, 51, 62–63,
70, 82, 84–85; nationalism of, 58,
121–122, 127, 131–132, 261;
resistance to, 51, 53, 69–80; rule
of, 51
Nicaraguan national culture: and
alternative bloc, 140; and black
Sandinistas, 177; chauvinism of,
172; and Costeños, 131; and
Creole culture, ix, 62–63, 66, 137,
142–143, 172; Creole resistance
to, ix–x, 70; and FSLN, 144; and
La Prensa, 278n.13, 281n.15; and
Sandinista revolutionary government, 146–149; and Somoza
regime, 140; and Spanish language, 66, 70; and subnational
cultures, 140, 149
Nicaraguas (ancestor culture), 122,
278n.9
Nixon, Richard, 278n.7
Nkrumah, Kwame, 178, 193
Nongovernmental organizations
(NGOs), 24, 153, 165, 186
North American popular culture, xi
Notice, Charles, 248
Novedades, 123, 124, 126, 130, 134
Núñez, Carlos, 146

Obeah, 19–20, 21, 49, 67, 266n.2
O'Laughlin, Bridget, 3
Olien, Michael, 32
Omier, Cyril, 207
Omier, Hennigston, 29
O'Neille, Tomás, 37
Operation PUSH, 186
OPROCO (Organización Progresista
Costeña—Progressive Costeña
Organization): and Anglo dias-
poric identity, 193; autonomy
within integration, 159–161; and
black Sandinistas, 218; and Black
September, 239; and canal

project, 179; and Creole culture, 169; and Creole intellectuals, 151, 165; and Creole populism, 196; and indigenous population, 193; and internal colonialism, 252; and Liberal Party, 155–156, 157; and Moravian Church, 158–159; and Moravian High School, 227, 240; and National Guard, 164–165; objectives of, 155–156; and Omier, 207; and PLN, 167; radical discourse of, 162–163; and regionalism, 164, 165–166; and Sandinista revolutionary government, 284n.15; and SICC, 188; and Somoza regime, 155–158, 159, 168; splintering of, 167–168, 178

Oral history: and British colonialism, 102; Creoles' attitude toward, 93; and European origins, 100–101; Gordon's use of, 94–95; and Great Britain, 115–116; and Jenelee Hodgson, 184; and Miskitu kings, 103–104; and Moravian Church, 104–105; and Mosquito Convention, 108–109; and Price, 275n.3; and Reincorporation, 105–109; and shipwrecked slaves, 96, 100; and slavery, 99; of Sui Williams, 277n.19; and Williams, 277n.15. *See also* Creole history

Organization of Black City Mayors, 186

Ortega, Daniel: in Bluefields, 282n.2; and Creole culture, 146; electoral loss of, 253; and MISUR-ASATA, 148, 231; and Murillo, 281n.13

Overthrow. *See* Reincorporation

Panama, 34, 265n.2
Panama Indian Council, 186
Parsons, Frank, 102, 276n.14
Pastora, Eden, 234
La Patria Club, 110
Patterson, Charles, 57, 268n.24

Patterson, Henry, 40, 268n.24, 269n.30
Patterson family, 52
Pearl Lagoon (district): as British colonial settlement, 33, 35; and Creole demographics, 66, 272n.29; and fisheries, 16, 24; FSLN control of, 215; and kinship relations, 191; and land rights, 65; and Miskitu Indians, 36, 260; and Mosquito Reserve, 268n.24; and resistance, 73–74; and SICC, 187; and U.S. enclave economy, 66; and U.S. troops, 78–79; Zambo Miskitu Indians of, 40
Pearl Lagoon (village): blacks in, 82; and CASIM, 185; commerce of, 38; Creole elite of, 59, 65; and Creole ethnogenesis, 39–40; Creoles' occupations in, 66; economy of, 56; education in, 55; emancipation of slaves in, 42; and Gordon, 16; Great Awakening in, 54; and Hodgson's former slaves, 37, 38; land rights in, 262–263; Moravian Church in, 54–56; population of, 42, 268n.26; and Reincorporation, 61, 65; Samboes of, 267n.13; trade in, 59; U.S. settlers in, 44
Pérez-Estrada, Francisco, 135–139, 278n.15
PESCANICA (seafood processing plant), 209–210, 211, 216
Pfeiffer, H. G., 47–48
Pineda, Roberto, 234
Pink Tea Party, 184
Pitt, William, 36
Planters Association, 72
PLN (Partido Liberal Nacionalista—Nationalist Liberal Party): and Creole politics, 151; and Frank Hodgson, 130; and Moravian High School, 227; and national hegemony, 51; and *Novedades*, 123; and OPROCO, 157, 160, 165, 167, 280n.4; and Red Cross, 207; and Rivera de Vallejos, 125; and

Sandinista Revolution, 214
POI (Policía de Orden Interno—
Internal Order Police), 235–236,
238
Porta Costas, Antonio, 35, 36
Porter, James, 268n.20
Power relations: and Anglo ideology,
198; and Anglo population, 52;
and British settlers, 43–44; and
Creole elite, 43; and Creole
history, 52; and Creole identity,
32, 260, 263; and Creole political
common sense, 189; and Nicaraguan rule, 69–70; on Atlantic
Coast, 51; and racial/cultural
identity, 45; and resistance, 199
La Prensa: and Atlantic Coast, 128–
129, 131; and black Sandinistas,
177; and Brautigam Beer, 96,
279n.17, 280n.11; and Chamorro
Cardenal, 127; closing of, 248;
and Costeños, 129–130; and
Creole culture, 139–140, 167,
175; and Creoles, 134–135, 138–
140; and FSLN, 145; and Great
Britain's cultural influence, 136;
on Johnson, 181; and Miskitu
Indians, 130, 134; and Nicaraguan
cultural nationalism, 131; and
Nicaraguan national culture,
278n.13; and racism, 179, 182;
and Somoza regime opposition,
141
Price, Richard, 266n.2, 275n.3
Price, S., 267n.16
Prinzapolka, 5, 61
Protestantism: and Creole identity,
xi, 55, 191–192, 193; and Creole/
Sandinista relationship, 227, 229–
230; and neocolonialism, 282n.2;
and SICC, 188
Providencia, 33, 38, 101, 117,
265n.2, 267n.17
Proyecto Piloto de Castellanización
(Hispanicization Pilot Project),
277–278n.3
Prussian immigrants, 268n.26
Puerto Cabezas, 82, 123, 126, 176

Puerto Limón, Costa Rica, 181
Punta Gorda, 33

Queen Victoria's Jubilee, 55–56
Quinn, Michael, 40

Race: in Bluefields, 206–207, 210,
212, 214–215, 220–221; and
Brautigam Beer, 168; and Creole
identity, xii, 18, 32, 39–40, 47,
166; and Creole politics, 176;
Green on, 83; in Latin America,
264; and Mestizo racialized
discourse, xi, 149; and miscegenation, 32, 34–35, 100, 117, 169–
170, 278n.10; and Miskitu
Indians, 34; and Moravian
Church nationalization, 154–155;
and Mosquitia, 34, 35; and
Nicaraguan history, 137; and
Nicaraguan socialist revolution,
5; racial Darwinism, 139; racial
hegemonies, xii; and racial
marginalization, 166; and racial/
cultural identity, 265n.3; in
Rama, 210; and social hierarchy,
45; and Somoza Debayle, 125; and
UNIA, 76. *See also* Mestizos'
racialized view of Creoles
Racial/cultural identity: and Anglo
population, 48; and black nationalism, 188; and black Sandinistas,
167, 218, 224; Brautigam Beer on,
169; and British colonialism, 33;
and class issues, 224; and Creole
identity, xi, 32, 40, 46–47, 190–
194; and Creole politics, 258; and
Creole populism, 231, 250, 251–
252; and Creole/Sandinista
relationship, 204, 210–211, 228,
230, 250, 282n.2, 282n.3; Creoles
versus Negroes, 67; definition of,
265n.3; and FSLN, 217; and Latin
America, 264; of Mestizos, 12; of
Miskitu Indians, 204; and
OPROCO, 156–157; and power
relations, 45; and Protestantism,
230; and regionalist identity, 81;

and Sandinista revolutionary
government, 148; and separatist
activity, 73
Racism: of alternative bloc, 134,
140–141; of Anglo entrepreneurs,
60; of Anglo population, 67–68;
and APSP, 4; and black Sandinistas, 175–178; Brautigam Beer
on, 169; of British settlers, 47;
and Creole/Sandinista relationship, 12, 224–225; and FSLN, 10–
11, 143; Daisy Garth on, 119–120;
Johnson on, 179–182; of Mestizos,
68, 119–121, 134, 148, 178, 179,
182, 188; and Nicaraguan nationalism, 137; and *La Prensa*, 134,
140, 281n.15; and racial/cultural
identity, 265n.3; and rastas, 219;
and Sandinista revolutionary
government, 8–9, 239; in United
States, 6, 8, 134, 169–170, 172,
174, 180, 195, 280–281n.12; and
U.S. imperialism, 6, 210. *See also*
Mestizo racism
Railroad, 74, 271n.19
Rama, Nicaragua, 13–14, 82, 84,
209–216
Rama Indians: and African intermarriage, 39, 98, 100, 117, 260,
267n.13; Creoles' attitude toward,
45, 193; and General Council of
the Reserve, 42; Green on, 111–
113; and Hodgson, 99; and land
rights, 65; Miskitu Indian
subjugation of, 33, 36; and
Reincorporation, 107; and SICC,
186; and social hierarchy, 69
Ramírez, William, 11, 223, 226, 228,
233
Rastas: and African origins, 97; and
Creole populism, 251–252; and
Culture for I, 218; and García,
275n.2; and González, 218–219;
and Reincorporation, 109; and
UCCOD, 184
Reagan administration, 244, 251
Red Cross, 207
Rediske, M., 282n.1

Reeves, Jim, 18
Reforestation Law, 129
Regional Autonomous Governments, 257
Reincorporation: and Bluefields, 60–
62; Brautigam Beer on, 105, 107–
108, 109; Cuthbert as political
adviser, 44; and OPROCO, 159–
161; oral history of, 105–109;
resistance to, 61, 105, 109, 110–
111, 195, 196; and U.S. troops, 62;
and Zelaya government, 63–64,
105, 108, 181
Reinke, Amadeus, 39, 47–48
Rener, Remy, 160
Rener Valle, Pablo, 157–158
Residual historical elements, 266n.3
Resistance: assumptions concerning,
30; and Creole history, ix–x, 52;
and Creole political common
sense, 50; and Creole populism,
194; decline in, 81; and enclave
economy, 71; everyday resistance,
52; and group letters, 73–74; to
Moravian Church's cultural
colonialism, 49–50; to Nicara-
guan national culture, ix–x; to
Nicaraguan rule, 51, 53, 69–80;
and power relations, 199; to
Reincorporation, 61, 105, 109,
110–111, 195, 196; role of, in
Creole politics, x, 31, 51; and
slavery, 266n.1; to white U.S.
entrepreneurs, 52; zero-sum
assumptions concerning, 52
Reyes, Juan Pablo, 274n.86
Rigby, Carl, 224, 279n.17
Río Coco region, 123, 129, 131
Río Escondido, 36, 38, 56, 64
Río Grande, 35
Río Hueso, 41
Río Kukra, 158, 188, 280n.5
Río Punta Gorda, 41, 50
Río San Juan, 41, 44, 62, 123
Río Tinto, 35
Ritmo, Bárbaros del, 279n.17
Rivera de Vallejos, Alba, 125–126,
157

Roatán, 101, 270n.8
Robert Charles Frederick (Miskitu king), 41, 42
Robert Henry Clarence (chief), 61, 62
Roberts, Orlando, 38, 39, 40
Roque Abarca, Subinspector, 37
Rose Girls, 184
Ruiz, Henry, 211
Ruiz, Horacio, 132–133
Ruiz y Ruiz, Frutos, 69, 272n.32
Rule, and hegemony, 51, 63, 270n.1

Sacasa, Juan Bautista, 78, 274n.76
Samarriba, Comandante Marcos, 229, 230
Samboes, 39, 100, 267n.13
San Andrés: Creole culture of, 265n.2; and Creole definition, 267n.17; and Hodgson's slaves, 37, 38; immigrants from, 38, 101, 117; and Maroon former slaves, 42; and Pearl Lagoon settlers, 39; and slavery, 268n.25
San José, Costa Rica, 152
San Juan del Norte, 82
Sandinista National Liberation Front. *See* FSLN
Sandinista Revolution, Triumph of: anniversary of, 2; and Bluefields, 213; and Creole populism, 206–214; and Creole expectations, 203; Gordon on, 18–19; and racial/cultural conflict, 217
Sandinista revolutionary government: and Atlantic Coast, 279n.21; and Catholic Church, 229, 246; confiscation of, 22; and consumer item distribution, viii; and Contra war, 25, 241–244; and Costeños, 145–147; and Creole politics, 258–259; and Creole/Sandinista relationship, viii; and Creoles, 148–149; Creoles' initial acceptance of, x, 22–23, 203, 205, 213–214, 221, 223, 282–283n.5; and Cuba, 232–233, 234, 235, 239; and economic development, 225;

electoral loss of, 253; and fisheries, 4; and Gordon, 7–9, 24–27; and internal colonialism, 239; legitimization of, 144; literacy campaign of, 231; and Miskitu Indians, 147, 148, 283n.10, 283–284n.15; and Moravian Church, 115, 246; and racism, 8–9, 239; and SICC, 240, 249, 284n.15; and social services, 229–230; and UNO, 275n.6; and Western cultural dependency, 147
Sandinista Youth (Juventud Sandinista), 220
Sandino, Augusto César: and FSLN, 144; and Gen. George Hodgson, 112–113; and Moravian Church, 105, 115, 153; U.S. against, 79, 107
Sandino Sun mural, 201, 230
Sandy Bay, 35, 242
Saramaka history, 275n.3
Savery, Hernan, 186, 218, 225, 231, 233–234
Schick, René, 155–156
Schneider, R., 282n.1
Scott, David, 266n.2
Scott, James, and "everyday resistance," 52
Seminario Bíblico Latinoamericano, 152
Senegambia, 96
Separatist activity: and Chamorro, 128; and Estrada, 73, 273n.56; and Miskitu Indians, 5; and Mosquito Reserve autonomy, 57; of Pearl Lagoon Creoles, 73–74; and Sandinista revolutionary government, 9; and SICC, 187, 234
Servicio Militar Patriótico. *See* SMP
SICC (Southern Indigenous and Creole Community): and African Diaspora, 193; and black diasporic identity, 191; and black Sandinistas, 218; and Black September, 238; and Blanford, 276n.10; and Creole political common sense, 187–188; and

Creole politics, 151, 207–208, 230–231, 233–234; and Creole populism, 196, 251; economic development projects of, 187; formation of, 186; goals of, 186–187; and Burt Hodgson, 276n.8; and Hooker's election, 207; and indigenous population, 194; and Moravian High School, 227; revival of, 247; and Sandinista Revolution, 225; and Sandinista revolutionary government, 240, 249, 284n.15; and Vance, 213

Sieborger, Br., 55

Silva, Fernando, 182

Slate, Alicia, 29, 282n.4

Slaves and slavery: and Africans' affiliation with Miskitu Indians, 33, 96–97; and Anglo diasporic identity, 50; and black diasporic identity, 30, 37, 48; and Bluefields, 42, 99; and British colonialism, 98; and British emancipation, 39; and Corn Islands, 91, 98, 274n.1; and Creole culture, 174, 260; and Creole elite, 42, 260; and Creole identity, 30, 48; and Creole politics, 30; emancipation of, 42, 100, 268n.25; and Great Britain, ix, 32; of Hodgson, 36, 37, 267n.9; Maroon former slaves, xii, 35, 37–38, 42, 260, 267n.10; and miscegenation, 35; in Mosquitia, 34, 35, 266n.6, 266–267n.7; and resistance, 266n.1; social memory of, xi, 96–100; Zambo Miskitu freeing of, 36–37

Sloan, Mike, 29

Small-scale production, 53, 56–57, 60, 64, 71–72

Smith, Alfonso, 242

Smith, Burti, 237

SMP (Servicio Militar Patriótico—Patriotic Military Service), 249, 276n.11, 283n.14

Smutko, Gregory, 212

Social hierarchy: Creoles' position in, viii, 45, 48, 67–69; and education, 82; of Mosquitian society, 45–50, 67–69; Ruiz y Ruiz on, 69; and skin color, 47–48, 67, 110

Social memory: and Bluefields Caribbean Festival, 184; and Creole history, xiii, 93–95, 96–118, 275n.5; and Creole political common sense, 118; and Creole politics, 118; and Jamaica, 193; of slavery, xi

Social organizations, 71

Socialism, 4–5

Solórzano, Carlos, 76–77, 274n.76

Somoza, Luis, 278n.7

Somoza Debayle, Anastasio (Tachito): and Atlantic Coast, 123; and Kennedy administration, 278n.7; and Miskitu Indians, 124–125; modifications in discourse, 141; and OPROCO, 157; and Somoza regime, 122

Somoza García, Anastasio, 80, 116

Somoza regime: and alternative bloc, 126–143; and Atlantic Coast, 122–126, 141–142, 279n.21; and Atlantic Coast university, 207; and black Sandinistas, 176; and Brautigam Beer's history, 96; and Creole accommodation, x; and Creole culture, 136; and Creole politics, 51, 207, 213; and economic investments of, 225; and FSLN, 141, 143–144; governmental control of, 80; and Great Britain, 129; and General Hodgson, 118; intercoastal canal project, 178; and Liberal Party, 83; and Managua, 6; and *mestizaje*, 121; and Miskitu Indians, 123–126, 134; and Moravian Church, 84–85, 117; and Nicaraguan national culture, 140; opposition to, 126–127, 167, 208; and OPROCO, 155–158, 159, 168; and oral history, 116–117; repressive nature of, 141, 184–185; and

SICC, 188; and United States, 107, 129, 143, 144, 278n.7

South Africa, 8

Southern Indigenous and Creole Community. *See* SICC

Soviet Union, 158, 188, 244, 247

Spain: Central American colonies of, 33; and Creole definition, 267n.16; and George II, 36; and Hodgson, 35; Hodgson's trade with, 36; and oral history, 102; and Providencia, 33; and slavery, 37; trade with, 38; treaties with Great Britain, 35

Spanish language: and education, 66, 70, 84, 272n.27; and Latin American nationalism, 121; and Nicaraguan cultural nationalization, 66, 70, 81; and Sandinista revolutionary government, 231

Stephen (prince of Zambo Miskitu), 267n.10

Stephenson, Alan, 29, 232, 248

Stephenson, Dicky, 29

Sui Williams, Francis, 105–106, 277n.15, 277n.19

Sujo Wilson, Hugo: and Black September, 236; and Creoles in government positions, 155–156, 179; and critical support of FSLN, 29; on PLN, 160; on regionalism, 164; as teacher, 256

Sumu Indians, 96, 100, 107, 112, 143, 147

Swope, Putney, 263

Tabouret-Keller, A., 267n.17

Tasbapaunie, 66, 241

Tawira Miskitu Indians, 34, 35, 36, 267n.10

Taylor, John, 57, 271n.23

Taylor, Markland, 58

Thomas, J. O., Jr., 52

Thomas, J. O., Sr., 52, 57, 58, 62, 70–71

Tobie F., Rollin B., 178–179, 182

Tosh, Peter, 18

Tourism, 122, 139, 279n.19

Traslado, 11–12

Troubleshooters, 283n.11

Twaka Indians, 45

Twenty-five Brave: attack of, 78; and Bluefields Caribbean Festival, 184–185; and Creole history, 183, 258; and Creole politics, 52, 150; photograph of, 90; and Reincorporation, 107; social memory of, 110–111

UCCOD (United Committee for Community Development), 183–186, 194

UDEL (Unión Democrática para la Liberación—Democratic Union for Liberation): and alternative bloc, 141; and Arana, 212; and CDC, 214; and Chamorro Cardenal, 143, 208; and Mestizos, 207; radical discourse of, 167

Ugarte, Mary, 29

Ulwa Indians, 33, 36, 45

UNAN (Universidad Nacional Autónoma de Nicaragua), 207

UNIA (Universal Negro Improvement Association), 75–76, 77, 109–110, 184, 191, 193

Union Club, 71, 72, 73, 76, 80, 110

Unión Democrática para la Liberación. *See* UDEL

United Committee for Community Development (UCCOD), 183–186, 194

United Fruit Company, 63, 115

United Nations, 233

United Nations Conference on Human Rights, 11

United States: and Anglo diasporic identity, 71; and Anglo ideology, 198; anticommunism of, 84, 85, 247; anti-Sandinista propaganda of, 251; and anti-Somoza opposition, 127; Atlantic Coast as economic enclave of, viii–ix; and Atlantic Coast economy, 196; and Atlantic Coast exploitation, 195; and banana exports, 56; black liberation movement in, 5; blacks' migration to, 82; and Bluefields population, 270n.8; capital of, 53; civil rights movement in, 123; and Conservative government, 79, 273n.66; and Contra war, 25, 244; and Creole elite, 74; Creole immigration to, 257; Creole support for, x, 204, 225, 240; Creoles' resistance and, 73, 78; and democracy, 197–198; education in, 57; and Estrada, 73; FSLN opposition, 205; Hodgson's trade with, 36; immigrants from, 66, 67; and interoceanic canal, 44, 62; military presence of, 12, 79–80, 105; and Miskitu Indians, 130; and Moravian Church, 84, 151, 274n.89; Moravian seminary training in, 152; Mosquitia dominance of, xi; and Nicaragua, 12; and OPROCO, 158–159, 165; and oral history, 102; racism in, 6, 8, 134, 169–170, 172, 174, 180, 195, 280–281n.12; and Reincorporation, 62, 105, 106–107; and Revolutions of 1909 and 1926, 114; and Sandinista Revolution, 23; and SICC, 240; social change in, 3; and Somoza regime, 107, 129, 143, 144, 278n.7; trade with, 38, 57; troops of, 78–80

U.S. imperialism: and Anglo hegemony, 59; and Anglo ideology, 247; and Atlantic Coast, 63, 270n.10; and CIDCA, 10; and Creole elite, 43; and Creole history, 19; and Creole identity, 282n.2; and Creoles' position in social hierarchy, 67; and enclave economy, 66, 71; military response of, 12; and Moravian Church, 151; and Nicaragua, 63; and OPROCO, 159; and racism, 6, 210; and Sandinistas, 142

Unity Synod, 153

Universal Negro Improvement Association. *See* UNIA

Universidad Nacional Autónoma de Nicaragua (UNAN), 207

UNO (Unión Nacional Opositora—United National Opposition), 203, 275n.6

Vance, Gayland, 213, 218, 231, 234, 236

Versailles, Treaty of, 35

Vivas, René, 211, 222, 225

Voice of America, 23, 213, 244, 251

Walker, Alice, 1–2

Walker, Patrick, 40–41, 268n.26

Walpasixa, 35

Waslala, 41

Waspam, 82, 123, 130

Weinberg brothers, 63

Weinberger, Charles, 271n.16

West Indian cottages, 15

West Indian immigrants, 67, 97, 260

Wheelock, Jaime, 209, 238

Whitaker, Rupert Linton, 157, 280n.4, 280n.10

White, Noreen, 29

White, Robert, 266n.6, 266–267n.7

Whitiker, Kevin: background of, 276n.12; and Contra war, 244; and European ancestors, 101; and Gordon, 19–22; and Jamaica, 98; on Reincorporation, 105; on Somoza regime, 116–117

Whitiker, Mabel, 19–22, 244

Williams, Lucy: background of, 275n.7; and Cayman Islands, 101–102; and Creole history, 92, 97; on Miskitu kings, 104; and racial mixing, 100; and slavery, 99

Williams, Raymond, 120, 125, 266n.3

Wilshire, Charles, 212

Wilshire, Eustace, 211, 218, 224–225

Wilson, Hedley, 279n.1, 280n.2

Wilson, Herman: background of, 277n.16; on class segmentation, 115–116; on Creole elite, 116; on Reincorporation, 108–109; on

UNIA, 109; on Union Club, 110

Wilson, John: and British influence, 102; Creole history of, 95, 96; and Creole/Sandinista relationship, 228; on Managua Treaty, 109; and Moravian Church, 104, 114, 279n.1, 280n.2; and Revolutions of 1909 and 1926, 114–115; and SICC, 186; on Somoza regime, 117; on Zelaya regime, 114

Women: and Anglo entrepreneurs, 34; and Anglo racism, 68; as anthropological scholars, 265n.1; in APSP, 5; and Bluefields calypsos, 21; and institutional leadership, 283n.9; as organic intellectuals, 258; in OPROCO, 158

Wong, William, 217–218

World Black Council, 186

World Council of Indigenous People, 186

World War I, 74

Wrights, Marvin. *See* Kalalú

Young Men's Union, 71

Young Women's Union, 71

Zambo Miskitu Indians: as African Amerindians, 34, 40, 278n.10; alliances of, 36–37; and Bluefields Maroons, 267n.10; and British dominance, 103; as Creoles, 39, 260; and FSLN, 143; as Samboes, 267n.13; and shipwrecked slaves, 96; and social hierarchy, 69

Zelaya, Department of, 65, 141, 162, 277n.15

Zelaya, José Santos: and Bluefield Steamship Co., 64, 72; Green on, 113–114; Hodgson on, 159; and land rights, 271n.19; monopolistic concessions of, 64, 72; and Reincorporation, 63–64, 105, 108, 181; and Spanish language, 70, 81; and trade, 61

Zumos Indians, 69